Jurist in Context

This is the engaging and accessible intel⋯ ⋯ memoir of a leading jurist. It tells the story of the development of his thoughts and writings over sixty years in the context of three continents and addresses the ironies and ambiguities of decolonisation, the Troubles in Belfast, the contextual turn in legal studies, rethinking evidence and the implications of globalisation which have been central to his life and research. In propounding his original views as an enthusiastic self-styled 'legal nationalist', Twining maps his ideas of Law as an exciting discipline, which pervades all spheres of social and political life while combining theory and practice, concepts and values, facts and rules in uniquely illuminating ways. Addressed to academic lawyers generally and to other non-specialists, this story brings out the importance and fascinations of a discipline that has changed, expanded and diversified in the post-war years, with an eye to its future development and potential.

Born in Uganda, educated in Oxford and Chicago and wanting to work in Eastern Africa, William Twining started in Sudan, because it had the only law school in acceptable Africa and teaching Law was all that he was qualified to do. After three years he moved to Dar es Salaam in the heady days of Independence, but later concentrated on Anglo-American Jurisprudence, based mainly in the UK and the United States. He is now well known transnationally as a leader of the Law in Context movement and as an influential thinker with a distinctive voice. Sceptical but committed, original and provocative, he is always nudging the mainstream and challenging settled assumptions. He is sharply aware of the parochialism of much Western academic law. His recent books include *Karl Llewellyn and the Realist Movement* (2nd edn), *Rethinking Evidence* (2nd edn), *How to Do Things with Rules* (with David Miers, 5th edn), *General Jurisprudence, Globalisation and Legal Scholarship*, and *Human Rights, Southern Voices*. As an intellectual autobiography, this book is a departure from these, but it provides a clear, vivid, often amusing context for all his writings.

The Law in Context Series

Editors: William Twining (University College London),
Maksymilian Del Mar (Queen Mary, University of London) and
Bronwen Morgan (University of New South Wales).

Since 1970 the Law in Context series has been at the forefront of the movement to broaden the study of law. It has been a vehicle for the publication of innovative scholarly books that treat law and legal phenomena critically in their social, political and economic contexts from a variety of perspectives. The series particularly aims to publish scholarly legal writing that brings fresh perspectives to bear on new and existing areas of law taught in universities. A contextual approach involves treating legal subjects broadly, using materials from other social sciences, and from any other discipline that helps to explain the operation in practice of the subject under discussion. It is hoped that this orientation is at once more stimulating and more realistic than the bare exposition of legal rules. The series includes original books that have a different emphasis from traditional legal textbooks, while maintaining the same high standards of scholarship. They are written primarily for undergraduate and graduate students of law and of other disciplines, but will also appeal to a wider readership. In the past, most books in the series have focused on English law, but recent publications include books on European law, globalisation, transnational legal processes, and comparative law.

Books in the Series
Acosta: *The National versus the Foreigner in South America*
Ali: *Modern Challenges to Islamic Law*
Alyagon Darr: *Plausible Crime Stories: The Legal History of Sexual Offences in Mandate Palestine*
Anderson, Schum & Twining: *Analysis of Evidence*
Ashworth: *Sentencing and Criminal Justice*
Barton & Douglas: *Law and Parenthood*
Beecher-Monas: *Evaluating Scientific Evidence: An Interdisciplinary Framework for Intellectual Due Process*
Bell: *French Legal Cultures*
Bercusson: *European Labour Law*
Birkinshaw: *European Public Law*
Birkinshaw: *Freedom of Information: The Law, the Practice and the Ideal*
Brownsword & Goodwin: *Law and the Technologies of the Twenty-First Century: Text and Materials*
Cane & Goudkamp: *Atiyah's Accidents, Compensation and the Law*
Clarke & Kohler: *Property Law: Commentary and Materials*
Collins: *The Law of Contract*
Collins, Ewing & McColgan: *Labour Law*
Cowan: *Housing Law and Policy*
Cranston: *Legal Foundations of the Welfare State*

Darian-Smith: *Laws and Societies in Global Contexts: Contemporary Approaches*
Dauvergne: *Making People Illegal: What Globalisation Means for Immigration and Law*
Davies: *Perspectives on Labour Law*
Dembour: *Who Believes in Human Rights?: Reflections on the European Convention*
de Sousa Santos: *Toward a New Legal Common Sense*
Diduck: *Law's Families*
Estella: *Legal Foundations of EU Economic Governance*
Fortin: *Children's Rights and the Developing Law*
Ghai & Woodman: *Practising Self-Government: A Comparative Study of Autonomous Regions*
Glover-Thomas: *Reconstructing Mental Health Law and Policy*
Gobert & Punch: *Rethinking Corporate Crime*
Goldman: *Globalisation and the Western Legal Tradition: Recurring Patterns of Law and Authority*
Haack: *Evidence Matters: Science, Proof, and Truth in the Law*
Harlow & Rawlings: *Law and Administration*
Harris: *An Introduction to Law*
Harris, Campbell & Halson: *Remedies in Contract and Tort*
Harvey: *Seeking Asylum in the UK: Problems and Prospects*
Hervey & McHale: *European Union Health Law: Themes and Implications*
Hervey & McHale: *Health Law and the European Union*
Holder & Lee: *Environmental Protection, Law and Policy: Text and Materials*
Jackson & Summers: *The Internationalisation of Criminal Evidence: Beyond the Common Law and Civil Law Traditions*
Kostakopoulou: *The Future Governance of Citizenship*
Lewis: *Choice and the Legal Order: Rising above Politics*
Likosky: *Transnational Legal Processes: Globalisation and Power Disparities*
Likosky: *Law, Infrastructure and Human Rights*
Lunney: *A History of Australian Tort Law 1901–1945: England's Obedient Servant?*
Maughan & Webb: *Lawyering Skills and the Legal Process*
McGlynn: *Families and the European Union: Law, Politics and Pluralism*
Moffat: *Trusts Law: Text and Materials*
Monti: *EC Competition Law*
Morgan: *Contract Law Minimalism: A Formalist Restatement of Commercial Contract Law*
Morgan & Yeung: *An Introduction to Law and Regulation: Text and Materials*
Nicola & Davies: *EU Law Stories: Contextual and Critical Histories of European Jurisprudence*
Norrie: *Crime, Reason and History: A Critical Introduction to Criminal Law*
O'Dair: *Legal Ethics: Text and Materials*
Oliver: *Common Values and the Public–Private Divide*
Oliver & Drewry: *The Law and Parliament*
Picciotto: *International Business Taxation*
Probert: *The Changing Legal Regulation of Cohabitation, 1600–2010*
Reed: *Internet Law: Text and Materials*
Richardson: *Law, Process and Custody*
Roberts & Palmer: *Dispute Processes: ADR and the Primary Forms of Decision-Making*
Rowbottom: *Democracy Distorted: Wealth, Influence and Democratic Politics*

International Journal of Law in Context: A Global Forum for Interdisciplinary Legal Studies

The *International Journal of Law in Context* is the companion journal to the Law in Context book series and provides a forum for interdisciplinary legal studies and offers intellectual space for ground-breaking critical research. It publishes contextual work about law and its relationship with other disciplines including but not limited to science, literature, humanities, philosophy, sociology, psychology, ethics, history and geography. More information about the journal and how to submit an article can be found at http://journals.cambridge.org/ijc

Jurist in Context

A Memoir

WILLIAM TWINING
University College London

CAMBRIDGE
UNIVERSITY PRESS

CAMBRIDGE
UNIVERSITY PRESS

University Printing House, Cambridge CB2 8BS, United Kingdom

One Liberty Plaza, 20th Floor, New York, NY 10006, USA

477 Williamstown Road, Port Melbourne, VIC 3207, Australia

314–321, 3rd Floor, Plot 3, Splendor Forum, Jasola District Centre,
New Delhi – 110025, India

79 Anson Road, #06–04/06, Singapore 079906

Cambridge University Press is part of the University of Cambridge.

It furthers the University's mission by disseminating knowledge in the pursuit of
education, learning, and research at the highest international levels of excellence.

www.cambridge.org
Information on this title: www.cambridge.org/9781108480970
DOI: 10.1017/9781108645911

© William Twining 2019

First published 2019

Printed and bound in Great Britain by Clays Ltd, Elcograf S.p.A.

A catalogue record for this publication is available from the British Library.

Library of Congress Cataloging-in-Publication Data
Names: Twining, William, 1934– author.
Title: Jurist in context : a memoir / William Twining, University College London.
Description: Cambridge, United Kingdom ; New York, NY, USA : Cambridge University Press, 2018. |
Series: The law in context series
Identifiers: LCCN 2018038595 | ISBN 9781108480970
Subjects: LCSH: Twining, William, 1934– | Law teachers – England – London – Biography.
Classification: LCC KD632.T86 A3 2018 | DDC 340.092 [B]–dc23
LC record available at https://lccn.loc.gov/2018038595

ISBN 978-1-108-48097-0 Hardback
ISBN 978-1-108-70367-3 Paperback

Cover Picture: The Thinker (Yerakdu), by Simon Gambulo Marmos and Jo Mare Wakundi
(1996.362.16)

© Iris & B. Gerald Cantor Center for Visual Arts at Stanford University; Gift of Joan Evans and George Gibbs.

The cover picture depicts a Papua New Guinea (PNG) interpretation of Rodin's 'The Thinker'. While we were
at Stanford in 1999–2000 we paid several visits to the open air Papua New Guinea Sculpture Garden on campus
(https://museum. stanford edu and other links). In the mid-1990s a group of PNG sculptors worked on trees
imported from PNG. At first, they carved their trees in traditional ways, but as they began to look outward, they
became curious about Rodin in the Cantor Museum also on campus. 'The Thinker', in particular, intrigued
them and Simon Gambulo Marmos is reported as saying: 'I can do this even better.' He and Jo Mare Wakundi
then transposed Rodin to the PNG imagination. The sculpture echoes some central themes in the book: North–
South relations in a post-colonial era; diffusion of ideas; hybridity; globalisation; and above all, the jurist as
thinker. 'Ironically, the Garden fostered the Western appreciation of non-Western art by substituting one
western category ['master-carver'] for another ['primitive' art]. One of the great aesthetic joys of the Sculpture
Garden is the visual contemplation of the ironies that arise from the cross-cultural dialogue and categorization
of artworks in the contemporary, transnational or globalized world.' (Wikipedia entry on Papua New Guinea
Sculpture Garden. See further www.facebook.com/pages/Papua-New-Guinea-Sculpture-Garden/
287527781305652.) Modern commentators have suggested that Rodin's original expresses grief rather than
reflection. Perhaps the background story suggests both: constructive thinking about the future after a disaster.

To Trevor Rutter

Contents

Colour plates can be found between pages 168 and 169

Foreword

For over sixty years, William Twining has been at the centre of legal education and legal scholarship in the English-speaking world. Beginning in East Africa in the early days of emergence from colonial rule, and going on to span several of the most influential law schools in both the UK and the United States, Twining's remarkable career has witnessed a transformation of legal education and of the scholarly world of the legal academy which has been, in its own way, quietly revolutionary to no less a degree than the political context amid which his professional life opened. The length, distinction and geographical span of this career would in themselves make its subject's observations and reflections on this period intensely interesting to legal academics, as well as from the point of view of intellectual and social history. But in Twining's case, this interest is intensified by the fact that he has been not merely a witness to but a key agent in the relevant transformation.

When I read law at UCL in the late 1970s, the curriculum – as was standard in most law departments at the time – was dominated by doctrinal legal scholarship, leavened by a moderate helping of analytical jurisprudence and sociology of law. This was still largely the case when Twining arrived as Quain Professor of Jurisprudence in 1983. But by then, the 'law in context' movement which he and his colleagues had nurtured at Warwick and in a few other departments had begun to change the shape of the discipline, with a smattering of socio-legal courses developing across the sector, enabled in significant part by new journals and by the distinctive and influential 'Law in Context' series which Twining and Robert Stevens had established at Weidenfeld and Nicolson. And that development has continued – and diversified – steadily, interacting with genres such as socio-legal studies and theory; feminist and critical race theory; and critical legal studies. Adapting the old saying about legal realism, contextualism is certainly *not* dead, and there is a real sense in which all legal scholars have to take aspects of context into account today.

In this memoir, Twining sheds fascinating light on the intellectual and – with small p – political origins of this approach in both his experience of living and teaching in the radically different legal and social worlds of colonial and post-colonial Africa, the United States, Northern Ireland during the Troubles, and England; in the key relationships which he formed with colleagues, mentors and students in each of these countries; and in the main intellectual resources which shaped his thinking from early adulthood on. Hart, Collingwood, Llewelyn and Mentschikoff emerge as perhaps the dominant figures in this intellectual history: but many others also feature prominently, underlining the ways in which the trajectory and impact of a single life are strongly shaped by both relational and institutional context.

Twining is beguilingly open – indeed self-critical – about aspirations which could not be met and projects which remain incomplete: the continuing lack of true dialogue and mutual respect between philosophically inspired jurisprudence and Twining's more socio-legal genre of legal theory being one; his ambitious multidisciplinary approach to evidence being another. And while he conveys forcefully his deep commitment to teaching, and the central role which pedagogy has played in not only the communication but also the formation and developing of his ideas, he modestly underplays his own impact as a mentor, institution-builder and supporter of younger scholars. Having myself been a beneficiary of these qualities of his, not least as someone he commissioned to write a book for the Law in Context series early in my career, it gives me great pleasure to write this Foreword to his intriguing memoir; to commend it to legal scholars as a fascinating window on legal academic praxis in the late twentieth and early twenty-first centuries; and to acknowledge and celebrate his influence, his scholarly contribution and his generosity.

Nicola Lacey
London School of Economics and Political Science
June 2018

Preface

Pick up today's newspaper and you will probably find law on every page not only accounts of transnational, international, regional, national and local news, but items that need a legal lens to interpret them or that use vocabularies drawn from the law: murder, in-laws, genocide, contract, mortgage, shares, corruption, hearing, rights.

That is how I have addressed English law students at the very start of their formal legal education. Before they have even registered in the University, they were asked to do some preliminary reading, to visit at least one court, and to complete 'The Newspaper Exercise'. For the former they were supplied with some questions to answer. The instructions for the latter asked them to read every word of a non-tabloid newspaper, such as *The Times*, *Guardian* or *Telegraph* – now *The i* will do – and to mark all passages that appear to be 'law-related' and then to answer a number of specific questions. On the surface this focuses attention on some particular points: that 'law-related' is an elusive category; that law, even narrowly conceived, features throughout a daily news-paper: footballers are bought and sold; the arts pages may contain issues of copyright, contract, and even libel; the business pages rely heavily on legal categories, such as companies, mergers and bankruptcy; contract is every-where; European Law and human rights pop up in unexpected places; and to understand foreign news one needs to know something about non-English traditions and systems of law. Even in England one encounters *shari'a*, *imams* and *fatwas*.

In some passages law is presented as a good thing; in others it may just be there as a fact of life; in others it may be presented as an instrument of injustice or oppression. What is law for the purpose of this exercise? In this context it may be best to beg such questions; if one defines the term 'law' narrowly it pre-empts reflective answers; if one defines it very broadly this makes the exercise more difficult. Most, but not quite all, of the examples above are examples of the kinds of 'law' that law students in England in fact study, even if the concept is not precise or coherent.

The underlying objective of the exercise is to remind students that they have experienced law throughout their lives, not only on TV but also as actors. It also suggests that it is interesting and relevant to them. A standard pedagogical device is to look at the entering class on the first day and say: 'Hands up anyone who has never committed a crime; . . . or libelled someone on Facebook or Twitter . . . Is there anyone here who has not entered into a contract in the last 24 hours?' If a hand goes up in regard to committing a crime, or a tort, an appropriate response might be: 'What never?', unless it would embarrass the student. If, as expected, no one volunteers, I go on to say: 'I have before me a bunch of contractees, trespassers, in-laws, tenants, owners, constitution-makers, copyright violators, twittering defamers . . . and CRIMINALS.' Law is not a new subject for them, as it is frequently portrayed. Rather the subject matters of legal studies are pervasive in social life, dynamic, important, and above all interesting – not esoteric, dry, abstracted from human realities.

It is important to distinguish between the discipline of Law (the name of a subject) and the subject matters of the discipline (law with a small l). In the previous paragraph I suggested that law (with a small l) is pervasive, dynamic, and so on. Theorising about law and 'law' in this sense is an important part of Jurisprudence, as we shall see. But phrases like 'the discipline of Law', 'Harvard Law School', or 'the Common Law of Torts' (in the syllabus of a Law degree) are merely field concepts; that is, rough labels for an area of study, usually with no firm or stable boundaries and little analytical purchase.[1] It would be strange, perhaps dangerous, to try to explain any of these phrases, by reference to a particular abstract theory or definition of law: for example, there is unlikely to be a consensus within the Harvard Law School about such matters and it would be foolish to try to impose or distil one. All that the word does in this context is roughly to differentiate one institution from others such as the Faculty of Arts or Cardozo Law School.

This point is significant here because this book is centrally about the health of the discipline of Law and only incidentally about the nature or essence or concept of law. The central thesis is that the mission of Law as an academic discipline, like other disciplines, is to advance and disseminate understandings of its subject matters, but that it has some way to go to realise its potential as a marvellous and important subject. Those subject matters are extensive, ill-defined and changeable.

This book advances a particular conception of Jurisprudence as a sub-discipline of Law and argues that so conceived it can contribute to the health of the discipline in several important ways (Chapter 1). In particular it can help both law and its study to respond to many challenges in a period of accelerated globalisation and technological change. In short, Jurisprudence can be an important engine for more particular activities within the discipline of Law, provided that it is treated as an integral part of the discipline.

Why *Jurist*? Oliver Wendell Holmes Jr said that 'The law is the calling of thinkers.'[2] 'Jurist' is a broad term referring to a thoughtful or learned person whose main subject, field or profession is Law, and who reflects about it strategically or in relatively abstract ways. The term applies to judges and reflective legal practitioners[3] as well as to legal educators, scholars and theorists. For all of them Law is their primary discipline and the main basis for their expertise.[4] I am one kind of jurist, in that I am a career scholar-teacher of Law who counts Jurisprudence among his special interests. I am not trained as a philosopher or a historian nor as a social theorist or social scientist, but I believe that all of the humanities and social sciences and even other subjects like Neuroscience and Psychology as well as the direct experiences of many legal actors, not only professionals, are relevant to understanding law.

This book is an intellectual memoir addressed to anyone concerned with law, in particular law students and academic lawyers in general. The aim is to present a restatement of my views as a jurist in the form of a narrative of the development of my ideas and a justification of a number of theses. When the idea for this book was first suggested to me, I thought immediately of R. G. Collingwood's *An Autobiography* which made a striking impact when I read it shortly after I first graduated. As we shall see it was seminal in my intellectual development from then on. Collingwood's memoir must be one of the most popular philosophical books in the English language, but when it was published in 1939 it was not expected to do well. The author warned Oxford University Press that it was 'destitute of all that makes autobiography saleable'. It was going to be a 'dead loss', he said, and in a preface he offered a pre-emptive apology: he was a philosopher by vocation – had been as long as he could remember – so the story of his life could not be anything more than a compendium of abstract ideas.[5] William Faulkner was more succinct, suggesting that the biography of an author should be short: 'He wrote books, then he died.'

Like Collingwood's *An Autobiography* this aims to provide a succinct, accessible and assertive restatement of a position. It will try to show where I am coming from, why I believe what I believe about law and its study, and where this might lead. It will be a narrative of ideas, not an intimate autobiography. However, I am more of a contextualist than Collingwood, so my story is firmly located in particular times and places.

My main academic subject, Jurisprudence, sounds abstract and daunting; much of it is, but my picture of the activity of legal theorising is that it should often be quite down-to-earth, realistic, practical and comprehensible. Since the subject seems esoteric and I have worked somewhat outside the mainstream, Chapter 1 summarises my conception of Jurisprudence for non-specialists. I hope that this will help both to make the rest accessible and persuade readers that it is relevant to them.

Chapters 2–4 give brief accounts of my formal and informal education up to the age of about 30, including apprenticeship in learning and teaching in Oxford, Khartoum and Dar es Salaam. These chapters introduce some of my African background and experience and three figures who played a major role in my early development as a jurist: Herbert Hart, R. G. Collingwood and Karl Llewellyn.

I chose to spend the first seven years of my career teaching in Sudan and East Africa because I was interested in education and Africa, and Law was the only subject I could teach. The experience of teaching, institution building, law reporting, and coming to grips with an alien culture and legal system led me to become interested in legal education, contextual approaches to understanding law and, after I had been responsible for putting Karl Llewellyn's papers in order in Chicago (1963–5), in intellectual history, archives and Anglo-American Jurisprudence (Chapters 4 and 7).

Chapters 5 and 6 describe how my ideas on understanding and teaching Law were germinated in Sudan and East Africa and how they developed mainly through activist debates about and politics of legal education in several countries.

Chapter 7 tells of my relationship with Karl Llewellyn and his formidable widow, Soia Mentschikoff, and about how I began to develop an interpretation of what is involved in being 'realistic' about law, without becoming a 'rule-sceptic' (i.e. someone who does not believe that rules exist or can have settled meanings).

Chapter 8 deals with my seven years as Professor of Jurisprudence in the Queen's University of Belfast (1966–72), where I had the opportunity to develop my teaching and thinking on Jurisprudence in three compulsory courses. One of these led to some in-depth thinking about rules and norms and their interpretation, out of which grew *How to Do Things with Rules* (with David Miers) and other ideas on the topics of standpoint, questions and reasoning (Chapter 10).

Chapter 9 deals with Normative or Ethical Jurisprudence. Recapping on my adolescent angst about 'the problem of belief', probably strengthened by early exposures to positivism, this chapter tells how, wrestling with Bentham under the influence of Hart, I became a moral pluralist and an uncertain modified utilitarian; and how later reacting to the local 'Troubles' in Northern Ireland I became intellectually engaged with issues relating to emergency powers and techniques of interrogation of 'terrorists'. This led to in-depth studies of Bentham's writings on torture and human rights, with JB being treated mainly as a sounding-board and even as worthy opponent. At the notable Torture Conference in Paris in 1973 I was dismayed when general empirical questions about its extent and the conditions under which torture flourished were dismissed as 'academic'. Nearly all intellectual attention was focused on abstract problems of legal definition and morality; this left me feeling that the practical problems of preventing and combating torture had not been properly diagnosed. Returning to this uncomfortable subject after a gap of nearly forty years, I have been pleased to find that some progress in prevention of torture has been made through more realistic approaches.

The next two chapters are more analytical. Chapter 10 explains why the idea of standpoint is important in my thinking and how it relates to questioning and reasoning in legal contexts. Chapter 11 on 'Social and Legal Rules' deals with theoretical and practical aspects of making, interpreting, using and otherwise handling all kinds of rules in everyday life, at home, in school or at work as well as in specifically legal contexts.

Chapters 12–14 cover my Warwick period (1972–82) as part of a new 'plate-glass' university in a Law School devoted to 'broadening the study of law from within' (Chapter 12). Chapter 13 tells how thinking about the potential contribution of Jurisprudence to this mission led me to clarify my ideas about the field. At Warwick each of us was asked to rethink a traditional field in a broader way. This stimulated me to develop 'law in context' and 'realism' as ideas and to rethink Evidence in legal contexts (Chapter 14). This became my main project for over twenty years, mainly in co-operation with Terry Anderson and David Schum.

After ten years at Warwick I moved to University College London (UCL) in 1983 to become Quain Professor of Jurisprudence for the (whole) University of London, a rather grand title for a quite demanding job (Chapter 15). Chapter 16 pauses to consider my contrasting relationships with four individuals who formed an important part of the background to my work, especially during the 1980s and 1990s: Jeremy Bentham, Ronald Dworkin, Neil MacCormick and Terry Anderson. At UCL from the early 1990s, while maintaining my interests in Jurisprudence and Evidence, I undertook a major project on the implications of 'globalisation' for understanding law in our rapidly changing world. At UCL I was also involved as both activist and commentator on many aspects of Legal Education policy and practice in many countries. Thinking about recent debates in England, following the important Legal Education and Training Review (2013), I have started to engage in some self-criticism along the lines that we as law teachers have only really paid lip-service to the twin ideas that we should focus more on learning than teaching and take the idea of life-long learning seriously; this has important implications for thinking, research, debate, regulation, diplomacy, policy-making and finance in this area, especially in a period of possibly revolutionary change in education generally, and in legal services and public understanding of law. That is still work in progress (Chapters 17 and 20).

Chapter 18 deals with my explorations on 'Globalisation and Law'. Starting with my uneasy relationship with the ill-named field of 'Law and Development', it links together my colonial childhood, African background, involvement with America and the difficulties of breaking away from the hangovers of colonialism and neo-colonialism, my scepticism about much globababble, and how thinking about law from a global perspective inevitably generates new ideas and uncertainties. It should also make us aware of the extent of our collective ignorance and incomprehension. Chapter 19 on General Jurisprudence considers the implications of a global perspective for Jurisprudence and its role in helping the discipline of Law to adjust to changing circumstances and to realise its potential as a great humanistic discipline. Since the early 1990s a high proportion of my writing and some of my teaching has been in this general area.

After fourteen years at UCL I became a Research Professor and a bit later moved to being half-time. My 'R/retirement' evolved over several years until, sans teaching, sans administration, sans institutional politics, I was on perpetual sabbatical, managing my own agenda. The last twenty years have been among my most productive ones. The book ends with some thoughts on unfinished business and how General Jurisprudence, as I conceive it, can help our discipline respond to the challenges in a period of rapidly expanding globalisation and technological change (Chapter 20).

It will be obvious that I have been in many situations that suggested a need for quite substantial re-examination of what had been treated as well-settled. In Oxford, Herbert Hart challenged the methods and aspirations of a modest kind of Particular Jurisprudence by bringing in the perspective of a lively school of Philosophy that claimed to be leading a 'revolution'; in Chicago an American law school brought to light important aspects of my dissatisfaction with my legal education in England; in Khartoum, and more explicitly in Dar es Salaam, we had to reconsider everything we had learned in the radically different contexts of two newly independent countries; in Belfast in addition to the Troubles the United Kingdom was experiencing a strong wave of legal reform; in my interview at Warwick in 1971, I was asked what subject I was going to 'Warwick-ise' – that is, rethink a field so as to 'broaden it from within'; I chose Evidence and I have been working on it ever since; from about 1980 I have been considering the implications of 'globalisation' for the whole of Law as a discipline. And in my travels, both geographical and intellectual, I have had to respond to numerous culture shocks. At no stage in my academic career have I been working within a really settled tradition. The futures look uncertain. This may explain why so many 'rethinkings' are scattered throughout the text.

As this is not an orthodox autobiography or memoir, I should explain some aspects of how it is arranged. I anticipate several kinds of readers. My intended primary audience is academic lawyers generally; my hope is to persuade them to see their own specialised work in the context of Law as a discipline as a whole and its challenges. Part of the message is that Jurisprudence, Evidence, Legal Education and Globalisation should not be viewed as specialist enclaves, but rather as a necessary part of the context of understanding law for all academic lawyers. A secondary audience is specialists in these and cognate fields. Here I hope that the particular chapters will explain where I am coming from and provide links with more detailed writings. I hope too that they will be stimulating or provocative and that I will be forgiven for letting my hair down from time to time, especially in the notes to the text.

Another important audience is 'non-lawyers', especially academics from other disciplines, but also anyone interested in law. I have tried to make the text accessible to general readers. For the most part, it tries to be readable, but there are a few dense passages that non-specialists may skip. There are notes to the text bunched in a ghetto towards the back. These serve two main functions: first, to provide links to publications by myself and others that deal in more detail with particular topics; secondly, to leave the text unencumbered by points which may be mainly of interest to specialists or by asides which would break the narrative flow. At the start of the notes to the text is a key to the abbreviations used to refer to the most-cited works (e.g. GJP for *General Jurisprudence* (2009)). Memoirists have some exemption from conventions against self-quotation or self-plagiarism. Nearly all of the text is original, but I have occasionally self-quoted or acknowledged passages that I have either adapted or reused, including some written for this book, but then used elsewhere.

This book is therefore about several areas of Law: Jurisprudence; Evidence; Legal Education; Law and Development; Comparative Law; and Globalisation and Law. Throughout my career, legal records and archives have been an avocation, as much as an activist as a scholar. These all began as interests early on, but the different contexts in which my ideas evolved are an important part of the story. I have tried to locate the products of my enquiries, writings and activities in the places and periods in which they were mainly developed through teaching and writing. Some of these areas will be of more interest to some readers than others and the structure allows some judicious skimming or skipping. However, I consider all of these subjects to be interrelated and central to the discipline of Law. *All* academic lawyers, not just specialists, should be concerned with and have a general awareness of trends and developments in all of them because they should be concerned with the relations between Law and other disciplines and the health of our discipline in years to come. All human beings are involved in education, learning, handling rules, solving problems, drawing inferences from evidence, legal relationships, decolonisation and adapting to increased transnational influences. These are central to this story, so I hope that it has a human interest.

Finally, why an autobiography rather than a summation of my ideas? For me that question is about publication rather than writing. I think with my pen and write in order to find out what I think. For many years I jotted down anecdotes and aperçus, as often as not as exercises in writing with no intention of publication. Over time this developed into a sort of scrapbook. I sometimes drew on these to lighten papers written for publication. Later I began to think of this scrapbook as a potential work of art, but only for limited private circulation. Then someone suggested that I should turn this into a full-scale autobiography. I resisted. I am a sceptical reader of such works. As a student of evidence, I see memoirists as unreliable witnesses to be viewed sceptically in terms of their veracity, reliability (especially in respect of memory) and bias. However, most of my sources are documentary. The unattractive motivations of the genre are several and obvious. Anyway, the lives of career academics tend to be very similar and rather boring.

However, at this stage I thought of Collingwood's *Autobiography*, which had been a game-changer when I was 20. I loved the book. Perhaps more important, I felt that many of my main writings have not reached what I consider to be my primary audience: academic lawyers generally. But Evidence is seen as esoteric by non-specialists, and my work is thought to be critical – even hostile – by some orthodox Evidence scholars; many colleagues think that Jurisprudence is too esoteric or difficult, which it often is as practised; even Globalisation is seen as a specialism or a threat or both; and many colleagues don't consider Legal Education as a serious subject worthy of theoretical or scholarly attention. I hope that this work refutes these ideas. A historical account of my intellectual development would not duplicate any of my other writings. So, after sketching an outline, I was hooked. It has been my priority project for the last two years. Nevertheless, I was ambivalent and quite secretive about the project, only going public when this manuscript was nearly ready to go. Why then did I decide to publish? Rather than waste time on further introspection, let me follow my near-contemporary Alan Bennett who, when asked 'why do history?', replied: 'Pass the parcel. That's sometimes all you can do. Take it, feel it, and pass it on. Not for me, not for you, but for someone, somewhere, one day. *Pass it on, boys.*'[6]

Acknowledgements

Collegiality is one of the blessings of academic life. As will be apparent from the text, I owe too many debts to friends, colleagues, students, librarians and others to thank most of them individually. I am particularly grateful to Niki Lacey for agreeing to write the Foreword; Tom Randall, Finola O'Sullivan and Sarah Payne at Cambridge University Press; and to Jem Langworthy, a superb and congenial copy-editor. Andrew Halpin, David Restrepo-Amariles, David Sugarman and others made helpful comments on particular chapters, as have Karen Twining Fooks and Peter Twining. Trevor Rutter and Penelope Twining read and made invaluable suggestions on several drafts of the whole book. They patiently discussed its conception and gave continuing support and encouragement without which it would never have been completed.

Abbreviations

(At p. 285 there is a further list of abbreviations for references in the notes to the text.)

AALS	Association of American Law Schools
ABA	American Bar Association
ALR	American Legal Realism
BNC	Brasenose College Oxford
CLA	Commonwealth Lawyers' Association
CLEA	Commonwealth Legal Education Association
cls	critical legal studies
CPD	Continuing Professional Development
ECHR	European Convention for the Protection of Human Rights and Fundamental Freedoms
EPF	Evidence, Proof and Fact-finding
FBA	Fellow of the British Academy
IALS	Institute of Advanced Legal Studies (University of London)
ILC	International Legal Center (New York)
JD	Juris Doctor (American first degree in Law)
JSPTL	*Journal of the Society of Public Teachers of Law*
KLRM	*Karl Llewellyn and the Realist Movement*
LLB	Bachelor of Laws
LLM	Master of Laws (postgraduate)
LSA	Law and Society Association (US)
LSE	London School of Economics and Political Science
LTP	Law Teachers' Programme (UCL)
MDGs	Millennium Development Goals
MWA	Modified Wigmorean Analysis
NGO	Non-governmental organisation
NIAS	Netherlands Institute of Advanced Study (Wassenaar)
NLR	New Legal Realism
PEAP	Poverty Eradication Action Plan
QUB	The Queen's University Belfast
SAS	School of Advanced Study, University of London

SLA	Socio-legal Studies Association (UK)
SLJR	Sudan Law Journal and Reports
SLS	Society of Legal Scholars (replaced SPTL)
SOAS	School of Oriental and African Studies (London)
SPTL	Society of Public Teachers of Law
TANU	Tanganyika/Tanzania African Union
UCC	The Uniform Commercial Code
UCD	University College Dar es Salaam
UCL	University College London
UM	University of Miami
YMG	Young Members Group of SPTL

1

Jurisprudence: a personal view

Jurisprudentia est divinarum atque humanorum rerum notitia, justi atque injustia. (Jurisprudence is the knowledge of things human and divine, the science of right and wrong.)

(Attributed to Ulpian)

... except law.

(The Hard-nosed Practitioner)

Perhaps sociology is not yet ready for its Einstein, because it has not yet found its Kepler – to say nothing of its Newton, Laplace, Gibbs, Maxwell or Planck.

(Robert K. Merton)[1]

Italo Calvino is one of my favourite authors. As a jurist I often identify with two of his characters, Mr Palomar and Marco Polo. Mr Palomar wishes to understand the universe. He decides to start with particulars. He tries first to see and fix in his mind one individual wave as a precise and finite object. He fails. He tries to work out how to control his lawn, by focusing on a single square metre of it (in order to count how many blades of grass there are, how thick and how distributed). Using statistical analysis, description, narrative and interpretation, he fails again. He becomes neurasthenic. Maybe, describing a constellation of stars viewed from the earth is easier than describing a wave or a patch of grass. But 'this observation of the stars transmits an unstable and contradictory knowledge'.[2] They move, they change, there are faint glimmerings. He distrusts the celestial charts.[3]

Many scholars have Palomar moments. Calvino's vision is anti-reductionist. It is futile to try to master the world or the universe; enquiry is endless. Later we shall encounter Calvino's Kublai Khan who thinks that he can gain control of his Empire by reducing it to sixty-four orderly squares of a wooden chessboard. In counterpoint, his guest, Marco Polo, starts on boundless imaginary journeys by contemplating the grain of a single square.[4] Particularity and generality, simplicity and complexity are relative matters. On a continuum of simplicity and complexity I am closer to Marco Polo than Kublai Khan, but I do try to think in terms of broad pictures and frameworks and hypotheses in order to set contexts for more particular enquiries.[5]

This book is based on a particular vision of Jurisprudence, which many do not share. I wish to start by making that vision clear. This is how I summarised my position recently: I am a jurist, although by necessity I dabble in other disciplines, including philosophy, anthropology and literature. My central concern here is with the health of law as a discipline.

I use 'jurisprudence' and 'legal theory' as synonyms. Some do not.[6] I treat the field of Jurisprudence as the theoretical part of Law as a discipline. The mission of a discipline is to advance and disseminate knowledge and understandings of its subject matters. The mission of the discipline of Law is to advance and disseminate knowledge and understandings of the subject matters of that discipline. These subject matters are neither static nor well-defined – nor should they be.[7]

The term 'Jurisprudence' is like the term 'Law' in phrases such as 'Law as a discipline' or 'the Harvard Law School' or a course on 'the Law of Torts'. These signify 'field concepts'; that is to say, they are rough labels or designations of fields or areas of enquiry with no precise or stable borders and very little analytical purchase.[8] 'Law' in Harvard Law School does not need and should not have a general theory or definition.

Jurisprudence (and Legal Theory as a synonym) is the theoretical part of that discipline; a theoretical question is a question posed at a relatively high level of abstraction; 'Legal Philosophy' broadly refers to the most abstract parts of Jurisprudence; in my view, this is just one aspect of Jurisprudence because understandings of legal phenomena and ideas require addressing questions at many levels of abstraction and generality from many different perspectives. For example, the topic of 'judicial reasoning', conventionally interpreted as reasoning about doubtful or disputed questions of law, can involve questions about reasoning in general (philosophical), judicial reasoning in general, judicial reasoning about questions of law, judicial reasoning about questions of law in common law/anglophone/American appellate courts or the US Supreme Court; reasoning about questions of law over a period of time in one court in a specific jurisdiction; or the reasoning style of one particular appellate judge. These are *all* theoretical questions, although the last two may be on the borderline depending on the approach adopted. Some of these questions need only a small acquaintance with legal matters; some require the lenses of more than one discipline. The more one moves down one or more such ladders of abstraction, the more engaging with such questions requires local legal and other knowledge.[9]

I view Jurisprudence as a heritage, as an ideology, and especially as an activity. The idea of *heritage* reminds us that Jurisprudence has a history and that, even within a quite narrow 'tradition', the total picture of extant texts, ideas and debates can be vast, complex and daunting. Most historical overviews of the Western tradition of jurisprudence extend back at least to classical Greece (Plato and Aristotle) and include different strands of Western Christianity (especially Natural Law), the secular enlightenment, grand social theory (e.g. Marx, Weber and Durkheim), several branches of philosophy as well as specifically jurisprudential studies.

Some student books attempt to classify and describe the main strands of modern legal theory in terms of crude, overlapping 'schools' and 'isms', such as Natural Law, the Analytical School, the Historical School, the Sociological School, Law and Economics, Realism, Marxism, Positivism, Feminism and Post-modernism.[10] For convenience of exposition it is sometimes useful to speak of three domains of Jurisprudence: Analytical, Normative and Empirical (including Historical) reflecting the idea that understanding law involves concepts, values and facts. In most enquiries in legal studies all three are combined. In some conceptual analysis, normative evaluation or empirical concerns may be paramount, but it is dangerous to treat any of these as separate sub-disciplines. Such 'domains' are merely broad kinds of field concepts.[11]

Looking on jurisprudence as a heritage emphasises continuity and the relevance of history. It brings into focus problems of selection and some of the difficulties of classifying and generalising about ideas and thinkers.[12] Viewing Jurisprudence as *ideology* is also helpful. The term 'ideology' is ambiguous: it can refer to a set (sometimes a system) of beliefs or, in Marxist usage, it can refer to beliefs that are distorted by self-interest. Both usages are relevant here: the first draws attention to the links between one's beliefs about law and one's more general beliefs about the world. My main aim as a teacher of Jurisprudence has been to stimulate students to align their own assumptions and beliefs about law to their other beliefs and to reflect on and refine both. The same kind of exercise is involved in critically examining the normative assumptions underlying a particular legal system or body of law, whether or not they are coherent.

The Marxist sense of 'ideology' is a useful reminder of the close connections between belief, self-interest and delusion. A central theme of critical legal theory has been to stress the close connections between law and politics and to put into question any claims to impartiality or objectivity in theorising about law. Some commentators even dismiss Jurisprudence as 'ideological' in this pejorative sense, as an inescapably self-justificatory or even obfuscating enterprise. By this they may mean that the main function of Jurisprudence has been to purport to legitimate law and its study by providing politico-moral justifications for legal systems, especially state legal systems. This may be partly true about some practices of legal theorising.

Viewing jurisprudence as heritage and ideology provides useful reminders of important points. However, in the present context, I see the field mainly in terms of the *activity* of theorising about the subject matters of our discipline; that is, posing, analysing, reposing, researching, reflecting on, arguing about and even answering general questions relating to these subject matters from different standpoints and at different levels of abstraction.

One kind of jurisprudential activity, especially in teaching, is entering into dialogue with significant texts selected from our vast heritage. The main objective is to clarify one's own views, but in order to do this sensibly one needs to understand the texts historically, for instance in ways that R. G. Collingwood and Quentin Skinner have pioneered. Dead jurists have other secondary uses as targets of satire or caricature or crude classification into schools or as exemplars of a particular perspective or tendency.

Theorising is a questioning and answering and reasoning activity. Some of the products of this are more or less tentative or confident answers to questions of many different kinds. Some substantial, carefully worked out answers may deserve the name of 'theories'; but very often the products of theorising are answers to quite modest or specific questions or the dissolution of puzzlements or clarifying concepts.

The term 'theory' is also bandied about to refer to speculative hypotheses or working assumptions or presuppositions or as a form of self-aggrandisement.[13] The term 'theory of law', which is ambiguous, is in my view greatly overused and abused. It has one specific meaning, as an attempt to answer the question: what is the nature or essence of law? I am sceptical of that enterprise for several reasons: I don't understand the question; I doubt if law has a nature or essence; I also doubt that any abstract theory of this kind can have much analytical purchase or organising function for our discipline – it is likely to be too abstract and reductionist. However, the main point here is that theories – and especially theories of law – are not, and should not be, the main products of legal theorising. *Jurisprudence is not a one-question subject.*

I do not have, and do not aspire to, a General or Grand Theory of Law.[14] Most of my work involves middle-range theorising in between detailed particularity and very abstract philosophising.[15] For instance, in my project on Globalisation and Law I have been quite sceptical of Grand or universal reductionist theories of either 'globalisation' or 'law', and have chosen to focus on sub-global patterns, and topics that are most appropriately dealt with at lower levels of abstraction, such as legal pluralism, diffusion of law[16] and 'rethinking' specialised fields such as Evidence,[17] Torts,[18] Land Law[19] and Comparative Law.[20] At these 'middle-range' levels, unlike Merton, I have not tried to fashion neat theories, but have rather thought in terms of the interaction between very particular enquiries and more general working assumptions that need to be articulated and examined critically from time to time. For me working assumptions are like planks of a raft more or less tightly fastened together to provide a temporary and more or less stable platform on a boundless sea which in turn has varying moods. The planks may have various origins and may or may not fit easily together.[21] One job of the theorist is to help to articulate these often tacit working assumptions, to examine them critically and, where necessary, to adjust, repair or replace particular planks and only occasionally to risk jumping onto a new or completely different set of rafts.[22]

What is the use of theorising? There is no single general answer. Of course, sometimes it is useless, sometimes very important or even essential. It can be an end in itself. In the present context I wish to emphasise its potential contribution to the health of the discipline of Law, the aim of which is to develop and disseminate understandings of the subject matters of that discipline. From that perspective, theorising has several functions or 'jobs':[23] constructing total pictures (synthesising); clarification and construction of individual concepts and conceptual frameworks; developing normative theories, such as theories of justice or human rights; constructing, refining and testing empirical hypotheses; developing working theories for participants (e.g. prescriptive theories of law-making or adjudication or advocacy in a particular legal system); and so on – wherever thinking at a relatively general level contributes to understanding.

For me the most important function is articulating, exposing to view and critically assessing significant assumptions and presuppositions underlying legal discourse generally and particular aspects of it – not only issues about law in general, but also the assumptions and presuppositions of sub-disciplines, as has been happening recently in fields obviously affected by globalisation, such as Comparative Law and Public International Law. This critical function can usefully be applied to one's own work as well as to others – there is a need for self-critical legal studies (Chapter 19). One conclusion of my project on 'Globalisation and Law' has been that these complex and varied processes challenge some of the mainstream general working assumptions of Western traditions of academic law (Chapter 19). An important reason for this, as we shall see, is that for at least two centuries these traditions have very largely focused on the details of domestic municipal or state law of particular countries, such as English Law or German Law or American Law, and have not developed much equipment for dealing with enquiries that cross national or other jurisdictional borders.[24]

From relatively early in my career I had to make 'the case for law' in respect of funding legal education and research, mainly in developing countries, often in competition with the claims of agriculture, economics, population studies and so on. In that context I became an advocate for my discipline, using a fairly standard argument:

> [T]here are certain tendencies in Law as an academic subject which justify cautious generalization. For typically it is (a) part of the humanities, not least because it covers so many phases of human relationships and (b) it is intellectually demanding and (c) it is directly related to the world of concrete practical problems and (d) it is concerned, as perhaps no other subject is concerned, with process and procedure from the point of view of participants, and (e) it has a long heritage of literature and resources. While none of these elements is on its own peculiar to Law, perhaps no other discipline combines them in the same way and to the same degree: thus Law can be as intellectually exacting as Philosophy, but more down-to-earth; as concerned with contemporary real life problems as Medicine or Engineering, but with closer links to the humanities; as concerned with power and decision-making as Political Science, but

more concerned with the how of handling process ... This being so, it is important that it should be done well.[25]

This is of course a piece of advocacy, perhaps a bit overstated, but nevertheless sincere about the potential of my discipline. This is why I call myself 'a legal nationalist'. However, I shall argue that Law as a discipline has some way to go before it fulfils that potential.

Few of the specific ideas presented here are unique. For example, others have argued for a better integration of Analytical, Normative and Empirical Jurisprudence; or for viewing theorising as an activity; or for constructing contextual intellectual histories of our heritage of legal thought; or for acknowledging the ideological function of much legal theorising; or for viewing theoretical enquiry both as an end in itself and as having several different instrumental functions. Combining these ideas may be unusual, but the important point in this book is, first, that all of these ideas are directly relevant to the health of the discipline of Law and, secondly, that the biggest challenge facing both Law and Legal Theory is taking the implications of globalisation seriously.

This book is by someone who is an enthusiast for his discipline, who believes that theorising can contribute greatly to understanding law at many levels and that this enterprise should be of interest to anyone who wishes to understand law in these confusing times – which should, of course, be nearly everyone.

2

Childhood and schooling (1934–52)

> Twinkle, twinkle tiny Twinks,
> Never mind what Daddy thinks,
> Mummie'll make you fat and sleek,
> You know she started Baby Week.
> (*Uganda Argus,* 24 September 1934)

I was born in Kampala on 22 September 1934. Brigitte Bardot and Sophia Loren were born on the same day, but shifted the dates as they could not stand each other: Sophia older, Brigitte younger. I am the only person I know who has been celebrated in this way in the *Uganda Argus*. There is evidence to support the message.[1] A colonial scene. My early life and education are no more than background. My mother was a doctor specialising in public health and child welfare. My father was a colonial administrator, largely because it was a condition of his marriage that he should cease to be a professional soldier and move into civil administration, preferably in Africa. At the time he was a frustrated anti-bureaucrat festering in the Secretariat in Entebbe.

My family background was a mixture of nuanced grades of the Victorian middle classes. My mother's family were mainly soldiers, merchants and comfortably off country gentlefolk: my maternal grandfather, William DuBuisson, had qualified as a barrister, but by chance inherited from a childless cousin a charming estate and farm (Glynhir) in Carmarthenshire, bought at an auction in 1770 by a Huguenot refugee called Pierre Groteste, son of Paul Groteste, Sieur du Buisson, the direct ancestor, we think, of all English DuBuissons.

The Twinings acquired the name when they emigrated from the village of Twyning (various spellings, meaning 'between two rivers'), so they are not all related. My father's side was a fusion of upwardly mobile West Country folk – labourers, and later millers and merchants. My entrepreneurial great-grandmother was registered as a merchant: she sold provisions on a wharf on the canal at Dudley (Worcestershire) and married a boatman, who became the local station-master. My paternal grandfather was vicar of St Stephen's, Westminster for many years; he married into the Bournes, grander, downwardly mobile country gentry. My grandmother Agatha was the eighth of nine Bourne children, including six daughters, none of whom married money. Agatha's eldest sister Ruth, whose eighty-volume diary is in the Herefordshire County Archive, wrote of my grandfather: 'Isn't it a pity that William did not go to Oxford or Cambridge; he only went to King's.' As far as I can tell my grandfather was the first Twining ever to go to University.

The most notable member of the family was Sir Samuel Baker, the explorer, who was my grandmother Agatha's uncle and much boasted about in the family. I was more attracted by his younger brother, Valentine (1827–87), who was a rising star in the 10th Hussars until he was convicted of assaulting a Miss Dickinson in a railway carriage, imprisoned and dismissed from the Army. His subsequent career in the Middle East was quite romantic. As an undergraduate I spent considerable time in the Bodleian analysing the evidence in Great-uncle Val's trial to test the family legend that he had sacrificed himself for the Prince of Wales. This was my first exercise in analysis of evidence; I regretfully concluded that the legend was wishful thinking.[2]

I spent the first ten years of my life first in Uganda and then in wartime Mauritius and for the next ten years being educated in England at boarding schools and in Oxford, while my parents were abroad. Both my parents had strong personalities and considerable talents and energies. My father eventually had a very successful career culminating in being Governor of Tanganyika for almost ten years and becoming one of the first life peers. My mother continued selflessly working for medical causes until a few days before her death in her late seventies. My parents' circles (family, friends and acquaintances) were populated by what used to be called 'strong women'.[3] This probably nudged me towards thinking of women as people. However, until I was about 20, girls seemed to be a different species. Within the family, sex was not discussed, passion was suppressed or lacking, praise was in short supply, sentiment was not done; but, as one friend observed in surprise when I tried to evoke my family to her: 'All that *affection!*'

I learned much from each of my parents, but I chose a career as a legal theorist and intellectual largely to move out of their shadows and to prove that I was capable of doing something well without their help. Both were intensely practical and one lesson I took from them was to reject any sharp distinction between theory and practice. I also learned from my father to think strategically in long time-frames and 'total pictures' and from my mother to keep my head down and get on with the job.

I have sometimes said that 'I had a colonial childhood, an anti-colonial adolescence, a neocolonial start to my career, and a post-colonial middle-age'. This succinctly captures an important theme in my story, but it is too glib, first, because the terms are both vague and ambiguous; and secondly, especially in respect of literature, because the last term has acquired a specific political meaning different from what I originally intended.[4] On the first three terms my usage should be clear from the context: my father was a colonial administrator and my upbringing was fairly typical of such children; the process of rejection of my parents' benevolent paternalism was a slow process which came to a head when I was 21, linked to both a growing political awareness, a concern for personal autonomy and mixing with embittered African students in London and Paris (Chapter 3); the ambiguities and ambivalences of working as an expatriate in two newly independent countries are explicitly dealt with in Chapters 5 and 6, including enthusiastic 'nationalism' and an underestimation of the power of path-dependency and the extent and complexities of hybrids.

My mother and I arrived in Mauritius in February 1939. We were joined a few months later by Evelyn, a cousin and close friend of my mother's and an intellectual sparring partner for my father. She was my godmother, and later guardian and de facto second mother. My parents' Guest Book contained an entry: E. S. DuBuisson, arrived May 1939, left August 1944. When war broke out in September, we were effectively marooned there for five years. My elder brother, John, had stayed in England for health reasons and saw his father once and his mother not at all until 1944.

During the war my father was mainly working undercover for MI6, my mother was engaged full time in public health, including attempting to eradicate malaria, and Evelyn worked in my father's office, among other things helping to intercept Japanese transmissions.[5] I knew nothing of this. Nor did the grown-ups let on that for long periods Mauritius seemed likely to be invaded by the Japanese. Rather I have blissful memories of growing up as, in effect, an only colonial child and lording it over younger 'European' children in the makeshift primary school that my mother organised in our garden.

We had arrived in Mauritius in February 1939 and left in June 1944, by boat to Durban, train to Cape Town and there we boarded the *Andes*, a troopship converted from a liner, bound for Liverpool. This was quite a dangerous journey: the small coaster that took us from Port Louis to Durban was torpedoed on its return journey. The *Andes* was in a convoy threatened by U-Boats, and made a break for Liverpool towards the end of the voyage. I was again kept in the dark about most of this.

My father had a 'good war' – that is, he was very successful and his career took off; my mother had a very busy one; Evelyn had an intellectually demanding one; and I had a blissfully ignorant colonial childhood in what, for me, was an island paradise. I have written up some unreliable memories, but only one remembered incident seems directly relevant here. This was my first research project.

'Let me see your thing', said Joe, 'and you can see mine'. 'I'd rather see your bum', said I. 'OK, let's toss for who goes first'. I lost. Joe had his look. There was a loud hammering on the bathroom door. *Cognitio interrupta.* 'Thing' did not seem quite right. So, what was its real name? I tried unsuccessfully to wheedle this out of my medical mother by indirection. How then to find out? My father had obtained a set of *The Encyclopedia Britannica* for his office. It was a black-bound copy of the landmark eleventh edition (1910–11) in twenty-eight volumes plus Index. The trouble was that only one volume could be borrowed at a time, so I started my research career with *A–Aus*. I worked through the early volumes. I could not explain my purpose – I was looking for the name of 'the thing'. They were impressed. I persisted, but my approach was methodo-logically unsound. I failed. But my parents may have got a hint that, despite their aversion to academia, I was destined for an academic career.

Until I was about 10 my only visual memories of England were of Woolworth's threepenny and sixpenny store in Godalming High Street (why were some things a whole shilling?) and about 1937, aged 3, being carried screaming from my first moving picture, *Snow White*. I have been averse to Walt Disney ever since. When I arrived in England from Mauritius in 1944 I found it very strange. I was probably two years behind my age-group academically, but I had acquired a taste for Dickens, and fluent local creole – a form of French with no grammar but a much richer vocabulary than the curriculum permitted. So, when I was deposited at a prep school, St Ronan's – rusticated during the war to East Budleigh in Devon – I was not only a displaced person, like many others, but also a colonial waif who had never encountered cricket or football or rugger or conkers or snow or algebra or a school of sixty or seventy schoolboys, let alone a charismatic giant called 'Harry' with large bushy eyebrows. I was bewildered and apprehensive, awed by the Headmaster and probably rather withdrawn. When a kindly grand-mother-substitute asked the new bugs if we were homesick, I reputedly said: 'I don't have a home to be sick on.' This innocently bathetic response was repeated within my family long afterwards. But it was true.

Holidays were difficult. My parents' house in Godalming was let. We were billeted on kindly – probably long-suffering – but uncomprehending relatives. Fortunately, my elder brother, John, whom I had barely met before arriving in England in 1944, took me under his wing, taught me how to be independent and fend off grown-ups, and over the next few years introduced me to cricket, humorous verse and some delights of middlebrow literature, including Bernard Shaw, Christopher Fry, James Elroy Flecker, Lorca, Lewis Carroll and Hilaire Belloc. John made me into an intellectual of sorts and then deserted the life of the intellect after he became engaged to his commanding officer's daughter while doing National Service in Gibraltar.

Both my brother and I have been fascinated with archives, and preserving legal and family records has been for me a lifelong avocation. I have dumped minor collections in several improbable places. I would never have made an archivist, because, like my brother, I love reading and 'playing' with them. How did this fascination start? The story is linked to John. It is too fantastic to be true in its details, but I lack the imagination to have made it up. Somewhere, maybe at the home of relatives on whom we were billeted, maybe when I was 11 or 12, there was a large cardboard box labelled 'family photographs'. It contained dozens of hardboard photos, mainly portraits and groups of elderly Victorians and other ancestors. With two, three or four players, we used to deal them out. Each played one photo. We then switched from being partisans to adjudicators. The ugliest individual won by acclaim, often after prolonged rational debate. This game was ahead of its time because it was collaborative and consensual, rather than competitive. It bore my brother's hallmarks and I am pleased to give the credit for this invention to John.

St Ronan's proved to be quite gentle and literate. In fact, it gave me a soft landing in 1940s England. The next stage, Charterhouse, was less easy. Many Old Carthusians, including Frederick Raphael, Simon Raven and Mark Frankland (as well as Thackeray and Robert Graves) have given it a bad press, mythologising the anti-intellectualism, unhappinesses and terrors of public school life. My memories are similar, but a bit more ambivalent. By the time I got there I had nearly caught up academically and was placed in the classical stream where I scraped along miserably, hating the masters and their approach to learning. Latin and Greek involved grammar, parsing, meticulous translating, without any emphasis on the classics as literature. The only bits I enjoyed were Ancient History and composing Latin verse. My first two years were overshadowed by a mixture of alienation, terror and humiliation as a classical specialist.

My nemesis was R. L. Arrowsmith, 'the Arrow', who taught us Latin and Greek and English for two years in the Remove. Reminiscent of Long John Silver, a wiry, one-legged tyrant, he was famous for his relentless discipline and biting sarcasm. Frederick Raphael describes him as follows: 'Arrowsmith had a lupine smile, a swinging limp and an exquisitely neat Greek script. His florid complexion and hawkish nose gave a confused impression of bonhomie and menace; he was capable of both.'[6] I only experienced the menace. He seems to have singled me out, perhaps because he thought that I was not trying, when in truth I was petrified. I was relentlessly called on, humiliated and verbally castigated in what seemed like every class. The Arrow almost single-handedly destroyed for me any hope of enjoying the classics and, for most of my time at school, any love of formal learning. It cast a pall over almost the whole of my experience at Charterhouse. This was genuine child abuse and a reverse role model for teachers. I tried at 15 to switch to history, but my House tutor persuaded my father that I should stick with Classics on the grounds that history is bunk. My father, himself an amateur historian, treated it as an avocation rather than as a proper subject. I stayed on at the bottom of the classical stream. By 15 I had developed techniques of survival and playing the system. During my adolescence I built up an elaborate system of defences against authority, intrusive peers, curious aunts and my parents. So there became two WLTs: one outwardly cheerful, humorous, frivolous, conformist, friendly; behind that anxious, resentful of authority, solitary and intensely serious.

One saving grace of Charterhouse was that it encouraged self-education. Classicists were given very little instruction in other subjects, which we had to get up almost on our own for the national exams, then known as School Certificate and Higher Certificate. These 'public examinations' were treated by the authorities as both an intrusion and a dilution of the pure stream of classical learning. We were left to do most of the preparation on our own, but were nevertheless expected not to let the school down by failing to get Distinctions in most subjects. We had to take papers in at least eight subjects, including one each in English Language and English Literature. Only two periods a week were assigned for English. The set books for the Literature paper were *The Tempest* and *The Nonne's Preest's Tale*. After a perfunctory introduction to the texts at the start of the year, the English master, Wreford-Brown, told us to get on with reading them on our own and we would discuss them in due course. Instead, the two periods were devoted almost entirely to a seemingly random stroll through tid-bits of English literature, including reading aloud some P. G. Wodehouse short stories, Masefield's *Reynard the Fox* and selections of Browning and Keats.

We enjoyed the classes, but by about February we began to worry about our set books. Wreford-Brown fobbed us off, saying that we would get around to them all in good time. So, we set up our own study group, bought a crib for the Chaucer, and although I had not previously conceived of literary criticism, I found some essays on *The Tempest* in the library. They were a revelation, but did not link the play to colonialism, resistance and dependency. The few classes eventually devoted to discussion of the set texts served mainly as revision and clarification. Most of us got Distinctions. I do not know whether this enforced self-education was inadvertent or deliberate on the part of our teachers – it was probably a bit of both. Ever since then I have believed in self-education and have been an auto-didact – with some of the strengths and weaknesses that entails.

At Charterhouse, I extended what the school offered by way of formal instruction and developed an idiosyncratic programme of self-education. By the age of 15 I was definitely bookish, but eclectic in my tastes. I did not read classics for pleasure. During holidays from school, I used to haunt Thorpe's second-hand bookshop at the top of the High Street in Guildford as well as Foyle's in Charing Cross Road and, a bit later, the wonderful second-hand bookshops in Edinburgh. I spent most of my pocket-money on books. Aged 14–15 my main purchases were humour, cricket, Latin and Greek 'cribs', a few novels and especially books on self-improvement. Over time this extended to detective stories (especially Simenon), and novels mixed in with history, World War II (Churchill, generals), Africana, and reference. By 18 I had become fascinated by African exploration and collected and devoured books by Livingstone, Stanley, Emin Pasha, Bruce and, of course, Great-uncle Sam (Sir Samuel Baker). What I hid and read under the bedclothes in my cubicle was not so much soft porn – apart from the occasional *Lilliput* – but books on hypnosis, self-improvement, and how to write short stories. Schoolboy prurience was forgivable; being caught taking oneself seriously was not.[7]

The school was divided into eleven separate units or 'Houses', each with its own distinctive traditions and culture. The Houses stood in much the same relationship to the school as Colleges at Oxford and Cambridge stand to the

University. For most boys it was the House rather than the school that was the hub of their pressurised daily existence. Outside the classroom life centred on these small communities for discipline, sports, free time, gossip and even military training. My House, Saunderites (about seventy boys), was even more autonomous than most because the House Master was also the Headmaster and his attention was elsewhere.

Three specific memories of Charterhouse are relevant to later themes in this book. They relate to micro-politics and legalism.

In Saunderites there was almost complete apathy about national and international politics. The Empire was taken for granted and the Conservatives were the good guys. Micro-politics was a different matter. Power and authority were perceived as much in terms of personalities as rules and top-down control. Tradition, the House Master and occasionally more remote authority prescribed the rules, but these were interpreted, enforced, adjusted, manipulated, applied woodenly or flexibly, or waived by boys at various levels of authority. Order was maintained, disputes were resolved and leadership exerted almost entirely by members of the House. One had to develop jungle survival skills, much was negotiable and the ways in which one protected one's private space can be interpreted in terms of resistance to authority and alien rule.

Macro-politics was of no interest. Rather, for most of my time, relations with other boys were a highly political process involving jockeying for position, bargaining, assessing character, and local ideological differences that sometimes deteriorated into factions and feuds.[8] One day, when our gorgeous Matron had allowed four of us to book the sick-room, we spent the whole time minutely analysing the character of each member of the House and predicting where they would be in ten years' time. We were proud of these skills.

The main political feud of my time centred on compulsory sport. The 'sporties' wanted to impose a strict regime of physical activity every day for the glory of the House; the 'bolshies' argued for a minimum of compulsion and tried to organise intellectual or otherwise subversive pursuits. As I was keen on sports, but not much good, and against compulsion, I often acted as a go-between among the factions. In my last year for several months I was the main channel of communication between two pairs of ideologues who shared a dormitory but were not on speaking terms. As an intellectual who was keen on games I held the balance of power among the monitors – as messenger, envoy, mediator, architect of truces and compromises. I enjoyed that role. It may be because of this, combined with my father's oft-repeated dictum that 'politics and dishonour are synonymous', that I have tended to approach politics through the lens of diplomacy and tactics more than ideology and commitment to parties or causes.

To its credit Charterhouse gave one a few freedoms. Cubicles and studies were private. One civilised rule was that we were free to go anywhere without express permission provided that one did not cross a railway line – an example of a well-crafted rule. There was sufficient free time to escape. Many boys cycled for hours in the Surrey hills. My parents had bought a house in Godalming about a mile from the school. To reach it did not involve crossing a railway line. The house was let, but I was allowed to keep my bedroom in consideration for reduced rent. This was my bolt-hole. There I kept my most private things and could play or do serious stuff on my own. My bedroom had a cork floor and I could spend hours playing battleships or STUMPZ (a cricket game) or patience or reading, even writing – always by myself.

Two incidents of my early teens are rather difficult to interpret. Some might see them as early signs of a nascent legalism. Baden-Powell, the founder of the Boy Scouts, was an Old Carthusian and the school had to have a thriving Scout Troop. As a new bug one was given the choice 'Scouts or Pioneers'? Pioneers looked after the grounds and involved manual labour. The incentive to join Scouts was that one postponed compulsory 'Corps', which trained boy soldiers. Almost by accident I led an unsuccessful revolt. In order to be initiated we had to be prepared to swear an oath, which has a long and convoluted history. The Charterhouse version involved promising to be clean in thought, word and deed, and to do a good deed every day. I teased my friends: 'You don't seriously intend to be clean in thought *and* word *and* deed, Young, do you? What about those filthy stories you were telling last night?' For the first time in my life I took a political stance: 'They can't force you to take an oath in which you don't believe.' Soon I had recruited perhaps half of the Scouts' new intake. We told the Scoutmaster that we did not feel that we could in good conscience swear a solemn oath which we neither wished nor were able to keep. The authorities were nonplussed until someone with a military background remembered that there are ways of dealing with conchies. Now only three or four in number, we were transferred to the Pioneers where we were made to dig holes and then fill them up again.

At bedtime at the start of one term there was a knock on my cubicle door: 'Confirmation or Boxing?' Although one had to do Boxing at least once, I chose to postpone it, so I joined the confirmation class. There was good cocoa at the first meeting after lights out, but then people began to get solemn. After a bit I caught the mood. We were going to be asked to swear to the Thirty-nine Articles of the Anglican Church. I was not sure that I believed any of those that made sense. We were being asked politely to testify to *belief* that we had voluntarily chosen. Choice and belief – two new concepts for me. The idea that the choice was free was, of course, treated with good-humoured schoolboy cynicism. Henry B., 'The Reverend', made it sound as if it was for real, but we would have a chance to voice any doubts we might have in private.

On my own I went through the Thirty-nine Articles one by one: a tick for the ones I believed in, a cross for those I didn't understand or accept (how can you swear to something you don't understand?) and half for those I had Doubts about. I don't remember the precise figures, but it was something like 3 – 12 –

24. The dilemma was acute: to swear that I believed in the ones I didn't believe would be blasphemy if God existed and lying if he didn't. I was so upset that I mustered the courage to ask for a private audience with 'The Reverend'. But I didn't have the face to tell him the true score. Instead I fudged it: there were some of the articles that I didn't understand and I had Doubts about the Trinity. To my surprise the Reverend was gentle and sympathetic; he took me through some troublesome articles explaining them carefully, and then, to my utter amazement, he complimented me. He conveyed some vague idea that reflective doubt, reading the small print and taking the detail seriously were commendable rather than sinful. He also suggested that some matters, like belief in God and the Resurrection and redemption, were central and that it was quite common for some people to have doubts about some of the lesser articles even after confirmation. How could they, I wondered? I did not play my Ace, the Holy Ghost, but went ahead feeling guilty. I had never heard of Jeremy Bentham, but like him, I resisted being compelled to take an oath. We both disliked oaths because we took them seriously. It never occurred to me that I was being asked to commit or accept as an act of will; to me it seemed that I was being forced into a lie. This led me to have a life-long problem with the idea of belief.

Was I as an adolescent exhibiting a precocious legalistic streak? If 'legalism' in individuals refers to being over-fond of rules or a tendency to very literal interpretation, neither of these is the point of these anecdotes. Like Bentham, I disliked being compelled to swear to something that I did not believe in, but that was not because of literal-mindedness about the meaning of the oath. Similarly, with Scouts I resisted being pressured into making a promise that I would not keep.

Classics, coercively taught by sour old men who had missed the war, only gave me a small portion of the supposed benefits of a classical education: a reasonable command of language, some analytical skills and a concern for accuracy. I trailed along reluctantly towards the bottom of the classical stream. The system cannot have been totally flawed, for at least three of my near contemporaries became distinguished scholars in Classics and Philosophy: [Sir] Geoffrey Lloyd, [Sir] Richard Sorabji and Richard Swinburne, all now Fellows of the British Academy. I have never been able to read Latin and Greek classics for pleasure. My experience made me draw a sharp distinction between public and private study: learning enforced through discipline and pain, on the one hand; and self-education, carried out secretly and eccentrically in my own sheltered private world. Insofar as I attained a broad general education and a love of literature it was in spite of Charterhouse, not because of it. As Mark Twain is supposed to have said: 'I have never let schooling interfere with my education.'

I left unevenly equipped to face the next stage on the easy path to success and riches. If I had never met a girl, I had seen two in the flesh, and many in *Lilliput*. I was confirmed and practised in my religion and had fulfilled almost all of the routines of low-church Anglican observance; I was disciplined in word if not in thought. If I never had actually been caned, I had imagined it all too often. If I had not been taught good manners at school, as my parents complained, I had learned some of the basic arts of diplomacy, courtiership, political manipulation and playing the system; I had learned some of the perils of friendship and the possibilities of power. I gained some insight into the complex ways of ordering and dispute-processing in a closed community. I had been taught that honour and fame go to the natural athlete, scholarship money to the well-disciplined swot, loss of privilege and advancement to the subversive. I had experienced, and rejected, an extreme form of nationalism: the value placed on loyalty to one's own House or tribe and of the inferiority of all outside it. Above all, I had learned to dissimulate, so that I could be witty, sarcastic or flippant without letting on that I was unhappy or afraid or pursuing a private agenda.

3

Oxford and after (1952-7)

Getting in

We were reading for Higher Certificate and were expected to do well. It was assumed by the family that I would go to 'BNC' (Brasenose College, Oxford), following in the footsteps of an uncle and my brother. Nevertheless, even in those days, one had to take an entrance exam and submit to interview. I had been well-drilled in Classics. For the interview, my brother's advice was: 'For God's sake, be interesting.' I prepared. Presented with a formidable array of gowned Fellows, with the ascetic Principal, Hugh Last, at the head of the table, I was nervous. When eventually the right question came, I was ready.

> 'Mr Twining, what do you do in your spare time?'
> 'Well, er, I read . . . and watch cricket' . . . and then
> quickly, but modestly, 'I am an erstwhile
> phillumenist.'

A rustle went around the table. None of them knew the word. Eventually a classicist spoke up:

> 'A lover of light?'
> 'Oh No. A collector of match-box
> labels.'

I had upstaged a bevy of dons. I was in. And grew more confident. I told them how my father had accepted a bet that he could not collect 1,000 different labels in a year. He won the bet, thanks largely to the Japanese. He gave the lot to me when I was 10. I had collected until I was about 14, but then retired. Hence the 'erstwhile'. I went on: 'But I have kept up. King Farouk of Egypt is the leading phillumenist in the world . . . ' Then, getting bolder: 'There are of course several magazines. The best is *Match Boxes and Match-Boxing*.' The last was a complete fabrication.

Getting on

I arrived in Oxford with a poor-to-middling academic record and no special interest in law. There was no thought of an academic career as a possibility. I may have been considered quite clever, but everyone including myself was surprised when I was awarded a State Scholarship, probably because I had written an answer on the economic policy of the Gracchi, having randomly borrowed a book from the library.

I had applied to read Law in Oxford for largely negative reasons. I was determined to escape Classics; my father had dissuaded me from History; my brother had read Law, narrowly missed a First, and offered me his notes. I had no curiosity about the subject. For my first five terms I did the bare minimum of work on law and continued to focus on literature, mainly twentieth-century literature under the tutelage of my closest friend, Trevor Rutter. I read voraciously and seriously – once resolving to read Virginia Woolf's *Between the Acts* five or six times in quick succession in order to try to understand it. My classical background made Roman Law easy, and there was plenty of that, but it had not helped with literary criticism or theory.

I did not enjoy my legal studies nor take them very seriously for my first two years, doing the minimum necessary for preparing generally second-rate essays and scraping through the start-of-term tests ('Collections'). My mind was more on literature, politics and East Africa. Unlike some other Colleges, which looked down on Law as somewhere between Geography and Agriculture, BNC had a strong legal tradition with a significant number of law students (fourteen or fifteen in our year). We formed a close-knit group, partly because the separate Law Library was also a social club. I attended very few lectures, the main exception being two series on defamation, one by Robert Goff (later Lord Goff) in Lincoln because they were brilliant, one by Alderman Brown (the Lord Mayor of Oxford) in Worcester instead of coffee – dirty stories from the Year Books, mainly about defamation. However, I had two expert and concerned tutors in Barry Nicholas and Ron Maudsley who may have taught me much more than I realised.

Then in my second summer term two things changed. First, in my autodidactic way I started to have a serious philosophical concern. I just could not understand how people could believe anything with confidence in the face of the variety of strongly held opposing beliefs and opinions that there were. Over the Easter vacation 1954 I spent most of my time struggling over an essay, written solely for myself, on what I called 'the problem of belief'. It was stimulated in part by my reading and being surrounded by political disagreements, but less consciously by an increasing tension between my 'Oxford self', represented by my private intellectual life and Oxford politics, and the very different atmosphere when I stayed with my parents on holidays in Dar es Salaam – still in awe of and dominated by my father and his firmly stated outlook on life. I had had previous concerns about theology and confirmation, but this time it was not so much about religion or cosmology as about the psychology of belief.

Enter Hart

The immediate stimulus for the second change was a typical piece of quiet inspiration by my main tutor, Barry Nicholas. Barry liked me, but had dropped some hints that I was not doing myself justice. In April 1954, at the start of the summer term, he told me that the new Professor of Jurisprudence, H. L. A. Hart, was giving his main series of lectures and nobody in the Law Faculty could understand what he was on about. Would I mind going to them and reporting back? I was not planning to attend any lectures that term, but flattered by the invitation, I set out proudly in my gown to walk to the Examination Schools, only to see almost all of the BNC 'lawyers', some of whom never attended lectures, walking purposefully in the same direction. Good tutoring.

Hart's lectures aroused my interest and set me on the path to becoming a jurist. For a long time, Jurisprudence had lost touch with Philosophy. Hart was part of a group of Oxford philosophers who pioneered 'ordinary language philosophy' or 'linguistic analysis' to bring about what was claimed as a 'Revolution in Philosophy'.[1] Hart's main role was to introduce these techniques of philosophical analysis into Law. These were in fact the second of the series of lectures which outlined the main themes that were to be developed in Hart's classic, *The Concept of Law* (1961). Hart was a charming, intellectual-looking, shambling man, with a mellow voice. He was very clear. I still have my notes of the lectures. My main visual memory is of a somewhat rumpled figure sitting at a table in one of the lecture rooms at the Examination Schools. The room was quite full. His legs were visible under the table and as he spoke he kept pulling at one of his socks. As the lecture proceeded he leaned further and further sideways, still fiddling with the sock, until by the end there was little to be seen above the table except one almost horizontal talking head, still audible and lucid, while underneath the action was more visible and enthralling.

At the time I kept an episodic, introspective, adolescent diary. Interestingly, this hardly mentions the impact of Hart. Here my memory is more reliable and more vivid. I was fascinated intellectually as well as visually. The first revelation was that words do not have a proper meaning and that the quest for a definition of law was futile because 'what is law?' and other classical questions of jurisprudence had been mis-posed. I quickly read Hart's inaugural lecture ('Definition and Theory in Jurisprudence'),[2] in which these ideas and Hart's basic method of conceptual analysis were first proclaimed. I was shocked, fascinated and converted. Most important, I was fruitfully puzzled. Questions could be wrong or poorly articulated; definitions of words could not be true or false; words do not have a proper meaning; often sentences rather than single words are the main unit of meaning; puzzles behind questions can be dissolved by careful analysis of ordinary language.

Final year: 1954-5

I set out to convert my tutor. I learned the basic technique and became obsessed with it. Tutored in turn by two friends, Trevor Rutter and Michael Woods, who were both outstanding philosophy students, I later wrote basically the same essay several times for Barry Nicholas, applying Hart's method to different concepts – sovereignty, possession, persons, rights and the like. During the long vacation of 1954 in Dar es Salaam, I spent many hours carefully analysing Hart's inaugural lecture and wrote an ambitious essay advancing his method as the basis for a general approach to Jurisprudence. Barry was impressed, but not converted. This may be the first time that he thought that I was seriously in the running for a First.

With his encouragement I set out to work towards that goal. This involved learning the basic English Law subjects almost from scratch – Contract, Torts, Property, Constitutional Law – in addition to tackling new ones. I embarked on a self-disciplined regime – working 8.30 to 12.30 and 4.00 to 7.00 six days a week, leaving time for sports or walking in the afternoon and for entertainment or reading in the evenings – a forty-two-hour week, generally adhered to far beyond the range of English undergraduates of the time, but nowhere near to that of eager American law students.

A description of a year of swotting is not likely to be interesting and it is not as if it produced any landmarks or epiphanies in my intellectual development. It was in effect my first year of studying Law. I learned a bit of private law doctrine; I tried to approach some topics holistically, for example treating the English Law of Torts, the Roman Law of Delict, and the development of Torts for the Legal History paper as one subject – this integrative approach was helped by attending a few classes led by Harry Lawson, the Professor of Comparative Law, who perkily juggled concepts and won my respect for his kind of analysis. I kept up my interest in Jurisprudence and I allowed some time for my continuing self-education in literature and music.

'Schools', the final examination, was a test of stamina as much as nerves, eight three-hour papers in five days. I came away exhausted but feeling quite confident, except that I knew that I had messed up my Land Law ('Real Property') paper. I had in fact prepared some ingenious theses on seisin, the doctrine of estates, and the rule against perpetuities, but the paper turned out to be a simple test of elementary knowledge, which I had omitted to mug up. I knew that if called for an oral examination ('viva') I would be questioned on this, so I was able to prepare. I learned later that Herbert Hart and Vere Davidge, a notorious anti-intellectual blackletter lawyer from Keble (the examiner in Land Law), had disagreed about whether I deserved a First. I had four alphas, one near miss in Torts (trying to be too original?) and a gamma in Real Property. At the viva my proponent, the Professor of Jurisprudence, had to quiz me on such matters as how many witnesses are required for a valid will, while Davidge snorted and the Chairman, Barry Nicholas, had to stay quiet because he had been my tutor. My mark in Property was moved up to Beta and I was awarded a First.

In the same examination, another candidate's paper on Jurisprudence so impressed Hart that he purloined the script. He spent the rest of his career worrying about Ronald Dworkin's challenge to his positivism and engineered his election as his successor. Apparently, Hart liked my paper, but not enough to steal it. If I had not got a First, I would almost certainly not have become an academic. My father said that it was the worst thing that had ever happened to me.

Later I heard another interesting rumour. It seemed a bit out of character that Herbert Hart should have opted to take on examining responsibilities so soon after his election to the Chair. One possible explanation, that I have not been able to confirm or refute, is that he realised that in Oxford it is almost impossible to change the syllabus in Law through normal procedures. Given that, even in Oxford, examinations are the main instrument of power over changes in students' and teachers' behaviour, how could Hart achieve a Revolution in Jurisprudence? Having accepted appointment as an examiner, he changed the rubric of the question paper in Jurisprudence: instead of 'Answer FOUR questions' out of eight, he substituted 'Answer FOUR questions' out of sixteen – roughly eight old-style Particular Jurisprudence topics and eight new-style questions. How else could he have succeeded? Nicola Lacey, his biographer, had not heard this story, but told me that it is plausible as Hart was an adept academic politician.

Undergraduate legal education in retrospect

As an undergraduate I did not think much about the kind or the quality of the process I was going through. Later Barry Nicholas said jokingly in an after-dinner speech that I had made my reputation by attacking my Oxford legal education. This was partly true. Early in my career I regularly attacked the dominance and narrowness of doctrinal approaches to understanding law. I have always been grateful to Barry and, as we shall see, I never rejected doctrine as such, but merely tried to set it in broader frameworks and contexts.[3]

At Oxford I encountered a rather casual kind of doctrinalism in my formal legal education. One studied the English Law of Real Property, Torts and Contract mainly by reading cases, given structure by textbooks, which were precise, clear, and focused almost entirely on concepts and rules. They were products of 'the common law mind' and so hardly 'scientific'. We learned mainly doctrine and how to apply it to particular, usually hypothetical, situations. Even the study of Roman Law, Legal History and Jurisprudence was generally positivistic and rule-centric, but not dogmatically so. Professor Hart provided a conceptual basis for doctrinal positivism by emphasising that the concepts of a rule and a rule system were important in understanding law theoretically – that is, a legal system is a system of rules combining primary and secondary rules validated by a 'rule of recognition' which exists as a social fact.

From Barry and others I learned to write essays, parse concepts, think clearly and a bit about constructing arguments. Hart aroused my interest in Jurisprudence and especially in linguistic analysis rather than in the concept of law as a system of rules, which never fitted my assumptions. From tutorials in

Legal History with Derek Hall of Exeter I learned that historians can fight acrimoniously about their interpretations of evidence. In my informal self-education, I rather preferred the grand historical vision of Sir Henry Maine, the politically sensitive approach of Wolfgang Friedmann and a Danish book on *The Right of Property* by Frederik Vinding Kruse because it contained pictures of houses and factories. Law books then had neither pictures nor conversation. It was not until later that I realised that each of these three indirectly subverted the doctrinal tradition.

Another Oxford: Law in some other colleges

I only learned about life in other Houses at Charterhouse after I left. Similarly, I was in BNC with its strong legal tradition and it was some years before I learned of the appalling state of tuition in some other colleges. At a conference bar some twenty years later, I listened to two of my friends reminiscing about their experiences as young college tutors not long after I had graduated. Brian Simpson, always a witty raconteur, told a series of scurrilous stories about Oxford Law colleagues when he was a Fellow of Lincoln.[4] Neil MacCormick, a Scotsman, in his first week as a Fellow of Balliol was tutoring law students from Trinity in Real Property.[5] Neil had recently read a new textbook on the subject by Megarry and Wade. Thinking that what one of his pupils was reading out as an 'essay' sounded familiar, he reached for the book and found that the passage – indeed most of the essay – had been copied out *verbatim*. He expelled the plagiarist from the tutorial. Panic spread round Broad Street and the Turl on the rumour that there was a mad Scotsman in Balliol who did not understand the culture – for students in some Colleges were expected to copy out the textbook *accurately* in their weekly essays. One story goes that in New College Jack Butterworth, the Bursar (and my future Vice-Chancellor at Warwick), would nod to a student to start reading, pick up the phone to discuss investments with the College stockbroker, occasionally interrupting the student to say 'You have left out a paragraph.'

There was another anecdote that I believe has more than a core of truth. At least one of the Law Fellows did not even have a Law degree (also true of Lewis Eliot, C. P. Snow's narrator in the *Strangers and Brothers* sequence, who was a Law tutor in Cambridge). This one had done well in Classics at St John's in 1922 or 1923, and was a good chap, but there was no vacancy for him, so his College suggested that he should read for the Bar and mug up some Roman Law. He was duly elected as a Law Fellow in 1923 or 1924, so that his study of law stopped before the major land law reforms of 1925. Even in the 1950s he refused to allow his pupils to refer to this intrusion on the common law. By then he was said to have published an article on Roman Law, but he was better known in Oxford for his performances on the tennis court. My friend Robert Stevens, an exact contemporary of mine, was at Keble. Vere Davidge, was his tutor, a keen oarsman, a caricature of a bibulous country squire, Master of a hunt and known as the worst law tutor in Oxford. This is the same Davidge who nearly brought me down in my Finals. Small wonder that private crammers did a brisk business with students from the weaker law colleges for their Finals – something that still persists in Germany, where the Professoriate are said not to prepare students for examinations.

I have not tried to research the details of these anecdotes. Apparently, Herbert Hart had a low view of most of his colleagues in the Law Faculty, which corroborates the thrust of this gossip. In a letter to his friend Isaiah Berlin he wrote:

> Of course what is odd about the whole faculty (there are 4–5 exceptions) is that they regard themselves as a pack of failed barristers and a weak version of the Real Thing in London. It's as if the philosophers regard themselves as merely propae-deutic to the Civil Service and the Stock Exchange. Hence the odious veneration and bootlicking attitude to the judges. So what they need most is self-respect. Shall I give it to them? You must hold a class with me one day (Hegel?) and so help.[6]

This illustrates how things have changed. How lucky I had been to go to Brasenose. And how successful Hart seems to have been in this project: for some legal philosophers in Oxford may now regard themselves as Kings of the heap – or, as Hart's successor Ronald Dworkin would have put it, 'the top bananas' – at least within Law.

1955–7

Three game-changers

Soon after going down from Oxford, three events were game-changers for me. First, between Schools and my viva, six weeks later, there was an epiphanic moment. On a post-exam visit to the Lake District with my mother, at Keswick I bought a tattered copy of R. G. Collingwood's *An Autobiography* for, I think, one shilling. I read it on the coach to London. I reread it several times that summer. About forty years later at a conference at Gleneagles, the conservative political theorist Walter Oakeshott invited two young jurists to have a drink with him before lunch. He turned to my colleague and asked: 'What was the most seminal book in your intellectual development?' 'Collingwood's *Autobiography*', said John Finnis, 'I read it when I was [8?].' Turning to me: 'And yours?' 'Collingwood's *Autobiography*', I said, 'I read it when I was 21.' Late developer. As we shall see, I was telling the truth. I learned later that Oakeshott had himself been influenced by Collingwood.

Next, I had decided to read for the Bar in a leisurely way while staying with my parents in Tanganyika. It would be a good cover for continuing my self-education. I called at the office of Gibson and Weldon, the private crammers, in order to sign up for their Bar Finals correspondence course. I was interviewed by a cynical man who made it clear that a First from Oxford was a disadvantage – no place for independent thought, speculation or, even worse, criticism or theorising or other academic waffle. Gradgrind personified: what was needed was facts, facts, facts. His attitude was indeed practical so far as the exams were concerned. The idea that studying law involves little more than rote learning of legal rules is still around today in some quarters. This became one of my main targets in the politics and polemics of legal education. I had great pleasure about thirty years later in being an active member of the Hoffman Committee that recommended abolition of the old-style bar exams and the substitution of a skills-based vocational course for a knowledge based, exam-oriented, crammer-dominated system (Chapter 16). The idea that skills could be learned in an institutional setting is still controversial, but no one tried seriously to defend the old system.

The third episode was even more important. Shortly after that bruising encounter, I spent a few days in a solicitor's firm that specialised in personal injuries cases. At Oxford *Salmond on Torts* (1953) had been my favourite text-book. It was a conventional, lucid expository work. When I mentioned this to a partner he told me to forget what I had learned in the books because nearly all of his cases were settled out of court with an insurance company or the Motor Insurers' Bureau involved. Anyway, the whole system needed drastic reform, especially damages. I suffered culture shock. I began to wonder: how could one *understand* the law relating to personal injuries if one knows nothing about insurance, settlement, the damages lottery and alternatives to the common law action for negligence (Chapter 12)? I felt misled, let down, even betrayed by *Salmond* and my teachers – a common complaint by law students in most modern legal systems.

This very elementary example of a divide between law in books and law in action was my first step towards legal realism. Back in Oxford, when I complained about this, the responses were as unconvincing as they were dismissive: we never claimed that we were being realistic (half-true); you learn about that in procedure (untrue); we are not a trade school (true); this is all mere common sense (untrue). This led to a question: how can one understand legal doctrine if one knows nothing about how it operates or is used in practice? Later I saw one challenge as being how to get more of the action into the books. On this one, Patrick Atiyah showed one way in 1970 (Chapter 12).

Dropping out

After graduation I had expected to have to do National Service (NS), but as that was running down in 1955 and I had been born abroad and only been in England for education, I was told I was not eligible unless I did a short-term commission for three years. For me this was a welcome way out, but a disappointment for my parents, who feebly urged me to accept the oppor-tunity. My bargain with my father had been that, if I went up to Oxford first, I would join the Territorial Army while there. I had done that and had completed basic training during vacations and even passed the War Office

Selection Board for Potential Officers. I had honoured my bargain. It had been most unpleasant and ruined several vacations. But, a regular soldier? Me? I said I would spend the next few months reading for the Bar.

In fact, ahead of my time I dropped out for two years. On my arrival in Dar I found a letter awaiting me from Barry Nicholas saying that Professor Hart had suggested that I try for a Prize Fellowship at All Souls because they had not elected a lawyer for some years and my approach to law was unusual. I was very flattered, but not as impressed as my parents were – it sounded very prestigious to them. We agreed that October 1955 was too soon and that I should plan to sit in October 1956. This was very welcome because now I had a cover for my private plans – reading for the Bar and preparing for All Souls and a similar, less prestigious research fellowship at Magdalen. So, unexpectedly, I had a year's sabbatical which turned into two. I took a few undemanding memory tests in my Bar correspondence course, but mostly I immersed myself in literature (mainly fiction), Collingwood, some other philosophy, and in African history, anthropology, politics and novels about Africa. I acted as a sounding-board for my father on evening walks, and attended his Sunday morning gramophone 'concerts' (Berlioz, Russian opera, Requiems on warped 33.3 rpm records). I also went on safari, visited out-of-the way places, and met an engrossing range of people.

Twenty-second birthday

At this time, I had no idea what I wanted to do to earn a living. I wanted to write, but that was not a job. Practice as a solicitor did not appeal at all, and I had taken a strong dislike to the culture of the Bar after a few ghastly dinners at Lincoln's Inn: indifferent food, patronising, often pompous, junior barristers and exploited, bitter, overseas students.[7] Academic law in England was neither highly regarded nor interesting. I wanted to work in Africa, but doing what was unclear. My parents thought that I would make a good 'administrator' and argued that there would still be some Empire left to administer, although by 1955–6 that looked unlikely. Anyway, I was moving into an anti-colonial phase. However, in September 1955 an alternative to administration came in view – working in an African university. The enthusiasm for education and eagerness to learn that one came across visiting schools contrasted sharply with the attitude of English schoolboys. There probably is not a term for 'swot' or 'banco fiend' in Kiswahili. I became fascinated by education, and later, through my interest in African students in UK, in higher education in Africa.

On my twenty-first birthday, 22 September 1955, while visiting the leading boys' secondary school in Tabora, I met Bernard de Bunsen, the Principal of Makerere College, the only university institution in East Africa. I sought his advice and he invited me to come to Kampala. I spent a few days at Makerere, staying with the Principal, meeting a range of staff and students, mainly hosted by Cranford Pratt, a young Canadian political scientist, who six years later became my boss. It was a strange and fascinating experience, not least because I had heard a great deal of criticism about both staff and students at Makerere and I was able to behave like an inspector – diplomatically, of course – asking sharp questions and getting robust answers. The outcome of my visit was that my interest in African universities was confirmed, but I also gained a quite realistic picture of the institution and its problems and the difficulty of finding a role there for a law graduate. There was no law to teach. None of the other possibilities sounded ideal – teaching public administration, researching customary law, acting as the warden of a hostel, or doing postgraduate work until a law school was set up somewhere. In those days English law graduates did not study for doctorates. Nevertheless, I now knew what I wanted to do – teach Law in Africa.

One interesting point: Law hardly featured in my career choice. My first priority was Africa, my second was education, and Law was the only subject I was qualified to teach. At no stage was private practice of law seriously considered. That explains why later I devoted so much energy to thinking and writing about legal education – not at the time widely considered a respectable subject for a serious jurist or scholar.

Back to Oxford

After five months this fascinating but artificial life in Dar es Salaam proved both lonely and stressful, so I took the opportunity to return to Oxford to do some tutoring at BNC (Barry Nicholas was on sabbatical) and to prepare for All Souls and Magdalen. By then National Service was no longer a serious prospect and I had virtually given up on the Bar.

En route to England I visited Rome in Holy Week, my first encounter with Italy. I had a privileged introduction: Father Walsh, a leading White Father in Dar (and a mentor of Julius Nyerere), gave me an introduction to Father Keane, a former missionary, now retired and living in the Vatican. Not only did he act as an enthusiastic tour guide, but he enabled me to penetrate quite arcane parts of the Vatican and even arranged an audience with the Pope. I was announced as 'Il Professore Twining from Oxford'. His Holiness looked quizzically at this pimply twenty-one-year-old and said, 'Ah, Oxford – my boooook is from Oxford', and moved on. I fell in love with Italy.

Tutoring

Back in Oxford, my immediate concern was teaching. I had about a dozen students at BNC, including for BCL Jurisprudence, John Davies and Tony Hughes, both older than me; both got outstanding Firsts and followed academic careers. I should have retired then. The rest were of mixed ability, mainly struggling with Roman Law. I took my teaching seriously, even kept a teaching diary, but I talked too much. The Oxford tutorial system – these were mostly one–one meetings – allows one to maintain credibility by appearing self-confident. As I got free meals, I ate in a lot, and got to know the bachelor dons, if anything too well. To hold up my end at High Table I followed the advice of my ex-tutor, Ron Maudsley, and mugged up on Mark Pattison's *Memoirs*, read the correspondence column of *The Times* daily, and showed polite interest in improbable train journeys in Continental Europe. This worked and I survived, but the experience left me as ambivalent as ever about Oxford.

It was not an easy period, full of doubts and uncertainties about my future and my commitments. As the exam drew nearer I felt overwhelmed by the prospect of being a Fellow of All Souls and hoped that I would not get it. I made a mess of my papers (and for a similar Fellowship at Magdalen), and joined the honourable company of 'Failed All Souls'. But this was a hugely educational period. I devoured books, widening my scope beyond literature to include some philosophy, a great deal about African history and politics, and some Law, especially Jurisprudence, and even a bit of substantive law.

Political awakening: 1956

I said earlier that I had a colonial childhood, an anti-colonial adolescence, and a neocolonial start to my career. The claim that I had an anti-colonial adolescence is only plausible if broadly interpreted. There are several complex strands in anti-colonialism – anti-racism, the struggle for self-government and other power struggles, a sense of injustice, nationalist pride, desire for genuine cultural and economic autonomy, hatred of foreign rule sometimes translated into hatred of foreigners generally and, in addition to political independence, a quest for democracy and human rights as aspirations. My parents subscribed to a benevolent 'multiracial' version of the imperial dream with a steady gradual path to independence; I accepted much of their ethos uncritically well into my teens, but by my mid-twenties I was a committed supporter of Julius Nyerere's version of African Socialism. This transition from one moderate ideology to another was convoluted and slow and did not involve a sudden conversion or complete rejection; it was tied up with a struggle for power with a dominating father and doubts about beliefs and values and what I should do with my life. This dragged on into my early twenties and ended with a rejection of benevolent paternalism.[8]

Students of the heady 1960s called their predecessors 'the Quiet generation'. True, very few participated in marches, we had not conceived of sit-ins and we were not interested in university governance. But the 1950s had their share of political excitement: the Cold War, self-determination, McCarthyism, the welfare state, the class system, nationalisation, concerns about Hiroshima and Nagasaki, and nuclear power were all on the political agenda. 1956 was the key year of my political awakening: that year saw the first Aldermaston march, Sudan and Ghana became independent and this was the year of Suez and Hungary.

'The wind of change is blowing through this continent, and whether we like it or not, this growth of national consciousness is a political fact. We must all accept it as a fact, and our national policies must take account of it'.

Harold MacMillan's famous wind of change speech was not until 1960, but this was public recognition of a situation that had been going on for some years. In Tanganyika African nationalism had begun to be prominent only about 1954 under the leadership of Julius Nyerere and by 1956 it was clear that the nationalist movement was gaining ground rapidly.

In January 1956 my father asked me to provide him with some notes on 'nationalism' for a speech he was giving to a Conference of Provincial Commissioners. To my shame, I provided him with a rather 'academic' argument, that stressed the strength of nationalist feeling, but did not sharply challenge his views that self-government should be evolutionary, with economic, social and political development 'marching in step' and that full Independence was a long way off. At that point I did not think of self-determination as a principle or a right and I did not immediately translate my own desire for autonomy into a principle for colonies.

At the time I was dissatisfied with my effort, and later I became embarrassed by it. During the next few months I read and thought constantly about nationalism. I had, of course, encountered and even debated these issues, but this exercise was the first time I had intellectualised them. My reading was extensive but unsystematic: Thomas Hodgkin's *Nationalism in Colonial Africa*, Arnold Toynbee's *The Study of History* (abridged), speeches and writings by Nkrumah, Kenyatta and other African leaders, an eclectic glut of novels about Africa, including by Joyce Cary, Joseph Conrad, Alan Paton, Elspeth Huxley, Peter Abrahams, Camara Laye, Amos Tutuola and Laurens van der Post. I also followed events in the press, observed developments in East Africa and reflected on conversations that I had had with African students in the UK, and later in Paris. After about four months I set out to write a rather academic essay, which could be said to be my first venture into political theory. The text and extensive notes survive. It is a mishmash – at once too 'academic' and not intellectually disciplined enough. But the process helped me to chart out a position of my own that became significantly different from my father's, perhaps more at the level of emotion than of abstract 'reason'.

In the second half of 1956, two particular events dominated my political consciousness: the Suez crisis and the Hungarian invasion – I was in Oxford at the key moments and for once I got really caught up in the political excitement of the day. I had a blazing row with my father over Suez in London in July, although I feebly acknowledged that there were two sides to the issue. I volunteered for Hungary (but was promptly rejected as I knew no Hungarian and had no medical qualification). In October I met an Australian postgraduate of Hungarian descent, who was studying East African history. For the next six months we had an intense personal and intellectual relationship, based mainly on shared commitment to 'Africa'. By the following spring I was a convinced nationalist.[9]

Anti-colonial adolescence? Well, if one grants that I was an apolitical adolescent until about 1956, one could say that by then I was anti-racism, pro-Independence, a Tanganyikan nationalist, and prepared to accept, even excited by, the winds of change, without being hypercritical about all aspects of British rule. I think there was an analogy between fending off my parents and other grown-ups (colonial children were forced by their situation to be independent) and feeling empathy for those who resisted and resented foreign rule even by benevolent paternalists – but the analogy can be pressed too far. So, a late-developer mildly rejects colonial rule as past its sell-by date? No, it was more than that: I came to the view that self-determination is a matter of principle. Thereafter I made modest contributions to lowering the flag.

Travel, Love, Marriage, Chicago: 1957

By January 1957 I had failed to get into All Souls and Magdalen, had decided on an academic career in Africa and was contemplating applying to do post-graduate work in the United States. During the next six months I did a Grand Tour of Europe on a shoestring and then, finding that I could extend my air fare for only £14, did another tour, this time of African universities – Salisbury, Accra, Lagos, Ibadan and Ahmadu Bello in Northern Nigeria. However, at Easter I fell in love at first sight, became engaged in July, married in August and whisked my bride off to Chicago in September. That period is a blur with almost no intellectual or academic content, but it was a wonderful culmination to an unforgettable two years.

Why Chicago? It was largely by chance that I came to work with Karl Llewellyn. By 1956 I had decided that I wanted eventually to pursue an academic career teaching Law in Africa rather than the UK. I also wanted to learn more about Jurisprudence and to see something of the United States. I heard that Professor F. H. Lawson, the Professor of Comparative Law at Oxford, was responsible for placing promising Oxford graduates in leading American law schools. When I told him of my interest in the USA and Jurisprudence, he advised me to think in terms of choosing a jurist rather than an institution: 'At whose feet do you wish to sit?' He then asked me which living American jurists did I most admire. I needed notice of that question, for apart from adulatory references to Holmes and Pound and denigratory dis-missals of madcap Realists – jazz jurisprudence for a jazz age[10] – American jurists had not featured in the Oxford curriculum. I went away and read Fuller's *The Law in Quest of Itself*, which I found enthralling, and Llewellyn's *The Bramble Bush*, which I thought intriguing, but mystifying. I returned to Lawson and told him that my first choice was Fuller and my second Llewellyn. I first wrote to Harvard saying that I would like to come and sit at Professor Fuller's feet, I was not interested in obtaining a degree but I needed funding.

Harvard responded kindly that they only had scholarships for degree courses, and I had missed the application date for the coming academic year. Anyway, I was a bit young for postgraduate work at Harvard. Having learned my first lesson about American law schools, I applied to the University of Chicago in a more conventional way and was awarded a Commonwealth Fellowship to start in September 1957. Newly married, Penelope and I set off for Quebec in the bilges of RMS *Ivernia*.

4

University of Chicago I (1957–8)

First encounters

I arrived in Chicago in September 1957, newly married, a mixture of diffidence and Oxonian arrogance. I was immediately subjected to culture shocks. One of these was the regimentation in the Law School. It was like returning to school. Soon after my arrival I was asked to go and see Roger Cramton, a young member of faculty who was standing in for Professor Sheldon Tefft as director of the Commonwealth Fellows Program. He made it clear that my choice of courses was subject to his approval and that I could not just sit at the feet of Karl Llewellyn or take only courses on Jurisprudence and Philosophy.[1]

After some wrangling we negotiated a package which included a mixture of 'hard' law and theory courses, with some private research with Llewellyn. But our negotiations nearly fell apart over a course entitled 'The General Theory of Price'. Cramton told me that this was required of Commonwealth Fellows as it was a foundation course for some of the most valuable courses on offer, such as Levi and Director's Anti-Trust. When told that this was a basic course on economics, I said that I was not interested. However, I consulted some fellow students. This was, they said, a fairly rigorous introduction to economics, but it was quite easy to pass provided that you agreed with the teacher, Aaron Director. What did he believe in, I asked? A free market, was the reply. This was the heyday of the Welfare State and Butskellism in the UK and Director's monetarist views were portrayed to me as being to the right of any party in British politics at the time. This description was essentially correct, for Director, as a hard-line doctrinaire disciple of Milton Friedman, presented a particular version of micro-economic analysis as if it were a science without any ideological underpinnings.

I was outraged and stormed back to see Cramton. I told him that I categorically refused to take Aaron Director's 'General Theory of Price' because my fellow students told me that, if you disagreed with the teacher, you failed. I disagreed with him. I told Cramton that I thought that I had come to the University of Chicago, not the University of Moscow (this was the year of Sputnik), and that I refused to be brainwashed by someone whose ideology was diametrically opposed to mine. I meant what I said. I was so shocked and angry, I was prepared to leave if I was required to take this particular course. If I had left, this would have been exceedingly foolish and probably the end of my academic career. That would have delighted my parents. Fortunately, Cramton crumbled before this onslaught and, after clearance from higher authority, I was exempted from the requirement. Things could well have been different if Sheldon Tefft, the tough old-school originator of the programme, had not been on leave. I won the exchange, was excused the course and never learned enough economics. A serious mistake.[2]

I felt vindicated when I met Aaron Director for the first time. A group of foreign students was taken to see a well-known local programme for urban renewal. This involved bulldozing acres of slums to replace them with 'low-cost housing'. It was clear to me that the former inhabitants could not have afforded the new rents. We were not told what happened to them. At a party after this outing, I raised this question within a group which included a small man with a Hitler moustache, who turned out to be Aaron Director. He said: 'They were not economically fit to survive.' At first, I thought this crass caricature of Darwin was intended as a joke. It was not. I never recovered from this first encounter with economic fundamentalism.[3]

The University and the Law School

I had come to Chicago to study under Llewellyn, but in fact most of my courses were taught by others and I was fully assimilated into the Law School, and to a lesser extent the University. So before relating my first encounters with Llewellyn, I shall sketch this broader institutional context. The University of Chicago, the Law School and the windy city all provided new experiences. The University, financed largely by Rockefeller money, ruthlessly paid for and pursued Excellence; it did this in an abrasive dialectical fashion, so that one found that whenever one opened one's mouth one's assumptions were liable to be challenged, even at breakfast. The Law School fitted that culture. It was also more grown up and professional than undergraduate Oxford.

At the time I did not realise that the faculty included some of the most famous names in American academic law: Dean Edward Levi, Harry Kalven, Max Rheinstein, Kenneth Culp Davies, Walter Blum and Malcolm Sharp, as well as Karl Llewellyn and his formidable wife, Soia Mentschikoff. I found nearly all of them friendly, approachable and not unduly concerned about their individual reputations.[4] The students were older, worked harder, and were more competitive and ambitious than those I was used to. Orally, they were more articulate and forthcoming than English students, but fortunately for a bemused Oxonian they had not learned how to write. The students acted like baby Wall Street lawyers, talked loudly, but wrote badly. When I arrived, I had simply assumed the superiority of Oxford and it took me a long time to learn otherwise.

For me, the main significance of our first time in America relates to the Law School, which made a profound impact on me. It was a strongly integrated, sociable and collegial community and students had quite close contact with most of this star-studded faculty, whether or not one took their courses. Dean Edward Levi had a deliberate policy of recruiting a diverse individualistic faculty representing a range of political, moral and juristic views. Almost the only thing that they most had in common was that they were anti-doctrinaire.[5] Levi can take some credit or responsibility for pioneering economic analysis of law, but in the late 1950s this was only one small part of a varied multidisciplinary programme in the School and it had not yet become the dogmatic Friedmanite free-market ideology that developed later under the influence of Director and Posner.

In his excellent book, *The Common Law Tradition: A Collective Portrait of Five Scholars*, written about the Chicago Law School in the 1950s and 1960s, George W. Liebmann, having emphasised the individuality and distinctive views of the subjects of his pen portraits, bravely tries to articulate a common ethos. Pointing out that they belonged to a generation that came to maturity during the Depression and in the shadow of war, these individuals were not disillusioned revolutionaries or bitter reactionaries, but constructive thinkers concerned to 'engage in hard thinking about how to reform, how to rebuild and how to avoid the destructive passions of an ideological age':[6]

> They did not reason backward from either ideology or received doctrine. They believed in an empirical approach to the law and heeded an admonition attributed to Judge Augustus Hand: 'Hold fast to the English tradition', by which he meant the common law tradition. It was that conviction that supplied the title of Karl Llewellyn's last book, the reason that Philip Kurland testified as he did at the Bork hearings, the explanation why Harry Kalven's writings were so fact-specific, the focus of Edward Levi's *Introduction to Legal Reasoning*, and the motive for Kenneth Davis' long interviews with administrators.
>
> They were convinced that law served best when it served its own values, and that predictability, incremental change, conformity to community needs and customs, respect for ascertainable legislative will were high among these. As for the Constitution, the darling of the modern law teachers' nursery, several, most notably Kurland and Davis, were explicit in saying that its primary bite was procedural ...[7]

I find this account plausible.

America opened up new horizons, but it is difficult to pinpoint how and how much it changed us. The one major exception is American legal education. This is how I summed it up in 1996–7:

> After I had recovered from the initial culture shock and shed some of my Oxford arrogance, I realized that I was in a more sophisticated, lively and demanding institution than I had even conceived as possible. The University of Chicago provided an alternative model to Oxford of an institution of higher learning devoted to excellence.
>
> Conversion to the idea of the American law school at its best and to the ideas of Karl Llewellyn at no stage involved a wholesale rejection of Oxford. It was, after all a capacity to write English and to study on my own that enabled me to cope with the pace and the bewildering range of new ideas and then to choose between them.

And Oxford rather than Chicago had taught me the importance of history. But this experience both exposed and provided for some key missing elements in my legal education up to then: the linking of law to the social sciences; a dialectical approach to every issue; a highly intellectualised but nevertheless realistic approach to legal practice and the law in action; a demonstration of the inter-dependence of theory and practice; and a concern for justice.[8]

Enter Llewellyn

Llewellyn was my second choice of an American jurist at whose feet I wanted to sit. My first choice had been Lon Fuller, but Harvard did not offer me money. I arrived in Chicago rather pleased with myself as an Oxford graduate who had done some tutoring, knowing little about the United States and American law schools, and less about Llewellyn.

By the time I first met Karl I was quite well-informed as a jurist. I had attended three lots of lectures in the area at Oxford, including Herbert Hart's; I had tutored in Brasenose for two terms, I had read widely in philosophy – linguistic analysis, political theory, philosophy of science and, above all, R. G. Collingwood (Chapter 3); I had developed some useful ideas on stand-point and questioning (Chapter 10); I also knew something about custom and customary law in East Africa. I considered myself rather sophisticated, even if I seemed to be caught in an endless regress, asking in sequence what do you mean by that? What do you mean by *that*? That? That?

Because I had to take a range of courses, I had fairly limited contact with Karl Llewellyn: I took one full course, audited another and he taught a small part of a third. I also wrote a paper under his supervision and had a fair amount of informal contact. I did not really get close to him until I put his papers in order in 1963–4. But he made an immediate impact. This is I how I reported my first impressions as I remembered them in 1963–4 – that is, about six years later:

> English friends who had been to the United States had emphasized the bizarre: the only American ever to have been awarded the Iron Cross; joint organizer of a verse competition for law students; histrionics in the classroom; eulogies of the 'beauty' of the letter of credit. First impressions did not quite fit this picture; a stocky man with fierce eyebrows and a limp; traces of a parade-ground manner (trying to frighten me?); primarily interested in how much of his work I had read; embarrassing questions about negotiable instruments. Not quite the reception an Oxford man expects. We exchanged writings. I gave him my proposals for a very ambitious research project. He gave me a bundle of his articles and teaching materials and sent me away.[9]

My proposal was a lengthy, muddled paper about conceptual analysis. I scampered over rather than through the offprints and prepared some critical comments about his loose terminology. When we next met he had read my paper carefully and had scribbled all over it. He had also diagnosed what was wrong with me. He had brought in a book on Gothic architecture and showed me some pictures of gargoyles and other carvings – some were striking, powerful and clearly works of art. The second lot were less crude technically, but inferior as art. Llewellyn explained that the first lot had been created by master craftsmen, using only the adze. The second lot, after the invention of the chisel, had been made using only that new tool. Llewellyn explained that I was suffering from 'Korzybskian paralysis'; I had found a bright new tool – conceptual analysis – and was now obsessed by it and over-using it.[10] After that I was more deferential and became his disciple.

I wrote some papers for Karl, but my main contact in 1957-8 was with his Jurisprudence course, called 'Law in our society'. Accompanying the lectures and classes was a set of materials which were going to form the basis for a series of lectures in Germany in the summer of 1962.[11] It is reasonable to infer that this was to be a final statement of his views. Sadly, he died in February of that year and the manuscript is still unpublished, offering a substantial challenge to some future editor. Apart from a few one-to-one meetings and a superficial skimming of some of his shorter works, this is where I began with Llewellyn. It was an eccentric course, uneven in delivery, and the materials were cryptic, but it made a profound impact on me. First, this was a purported development of Llewellyn's 'Whole view' – but it clearly did not claim to present a Grand Theory of Law. Indeed, he denied having one. But it did give a coherent, if elusive, picture of his conception of Jurisprudence. Having dismissed 'Jurisprudence for the hundred' (he said to one student: 'what the Hell has Kant to do with my course on Jurisprudence?'[12]), he developed 'jurisprudence for the hundred thousand' (the Bar and intelligent laypeople). This is I how described it in 1973:

> In working at the level of 'jurisprudence for the hundred thousand', Llewellyn tended to make certain disclaimers about what he was doing. For instance, in *Law in our Society* he explicitly excluded 'professional' philosophy; he maintained that his descriptive generalisations were pre-scientific'; the values he accepted were no more than 'fighting faiths', bolstered by 'the best reason we can muster'; his concepts were expressed in 'roughly workable, not "accurate" phrasing'; the basic approach was that of 'horse-sense' [a favourite concept]. The title 'Law in our Society' emphasised its American orientation. In short Llewellyn claimed neither universality nor refinement for his ideas in this context.[13]

This was not self-deprecation. Nor was it as unsophisticated as it claimed. Nor was it anti-intellectual. Rather this kind of jurisprudence was intended as a working theory for practitioners and other participants – it had to be simple, usable and useful. For this purpose most abstract theory was too far removed from first-hand experience and particular cases and problems:

> Jurisprudence means to me: any careful and sustained thinking about any phase of things legal, if the thinking seeks to reach beyond the practical solution of an

immediate problem in hand. Jurisprudence thus includes any type at all of honest and thoughtful generalisation in the field of the legal.[14]

It is a mistake to think that Llewellyn was mainly reacting against abstract theorising. His main target was the unsophisticated, and mainly unexpressed, working assumptions of 'formalistic' academic lawyers such as Langdell and Beale of Harvard, and Formal Style judges and practitioners, all of whom, to paraphrase Filmer Northrop, had legal philosophies in Llewellyn's sense even if they did not know what their philosophy was.[15]

During the course he set us several short exercises: two of which I remember vividly:[16] the first was to take three volumes of law reports at random from the same court with gaps of forty to fifty years between each, read the first 100–150 pages of each volume and describe the differences. This immediately produced a new lens on the law reports: the length of the judgments, their style, the kinds of cases that reached the court and something that one might call 'the culture' of each court were strikingly different in each period.[17] Llewellyn used this approach extensively in his first-year course on 'Elements', giving students sequences of cases from one court (typically New York) to show how judges worked their way through tricky doctrinal problems over time, often quite like a team. So far as I can see, this approach has not been as influential on students of adjudication, especially in Comparative Law, as it should have been. It was an embodiment of Llewellyn's main realist precept: 'See it fresh, see it whole, see it as it works.'

The second exercise that I remember involved testing the law-jobs theory against any group of which each student had had intensive first-hand experience. The bare bones of the law-jobs theory can be restated as follows:[18] all of us are members of groups, such as a family, a club, a teenage gang, a sports team, a school, a commercial organisation, a trade union, a political party, a nation, a nation state, an international non-governmental organisation (NGO), the world community. In order to survive and to achieve its aims, insofar as it has aims, any human group has to meet certain needs or ensure that certain 'jobs' are done. These, for purposes of study, can be broken down into five or six rough categories.

First is adjustment of the trouble-case (dispute, grievance, offence).[19] When conflict or other trouble arises, it has to be resolved or, at least, kept to a tolerably low level, or else the group will disintegrate or its objectives will be frustrated or impaired. The second job, and perhaps the most important, is the preventive channelling of conduct and expectations to avoid trouble. The third, as needs, conditions and relations change, is the re-channelling of the conduct and expectations of the group. The fourth is the job of 'Arranging for the Say and the Manner of its Saying'; that is, the advance allocation of authority and the regulation of authoritative procedures for decision. This job is prototypically the primary function of a 'constitution' of a club or organisation or a nation-state. Where power and authority diverge there tends to be a gap between what in fact happens and what is meant to happen. Giving a realistic account of a constitution as a kind of institution is accordingly problematic.[20] The fifth job is that of 'providing Net Positive drive: Integration, Direction, Incentive for the whole'. Llewellyn, like Bentham, explicitly linked positive and negative sanctions (rewards as well as punishments, for example) within his conception of law-government. Finally, in any group – but especially in complex groups – techniques, skills, devices, practices, procedures and traditions need to be developed, institutionalised and adjusted if the first five needs or jobs are to be dealt with adequately or well. This is what Llewellyn called 'the job of juristic method'.[21]

The central question was *how* were dispute prevention and settlement handled in this group, how was power and authority distributed, how far were the procedures and techniques of creating and maintaining order institutionalised and so on. Llewellyn never denied that rules play a role in the doing of the law jobs, but they were for him one of a variety of means. Most students reported that they had found that the exercise helped them to understand better the dynamics of their respective groups as well as the theory. Trying to be clever, I chose to try to falsify Llewellyn's theory by applying it to Maeterlinck's *Life of the Bee*.[22] The idea that bees do not have many disputes but lead orderly, seemingly regimented existences, suggested to me that there might be groups for which co-ordinating behaviour, expectations and relations were not 'problematic'. My idea was half-baked, but I learned one lesson: Llewellyn's law-jobs theory was not really an empirical theory; it was not interestingly falsifiable or verifiable because it had almost no empirical content, except perhaps some such proposition as: all human groups have potential and actual disputes that need to be dealt with if the group is to survive and flourish. The law-jobs theory provides a perspective and set of lenses for asking about the particular ways and techniques these problems are handled specifically within any particular group.[23] The main puzzles are about the concepts: especially group, job, dispute and institution. The theory provides some useful questions for studying the how – what within jurisprudence fits under the relatively neglected topic of legal technology.[24]

Llewellyn's down-to-earth approach, his concern to link theory and practice and his interest in the details of what lawyers actually do were, not surprisingly, attractive after my experiences with the gap between law in books and law in action and with the canned doctrine of the English bar exams. But there were even more important rewards. Llewellyn's emphasis on skills, crafts and legal technology as a serious subject of study; his undogmatic stance on values ('can't helps')[25] whilst emphasising the central role of ethics, justice and idealism as concerns in legal practice; and, most important of all, his insistence on developing one's own ideas and beliefs towards something approaching a personal 'whole view' provided much of what I had felt lacking in my earlier legal education. The avowed purpose of this course was to help each student to integrate their assumptions or beliefs about law with their beliefs about the world (cosmological, religious, political moral, epistemological, linguistic). It was probably this perspective more than anything that won me over. The first step in Jurisprudence is clarifying one's own beliefs about law, justice and everything else. In teaching Jurisprudence, I have ever since tried to pursue this objective, whether in getting students to converse critically with classic texts in a Collingwoodian way, or to construct arguments justifying their normative conclusions, or reflecting on what is involved in understanding a topic.

Llewellyn and I got on very well together: he was intrigued by my interest in Africa and found my loyalty to Hart's Jurisprudence a challenge. In retrospect, I recognised that his vision of law offered to fill some major gaps in my early legal education and that we were in important ways kindred spirits intellectually, though not culturally. Obviously, there are specific ideas that I have assimilated, used or even refined in my own work: the law-jobs theory; juristic method; styles of judging and argumentation; type fact situation; horse sense (uncommon sense based on experience) and so on. Later I shall have much more to say about Llewellyn and his wife, Soia Mentschikoff – the two most important people in my professional life (Chapter 7). By the time I graduated from Chicago in June 1958, I was a Llewellyn disciple. He influenced my teaching in Khartoum and Dar es Salaam, but I did not really get to grips with his ideas in depth until later, when I put his papers in order and wrote his intellectual biography.

I was in Chicago as much to learn about America as about law, and we spent weekends in museums, theatres, jazz dives and at sporting events as well as travelling to New York, Washington DC, Southern Illinois, and – I don't remember why – Albany, NY. Although I worked steadily, I did not take my studies as seriously as the American students did. They worked very long hours, they were highly competitive, and they were very intense. We lived in a married students' building and disconcertingly heard marital rows seemingly all around us on the infrequent occasions that spouses encountered each other. I took my studies more lightly, and even attended some meeting of the Law Wives Club, which eventually awarded Penelope a PHT (Putting Hubby Through) certificate. Penelope also worked as secretary/PA to a sociologist on the Chicago Jury Project, one of the first large scale socio-legal projects. Naturally I found this intriguing.

Looking ahead, I had heard that the University of Khartoum had a Law Faculty, the only one in acceptable anglophone Africa in 1958. I learned that they had vacancies; I applied, and was appointed to a Lectureship in Private Law from 1 September. We spent June through August in Ireland and London, where I was busily preparing lectures on Torts, Jurisprudence and Sudan Legal System. By then Penelope was pregnant and could not join me until November, where she coincided with our First Revolution.

5

Khartoum (1958–61)

Introduction

Three years in Sudan was stage I of my apprenticeship as an academic lawyer. This period involved several firsts for me: first full-time job; first (and second) child; first experience of Arab culture and Islam; first teaching of students from another culture and another educational tradition; first *haboob* (dust storm); first locust storms; first experience of a judiciary at close hand; many political firsts: a newly independent country, student politics and my first revolution. That my attention was largely focused on coping during the first year is hardly surprising; during my second year I was mostly concerned with fatherhood, teaching and editing law reports; by the third year I was unsettled, but could speak to newcomers as confidently about the local scene as any ill-informed expatriate – indeed better than some. I came away with a few anecdotes and flashes of insight. Only in retrospect did I grasp the full extent of my incomprehension.

Sudan achieved Independence on 1 January 1956. I went to Khartoum in September 1958, having spent the summer in Dublin and London preparing lectures. Penelope joined me in November, on the eve of General Abboud's bloodless coup; we left Sudan in September 1961. I have told the personal aspects of the story of our time in Khartoum at length in a private memoir. Here I shall focus mainly on what I learned professionally. The account is episodic because the experiences were bewildering, my memory is fragmented and the written sources, including an occasional diary, are quite limited.

Context

Over time I got to know greater Khartoum quite well. 'The three towns', divided by the White and Blue Niles, were quite distinctive: Omdurman, the Arab city; Khartoum North, the industrial area; and Old Khartoum, the imperial and commercial centre, containing the Presidential Palace, Government buildings, the Grand Hotel, and the University which had recently evolved from Gordon College. In the 1950s the desert (sometimes inaccurately described as *tundra*) came right up to the edges of all three towns;

today a massive suburban expansion and refugee camps surround the con-
urbation for miles. The Faculty of Law had evolved from a course run by the
Legal Secretary in 1934 and repeated in 1938. This resulted in the first generation of Sudanese lawyers, including the Chief Justice, several High Court
judges and ministers and some leading politicians.

The Faculty had started teaching for the London External LLB (a four-year
degree) in 1946. In 1958 it was quite small, the staff consisting of four
expatriates, four Sudanese and two Egyptians (teaching Islamic Law –
Shari'a). The expatriates comprised Elcana Tenenbaum, the Dean, a British
citizen of Hungarian origin; Patrick Atiyah, who had been brought up in
Khartoum by a Scottish mother and a Lebanese father; C. d'Olivier Farran,
who had recently arrived, a good scholar of international law, affected by polio;
and myself. There were two Egyptian teachers of Shari'a who spoke almost no
English. Two of the Sudanese colleagues were abroad on postgraduate studies,
but two were there: Karamalla Awad, a senior civil servant seconded to run
a Diploma in Public Administration – very pleasant and helpful in explaining
things; and Hasan al-Turabi – on whom more below.

In the late 1950s there were two university law schools in Khartoum.
The University of Khartoum, the more prestigious, taught largely English
Law in English; the University of Cairo in Omdurman taught mainly
Egyptian Law in Arabic. Broadly speaking, the University of Khartoum
was the favoured choice for better students and they tended to get the best
jobs on graduation. First choice for most was the judiciary, second the
Ministry of Justice, with private practice a poor third, at least at the start of
one's career. The outcome was that nearly all of the judges were common
law trained, as were half of the Ministry of Justice, whereas the other half
of the Ministry's intake and the bulk of the bar were brought up in the civil
law tradition. The major exception to this pattern was that a few leading
advocates (including some leading politicians – such as Mohamed Ahmed
Mahgoub, a former Foreign Minister and future Prime Minister) had
moved into private practice after a period in the public service. One
Attorney-General told me that it was easy to tell a recent Khartoum
graduate from a Cairo graduate: when given a problem the former would
go to the library; the latter would sit down with a blank sheet of paper and
start writing. Since basic legal education is an important part of the
intellectual capital of lawyers, the common lawyers tended to favour the
retention of the common law; the civil lawyers supported a switch to
Egyptian law, especially the Civil Code, based on the Code Napoléon.
While I was there the senior members of the legal establishment were
almost all common law trained. Matters were complicated by a sharp
division between pro- and anti-Egyptian factions. Thus, Judge Babiker
Awadalla (later Chief Justice and Prime Minister) was pro-Egyptian and
the leader of the movement to switch to Egyptian law, even though he was
common law trained.

People

In Sudanese culture, both North and South, personal relations are of supreme importance. My most vivid memories are of friendships and close relations with Sudanese and expatriate colleagues, my students, several judges, Mohamed Omer Beshir, the Secretary/Registrar of the University,[1] diplomats and our cook-suffragi, Abdullah Mohamed Abdullah, who ruled our household. Let me start with a few individuals.

Elcana Tenenbaum, the Dean, and Patrick Atiyah were my closest colleagues. Both they and their families were very supportive. Both spoke quite good Arabic, which – alas – I failed to master. Patrick became my main mentor. Since he features later in this story, it is relevant to say something of his background. His father, Edward Atiyah (1903–64) of Lebanese origin spent most of his career in the Sudan, first as a schoolmaster, later in the politically ambiguous role of liaison between the Sudanese intelligentsia and the liberal wing of the Condominium administration. Later, he was Secretary of the Arab League and a prolific writer. He was married to a Scot and wrote a semi-autobiographical novel about a mixed marriage in Sudan in the 1930s and 1940s[2] which I consider to be his best book, although he is better known for *The Arabs* (1958). Three of the four children of the marriage grew up in Khartoum. Selma, the eldest, emigrated to California. Michael and Patrick were sent to boarding school (Victoria College) in Egypt on Sudan Government scholarships with the understanding that they would return to the Sudan to work for a period. Michael was a brilliant mathematician. Since mathematics did not flourish in Khartoum, he was not required to work in the Sudan, but Patrick, who obtained a Double First in Law in Oxford, returned to serve his time, before going on to a distinguished career first as a civil servant, but for the most part as an academic lawyer.

The Atiyahs were our neighbours. After finishing teaching about 1.00 or 2.00 p.m., we often went round to cool off in their 'swimming pool', which was about 10ft x 4ft x 3ft, but *cooool*. Patrick had already published the first edition of his book on Sale of Goods and was writing an introduction to Contract.[3] He was frustrated. He splashed. He wanted to know how businessmen and other actors actually *used* the Law of Contract. Splash. 'How can I write about sales or contracts in this benighted place?' Splash! 'How can I know whether businessmen take consideration seriously if I can't ask them? I want to know how the law actually works' ... Splash. He was already moving from being a conventional, but brilliant, doctrinal scholar to becoming a committed and quite radical contextualist or realist. For two years Patrick played an important role in my intellectual development. Later he contributed the first book to the Law in Context series, a radical alternative to *Salmond* (Chapter 12) and after that I recruited him to Warwick, where he nearly completed his *magnum opus* on the history of Contract before moving on to the Chair of English Law at Oxford.[4]

Two students were my main guides to local cultures and remained lifelong friends.

Francis Mading Deng was in his second year in 1957–8, one of only four or five Southern Law students. He was one of the favoured sons of Deng Majok, the well-known Paramount Chief of the Ngork Dinka of Kordofan, the only Nilotic people to live in Northern Sudan. Francis was quite short for a Dinka, only about 6 foot, but he was recognizably Nilotic and, without putting on airs, had a dignified, aristocratic bearing. He spoke very good English and Arabic and, in some respects, became a leader of the whole class, not just the few Southerners; for example, leading an expedition to Germany during one long vacation. Oliver Farran and I encouraged him to gather information about Dinka custom and this turned out to be the start of his life-long involvement with writing about Dinka culture. In 1965, in New Haven, I helped to record his memories of his childhood and education from his father's compound through village, primary and secondary school to universities in Khartoum, London and Yale. This became an intimate memoir, the publication of which awaits his retirement from public life. Francis later followed a very distinguished academic, political and diplomatic career as well as publishing about forty books. After sixty years we are still close friends.[5]

Zaki Mustafa was slightly older than me. He looked much older. He was married with one child and generally seemed more mature than other law students. He was solidly built, fairly light-skinned, with a moustache. He graduated top of his class in 1959 and went on to postgraduate work in London (LLM, LSE 1961; PhD 1969). His style was laconic, with a wry sense of humour. He shrugged his shoulders more than anyone I have known – *Insha'Allah* (it is the will of God – this is how it is). Even as a student, he had an air of authority. In his photographs he looks resigned and withdrawn. Perhaps because he was often an informal spokesman for and interpreter of the students, we saw a lot of each other and became good friends. I went to stay with his family in Wadi Halfa one vacation.[6] He was the author of the best book on Common Law in the Sudan. In time he became Dean of the Law Faculty, later Dean of Law at Ahmadu Bello in Nigeria, Attorney-General of Sudan and, towards the end of his life, a partner and manager of the law firm of Sheikh Ahmed Zaki Yamani the oil magnate – my first former student to become a millionaire. Zaki died in 2003. These two were my main guides to Southern and Northern Sudanese cultures.

Hasan al-Turabi, after completing his doctorate in Paris, returned to Khartoum where he soon earned a reputation as a scholar of *shari'a* and a potential leader.[7] He involved himself in politics and, after participating in the 1964 Revolution, became leader of the Muslim Brothers. Thereafter, he exerted enormous influence on the Islamisation of the Sudan. As a jurist he argued for a flexible interpretation of Islam, claiming to be a liberal Muslim professing to support the rights of women, democracy and religious freedom for non-Muslims. His political career is bewildering in the number of shifts in alliances, his critics maintaining that he was an opportunist who pursued a fundamentalist line in practice, with scant regard for human rights or genuine democracy.[8] He served with the Nimeiry regime and then fell out of favour, and this was repeated under other regimes. From 1999 onwards, he was imprisoned several times, becoming Attorney-General and a minister in between. I only met him once after leaving the Sudan. That was in 1991 when as Attorney-General he gave me an audience, which was entirely formal. He firmly told Penelope that she could not meet his wife, a former law student whom we had got to know quite well. Turabi was associated with Omer bin Laden, during his ten years in Khartoum, and this has affected his image in the Western press, who tend to portray him as a Machiavellian *eminence grise* and an extreme fundamentalist ('the Robespierre of the Sudan'). My sense is that he is a more complex phenomenon, a principled but not extreme Muslim, very pragmatic and very clever. I have watched his career from afar with bemusement. Naturally, none of us foresaw the complexities of his political career, but my original impression of him as very intelligent, subtle, devious and pragmatic still holds good.[9]

Taking teaching seriously

The hierarchy of reasons that I gave for my choice of career was: (1) Africa, (2) Education, (3) Law. Over time that order got reversed. Even in Khartoum I showed occasional signs that my professional interest in (1) was tailing off; later, in 1961–5, I switched my scholarly attention from customary and received law to Llewellyn and, over time, through teaching and involvement in outside legal activities, I became genuinely interested in Law as a subject of study and evolved into a self-proclaimed 'legal nationalist' or evangelist for its great potential as a humanistic discipline which is inevitably involved with 'real life' problems (Preface). However, my interest in education, especially higher education, never wavered.

I read quite a lot about education generally, especially higher education and pedagogy. I was particularly influenced by Gilbert Highet's *The Art of Teaching* (1950).[10] Highet is now seen as the apotheosis of the gentleman amateur and is criticised, sometimes justifiably, by those who espouse a bureaucratic rationalist approach to pedagogy. I found it very helpful as a start. In those days there was no formal instruction in educational theory or pedagogy for young academics and although internal divisions within Anglo-American academic law were a constant focus of attention, debates and writings of the time owed almost nothing to a wider educational literature. One self-educated and picked bits up as one went along, which mainly meant imitating one's elders, who generally wanted to replicate their own legal education. As I later wrote in my first reflective paper on legal education: 'The urge to reproduce one's kind is not limited to the sexual instinct.'[11]

One of Highet's messages was that you should treat your students as individuals and get to know them. I did not follow his particular method, which involved classifying them into body types and temperaments. I soon became aware of the barriers that our students had to overcome: they were studying mainly foreign, indeed imposed, law in a foreign language out of its social context, taught mainly by foreigners. They were very highly selected and had been taught in English in the last two years of secondary school, but they had not escaped very far from Middle Eastern and Islamic traditions of rote learning. Their teachers were well-qualified, perhaps too well-qualified. They upheld the notional 'standards' of the London degree and during my time in Khartoum only one student was awarded an Upper Second. The students' career expectations were uncertain, for by now there was competition among graduates, but there was hardly a culture of hard work or independent study, and the political atmosphere was volatile. Some of my colleagues, not only in Law, spoke disparagingly of their students – lazy, with a poor command of English, only wanting dictated lecture notes – indeed there was a thriving market for the latter. I did not accept this opinion, especially of the better students, who seemed to me to have done remarkably well to get this far. Teaching them was a challenge, but I set out to get them interested and to encourage them to think for themselves. To do this one had to get to know them as individuals. So I socialised with them and tried various pedagogical devices.

As soon as I had settled in my main personal contact was with my students, especially the older ones. Most of the third and fourth years were about my age or older than me. They often told me that I was too young to teach them, so I made them my friends. There were three cohorts with whom I was close. I have found the class lists for the third and fourth years when I arrived. I knew all their names, most of their personalities and some of their nicknames – though I never learned mine. I can still recall nearly all of these. I went on field trips with them, drank in cafés and quite a few would drop by about 5.00 p.m. for a coffee or *limoun*. I maintained contact after they had graduated and saw several in the United States and UK. When I returned to the Sudan in 1981–2, I was asked by a journalist why I had come back. I replied: 'To see my daughter and my students.' He told me that I had come to the wrong country because most of the latter were in Saudi Arabia or the Gulf states.

I was mainly responsible for three courses and a few bits and pieces, including teaching Local Government Law, about which I knew nothing, to mid-career civil servants, who knew quite a lot. In Introduction to Law I devoted most of the time to outlining the court system and setting law in Sudan in a broader geographical context. However, I made one modest advance. In order to set a context for the study of the Sudan Legal System, I began by presenting the class with a map of law in the world as a whole.[12] This map suggested that almost every country belonged either to the common or civil law family. It indicated that some civil law countries were socialist (this was the period of the Cold War) and that many countries, mainly colonies and ex-colonies, recognised religious and customary law for limited purposes, mainly in respect of personal law, such as family and inheritance.

This simple map served a useful purpose in setting a broad context for the study of Sudanese law, in interpreting legal patterns in Cold War terms, and especially in emphasising the impact of colonialism on the diffusion of law. It explained, but did not purport to justify, why we were mainly studying English-based law. It also identified the Sudan legal system as an example of state legal pluralism (officially recognising parts of Islamic and customary law), and it provided a starting point for discussing the future development of local law.

Today that map would look primitive, partly because the world has changed in fifty years, partly because cartography is more sophisticated, but mainly because it was based on assumptions that were dubious even then. For example, in orthodox terms, as a depiction of municipal state legal systems it could be said to have exaggerated the importance of the civil law/common law divide; it underplayed the differences between legal systems within the common law and Romanist traditions; it had a private law bias; and it paid too little attention to hybrid systems. My map depicted all the national legal systems of the world as belonging more or less fully to either the common law or the civil law 'families', largely from the perspective of exporters. This was a picture that assumed massive transplantation. But, in addition to being naïve about what I was mapping, I accepted uncritically an equally naïve model of legal receptions. My first ever article, fortunately published obscurely in the *Sudan Law Journal and Reports*, was called: 'Some aspects of Reception'; fifty or so years later I criticised this for being based on a naïve model of reception/diffusion, thereby starting the Self-critical Legal Studies Movement (Chapter 19).

The rest of the course was quite conventional, more descriptive than contextual, but I did try to include something on customary law, both the limited amount that was recognised as part of municipal law, and the much more extensive traditional customs that still were of great importance in rural areas. I asked students to bring back reports from their own localities when they went home; on the whole this worked well with Southerners, but with only a few exceptions aroused little interest among Northerners, even though customary land tenure and some other topics were still important in the North. My successor, Cliff Thompson, made a much better job of this, as did Olivier Farran in respect of family law. Later Francis Deng went on to write several books on 'Dinka law'.

These experiences taught me that equating 'law' with state or municipal law is quite inadequate, especially in countries like the Sudan. If I were to try to give an account of the Sudan Legal System today, it would be radically different from my superficial effort in 1959–61, not so much because it has changed (which it has), but because my ideas about legal systems have changed. Then I did little more than give a formal account of state legal institutions, mainly courts; today my account would be more like Mark Fathi Massoud's incisive account, much more historical, political and contextual with a far greater emphasis on the personnel of the state legal system.[13]

In Jurisprudence I struggled to find a way to make the subject relevant for Sudanese students. We had fun discussing issues about law and morality, I devoted some more time to custom and other local sources of law, but I did not deviate far from conventional historical approaches to Western legal theory. I used parts of George H. Sabine's classic *A History of Political Theory*[14] and included some legal anthropology, but there were no Southern voices, almost nothing on religious traditions, legal pluralism, or on the underpinnings of colonial law. Although Jurisprudence was my main expertise I had yet to find my feet in trying to teach legal and political theory that was less North-centric and more directly relevant to Sudanese law students. I did only a bit better in Dar es Salaam.

I was also responsible for Torts. I still loved the subject, despite the *Salmond* episode (Chapter 3) and even used *Salmond* along with a Canadian case book. It was easy to teach, not least because the students loved the plethora of interesting stories in the (mainly English) cases. There were almost no reported cases on the Law of Torts in the Sudan and only a few relevant ones from other parts of Africa. My main problem was not so much localising what I was teaching as just keeping up with preparation. In my first year in order to spin things out I spent an inordinate time on defamation and the esoteric law of liability for animals. Once I had only thirty minutes to prepare a lecture on strict liability from scratch. In a panic, I spent most of that time wrapping my copy of *Salmond* in a brown paper cover, as if it contained soft porn. Then I slowly dictated word by word the Rule in *Rylands v Fletcher* as if it were a statute, with a few obvious comments, and ended the class early. Afterwards two students came up to me and said this was the best lecture I had ever given them. Why could I not go on like this? I nearly gave up – but, fortunately, I persisted.

Later we came on to that absurdity, the English law of liability for harm caused by animals: we had fun discussing whether cows and sheep were 'cattle'; they loved *Filburn v People's Palace* in which a circus elephant trampled a dwarf; they were excited by the question whether the owner of a talking parrot could be liable for the parrot's slanders; then we came to a case in which a camel bit the hand of a child in the London Zoo. Most of the case turned on whether camels were by nature tame or wild. There was a zoo in Khartoum and Sudanese are familiar with camels. 'Aha, I thought, better than horses jumping over hedges where there are no hedges.' Unusually, a hand went up: 'Please, sir, why was the camel in a *zoo*?' My immediate reaction was that the student was missing the point. Then the scales fell from my eyes – neither in this case, nor most of the other Torts cases we had studied, could the facts arise in litigation in the Sudan context. To be sure there were roads and factories and accidents, but hardly any Torts cases reached the courts – indeed I wrote a whole article about a solitary case in which an expatriate judge fell into an open ditch on the way to a party and sued the Khartoum Municipal Council in negligence, claiming almost the equivalent of their annual road budget in damages.[15] I concluded that the English Law of Torts was largely irrelevant to Sudan.

I later wrote an article under the rubric 'The Camel in the Zoo'.[16] This was my first explicit attempt to outline a 'law in context' perspective in print. It raised questions about how Sudanese dealt with wrongful harms and other risks. 'It is governed by custom', said the students. How could I find out about these customs? I asked. 'Ask the people', came the reply. I encouraged the students to do just that, when they went home, with mixed success. I even attempted an absurd piece of field work in a village in the desert outside Khartoum, but this merely convinced me that I was no more fitted to serious empirical research than my guru, Karl Llewellyn. Meanwhile, I went on teaching the English Law of Torts from *Salmond*, as I was required to do. It took me some time to realise that the fatalism of Islamic culture embodied in *Insha'Allah* (God wills it) provided a coherent basis for a law of obligations suited to the Sudan: '*Insha'Allah* – the loss lies where it falls.'

Context, context, context. As soon as my eyes were opened I could see it everywhere. When a train-driver slaughtered some cattle lying on a railway on an open plain, this was held to be sufficient provocation to reduce murder to manslaughter for the cattle-owning Baggara people. Under English law at the time, damage to property could not be a basis for the defence of provocation in homicide, but the test in the context was held to be 'the reasonable Baggara'. Abu Rannat CJ explicitly distinguished the case of a minister killing someone who had damaged his new Cadillac, but did not specify how to categorise the defendant (urban-dweller? Evolué? Westernised?).[17]

SLJR and the Sudan Law Project

The *Sudan Law Journal and Reports* (SLJR) was founded in 1956 by Egon Guttmann, my predecessor, with whom I overlapped for a few days on arrival. It was the result of an enlightened deal under which the government paid for the whole publication and members of the Law Faculty edited the Law Reports and produced a journal devoted to law in the Sudan on a voluntary basis.[18] Patrick Atiyah took over from Guttmann and handed over to me when he left for Ghana in 1959. I had no experience of editing or law reporting and had only published one article (in the SLJR). This also proved to be an invaluable apprenticeship in at least three ways.

First, I had to spend a lot of time in the High Court, working closely with Chief Justice Abu Rannat, on whom more below. For two years I was in a similar position to a recent American law graduate clerking for a Federal judge. Secondly, I had to do much more than write headnotes, check citations and compile indexes. I had to chivvy reticent judges and rein in publicity-seekers. All of them wanted me to monitor their English, some wanted me to check their law, and a few even tried to get me to write their judgments. I was in and out of the High Court four or five days a week and got a real sense of how it operated. Thirdly, I soon noticed that the SLJR was not publishing a representative range of cases. Almost all the judgments I received or extracted were from criminal cases and a very high percentage were about homicide. The main defence against a charge of homicide was provocation, which would reduce murder to a lesser offence and mitigate the sentence. We were accumulating a rich vein of precedent on provocation and on almost nothing else. I persuaded the Chief Justice to broaden the range of courts from which we could select cases and to stimulate his brethren and subordinates to write judgments for publication on other legal issues.

On one occasion I nearly went as far as to encourage litigation. I discovered that the offence of 'House Trespass', modelled on the Indian Penal Code, was being interpreted differently by different courts in the Three Towns: in Omdurman 'house' was interpreted to include the *hosh* – the wall enclosing the property (rather like the English 'close'); but in Khartoum trespass involved entry into a building – like breaking and entering in English law; and in Khartoum North it had been ruled that breaking and entering was not necessary in a go-down or factory that had a roof but no walls. This probably broadly reflected the different cultures of the Arab city, the expatriate quarter, and the industrial area. It meant that when we slept in the garden, if someone came and started tickling our feet – a practice not unknown – this did not constitute house trespass. Similarly, when people daily took a short cut through our garden, as if they had a right of way, they were not committing an offence. This did not make for uniform law. My interest was in improving communication within the judiciary as well as publishing cases for use as precedents. So I persuaded a former student, then a Third-Class Magistrate, to obtain jurisdiction over some cases of House Trespass and to write a serious judgment analysing the offence. This he did, but his superior was horrified, insisting that it was above the station of a Third-Class Magistrate to presume to be capable of writing a judgment, let alone having it published. Editing the SLJR made me very aware of how unrepresentative and uninformative law reports generally and inevitably must be. They are not representative of the law, let alone of society and they rarely tell the whole story of a dispute or event, a theme later brilliantly developed by Brian Simpson.[19] They can be wonderful anthologies of stories and arguments, but they are typically atypical.

A fourth concern fortified my life-long interest in archives. The SLJR was dealing with recent cases from 1956. There had been two selective volumes of law reports published before Independence. They were the result of private initiatives by frustrated public servants. I argued for a project to publish the backlog of unreported precedents from the Condominium period. This had strong support, but how to get hold of the cases? There were some in personal collections of retired judges. Some advocates hoarded them as ammunition for 'pocket pistol law', using them to take their opponents by surprise. Most of the material was scattered in store rooms spread across the whole Sudan. I undertook a pilot project. The Chief Justice authorised me to inspect and, if necessary, sort the store in Wad Medani Provincial Court. The Province Judge was reluctant – perhaps because he feared that the store might reflect badly on him – but orders were orders. With two court clerks I attacked the store. It was full to the ceiling of a jumbled mass of files, loose papers and other relics, dumped there with no attempt to put them in order. One of the first things we found was a *panga* (machete) wrapped in a bloodstained cloth – an exhibit from a homicide case? We met many insects and a few scorpions, but no snakes. When we had emptied the store, we found that there were almost complete files going back many years and a valuable collection of judgments made by Judge Bodilly, a former Province Judge. This pilot study enabled Oliver Farran and me to draw up an ambitious plan to create a national legal archive, in first instance as a basis for law reporting, but also as a resource for law teachers, historians and social scientists. We obtained the support of the Chief Justice and approached the Ford Foundation, which had recently begun to take an interest in legal education in Africa. Within a remarkably short time we were awarded a grant of over $100,000 – an unbelievable sum in our eyes. In the following years the Sudan Law Project was brilliantly carried out by Cliff Thompson, who was in effect my successor on the Law Faculty. Not only was law reporting in Sudan transformed, but many law students and junior members of the judiciary were involved as part of their practical training.

The Sudan Law Project had two important repercussions for me personally, even though I left Khartoum soon after we obtained the Ford grant. First, this was the start of a long relationship with the Ford Foundation.[20] This, among other things, led to involvement in a New York-based committee on legal education in the world as a whole that has influenced my thinking and writing about legal education ever since (Chapter 17). Secondly, this reinforced my fascination with archives (Chapter 2). For the rest of my life I have been drawn to archival work of different kinds, in Dar es Salaam, the Llewellyn Papers in Chicago, the Bentham Project in London, the Commonwealth Legal Records Project, legal literature and legal records in small jurisdictions (in the Republic of Ireland, Scotland and Northern Ireland), latterly with family papers, including my own Augean stables, and a project on Legal Records at Risk in England and Wales.[21] Although my main object has been to save them from destruction, my fascination leads me to read them – which is one thing a real archivist must not do!

Chief Justice Mohammed Abu Rannat

El Sayed Mohammed Abu Rannat had been one of the first group of eight junior officials to be selected in 1934 to take an intensive part-time course in Law, taught by an enlightened Legal Secretary. Sudan had a mainly career judiciary and he worked his way up the ladder, becoming a High Court Judge in 1950 and the first Sudanese Chief Justice in 1955, the year before Independence.

Appointed by the Azhari government, Abu Rannat accepted the transition when they handed over power to the military in November 1958. Abu Rannat was highly respected as a competent, fair and upright judge, but had few intellectual pretensions. He was thoughtful, modest and kind and he taught me a lot. He also used me on two or three occasions as a sort of speech-writer, including doing the first draft of an article on the relationship between Islamic law and customary law.

As a judge, Abu Rannat CJ was notable for using the controversial 'repugnancy clause' to modify imported common law doctrines that he held to be unsuited to local conditions and therefore contrary to 'justice equity and good conscience' – a phrase that had empowered British judges to strike down customary and religious rules that they disapproved of.[22] He played a major role in reforming the court system and helped to introduce a (modest) element of democracy into local government. A sincere Muslim, he favoured cautious gradual evolution of law rather than radical Islamisation. He maintained the independence of the judiciary during the Abboud period and ensured a smooth handover of power during the 1964 Revolution, which ended his judicial career. I worked closely with him on law reporting and related matters and always found him accessible, friendly and supportive. His backing gained me immediate access to all the senior judges. I learned a lot.

Scrapbook

First revolution

In November, still waiting for a house, we were billeted with the Dean, Elcana Tenenbaum. On 17 November, I had an 8.00 a.m. class, so we had breakfast at 7.00 a.m. The telephone rang. Elcana answered it. 'There has been a revolution; the Army has taken over.' For all of us, this was our First Revolution – so we did not know what to do. Tenenbaum had no doubts about the first priority: 'I must tell Peter Kellner' (a journalist, the stringer for the London *Times*). That was the first PK had heard of it. My first question was: 'Will there be lectures?'; 'Why not?', replied the Dean.

So I set out on foot to the Law Faculty, about half a mile away. Sharia Al Gamhuria, the main road into Khartoum city centre, was completely deserted and silent. As I came to the Faculty, I saw several students standing around outside – about one-third of the class. They told me excitedly that there had been a Revolution. 'I know', I said. 'Are there lectures?' they asked. 'Why not?', I replied and strode confidently into the lecture room.[23]

Early accounts of the Revolution have become a pastiche: 'You send the tank to the Blue Nile Bridge, the armoured car to the White Nile Bridge and you hail a taxi and drive with your speech to the Radio Station.' There was some truth in this – in a failed coup nearly a year later, one of our law graduates was arrested in a taxi, with his speech neatly typed. He did not (yet) control the tank or the armoured car. It was said that General Abboud – a small, quiet, reputedly easy-going man – was woken up in the middle of the night and told: 'General, you are now the President.' Accurate or not, this apparently also had a core of truth. He was the figurehead of a quite disciplined military junta who ran the country for nearly seven years, until overthrown by a popular uprising in 1964, taking the form of a massive demonstration in Khartoum – another bloodless coup. In 1958 the democratically elected government – a fractious conservative coalition – had handed over to the military rather than call an election that they would probably lose.

All power – legislative, judicial and executive – was vested in the Supreme Army Council, then delegated to the President. For the next three months the courts continued to operate as if nothing had happened. After that, General Abboud delegated power to 'the Chief Justice' with retrospective effect. During this period no one publicly challenged the authority or jurisdiction of the courts. The General continued to rule by decree for several years, and the regime was generally accepted to start with. There was a delay before the students reacted, so the annual student demonstration did not take place in November, the scheduled month.

Book burning

After a siesta we used to sit out on the patio overlooking our garden and have tea. This was the hour at which students quite often dropped by to seek advice or just for a chat. They would have a cup of tea or a glass of *limoun* and move on. One afternoon a student we knew well dropped in. He seemed unusually reserved, even embarrassed. He even refused a *limoun* and left after a few minutes. Then came another who behaved in the same way. Then more, each coming on his own. Something was up, but they would not tell me. It transpired that they were on their way to a book burning. The military regime, to distract attention, had once more whipped up anti-Zionist fever. The students had decided to burn all library books published in Israel, even though scholarly books were specifically exempt from import restrictions. When I heard this, I remembered that I had met Hassan Omer Ahmed, one of our brightest recent graduates now a tutor, coming out of the library brandishing a book on precedent published in Israel. 'Who ordered this?', he asked angrily. 'I did', I said fiercely. 'Have you checked it out?'

Mine was the first book to be burned, before they went after bigger fish – the University Librarian was Jewish. Our visitors had called in en route to this event in order to make it clear that this was not a personal attack. This incident affected me quite sharply: first, I have a visceral disgust at book burning, not just the Nazis, but also because of one's special relationship with books. Book burning is destroying ideas, especially when the books are irreplaceable, so it has a different meaning from dumping Xeroxes or one's surplus offprints. Secondly, I had difficulty coping with the Sudanese way of drawing a sharp line between personal and political relations. I was also made to realise that the students just did not have the same cultural associations with books or book burning or, as I already knew, the ritual significance of demonstrations.[24]

First Examiners' meeting

In May 1958 I attended my first Examiners' meeting as a lecturer. It was in London. My most distinctive memory is that all of the Internal Examiners were senior academics of the University of London, that the names of most of them were familiar and that almost all of them had taken the trouble to turn up. Furthermore, they had devoted a lot of time to commenting on draft exam papers, reading quite a high proportion of scripts, and giving advice and encouragement to the teachers, who were co-examiners. The students were formally taking the London LLB and London standards were applied with no concessions. It was a tremendous boost to confidence to have nearly all our marks confirmed – occasionally upgraded by the London Examiners. During my time at Khartoum no one obtained a First; only one was an awarded an Upper Second; and the best students nearly always got Lower Seconds, which qualified at least some to go on to postgraduate work. The fact that I had a senior 'Internal' Examiner looking over my shoulder spurred me to mark very carefully and perhaps rather strictly. A very useful apprenticeship.[25]

A summer term in Oxford

Generally, things were very unsettled in Khartoum and so was I. On leave in the summer of 1960 I again stood in for Barry Nicholas and taught Jurisprudence at BNC, partly to decide whether to apply for Oxford Fellowships. There were three coming up. I was particularly attracted by Univ. (the Jurisprudence College). I was still very ambivalent about Oxford – the flummery of gowns and rituals and the conservatism of the syllabus, over which college tutors had almost no control. I had enjoyed teaching, including giving tutorials at BNC, but the grind of heavy tutorial teaching – often fourteen to sixteen hours a week – on a narrow syllabus was unappealing. Mainly for this reason I decided not to apply.[26] The decision proved to be a good one and for the right reasons. For the remainder of my career – in Dar es Salaam, Belfast, Warwick, UCL and several American law schools – I designed and examined my own courses. Oxford boasted that its strength lay in the fact that students were examined by people who had not taught them. This may do something for maintaining standards, but it almost completely stifled innovation.

First article

Diary, March 1959: '. . . in bed with symptoms of malaria ("There is no malaria in Khartoum," insist the medics). I finish my first academic article on "Some Aspects of Reception". It is published in 1957 *Sudan Law Journal and Reports*, which is two years behind schedule – "the prediction theory of law" in action? Patrick Atiyah doubted whether there was much to say about reception as a topic.' I agree, it is about influence and, like artistic or literary influence, there is not much illuminating to be said. Studying influences on Van Gogh is not as interesting as studying Van Gogh. Nevertheless, my interest in the topic has continued.[27]

The start of American interest in Law in Africa

I encountered American interest in Law in Africa about 1960, first by meeting and becoming friends with Jim Paul (University of Pennsylvania), who was on a mission to consider prospects for American involvement in legal education in Eastern Africa. His report suggested that the British had already established a sphere of influence in Sudan (and were about to in Tanganyika) and recommended that US efforts should be focused on Ethiopia.[28] In 1963 Paul became the founding Dean of the Addis Ababa Law School. As a graduate of Chicago and in reaction against narrow British conceptions of academic law, on the whole I welcomed the American involvement; indeed, from the early 1960s until the late 1970s I could be said to have been a minor, but quite sceptical, player in the American Law and Development Movement.[29] Starting with the Sudan Law Project, I had close contact with the Ford Foundation for nearly twenty years, mainly with the SAILER Program and the International Legal Center in New York. From time to time rumours would go round, suggesting that these institutions were created or infiltrated by the CIA or the State Department, or that they were disguised instruments of colonialism.[30] Clearly, they were concerned to spread American influence, but they seemed to be working through independent governments in a spirit of co-operation. Since they supported my work and helped the Law Faculties in Khartoum and Dar in ways that I approved, I welcomed their advice and funding. In my experience, it was some American academics who were more evangelical than the Foundation officials – often crudely assuming that the American Constitution and American legal education had no rivals and not paying much attention to local history and conditions. Some of those who only stayed one or two years were treated as 'experts' on 'Africa' on their return, whilst the few who spent many years in one or more countries, such as Cliff Thompson and Jim Paul, were well aware of how little we understood. Beyond this I have no evidence either way of CIA or other sinister influences. If it was there, it operated in very indirect ways.

I maintained contact with Sudan for many years afterwards mainly through Sudanese friends and news reports; we visited our daughter twice when she returned to the country of her birth after graduation – about twenty-one years after she had left. She worked first in Ahfad, essentially a girls' finishing school; then briefly as a civil servant monitoring NGOs (she came away thinking well of only about three out of over sixty); then after helping Tigrayens in exile she secured an appointment with OXFAM and stayed in Sudan for several more years. After that I still maintained a more spasmodic interest, mainly through contact with Francis Deng and Abdullahi An Na'im, about whom I wrote a certain amount in their roles as 'Southern jurists'.[31] So Sudan has been a concern mainly from afar through a turbulent and often tragic history and my memories are to some extent jumbled up with later gossip, rumour, reading and appalled following of news of disasters, coups, repression and apparent genocide.

Last night in Sudan

Diary, Sept. 1961:

> Juba, in a hotel that was, and still is, notorious for its discomforts. I am genuinely sad to be leaving Khartoum, but excited by the prospect of taking up a post in the University College, Dar es Salaam (UCD) which is due to open in about a month.
>
> At the bar, I fall into conversation with a Sudanese doctor, a Northerner. I tell him that it is my last day in Sudan and of my mixed feelings about leaving. 'As you are going' he says 'you can now speak frankly about the Sudanese. What do you think of us?' By now I am used to this style of direct questioning and I go through my litany on the friendliness, generosity, sensitivity in personal relations of the Sudanese. 'But were not your students lazy and ill-behaved, always making trouble?' he asked. I acknowledged that it was difficult getting them to work and that the university had suffered from endemic strikes, demonstrations and closures. But, on the whole, I was prepared to defend my students against his charges. He pressed me to say something critical; so I countered by saying that there was one thing that puzzled me and this was the sharp distinction Sudanese made between public posture and private relationships, sharper even than British MPs who attack each other on the floor of the House of Commons and then drink together quite amicably ... I had been a minor target of one such incident and I had found it hard to stomach. The book-burning episode was an example. But the most famous occasion had been just before Independence when a big demonstration had been held to demand the immediate repatriation of all expatriates and an instant Sudanisation of all senior posts in the University. The officers of the Students Union, as leaders of the demonstration, had spent the night before writing personal notes to every expatriate member of staff in effect saying: 'We think that you are great and are doing an excellent job; we love you very much and we hope that you will stay for many years.' Some expatriates, I suggested, found such conduct incomprehensible. He looked concerned and

pleased: 'I was President of the Union at that time and it was the best demonstration we ever organized. I can easily explain to you our attitude: we love you and/or hate you and we want to express both emotions. Why not?'

Retrospect

In his autobiography, Patrick Collinson, a near-contemporary and good friend in Khartoum, dismissed his five years in Sudan as a time of 'falsity, futility and self-delusion'. Pat was a devout Christian Socialist, a prodigious walker, who became a distinguished and popular Regus Professor of Modern History at Cambridge, and a lovely man. I was surprised by the intensity of his rejection of his time in Khartoum.

I came across his memoir, *The History of a History Man* (2011), after I had nearly completed a first draft of this chapter. He arrived in the Sudan to teach history two years before I did and left about the same time. I was quite shaken. How come that our accounts of our experiences of Sudan during this period have such a different emphasis? I think that it is worth quoting him at some length:

> To follow from a distance its unutterably tragic history over the ensuing decades is to be constantly reminded that our years there were years of falsity, futility and self-delusion. Neither we, nor above all the Sudanese, of so many ethnic and linguistic identities (175, with 325 smaller groups), had yet come to terms with how, and whether, such a state, if it was a state (rather, the anomalous outcome of colonial history), could be made to work; although those in power at any time knew what the answer to that question was – for themselves.[32]

After summarising the unending, appalling story of military regimes, ruthless Islamisation, famines and genocide in Darfur, Machiavellian 'Peace Agreements' masking battles over control of oil, inter-tribal massacres in the South carried out in the name of different strategies of emancipation, potentially ruthless Chinese intervention in pursuit of oil, Collinson concludes:

> The verdict of Julie Flint and Alex de Waal on Sudan in the early twenty-first century is chilling:

> The serial war criminals at the heart of Sudan's present government once sought absolute power in pursuit of an Islamic state. Now they seek power for its own sake. Today, as yesterday, the people they perceive to be challenging that power count for nothing. They can be subjugated, shot or starved without compunction. If local allies have different axes to grind, they are free to grind them, no matter how much blood they shed. Mass killing has become so routine that it no longer needs conspiracy or deliberation. It is simply how the security elite does business. It is ingrained intent, atrocity by force of habit.

> It is no less chilling to reflect on the fact that for five years Patrick Collinson was cheerfully working in the delivery room where this appalling future was gestating.

I agree with Collinson that the political and other aftermath at the macro-level were in many ways appalling and tragic. I probably followed events in the 1970s and 1980s more closely than he did through my daughter, who worked there as an aid worker and from former students, especially Obeid Hag Ali, Francis Deng and Mohamed Abu Hareira (whose PhD I supervised at Warwick). But was my time in Khartoum three years of 'falsity, futility and self-delusion'? *Falsity*? At the time I was ignorant and naïve about national politics, cut off from reliable information, more focused on micro-concerns than macro-politics. I was often bewildered, but not to the extent that I now think I was as deluded as my friend suggests. Too sanguine perhaps and mainly concerned with my own little patch. *Futility*? No – I do not think that my engagement with students in teaching and friendship was futile. I taught some things and learned a lot. I still think that the SLJR and the Sudan Law Project were worthwhile at the time and for a period afterwards. However grim the broader picture, this was not all futile. *Self-delusion*? It was only later that I realised the extent of my incomprehension at many levels. When there I suffered frequent culture-shock; I knew that I was bewildered and unaware of a lot that was going on. Teachers need to understand what they are talking about: if I were to try to teach about the Sudan legal system today I would use Massoud's book rather than Egon Guttman's article;[33] but I got the bare facts right, even though they told us nothing about what law in the Sudan was really like. It was only law in rather sparse books. I got only minor flashes about the law in action through my law reporting activities and professional and student gossip. I did my best.

Our strongest memories of our time in the Sudan were of friendships, which lasted long afterwards and I refuse to disown these as delusory. And I don't think that most of my anecdotes, especially those recorded in my diary, are merely self-delusory, although they are open to multiple interpretations. I claim to be a 'realist', but humankind cannot bear very much reality.[34]

6

Dar es Salaam (1961–5)

Hekima ni Uhuru (Wisdom is Freedom)
(The motto of the University of Dar es Salaam)

Introduction

I was appointed to a Senior Lectureship as one of the founder members of the Faculty of Law in University College Dar es Salaam (UCD) in May 1961. I took up my appointment in September 1961 and left in 1965. If the first stage of my apprenticeship as an academic in Khartoum was mainly about teaching, the second stage in Dar was more about university administration. For the first year we were working in a brand-new institution consisting of three law teachers, fourteen students and a few administrators. This was exciting enough; the fact that this was Independence year made it doubly so.[1]

Tanganyika (later Tanzania) had achieved self-government in 1960 and Independence was scheduled for December 1961 in a remarkably rapid and smooth hand-over of power. Julius Nyerere, the leader of the Tanganyika African National Union (TANU), was Prime Minister then First Minister during self-government and the first year of Independence, then the first President of Tanganyika when it became a Republic in December 1962. In 1964 the country merged with Zanzibar to become the United Republic of Tanzania.

One of Nyerere's first acts as First Minister in 1960 was to announce the need for Tanganyika to have its own university. The University College Dar es Salaam Act (Provisional Council) Ordinance was passed by Legislative Council on 16 February 1961. The first Principal was appointed in March/April. He was Cranford Pratt, the Canadian political scientist who had hosted my visit to Makerere in 1955. He and the first Registrar, Jock Snaith, started work in July. I arrived from Khartoum in September, having taught there for a final term. The first students arrived in early October, just two months before Independence. By then staff had been recruited, accommodation arranged, degree regulations drafted and a curriculum for the first Faculty (Law) approved. In October fourteen students from Tanganyika, Uganda, and Kenya had been drafted, some of them diverted from programmes of study abroad.

There were several reasons why Law was chosen as the first Faculty. Lord Denning had chaired a UK Government Committee on Legal Education for Students from Africa, which reported in December, 1960.[2] It was highly critical of the practice of sending African students to the Inns of Court to qualify as barristers and recommended that local institutions of legal education should be started as a matter of urgency in several African countries. The report specifically advised that a Faculty of Law should be set up in Tanganyika with all possible speed. One attraction for Nyerere was that Law was one of the major subjects not covered at Makerere or Nairobi, so that UCD could start the subject from scratch. Legal education was given a low priority in the colonial period, partly because law was not seen as 'developmentally relevant', partly because law students and lawyers were seen as potential troublemakers – they had played a major role in independence movements in India and West Africa. The outcome was that, at Independence, Tanganyika had only two African lawyers, and the numbers were not much higher in Kenya and Uganda. Another factor was that Law was and is perceived as a cheap subject, requiring no laboratories or special equipment or special accommodation. On this view, all it needed was a room, a blackboard and some chalk (and in time a duplicating machine with stencils). In fact, a great deal of our early efforts were devoted to building a good law library, the need for which was regularly underestimated by higher education planners. The College had no accommodation of its own until TANU, the ruling political party, agreed to lease its new and as yet unoccupied party headquarters to the College Council for three years – a gesture that symbolised the high priority attached by the government to education and the close relationship with the new political leaders.

To start with our students were registered for University of London degrees under a 'special arrangement' that was already in place at Makerere and Nairobi. This had some obvious advantages: it virtually guaranteed international recognition at the outset and many practices and regulations could be replicated rather than invented from scratch. It provided a framework, but allowed reasonable scope for teaching local law. However, UCD aspired to be distinctive. The main inspiration for this came from First Minister, Julius Nyerere.

Establishing a university was one of Nyerere's priorities. It was a symbol of nationhood, it was an important part of nation-building, and he was determined that the educated elite should share his vision of the ethos of an independent Tanganyika. Nyerere was a socialist and a committed egalitarian, but he recognised that a well-educated elite was essential to lead, administer and develop the country. He was also a scholar and teacher. He had studied at Edinburgh and admired the Scottish university tradition; he believed in academic excellence, a fair degree of academic freedom and, above all, teaching and research directly relevant to African problems and needs. Nyerere also expounded a philosophy of law that some interpreted as more liberal than socialist. At the opening of the College he said:

> I believe that law is one of those subjects that can only effectively be studied in the environment in which it will be used. Up to now, the Government has insisted that

those called to the Bar in England should have a period of reorientation on their return to Tanganyika before they begin to practice at the Tanganyika Bar. Although many of our graduates have found this an irritating and frustrating regulation, I believe that it has a lot of sound reasons behind it. But these reasons no longer apply when the whole training is done within the Territory ... We are undertaking a Herculean task, the task of building a united, democratic and free country. An essential part of our national philosophy must be a legal profession of great integrity which not only knows the formalities of law but also understands the basic philosophy which underlies our society. Our lawyers and our Judiciary must, in other words, not only appreciate that law is paramount in our society, they must also understand the philosophy of that law. It is essential in a democratic society that every individual believes in the equality of all its citizens that every individual should be subject to the law. Further, it is of paramount importance that the execution of the law should be without fear or favour. Our Judiciary at every level must be independent of the executive arm of the state ...[3]

The mandate for UCD and the Law Faculty was clear. The University should aspire to international standards of excellence, to traditional (Western) academic legal values, but it must contribute to nation-building, focus on African problems and conditions, and study law in its local context. These were not empty words and Nyerere was a charismatic leader. Inevitably, over time there were tensions between elitism and egalitarianism; between academic freedom and commitment to national ideology in the context of a 'war on poverty, ignorance and disease'; and between safeguarding security and national sovereignty and liberal ideas of the Rule of Law. There was a continuous tension between building on traditions of higher education of the former colonial powers and developing genuinely African institutions. All of these stresses were present from the start, and they surfaced from time to time, but in the early days the founders had a clear and inspiring mandate. Furthermore, Nyerere's reputation and charisma attracted bright and adventurous people who might have been less comfortable in more staid and traditional places, such as Makerere. Nearly all recruits to the academic staff in Dar were in tune with the goals and ethos of the institution and were trying to break free from a narrow and formal style of legal education.[4] Nyerere's emphasis on independence, nation-building, law in context, Rule of Law, academic freedom, liberal education and excellence were all appealing and being involved at the start of a brand new, innovative institution was immensely exciting. Later, when UCD became a centre of Marxist critiques of Nyerere's pragmatic socialism, I would have been less comfortable and, indeed, in one period from 1975 the Faculty was sharply divided between Marxists and others and there was a rapid turnover of staff.

Historians of the Dar Law Faculty – there have been several[5] – have categorised the early days as 'the nationalist period' implying that there was no overt political ideology, in contrast with the phase following the Arusha Declaration[6] and the later phases of noisy Marxism and structural adjustment. Given the emphasis on independence, nation-building and forging a national identity this may be an apt categorisation. But there was a bit more than that. In 1963–4 Patrick McAuslan and I were asked to draft what would now be called a 'mission statement' for Law to be included in a prospectus for schools. This is what we wrote:

> In the Faculty of Law at Dar es Salaam, lecturers have been appointed, syllabuses planned and methods of teaching devised, with a single important consideration in mind: the fact that the lawyer in East Africa has to be much more than a competent legal technician. With the coming of independence, the manifold problems that beset developing countries have to be faced and, in doing this, great changes will have to be made in the framework of society. Lawyers have a vital role to play in these developments for upon them will fall a major share of the work of putting into practice the principles and ideas of their colleagues in the fields of politics, economics and science, and ensuring that the resultant system works fairly and efficiently. Legal education must take account of these facts, and see that students are made aware of and prepared for their future role.
>
> Legal education for East African lawyers must therefore entail more than the accumulation of knowledge about rules of law – to know much law is not necessarily to be a good lawyer, although it is the foundation upon which most legal education must rest. The good lawyer is the one who knows also something of the society in which the law operates and the processes by which the law may change and be changed by that society. Thus, we teach the law as it exists in East Africa today, but we do not stop there; we use this law as a firm base upon which future developments may be considered. In this way we hope to be able to produce lawyers who will have thoroughly mastered the techniques of the law: how to search out all the relevant authorities on a particular point and marshal them in a coherent form; how to read a case in order to understand it fully; how to analyse and interpret a statute; and how to put across one's point of view in speech and writing. But over and above all this, they will have studied that law against the social and economic background of the East African jurisdictions; and will be in a good position to offer useful contributions to discussions of what the law ought to be in East Africa.[7]

There are several key terms in this statement that became central themes of our early efforts: technical competence plus local law, local context, skills, policy, including practical implementation of policy and the contested concept 'development'.[8] Looking back, we may have been naïve, idealistic and too much in a hurry, but I think that we can say that we did our best. We scoured the local law reports for East African cases, we set up an archives project for local legal records; we gave priority to preparing local teaching materials and developing a local legal literature. We tried to be sensitive to social, political and economic context: most of the law we taught was imported, but every doctrine, every statute, every case or other transplant had to be subjected to critical scrutiny: does it fit local conditions?

In fact, in the early years after Independence we could not have ignored context if we had wanted. In UCD there was a challenging, critical 'common course' focused on development: interdisciplinary, university-wide, sometimes attended by the President himself. The fact that we had students from Kenya,

Uganda, Zanzibar and Malawi, as well as locals, forced us all to be comparative and contextual. Similarly, the situation was one of dynamic change. The absence of textbooks, the fact that we were dealing with several countries and jurisdictions, the heady political atmosphere and the rapidity of change combined to make it virtually impossible to teach or learn law as a static system of abstract rules. We were forced by circumstance to be contextual, critical, comparative and to be concerned with how to think about dynamic problems and values; both teachers and students had to study primary sources rather than to rely on textbooks that encourage rote learning of dry facts and bare rules. We felt that we were pioneers and truly radical. But looking back, Issa Shivji was right – even the most committed radicalism has severe limits, especially for law in which tradition is a central characteristic. We were subject to path-dependency. We had of necessity to rely heavily on English secondary literature – and even fifty years on the new curriculum in Dar es Salaam depends rather a lot on English and American texts.

During the next four years I was kept very busy researching East African Law in order to teach it, drafting memos and regulations, visiting secondary schools throughout the region to publicise the Faculty, helping to recruit staff and sitting on numerous committees at Faculty, College and University levels. When A. B. Weston (known as AB) was away on leave (for a total of about eighteen months) I was Acting Dean. In addition, the original three academic staff were involved in discussing buildings with the architects (including helping to design housing for staff), debating the use of vacations, gowns, methods of assessment, legal records and law reform. Conscious of the need to innovate, we made many adjustments and proposals that deviated from tradition, but in retrospect many of these ideas look quite commonplace and minor. Most of the activities I was involved in were part of the bread and butter of academic life. They are quite well documented, but if they are at all interesting that is mainly for specialists. So rather than try to give a comprehensive account, I shall merely sketch a few anecdotes that put some flesh on the bare bones of this kind of academic administration.

People

A. B. Weston

Our first Faculty Meeting was held on a bench in the park in Russell Square in London in May or June 1961. The three founder members – AB, Patrick McAuslan and myself – were in process of rebelling against our English legal education. AB had started in Australia, spent two years in Oxford, en route to Canada, where he was already known for his unorthodox views. Patrick McAuslan had also been at Oxford, but had spent part of his National Service in Nigeria. A year in Chicago and three years in Khartoum had almost cured me of Oxford. So there were three Oxford graduates, sitting in a park in London, devising the first curriculum for a new institution that none of us had seen. A prototypical neocolonial scene – except that we thought we were radicals.

We drew up the world's greatest curriculum in less than half an hour – perhaps the shortest ever meeting of the Dar Faculty of Law? There was then a lull in conversation. To fill the gap, I asked my new Dean deferentially: 'What are you working on?' He replied: 'I am writing a book on John Austin' (the nineteenth century jurist). This was mildly embarrassing and rather disconcerting, since Austin stood for all that I – and Dar – should be against. Still better keep on the right side of the Dean. 'How far have you got?' I asked. 'I am starting tomorrow morning', said AB.

Eighteen months later, AB was on leave, sailing on his yacht in the Mediterranean, when he was involved in a collision with an even bigger yacht. Not much harm was done and the two captains tied up and had a drink. 'What do you do?' asked AB. 'I am a writer', said Leon Uris, the novelist. 'What do you write?', asked AB who should have known better. Leon Uris was rather surprised that AB did not recognise his name: 'Oh, pot boilers', said Uris who had made millions from *Exodus* and other big fat books:

'Where have you got on the present one?' asked AB.
'Oh, I am only at page 250', replied Uris, 'what do you do?'
'I write, too', said AB.
'What do you write?'
'I am writing a biography of John Austin, the jurist', said AB.
Uris laughed: 'There can't be much money in that. How far have you got?'
'I'm starting tomorrow morning', said AB.
This is repeated in other parts of the Mediterranean.

This is one of many A. B. Weston legends that he fostered himself.[9] Even if the stories are fanciful, they catch some of his character: he was an adventurer, charming, unconventional, breezy, very clever, charismatic and a brilliant linguist. Furthermore, he did not take himself too seriously. He had been a pilot in the Australian Air Force and I remember vividly his trying to commandeer the controls of a bumpy single-engine plane over the Northern Region as three of us flew up to represent UCD at a meeting of the University of East Africa at Makerere. We survived the journey, but arrived like three cowboys in safari clothes late for a meeting at which almost everyone else was wearing ties and business suits.

As Dean, AB took on some tasks with great energy, but left the rest to us.

Students

The first fourteen students came from four countries (including Zanzibar).[10] The second cohort which was more than double the number also had students from Malawi. They formed the first generation of locally educated lawyers in East Africa. They were a well-educated elite from the leading secondary schools in the region, their English was excellent and they were highly motivated. It is not at all surprising that most rose to prominent positions in law and public life. They include, I think, one Prime Minister, One Chief Justice, one President of Malawi, many judges, law officers and some substantial academics. As teachers we got to know them quite well and kept in touch with many of them afterwards. A study of the subsequent careers of the first three or four cadres and how they fared in their respective countries, and internationally, would make fascinating reading.

For example, Julie Manning was the only female in the First Fourteen. In 2011 she was one of the six people honoured at the University's Fiftieth Anniversary Celebrations. Her encomium states:

> [H]er educational career story is incomplete without mentioning how – as the only university female student [others would say as an only female among male 'wolves'] during that time – she coped and managed to survive the currents!'[11]

She worked in the office of the Administrator-General and then moved to the Attorney-General's Chambers as a Parliamentary Draftsman. In 1973 she was appointed the first lady High Court Judge (Acting), but in 1975 she was nominated as a member of Parliament and became successively Minister of Justice, Minister Plenipotentiary of the Tanzania Hugh Commission in Ottawa, member of the National Electoral Commission, Commissioner of the Law Reform, Chairman of the Parole Board and so on. Not surprisingly, she was the first, and often the only woman, to hold these posts. Soia Mentschikoff, as a lawyer, was called 'the first woman everything'. Although a very different personality – quiet, self-contained, efficient – this equally fits Julie Manning. At the Celebrations it was announced that a student Hall of Residence would be called Julie Manning Hall.[12]

The careers of many of her peers were equally remarkable.

Colleagues

Patrick McAuslan was scholarly, politically committed and dedicated to UCD.[13] He was also indefatigable, stimulating a new verb in Kiswahili – KuMcAuslan. Kiswahili is a wonderfully inventive language especially in its use of prefixes: *mhuru* means a free man; *kihuru* the language of freedom; *acha* or *weka huru* (to make free, liberate), *uhuru* the concept of freedom (independence). The students tended to give all staff Kiswahili nicknames: for example, Jim Reid was fittingly known as 'Bwana Twiga' (meaning Mr Giraffe); others were less complimentary; I never learned mine. But I did learn that the students coined *KuMcAuslan* (i.e. to do a McAuslan), meaning to lock yourself in your room and concentrate on your work for seventy-two hours without a break. If they had extended this to *UMcAuslan* (the essence of McAuslan) it would have carried the connotation of relentless, concentrated work over substantial periods of time. Patrick and I were close colleagues again for ten years at Warwick and remained friends until his death in 2013.

Our first local appointment was P. J. Nkambo Mugerwa from Uganda. He had recently graduated from Cambridge, but unlike the Dar Oxonians, he had not rebelled against his legal education. He was visibly uneasy about our 'radical' approach, but we got on well enough. He claimed to have discovered Sweden, as the first known Ugandan to have been there. After a short time at Dar, he was appointed Solicitor-General of Uganda, later Attorney-General. He was still in post when Idi Amin took over. He had a difficult and dangerous period until he quietly retired to take up farming and private practice. Several colleagues became friends and continued to have close contact long afterwards. Jim Read became the hub of the study of Law in Africa at School of Oriental and African Studies (London) (SOAS) and was famed for his capacity for friendship. Sol Picciotto, who like me had studied law at BNC and Chicago, was politically involved on campus in Dar and helped design the interdisciplinary course on 'Development' which the whole UCD community was expected to attend. Like McAuslan, he became a founding member of the Warwick Law School. Yash Ghai, was a Kenyan citizen and an Oxford graduate. I was sent to Harvard to recruit him in 1963. He remained in Dar as a core member of the Faculty until 1971, including being Professor and Dean during a very difficult period. Yash, who is still a close friend, followed a stellar career as a public lawyer and as a constitutional adviser, the architect of many post-Independence constitutions, including chair of the Kenya Constitutional Review Commission (2000–2). He will feature again at Warwick.[14]

Visitors

If Khartoum in the late 1950s was more central than Aberdeen, during 1961–65 Dar es Salaam was even more central than Khartoum. It had the same kinds of visitors who turned up in Khartoum, except for fewer Middle Easterners and more Americans. This was the period when America discovered 'Africa'; but Tanzania was also a magnet for donors, boondoggling academics, improbable salespersons, politicians, journalists and other tourists. It also attracted political exiles from further south: members of the Mozambique Liberation Front (FRELIMO), founded in Dar es Salaam and led by Eduardo Mondlane, who was often seen on campus; Terry Ranger, deported from Southern Rhodesia, who became Professor of History in 1963 and pioneered oral history in Africa;[15] Herbert Chitepo, a distinguished lawyer, in exile from Malawi; and, after I left, the radical historian, Walter Rodney, whose *How Europe Underdeveloped Africa* (1972) became a classic of anti-colonialism.[16]

As in other contexts, when a place becomes fashionable, Americans predominated. They would have threatened to swamp us, except that few Americans stayed long enough to make a lasting impact. Just before we realised – perhaps because of this occasion – how very inappropriate the institution of even semi-informal High Table was in this context, we sat down one night with Philip

C. Jessup, Judge of the International Court; Justice Thurgood Marshall of the US Supreme Court; Samuel Rosenman, influential adviser to Roosevelt and Truman; Murray Schwartz, later Dean of UCLA Law School; and a number of less well-known academics, diplomats and politicians. It was interesting, it was exciting, it made us feel good – but it was not symbolically appropriate and it was as evanescent as any other examples of tourism. High Table went and with it an element of *communitas* that never got replaced.

Ambiguous symbols

Gowns: symbolic – of what?

The first controversy in UCD was not overtly about neocolonialism or ideology or the meaning of 'development', or different approaches to teaching law. It was about gowns. It rumbled on for a long time.[17] Briefly the story goes as follows: all of the founding members were determined to create a distinctive institution suited to local needs and aspirations that was clearly different from the elitist, traditionalist sister institutions in Kampala and Nairobi. The very first testing ground for this ambition centred on academic gowns. Before any academics arrived, the senior administrators had asked: what colour should the gowns be? What would clearly differentiate our students from those at Makerere (Kampala) (red) and Nairobi (blue)? They decided on saffron – like the robes of a Buddhist monk – and ordered fifty. As soon as the first academics arrived, the very idea of having gowns was challenged – but for a variety of reasons. The first objection came from a pragmatic Englishman (guess who?): 'The climate in Dar es Salaam is much hotter than it is in Kampala and Nairobi – gowns are unsuited to our context.' The administration retreated and proposed that gowns should be optional at lectures and at meals (other than High Table). An American Professor objected: 'Gowns are just an outmoded British idiosyncrasy – like wigs, pinstriped suits, rolled umbrellas, and High Table. No American student would be seen dead in a gown – so why impose this on Africa?' The next objection came from a Danish Professor of Economics: 'Gowns exactly symbolize the kind of neo-colonialism and elitism that we are determined to avoid. They are politically incorrect.' A senior Tanzanian administrator, bemused by these squabbling expatriates, pointed out that colourful ceremonies and dress are an important part of African tradition and that a degree ceremony without gowns would be considered very alien. In the end pragmatism trumped climatology, tradition, ideology and local custom. The administrators said: 'We have already paid for 50 gowns out of public funds and there will be a scandal if we do not use them.' The Academic Board reached a typically British compromise: 'Gowns should only be worn on formal and festive occasions.'

In a witty memo, Professor Eric Svendsen, an economist, caught the spirit of the debate:

In this wider framework gowns may be said to be a minor matter. In this I cannot agree, however. To me gowns tend to stress the distance between students and other members of society. They help to create a feeling of belonging, not to society in general and taking part in this society's endeavours to change and develop itself, but rather to a group of higher educated people whose privileges and special conditions are anyway so different from those of other young people that they should not be stressed again.

And I fear that gowns may lead to manners and behavior which like the gowns have not been created or have matured on African soil, but come from somewhere else . . .

Finally, I would myself – as a graduate of a Danish University not possessing a gown – rather raise this, than hear it be brought up by somebody else as a semi-argument against my view of gowns. I think that it is a fortunate thing that we originate from different sets of traditions, even if I have to turn the Old Danish fairy tale upside down and let the gownless boy speak to the bewigged emperors.[18]

That was not the end of the story. When the first students arrived, immensely proud to be joining a real university, they accepted their gowns with delight and wore them whenever opportunity arose, including when they went to discos or shopping. The administration put a stop to that – it was too conspicuously elitist. Shortly afterwards the TANU Youth League adopted green shirts as a form of uniform and decreed that these should be worn by Tanzanian students on suitable occasions. This was interpreted as including lectures, shopping, movies, discos and demonstrations. The Tanzanian students conformed, but considered this uniform to be second best. Meanwhile for academic staff ties, suits and shorts became taboo.

The TANU Building, 1961–3: national pride or political subordination?

UCD's first home was the TANU Building, the brand-new headquarters for the ruling party.[19] That fact alone has, and had, potential as an ambiguous symbol: a leftish university from the start under the wing of the political party in a de facto one-party state – TANU was short of funds, said the cynics, and a homeless, hastily planned university was a soft touch; or it symbolised the high priority and the pride attached by Tanganyikans to having OUR university – a compliment and an act of faith, said the idealists; or it was a contingent matter of chance, said the pragmatists – the building fell vacant just as the College was looking for temporary accommodation. Take your pick.

The place and design of the building were also symbolic. The front looked out on Mnazi Moja – an open space where some of the most important pre-Independence rallies were held. The back looked over Kariokoo – corrugated iron and rusty petrol-can roofs of a quintessentially African shanty town, a bit upmarket from Magomeni and other 'African' areas. The boasts of multi-racialism and non-racialism in the colonial period did not disguise the de facto zoning – the building was on a clearly marked boundary of an African area, the front looking out towards the largely Asian commercial sector of Dar es Salaam. Though hardly a sky-scraper or even a tower block, the TANU Building, modern and clean, stood out above all the rather shabby surrounding houses and commercial buildings and commanded revealing views in every direction. To the front one could just see Dar es Salaam harbour over the shops and offices of Acacia Avenue; to the north one could see over 'the African quarter', houses, small shops, Kariakoo market right to Observation Hill, 6 miles away where the permanent site was to be – who would observe whom, we wondered? Snuggling against the back wall of the College was the first of a street of brothels – one of Dar's classiest red-light districts – where watchers on the roof could peek down and see sailors, many locals and the occasional tourist haggling and maybe hope to catch a glimpse of a student or even an uncircumspect colleague sneaking in. How convenient for the students, said the cynics; how shocking, said the strait-laced; sums the place up, said the critics.

The TANU Building proved to be a quite functional office block – short of suitable rooms for teaching, but otherwise quite convenient to start with. In the second year, when the Law Faculty were moved out to an old German Bank building in Acacia Avenue, both students and staff complained. Lectures were in a vault with no windows, the ceilings were low and the whole place was unbearably hot and stuffy, inducing everyone to spend as little time there as they could. The TANU Building was cool, spacious and elegant by comparison and after very a short time it seemed so much like home that we hardly noticed the incongruity of having High Table on Thursday nights, complete with gowns, grace and wine, on the top floor of a socialist party headquarters at the edge of the red-light area of an African seaport.

Architecture and elitism

Observation Hill is 6 miles from the centre of Dar es Salaam. The government presented UCD with a site of 850 acres on two ridges at heights varying from 105 ft to 350 ft above sea level. It overlooks the city and the ocean and in most parts catches cooling breezes or more vigorous winds. Planning for the site began immediately. Norman and Dawbarn, who claimed to specialise in tropical universities and airports, were appointed architects. Their brief was to design and oversee the building of the first stage of a self-contained campus including teaching, administration, library, student accommodation, staff housing etc., as far as possible using local materials and local craftsmen. It was to be excellent without being ostentatious. The first stage was completed by 1964 in time to welcome the fourth intake of students, the first for Arts, Social Sciences, and Science – a remarkable achievement.

'Only the name of the airport changes', says Calvino. Much the same is true of modern campus architecture. The architects and planners had to balance functionality with economy, excellence without conspicuous grandeur. The result is immediately recognisable as a modern university. Concessions were made to economy by providing almost no air-conditioning, in the use of materials and by accommodating most of the students in tower blocks which were understandably unpopular. I very much enjoyed following the architects around on the splendid site while it was still bush (there was said to be a lioness in the vicinity), sitting on various planning committees, and helping to design the first staff houses, probably too enthusiastically – the first ones, including ours, had prime sites and were very agreeable. Later ones were rather less enviable.

I found the exercise fascinating. The buildings fitted the magnificent site and the end-result was fine, but not architecturally distinguished. There was one exception to this. One day the Aga Khan, leader of the Ismailis, asked for an appointment with Cran Pratt, the Principal. During the meeting he indicated that he would like to fund a non-sectarian mosque on site. This was embarrassing because there was an issue about how secular the institution should be – shades of UCL. The idea of a chapel had been rejected. So Cran thanked him but prevaricated. The Aga Khan indicated that he would ask his architect to make some preliminary sketches anyway. 'My architect' was Walter Gropius. In time a Gropius mosque was built and a single chaplain and various other religious dignitaries were appointed. Critics of the institution still called it conspicuously elitist – which, of course, it was by local standards.

Academic matters

First class

I gave the first lecture of the whole institution. There is a slightly schoolboy-ish element about the story, but it makes the point that we were not going around all the time thinking 'we are making history' – at least some of us weren't. AB was preoccupied with ordering books for the library, and begging them from embassies and High Commissions, a task he insisted on dealing with personally. He was determined to have 'the best law library in Africa' – he still talked about 'Africa' as if it was one place. As he seemed a bit pressed, I offered to take his lecture for him on Tuesday. It was only afterwards that we realised that it was the first lecture in the history of the institution.

The first class was just the start of the course on Introduction to Law – not really a lecture at all – just fourteen students and I getting to know each other. There is no record of that event. However, there is a film of another class shortly afterwards. Not surprisingly, the early weeks of the first term had quite a lot of razzmatazz – opening ceremonies, press photographers and public relations exercises. A Canadian TV crew came to make a film for the first weeks of the College and asked permission to come into my class. I agreed, provided that they did not disrupt it. Although I had to make three entrances and start my presentation four or five times, I was quite pleased. Unfortunately, the topic for the class – half lecture, half discussion – could hardly have been less appropriate as a means of signalling what we were trying to do in teaching law differently. It was Hohfeld's analysis of the concept of 'right' – an important subject, I still think, but associated with the kind of dry, abstract analytical approach which we were meant to be breaking away from. I never saw the TV film, but a still photograph from it appeared in several Ford Foundation publications, showing me sitting at the head of a seminar table with the First Fourteen and this very formal analytical scheme prominently displayed on the blackboard behind me. AB was probably the only person who noticed this and he teased me about it for a long time (not least because I had been rude about his beloved John Austin, another analytical jurist), but he always added: 'At least you weren't *lecturing.*' Significantly, I was wearing an Oxford MA gown and a tie.

Custom and customary law

In both Khartoum and Dar es Salaam I tried to study and teach about 'customary law' and custom, both the limited amount that was recognised as part of state law, and the much more extensive traditional customs that were still of great importance, especially in rural areas. It was very difficult to do so. There was some good work on this in both regions by social anthropologists.[20] These were local, episodic and did not provide much insight into the interaction between state law and custom. More important, there were conceptual problems about custom and customary law and methodological problems about how to describe or expound them. In particular, did customary law consist of rules in the same way as modern state law was said to do?

During my time in Dar es Salaam both the Kenyan and Tanzanian governments were trying to accommodate customary law within the state system, both to give it more prominence and to control it. In Kenya the Restatement of African Law Project (based on SOAS) tried to record and 'restate' selected branches of law of particular peoples ('tribes') into code-like forms; in Uganda the policy was less clear, but over the years the trend was towards assimilating or replacing custom and customary law within the state system. Some of the Ugandan students were quite patronising about custom. In Tanzania – more radically – they asked Hans Cory to 'unify' the customary law of over a hundred peoples. Cory was a Viennese who had come out to work on a sisal estate in Tanganyika in his twenties. He claimed to have attended Freud's lectures, but he never obtained a degree. However, he was fascinated by the local people and he wrote copious notes about their customs, religions and practices. After some years he had spent much more time doing genuine field-work than most anthropologists have the opportunity to do and, though he was self-taught and his methods were elementary, over many years he collected a vast amount of data. Eventually, Cory published two books on the law and custom of the Sukuma and the Haya and one on African figurines.[21] During the colonial period he was employed as a government anthropologist to advise officials about local custom and public opinion when government policy seemed to be running into opposition.

Government anthropologists were widely regarded as colonial spies but, after Independence, Julius Nyerere employed Cory to try to unify customary law by producing a code that combined or harmonised the disparate values of allegedly 120 different peoples. The motive was political: to unify law as part of building a unified nation. The means were controversial, for two main reasons. First, there were severe doubts about the extent of uniformity or of public consensus about quite a few rules; for example, whether bride wealth should be a condition of validity of marriage, whether adultery should be punishable as a crime as well as a civil wrong; and the rules of inheritance. Secondly, 'codifying' customary law both imposed an artificial rigidity on what was generally a very flexible set of norms, and translating custom from dispute processes that usually ended in compromise to the all-or-nothing forms of Western adjudication involved a radical change of procedural context. As one Minister of Justice put it: 'People leave colonial courts as enemies, they leave African processes as friends.'[22]

Knowing about Cory's project and the controversy, I invited him to give a seminar on the subject to our first cohort of students. I had briefed them about the controversy and some of them, especially the Ugandans, were quite hostile to the idea of unifying and codifying customary law. Cory had brought with him from Vienna an image of the Germanic Herr Professor whose wisdom was accepted unquestioningly by his students and he was quite put out by the sharp questioning he faced when he had finished speaking. He had argued that the general principles of African customary law were indeed uniform, the differences were trivial and that he had had no difficulty in reaching consensus and gaining acceptance of his draft when he went around the country holding *barazas* – public meetings – to discuss it. The students were sceptical and there came a point when the exchanges were becoming acrimonious. Suddenly Cory started drumming on the table, using a recognisable rhythmic beat; soon the students joined in and everyone was drumming in time. 'Look,' he seemed to say, 'it is easy to get consensus.'

The unification project was based on the questionable assumption that rural customs were nearly all much the same and it clearly involved dubious methods. When I visited Chicago in 1963 my trip was financed by three public lectures on 'The Place of Customary Law in the National Legal Systems of East Africa' in which I was quite critical of both the Kenyan and Tanzanian approaches.[23] The main ground was that divorcing customary 'rules' from the context of the social processes in which they traditionally operated changed both form and substance of these 'rules' significantly. The processes rarely involved pure forms of third-party adjudication. Philip Gulliver was surprised to find that among the Arusha of northern Tanzania the outcomes rarely accorded with the articulated rules. When he returned to England he realised that this finding was not as surprising or original as he had thought, for the outcomes of personal injury litigation in England rarely accorded with the rules as expounded in *Salmond on Torts*.

In East Africa there was, admittedly, a policy dilemma: how could local courts apply local custom without reliable information about it? And, what if the magistrates were not local?[24] But reducing them to written, code-like form changed their nature. How people articulate, invoke, use or interpret rules depends on context. And can one assume that a people's 'customs' are monolithic or part of one coherent system? For example, a well-known anthropological anecdote in East Africa concerned the naïve reaction of a researcher observing the dispute processes of a coastal group who regularly invoked two well-established sets of norms: one claimed (not always convincingly) to be rooted in tradition, the other in religion, mainly Islam or Christianity.[25] Typically in group decision-making processes concerning such matters as marriage formation, inheritance, and family disputes, one party (and his or her supporters) invoked 'traditional' norms, the other invoked religious ones. The outcomes bore some connection with the norms, but there was no obvious pattern of lexical priority or choice of norm rules. Often there was compromise. When asked why the group did not simplify their social life by deciding which body of norms had priority or by integrating the two sets into a single consistent code, the interpreter was amazed: 'How could we possibly proceed if we had only one body of rules?' As one of my Belfast students remarked, the observer's question was perceived to be rather like asking: 'Why don't they decide which is the best football team *before* the start of the season?' Recent anthropological research reports similar phenomena as quite widespread.[26]

In Ethiopia I learned that Professor René David, while 'adapting' the French Civil code for local enactment, claimed that he 'hated customary law' and wished to abolish it (how is that possible?).[27] Some scholars began to suggest that 'customary law' was largely an invention created by interaction and negotiation between colonial rulers and indigenous leaders pursuing their respective interests, rather than long-established tradition.[28] This fitted in nicely with my views, but made it even harder to teach about the subject. These experiences also taught me that equating 'law' with state or municipal law is quite inadequate, especially in the countries of Eastern Africa. That is one reason why jurists need to take the concept of 'non-state law' seriously.[29]

Later these African examples led me to dig deeper into the very influential American *Restatements*, on which the Restatement of African Law was purportedly modelled. In fact, the context was rather different. I concluded that the American version was a form of private quasi-legislation calculated to by-pass state legislatures to produce a virtual system of 'American Private Law'. This product of teams of jurists became influential partly because the Restatements were quoted as persuasive authority in the courts but, perhaps more importantly, because elite law schools and advocates used them as a source of a fictional unified 'American law', despite the fact that private law was constitutionally largely a matter for the fifty-one semi-autonomous states. The legal establishment wished to maintain the unity of the common law in the United States; the elite law schools aspired to be, and became, national rather than local institutions on the foundation of a controversial juristic hybrid – a virtual body of substantive law.[30]

Continuity and change in legal education

My period in Dar involved me in a number of issues relating to legal education policy and cemented my interest in the subject. The gowns controversy is one of many stories that illustrate how difficult it is to break away from foreign models. With an institution like a university one can make adjustments at the margins, as with gowns, but basic structures, attitudes, habitual practices and entrenched traditions are much tougher to change, or even to adjust to fit local conditions. This is also true of teaching law. UCD was in a special relationship with the University of London and the first law graduates read for a London LLB. The authorities in London, while insistent on the 'standards' of the University of London, were surprisingly flexible about content. They positively encouraged us to teach about the legal systems and the constitutions and the laws of East Africa, so far as this was feasible, and we tried very hard to do this. The problem was how. For example, we had a course on the Constitutions and Legal Systems of East Africa – in 1961–3 Kenya, Uganda and Tanganyika all had new constitutions and were in process of debating and reforming their court systems, sometimes in strikingly different ways. In my second year, I was again teaching Torts – but how does one teach the East African Law of Torts, when there were only a handful of reported cases and no books?[31] Even today, how does one teach about local customary law of wrongs in detail and depth? These are real – and to some extent continuing – problems. We did our best and, in some respects, we made a virtue of necessity.

The task of gathering local materials was hard, especially in relation to customary law, but it was made harder by the fact that this was the immediate post-Independence period and people talked as if everything was up for grabs.[32] In fact we were more subject to path-dependency than we realised. For us the central question was: how could one sensibly teach about law in East Africa in the absence of a secondary literature in a period of momentous change? It seemed to us that there were two main options: first, to prepare elementary local textbooks and study aids so that the students could have some solid information to learn; or, secondly, to teach about problems of law in East Africa, sacrificing coverage of technical detail and focusing critically on the suitability of the existing state legal systems to the circumstances and needs of the various countries in the run-up to and aftermath of Independence.

In Nigeria, the local law schools, which were founded in the same period under the leadership of Jim Gower, gave a high priority to producing basic expository works and outlines on aspects of Nigerian Law. In Dar, we followed a different strategy. We used English-language textbooks and casebooks[33] supplemented by local materials. Where the course had distinctive local dimensions, we emphasised the materials. It is sometimes suggested that we followed an American model of cases and materials rather than a British model of textbooks. That is only partly true: like American law teachers, we emphasised primary sources; we were not too concerned with coverage, and we tried to proceed by discussion as much as lectures – which was easy with our First Fourteen. But conditions dictated that our approach was distinctive in several ways: first, it had to be comparative because we were dealing with five different countries from which our students came; secondly, transition from colonial rule and the resulting pressures for change linked with the lack of a developed literature virtually compelled us to adopt a historical approach – which was anyway congenial to Patrick and myself;[34] thirdly, since we were dealing in large part with imported legal ideas, institutions and doctrines, their suitability to a new context was continuously put at issue – we *had* to be contextual. In our jointly taught course, Patrick McAuslan dealt with the Constitutions, I took on the court systems and a bit about customary law. We systematically combed the local law reports, the statute books, official reports and newspaper accounts of public debates to supplement the almost non-existent secondary literature.

Path dependency again: the Western academic year

From early on as a teacher I have had a bee in my bonnet about students' use of time – the amount of time they were meant to spend studying during a calendar year. In Oxford there was a clear distinction drawn between holidays and vacations. A reasonable amount of the vacations was to be devoted to academic work and we were accountable for this through examinations and 'collections' at the start of term. In Khartoum I realised that the students' living conditions at home did not allow for doing much academic work during vacations, but the length of terms were much the same as in provincial universities in the UK. This was embedded in the structure of the University. We tried to encourage reading and research into local custom with variable results. In Khartoum, *faute de mieux*, I had supported the move from a four-year to five-year degree in order to ease pressure on the curriculum and to reduce the failure rate (which it did substantially). Without a period of apprenticeship or bar exams, Sudanese law graduates were eligible to practice at an earlier age than lawyers in most Western countries. Why were students studying for less than thirty weeks a year?[35] In Dar my argument was met with strong resistance. However, we did get some funding to enable students who had been accepted for the Law Faculty to have placements in law-related institutions and to do some preliminary reading during the six-month gap between leaving school and entering university.

In the end Dar students got a three-year LLB and a promise of one year of vocational training (on the Gower model). The students coped well with the academic side and there was a much lower failure rate than Khartoum. Provision was made for Kenyans and Ugandans to have a year's vocational course in their home countries, but nothing materialised to start with in Dar. This was a bad mistake, somewhat mitigated by the fact that almost all Tanzanian law graduates were bonded to the public service, so they were not let loose on the public immediately. They got some in-service training, but not as much as was needed, until some years later when AB was asked to set up a post graduate training programme on his return to Tanzania.

The Kenya Council of Legal Education (KCLE)

From 1962–5 I was a member of the Kenya Council of Legal Education, the statutory body concerned with all matters to do with admission to the Kenya Bar. It was chaired by the Chief Justice. It included one other judge and the Attorney-General *ex officio*, four representatives of the Law Society of Kenya and one law teacher. It was an intensely political body dealing with quite technical matters, such as recognition of foreign Law degrees. There were three recurring issues: first, all of the Law Society representatives had qualified through the apprenticeship system (two, I think, in Ireland). They were deeply suspicious of academic law. Secondly, this was a statutory committee on which they did not have a majority and they strongly asserted the traditional autonomy of the legal profession. Thirdly, they were white Kenyans and were suspicious of all things Tanzanian, including UCD, which they viewed as a hotbed of socialism. They believed that Kenya should have its own law school, based on the apprenticeship system and that all Kenyans should qualify there. I also suspected a latent racism, which was generally well-concealed.

On all of these issues I was potentially in a minority of one (and half the age of all the other members, except the Attorney-General, Charles Njonjo). But I had one trump card: I knew quite a lot about legal education in the UK, USA, Dar es Salaam and other parts of Africa. The Law Society members were ignorant: they had not heard of the Denning Committee or Jim Gower or developments in Ghana. When I suggested that some credit should be given to a Harvard Law degree, one solicitor commented, inadvertently echoing a famous clanger/gaffe reported to Holmes by Harold Laski when he had suggested that legal education in England might learn from Harvard: 'The crime rate in America is a sufficient comment on the Harvard Law School.'[36] He had probably not heard of Holmes or Laski.

I soon learned how to out-manoeuvre them – not by flaunting my own learning, but by emphasising practicalities: how could apprenticeship be the only route to qualifying in Kenya, when there were already dozens of

Kenyans studying law abroad, including in Dar and Moscow? There had to be provision for post-degree training for such people. In particular, Kenya needed a safety net to test for quality as it would be an impossible task to discriminate between English, Scottish, Irish, Russian, Australian, Indian and American Law degrees for the purposes of recognition. The Kenyan government had already pledged to recognise the Dar degree, but Dar graduates would need at least six months' practical training on top of that. No one had thought through the conditions and costs of apprenticeship, nor the library and other needs of a local law school. Crucially, would this be funded by the profession or government? Ghana provided one possible model, Australia another. And so on. Over time I gained their respect, if not their agreement, and I was quite often supported by the *ex officio* members, especially Sir John Ainley, the Chief Justice, who had more power than just a casting vote. Eventually a Kenya School of Law was set up, with an apprenticeship scheme and provision of a full-time conversion course for those with overseas qualifications. However, the battles continued. When the First Principal of the Kenya School of Law was appointed, there was a move to get me to resign in his favour – as there was only one place on the Council for a teacher of law. I fought this vigorously, with the support of the Chief Justice, and won – seemingly on the ground that the Council was the Principal's employer, so he should not be a voting member, but could be invited to attend meetings.

I thoroughly enjoyed my time on the Council. This rather parochial and arcane body provided me with a useful apprenticeship in the politics and diplomacy of legal education and training. Ever afterwards I adopted the role of professional legal educator who knew much more about the subject and developments elsewhere than any local practitioner could reasonably be expected to be aware of (see Chapter 16).

Disengaging

I suppose, in retrospect, that it was almost inevitable that I should leave Dar sooner than I expected. When one started one did not think much about even the medium-term future, but it seemed bound to be temporary. Despite my birth and background, I was still an expatriate, though one without an emotional home. I had expected to stay in Dar for five or six years, but chance intervened. Two main episodes led me to decide to look elsewhere and a third determined where I should go.

First, Karl Llewellyn died suddenly in February 1962. I heard about it shortly afterwards. From then on, my main scholarly attention was devoted to him and his ideas. It is as if I deserted Africa so far as my scholarship was concerned. In fact, this was largely a matter of chance. I had not intended to write about him, but a short obituary became an article which led to my being lured to put his papers in order in Chicago and this made writing a book about him almost unavoidable. I tell that story in the next chapter.

Secondly, I had to make a career choice. My stay in Oxford in 1960 had resulted in the decision not to try for tutorial Fellowships there. But where should I go next, doing what? In September 1964 I went on my own to stay on the slopes of Kilimanjaro to take stock and make plans for the future. The document marked 'Kibo' is uncomfortably revealing about my confusion and uncertainties, but it showed a clear commitment to continuing to be an academic. Yogi Berra said: 'When you come to a fork in the road, take it.' I combined or conflated both at Kibo in 1964 combining Africa and Jurisprudence: I contemplated 'doing' a major work on African Jurisprudence ('*after* the Llewellyn book? (huh!)'),[37] which I did not follow up, but the real issue was about my scholarly agenda. Soon afterwards I settled for Jurisprudence rather than for being an Africanist or more academic administration (there were emerging possible deanships in other parts of Africa) or other activist possibilities. Rather, I decided to concentrate on Llewellyn and complete this project as a first apprenticeship in scholarly writing.[38] But where should I do it? The UK had never been 'home'. A year at Yale seemed the best prospect. Dar had a fruitful link with Yale and this had been hinted as a possibility. So, I accepted an invitation to spend the academic year of 1965–6 in New Haven.

Then, thirdly, out of the blue I received an invitation to apply for the Chair of Jurisprudence at the Queen's University Belfast, I was offered it and accepted. That was almost entirely serendipity. I tell that story in the chapter following my re-engagement with the United States.

But why did I give up on Africa so fast and so sharply? Penelope explains it as follows: in Sudan I was fully involved not only with teaching and the University but also in practical extra-curricular activities – editing the law reports, starting an archive, writing about Sudan law including the future of the Sudan legal system (which was already quite political). In Dar I involved myself in the University and Law School, but deliberately – in her view obsessively – kept a low profile because of my background and fear of being attacked as a colonialist.[39] So, unlike Yash Ghai and Patrick McAuslan, I did not write on controversial public issues such as the one-party state and preventive detention. Her points are valid, but it is more complex than that. For one thing, while nearly all my published writings in both Sudan and Dar periods were about local legal issues, my reading and thinking were focused elsewhere – for instance my commonplace book for 1958–9 is mainly about Jurisprudence (and occasionally about teaching) and hardly at all about local law. More important, I did not have a long- or medium-term research plan. It was not part of the academic culture at that time. I was an auto-didact as a scholar (no research training), and most of my writing and publication were based on activist concerns. After I left in 1965 I continued with activist matters – external examining, postgraduate students from Africa, CLEA projects (archives, access, skills, legal awareness) (Chapter 16), and later consultancies and writing reports on legal education and law schools. I did not see these as *scholarly* activities.

I also saw my period of teaching in Africa as *temporary*. By now I knew that I was an expatriate – this defined me as being English; East Africa was not home. It never occurred to me to take out Tanzanian citizenship. Part of our mission was to train others to take over. In both Khartoum and Dar, we were unsettled for most of the time. I taught in Oxford during one long vacation from Sudan in order to decide whether to apply for tutorial Fellowships. In 1963–4 I spent first three then six months in Chicago in quest of Llewellyn. By 1964 I was thinking of leaving Dar. Until the opportunity at Queen's turned up, the main options seemed to be a lectureship at Southampton or a Chair at Lagos. There were also pressing family reasons: by 1965 Karen was 6 and Peter was 4, so there were not many years left before educational concerns would kick in and we did not want to treat them as colonial children, packed off to boarding school. On scholarship I took a rather strict line: reacting against Americans who claimed instant expertise after a mere year or two, I felt that to be a serious 'Africanist' one had to live in Africa or one would be out of touch within a month. That was taking purism to an extreme, as if serious scholarly work depended largely on local gossip. Probably more important was the fact that in my first seven years as an academic I had not had time to do any sustained research.

Aftermath

I left Dar in March/April 1965 first to spend six months at Yale, mainly working on Llewellyn, and then to Belfast – where I stayed until 1 April 1972, when I moved on to Warwick, a new law school, similar in conception to Dar, and, indeed, a bit like a retirement home for ex-Dar es Salaamites – McAuslan and Picciotto were already there and several others (notably Yash Ghai and Abdul Paliwala) were at Warwick before or after a spell in Dar. After that my career was much like that of late twentieth-century academics and insofar as there is much to recount, it is mostly to be found in my published writings. However, I kept in touch with East Africa and the Sudan and expanded my experience of Africa to Botswana, Lesotho, Swaziland, Ghana and Nigeria mainly through external examining, consultancy, research on legal records and some public lectures. Our daughter Karen spent 'a gap year' in Kenya after leaving school and, having caught the Africa bug, spent fifteen years in Sudan, Rwanda and Kenya mainly as an aid worker. Although based in England, she is still involved. So we maintained fragmented contact.

7

Llewellyn again: American interludes (Chicago 1963-4, Yale 1965, Philadelphia 1971)

Chicago II: Spring 1963

Almost my only direct contact with Llewellyn after I left Chicago was that he sent me a copy of *The Common Law Tradition* (1960), with a characteristically generous inscription. Soia Mentschikoff later sent me his posthumously published collection of essays *Jurisprudence – Realism in Theory and Practice* (1962), also with a nice inscription. I was generally preoccupied with institution-building in newly independent countries, adjusting common law ways of doing things to local conditions, and keeping a few pages ahead of the class. However, by then Llewellyn was profoundly influencing my approach, not only to teaching Jurisprudence, but also more generally to thinking about law in its social, political and economic context. A single episode exemplifies this influence. In Oxford Hart had first aroused my interest in Jurisprudence and had introduced me to the then prevailing methods of analytical philosophy. A year in Chicago had modified, but not weakened my attachment to Hart's approach. When Hart's *The Concept of Law* came out in 1961, I recognised this as an important book, but unlike many others I was not overwhelmed by it. I remember spending an evening in Dar in December 1961 in heated discussion with a visitor from Oxford (Ian Brownlie) who maintained that it was self-evident that Hart's book would from now on be the starting point for all serious jurisprudential discussion. I do not remember exactly what I argued, but in retrospect it is clear that it must have been Llewellynesque. Unfortunately, he proved to be right and what Hart later called 'that wretched book' became an obsession that still continues after fifty years.[1] Whether or not this was an epiphanic moment, it revealed an underlying tension in my attitude to my two jurisprudential mentors: is it possible to be a loyal disciple of both Hart and Llewellyn? I have written about that in the 'Afterword' to KLRM.[2]

Karl Llewellyn died suddenly on 13 February 1962. I heard the news quite soon afterwards in Dar es Salaam. In 1985 I recounted the next stage as follows:

It may have been on a beach in Dar es Salaam that I heard the news of the death of Karl Llewellyn. It was quite possibly the same beach on which we later played Frisbee with the late Wolfgang Friedman, who had come out to teach about Law and Economic Development . . . the same Wolfgang Friedman who in an earlier era had been a forerunner of the English Realist Revolution . . . if indeed England has undergone something that can be so described.

It was February, 1962. Academic news travelled fast in those days, for this was the peak period of American, indeed Western, interest in Africa . . . the brief era of the neocolonial honeymoon. This was the period in which a Scottish philosopher could justify his transfer to the Sudan on the ground that Khartoum was more central that Aberdeen. Almost every week we entertained at least one visiting fireman from the United States who was clocking up mileage, buying local carvings, selling American legal education, and passing gossip along the circuit.

I was upset by the news about Karl. I had found him an inspiring teacher; I was fond of him and I knew that his premature death meant that his final statement of his most general theory would never be completed. At the time I saw him as only one of a number of teachers from whom I had learned much. But Llewellyn's impact on me was growing as I reflected on the implications of his ideas for academic law in East Africa. They had more resonance than most other juristic ideas for young expatriates who were trying to make sense of the bizarre unrealities of the common law in a social context, nay a climate, that was not hospitable to Carbolic Smoke Balls.

As an expatriate Englishman I naturally subscribed to the airmail edition of the [London] Times. When it became apparent that the Times had not noticed Llewellyn's death, I quickly drafted an obituary and sent it off. In due course I received a curt rejection, which implied that readers of the Times were not interested in obscure American jurists. I was already well aware of the caricatures and sneering critiques of American Realism in English textbooks of the time. Incensed, I decided to convert the British public to Llewellyn by writing an article about him. Wishing to quote from his marvelously rich, if cryptic, course materials on Law in our Society, but retaining a gentlemanly concern for the niceties of copyright, I wrote to Soia Mentschikoff, Llewellyn's widow, for permission to quote from them. With a promptness never to be repeated, she replied almost by return, suggesting that I should come to Chicago to consult 'one or two unpublished manuscripts.' She would fix it. So in 1963 I set out from Dar es Salaam to Chicago, earning my fare by delivering a series of lectures on customary law in East Africa, a late example of armchair legal anthropology.[3]

This account from 1985 is essentially accurate. The flippant and slightly sardonic tone was intended to signal the unreliability of memory and the elusiveness of 'realism' and as a nod towards 'post-modernism', which was just coming into fashion in law at the time.

Culture shock again

I arrived back in Chicago in April 1963, nearly five years after I had graduated. My very first encounter was not with Soia Mentschikoff, but with Aaron Director again – a nearly traumatic reminder of the gulf between the University of Chicago and University College Dar es Salaam. In Dar we were all committed supporters of Nyerere. As soon as I arrived back in the USA, I was submitted to Chicago-style questioning: was Tanganyika better off than before Independence? Was the government committed to development? Did its policies make sense? Where did Nyerere stand in the Cold War? Why were we imposing an English-style legal education, when we had experienced the vastly better American way? My unease came to a head the day after my arrival in Chicago. Another confrontation with Aaron Director.

To finance the visit, I was due to give some lectures in the New Nations Program, which was run by Denis Cowen, a former dean of Cape Town Law Faculty and a substantial jurist. I arrived jet-lagged from Dar es Salaam via Europe to be hustled into a lecture by Director on 'Law and Economic Development in Africa'. The lecture began with a familiar kind of statement: 'I take it as axiomatic that economic development can only take place in the conditions of a free market.'[4] And he proceeded to build up a rigorous abstract, theoretical analysis which followed from this premise. I knew that Director was averse to travel and had never been to Africa. I was caught between jet lag and culture shock. The first was beginning to win, when Denis Cowen slid across to me and whispered that he hoped that I would reply to this. When the time came for questions, I reluctantly stood up and said: 'I have not visited *all* of the countries about which Mr Director has been talking, but I can say categorically that none of the newly independent African states with which I am familiar at first hand has ever had or is ever likely to have a regime that accepts his basic premise.' To which he replied dismissively: 'I was talking economics, not politics.'

The classic denial of ideology. I considered that I won that exchange, not least because of his reply. But I was shaken, for I began to realise that in Dar we were all so taken up with our mission that we never questioned our assumptions. Some of the questions I had to confront in conversation in the Chicago context would not have been politically correct in Dar. I began to wonder whether I too had been brainwashed. I did not radically change my views or commitments because of these encounters, but I was forced to think about justifications for my positions. It was a sobering experience.

The Karl Llewellyn Papers

My immediate task was to locate 'one or two unpublished manuscripts', as Soia had indicated. Karl had died suddenly and unexpectedly on the night of 13 February 1962. It was term-time and he was due to teach a class the next morning. His death came as a shock to many. Soia was, I think, traumatised. Fourteen months later, when I was given the key to his office, I was told that no one had been inside it since his death, not even a cleaner. It was indeed exactly as he had left it, except that a thin layer of black Chicago grime covered everything on the desk. If it was like a shrine, I behaved more like a grave robber than an archaeologist or a scene-of-crime officer. I made no attempt to leave things in their place until a record was made of their location. I did, however, notice that the very top piece of paper (on a yellow pad) was a handwritten poem in both English and German.[5] I rummaged through the papers on the desk and in the drawers and a filing cabinet, until I found what I was looking for – two or three drafts of unpublished pieces and some transcripts of lectures that had been recorded. I took these to Soia, implying that my mission was accomplished. She pointed out that Karl had a study at their home, 4920 Kimbark Avenue, and I should also inspect that. There was more there including some sets of teaching materials. When I reported that I had finished, she said that she thought there was also a cupboard with more paper in it. There was. At this stage, I realised that Soia was leading me on. I responded by moving in. I planned that when I was alone in the house I would case the joint from basement to attic. Sure enough, the basement held more boxes, including at least one unopened tea-chest indicating transport by rail from New Haven to New York. Karl had moved from Yale to Columbia in 1924. I worked my way up through the house, searching methodically and relatively free from inhibition, acting like a professional burglar. I found a few more enclaves of material. As I reached the attic, a door opened and out popped the head of a little old lady. We were both shocked. She looked afraid. I did not know that anyone was there, but I realised that this was probably Soia's mother. She had arrived from Russia in 1916 and knew (or claimed to know) no English. I know no Russian. All I could do was repeat 'Szoia, Szoia, Szoia'. She did not shoot me.

I am an archivist manqué (Chapter 2). I had no training, but I had been involved in projects for preserving legal records in both Sudan and Tanzania, so it did not take much to persuade me to try to put Karl's papers in order. The Law School financed the project in exchange for the return of Karl's office.[6] Intermittently over the next two years (1963–5) I supervised the exercise, assisted by Raymond Ellinwood (a former pupil of Karl's), Dori Dressander (a former secretary), and my wife, Penelope. We did not think to consult the University Librarian or those responsible for archives. They might not have approved of the idea of the project, let alone our rough-and-ready methods. But at least the job got done.

Rootling through a person's papers, especially those of an untidy magpie, is one of the best ways of getting to know them. I learned more about Karl from this exercise than I did from my direct contact with him in 1957–8, or from interviews, or even from casual reading of his works. Of course, it was not a substitute for careful reading, but it was a marvellously illuminating way of getting inside his mind. This is how I tried to evoke the experience in 1965, shortly after completion of the project:

> The amount of material was daunting. Seven large filing cabinets, tightly packed, have not sufficed to house the collection in its ordered state, even after the removal of irrelevancies, duplicates, and 'such lumber as was not literary'. Originally three or four times as much space had been taken up. The disorder was magnificent. Little pockets of order, occurring in periods like geological

strata, remained as evidence of the efforts of valiant secretaries to introduce a system, but more often than not even these had been subverted by a poltergeist whose capacity for subtle misplacement amounted at times to genius.

It is impossible to work with the papers without being made acutely conscious of Llewellyn's personality, always vivid, sometimes dominating, easily tempting one from the path of conventional legal scholarship. I confess to having indulged myself so that sometimes my quest for Llewellyn the jurist has become a quest for Llewellyn the man. In the early stages this was almost inevitable. The disorder was in itself revealing and produced juxtapositions that accentuated certain aspects of his personality. Lying cheek by jowl with an unpublished manuscript in German or a comment on a section of 'the Code' would be a newspaper clipping about a lecture to a Bar Association on its failure to meet the public's needs or an unfinished poem or the draft of a letter, probably never sent, lambasting a well-known jurist about some unwarranted idiocy.

Such juxtapositions give color to one of the more popular images of Llewellyn: Renaissance Man, full-blooded, rumbustious, 'universal,' a sort of Benvenuto Cellini of the law schools. Mercurial of temperament, he generated anecdotes almost as fast as he generated ideas. There are stories of heated clashes with his superiors; of a rhapsody over the magnolias in bloom interfering with the drafting of the Uniform Commercial Code; of flights of oratory that his audience never forgot. The best known is the story of his adventures in the German army from which he emerged with the Iron Cross. Several contradictory versions exist, and the task of piecing together an authentic account has not been made easier by the fact that Llewellyn, who was normally reticent about the episode, gave currency to two versions – one of which reads like a military romance, the other tending to the mock-heroic.[7]

Chicago III: January–June 1964

I returned to Chicago with my family for six months from January to June 1964. I earned my keep by teaching a rather eclectic course on 'Problems of Law in Africa', but most of my time was devoted to the Llewellyn Papers Project, working with an excellent team. We almost completed the project, including a detailed catalogue, and I began drafting a rather exuberant short book on the papers.[8] This was published by the Law School in 1965, although looked down on by Philip Kurland and one or two other colleagues. Indeed, while the Chicago faculty were all polite to me (unusual for Chicago), I sensed that some had reservations about the project. Intellectual biography was almost unknown in American Law Schools at the time,[9] and one or two senior members of the Faculty gently suggested that this kind of work would not further my career; others seemed to be asking 'Why Karl?' – sometimes with an implicit coda: 'Why not Me?' Alison Dunham and Grant Gilmore who had worked with Karl on the Uniform Commercial Code were reticent about its politics; but others, including Max Rheinstein, Malcolm Sharp and Gerhard Casper, were very supportive. But, of course, the key figure was Soia.

Excursus: Soia Mentschikoff Llewellyn

At this point I need to pause to evoke Llewellyn's third wife and widow, Soia Mentschikoff Llewellyn, who hardly features in KLRM and then mainly in relation to the UCC. That was probably appropriate for the book.[10] But Soia was both an extraordinary person and a central actor in the present story: she invited me to come to Chicago to look at Karl's papers; she fixed the funding; she lured me into putting them in order; she was an essential source of information and reference point in writing about Karl; and she did much to keep his memory alive after his death, not least when she was Dean of the University of Miami Law School (1974–82) and as co-author of the book based on his materials for *Elements*.[11] My wife became her intimate friend. Soia treated me like a somewhat wayward son – bright-eyed and bushy-tailed, but with some quirky ideas of my own.

Soia Mentschikoff deserves at least one full-scale biography and it is sad that none has yet been completed. First, the basic facts: born Moscow 1915; settled in New York, 1918; Hunter College, AB 1934; Columbia Law School, LLB 1937; private practice in New York 1937–47 (partner, Spence, Hotchkiss, Parker and Duryee from 1944); Associate Chief Reporter, UCC;[12] married Karl Llewellyn, 1947; Harvard Law School 1947–9 (Visiting Professor); University of Chicago 1951–74 (professorial lecturer, then Professor, 1962);[13] University of Miami Law School 1974–82 (Visiting Professor from 1967 and then Dean); died 1984.

Her public image is replete with hyperboles. Franklin Zimring called her the 'first woman everything':[14] inter alia, she was the first woman to teach at Harvard Law School; the first woman partner of a major US law firm; the first woman President of AALS; and the first woman listed as a possible US Supreme Court nominee.[15] In Miami she was known as 'the Czarina' and as Snow White, who brought in seven dwarfs, mainly young graduates of the University of Chicago Law School and Harvard, to transform the University of Miami according to her own lights – or her interpretation of Karl Llewellyn's. She was persuasive, inspiring, autocratic, tough-minded, funny. She was a brilliant practical lawyer and a superb fixer. She was repeatedly called 'an artist in the law', but she wrote little.[16] In 1971 she was judged by *McCalls* magazine to be one of the fifty women who had made the greatest contribution to American society. She refused to be labelled a feminist.

She was formidable and shrewd, she read people well and she could be very effective – some called it forceful or cogent, others manipulative or domineering. One of her favourite precepts was reputedly: 'In any transaction, when you push the button, you'd better know who's gonna die over there – because if you *don't*, it might be you.'[17] Karl, who adored her, is reported as introducing her as a speaker with the words: 'but you shall hear Soia, my gal can sail ships'. One Miami colleague is reported as saying: 'She always sets the terms of discussion, and in such a way that she cannot lose ... You have to watch her all the time. She can smile and eat you alive.'[18]

Of course, I had a different angle on Soia. As a student, my first impression was of a large, imposing, grey haired woman, soft-spoken, with a no-nonsense style. I had difficulty following her teaching, both because her voice was very low and what she said assumed a commercial background that I lacked. The Llewellyns threw good parties and in 1957–8 we went to their house several times. Penelope said that she had no dress sense. I did not see her as a dominant character in the Law School and I had little idea of her legendary reputation.

Later, especially after the completion of the book, we became part of the family. We saw her in the roles of dutiful daughter, relaxed hostess and intimate friend. Many viewed her as a Russian Earth Mother. She and her mother attended the Russian Orthodox church regularly and on one memorable Easter we went with them. 'Mama Toia' made her daughter speak to her in Russian. We went walking with her in Ireland, except we were more behind than with. Soia longed to revisit Russia – she had not been back since she left and Karl had been worried that she would be held to ransom by the Soviets. One year at her house in Coral Gables we planned a Grand Tour, sitting on the floor round a map of Russia. Soia had very grand ideas about the itinerary, including going from Leningrad to Tashkent by train. When I pointed out that there was no railway connection, she took a pencil and drew a line on the map: 'There is now', she said. Somehow, that epitomised Soia. She did visit Russia once before she died, but to our great regret we were unable to go with her.

I loved and respected Soia. But there was one difficulty: I had to cope with the biographer's problem of a living widow – to maintain professional detachment while ensuring her co-operation. She was one of the two most formidable women I have ever had to deal with – the other being my mother. How did I manage? First, she liked and trusted me and left me to get on with it. Secondly, she did not take archives (or history or biography) very seriously. If I had not become involved, she would probably have dumped most of Karl's papers. She looked on them as 'relics' and was amused by my fascination with them. Thirdly, she genuinely respected my independence. She realised that I was sympathetic to Karl, but that I needed to be free to criticise, and that it was important that the book should not be mere hagiography. And, fourthly, she often seemed apathetic or indifferent. She would answer my questions face-to-face, almost never by correspondence; she made some suggestions about people to contact, but she was quite reluctant to look at drafts; and I suspect that she never read the completed book – certainly, she never commented on it and I did not ask her. I felt that in an important sense she did not want to know. For some time, she was devastated by Karl's death, and later she did not seem to want to dwell on the past. All this might have counted for little, but for the fact of distance. In Chicago I put the papers in order and collected material, but my research also took me to New York, New Haven, Philadelphia, Minneapolis, New Mexico and California. Nearly all of the writing was done away from Chicago and Coral Gables, first in New Haven in

1965, later in Northern Ireland in the period 1965–71. During that time, I only saw Soia on brief visits once or twice a year. Moreover, I was under pressure to produce a work of serious scholarship: I had been appointed to a Chair in Belfast largely on promise and the book was to be the means of proving myself.

Accordingly, dealing with Soia turned out to be less of a problem than I had feared. Insofar as I am perceived as being too loyal a disciple, one need not blame Soia's influence.[19] There is, however, one exception to this – the story of the Uniform Commercial Code.[20] I am not a commercial lawyer and have very little business sense – Soia once told me that I would never understand the credit economy. She was as anxious as I was to get the UCC chapters right. One day, after I had asked some questions that showed I was struggling with the Code records, she shook her head and in effect said: 'I don't see why you are bothering with all those papers; all of the important decisions affecting the Code were taken on the phone – I was at one end of the line, and the person at the other end is DEAD.'[21] I knew that the making of the Code had been controversial, both within the team and in getting it approved and enacted, but I had no means of checking. I was anxious to hear all sides of the stories, but I was regularly frustrated. Soia was correct in suggesting that the papers were not very informative about disagreements and that some of the main players were dead. Other key figures, such as Bill Schnader, Homer Kripke and Walter D. Malcolm, died before I could meet them or were otherwise unavailable. When I interviewed two others, Grant Gilmore and Alison Dunham, both Chicago colleagues, they seemed quite reserved about disagreements. By 1970–1 I had failed to get enough detailed material of significance on the internal tensions within the Code team, so I made two decisions: first, that I would candidly present the Llewellyn-Mentschikoff version of events and, secondly, I would try to stimulate an oral history project on the making and enactment of the Code whilst memories were fresh and while there were still survivors. I attempted to make it clear in the endnotes to chapters 9 and 10 of KLRM that I was recounting Soia's version of events by repeatedly indicating that my main source was 'ex rel. Soia Mentschikoff Llewellyn'. Later with the help of Professor Robert Summers I tried to stir some interest in the history and politics of the UCC and in a footnote I urged surviving participants to record their memories of the project.[22] As far as I can tell, these efforts failed.[23] It is now too late as nearly all of the actors are indeed dead. It might be possible to piece together an alternative story, if enough of their papers survived. Commercial lawyers showed little interest in the topic and even to this day I am told there is no adequately researched general history of the making of the Code.[24]

Writing KLRM: 1963–73

Once enmeshed in the project of dealing with Karl's papers, it was perhaps unsurprising that I should write a book about him. I was determined that this should not be hagiographic. It was to be a scholarly intellectual biography, focusing on particular works and setting them in the context of his life and intellectual milieu.

I have published over 1,000 pages about Karl Llewellyn, who has been the most important academic influence on my thinking. I shall not try to summarise them here: *The Karl Llewellyn Papers* (1968) (KLP) describes the collection that I helped to save and put in order in 1963–5. That is now in the Special Collections of the University of Chicago. There is a partial 'shadow collection' in the Perelman Institute of the University of Brussels. *Karl Llewellyn and the Realist Movement* (1973) (KLRM) gives a detailed account of Llewellyn's life and works, set in the context of the development of elite American law schools between about 1900 and 1962, the year of Llewellyn's death. The substantial 'Afterword' to the new edition (2012, the original text was reprinted but not revised), tells of my relations with Llewellyn and Soia Mentschikoff and sketches some of the relevant developments in the fifty years after his death. In the Dewey Lecture on 'Talk About Realism' at New York University Law School in October 1984[25] I critically examined various interpretations of Llewellyn and the Realist Movement and concluded that most generalisations about 'the [American] Legal Realists' are false or trivial or both. In 1993, for the centenary of Llewellyn's birth, I made an extensive analysis of the idea of 'juristic method', his theory of the crafts of law and the idea of legal technology.[26] There are also several other papers and encyclopaedia entries. In 2015 I summarised my own views on R/realism and what it means to be 'realistic' about law. This will be considered below in Chapter 13.

Most of these publications are easily accessible and it would be inappropriate and unnecessary here to give a detailed account of Llewellyn's life, his major writings, or a history of American Legal Realism. I have already discussed his conception of Jurisprudence and how he taught it in Chicago and my relationship with his widow. Here I shall try to explore why his ideas and mindset have been, and still are, important to me, and how my views have developed or diverged from his. Some of his specific insights and dicta are scattered through this book. However, this section does require some background on Llewellyn's career, personality, style and general approach.

I began the Preface to KLRM as follows:

> At first sight it may seem that few jurists can stake as strong a claim to singularity as Karl Llewellyn: the only American ever to have been awarded the Iron Cross; the most fertile and inventive scholar of his generation; legal theory's most colourful personality since Jeremy Bentham; the only common lawyer known to have collaborated successfully with an anthropologist on a major work; a rare example of a law-teacher-poet; the chief architect of the most ambitious common law code of recent times; the most romantic of legal realists, the most down-to-earth of legal sceptics; the most unmethodical of methodologists; and least controvertible of claims, the possessor of one of the most exotic prose styles in all legal

literature. Yet for all his idiosyncrasies, Llewellyn was to an extraordinary degree representative of the best of his generation of American law teachers.[27]

Allowing for youthful exuberance and for a gap of more than forty years, this will do as an explanation of why I became fascinated by Llewellyn. More prosaically one can summarise the basic facts: Karl Nickerson Llewellyn (1893–1962) was born in Seattle, went to school in New York and Germany, fought briefly on the German side in 1914, was wounded at Ypres and awarded the Iron Cross (second class), graduated from Yale College (1915) and Yale Law School (1920), practised for two years in New York and then taught at Yale, Columbia and Chicago until his death in 1962. Today he is remembered mostly as the Chief Reporter of the Uniform Commercial Code, for the best-selling introduction to law, *The Bramble Bush* (1951 [1930]), as a leader of the American Realist Movement, and author (with E. Adamson Hoebel) of *The Cheyenne Way* (1941), and of *The Common Law Tradition: Deciding Appeals* (1960). He also wrote a book in German which was destroyed by the Nazis and later partly translated into English.[28] He published many articles and lectures mainly on commercial law, jurisprudence, sociology of law and various social and political issues.

My work on Llewellyn altered the trajectory of my career. It was the main reason why I accepted a post in Belfast rather than at Lagos or elsewhere in Africa. I first published two articles in the *Modern Law Review* that were drafts for sections in the book.[29] I underestimated the challenges and the whole project took nearly ten years.

Writing about Llewellyn in Belfast had its difficulties, although it helped me to attain some distance from Soia, who left me to get on with it on my own. The dilemmas of reconciling intimacy with relative detachment were largely resolved by distance and Soia's scepticism about archives and biography. My Llewellyn research involved several more visits to the United States, including six months at Yale in 1965 and a semester at the University of Pennsylvania Law School (Penn) in 1971.[30] It progressed slowly because I was not satisfied with what I was writing and from January 1966 I had many other calls on my time. By 1967–8 I had an almost complete draft of the chapters on Llewellyn's life and works. Over several years, when I could make time from other commitments, I had ploughed through each of Llewellyn's other main writings. This produced careful, accurate introductions to each text, but I knew that it was pedestrian. I sought advice from Arthur Leff, a friend at Yale Law School. He wrote back saying that he would give it to his reading group that semester. The group of three, in addition to Leff, included Duncan Kennedy, who later became the unofficial leader of critical legal studies, a movement that developed 'trashing' and deconstruction into an art. Some months later, I received a letter which was fairly polite, but made clear that they thought it dull. At least they did not trash it. Apart from a few detailed comments they made two suggestions: first, that I should drop the biographical detail as being irrelevant to a jurist's ideas and, secondly, that I should set Llewellyn's work in the much broader political, social and educational context of the time.[31] I rejected the first piece of advice – I am a committed contextualist and believed that each of Karl's works should be set in the context of his situation and concerns at the time. I accepted the second with alacrity and in a relatively short period – mainly in a cottage in the Mourne Mountains – I dashed off the first draft of what are now the first five chapters of KLRM. I was on top of the material and wrote a coherent narrative mainly from my head. Several commentators have said that they are the best chapters in the book.[32]

After the criticisms from Leff's reading group, I added the first five chapters, tried to invigorate the others, while retaining the biographical aspects. In 1971, I put the finishing touches to the manuscript while visiting the University of Pennsylvania Law School for a semester, and then unburdened this albatross on Weidenfeld and Nicolson, the publishers of the Law in Context series. It was another eighteen anxious months before it was finally published. The book was well received, but I would have preferred more controversy.[33] It was thought strange that a study of one of the two or three leading American jurists of his generation should have been written by a foreigner and published in London. But it became a standard reference point in the United States and gained me a reputation as a serious, if unconventional, jurist.

Over time, especially because I was teaching in very different contexts from his, my conception of Jurisprudence developed away from Llewellyn's. I wished to retain an important place for elucidation and construction of concepts; I was less dismissive of some strands in Legal Philosophy, especially in relation to Bentham and Hart; a lot happened in Jurisprudence as a field between 1962 and today; from the early 1970s I became interested in the relations between theory and detailed scholarship and I developed my ideas about the variety of 'the jobs of jurisprudence' (Chs. 1 and 13) and from the early 1990s I began to take globalisation seriously. But the general approach was based on Llewellyn: keeping theory in touch with particular enquiries and social reality; seeing the field as being concerned with beliefs and working assumptions about law related to other beliefs about the world, politics, morality and society; viewing 'realism' as ranging from empirical science to making one's own judgements as well-informed as one can on the best sources available including experience and 'horse sense' ('knowledge . . . .. does not have to be scientific to be useful and important');[34] keeping in touch with the viewpoints, understandings and practices of providers of legal services (including judges) and other actors, users and victims; and maintaining continuity between conceptual, normative, doctrinal and empirical approaches (e.g. his favourite aphorism: 'technique without ideals is a menace; ideals without technique are a mess').[35]

I was not uncritical of Karl. I thought that his early interpretations of Realism inadvertently obscured the strengths of the movement by including a diverse list of individuals and looking for shared ideas; I argued that *The Common Law Tradition*, the last major work published before his death, should have set the study of state appellate courts in the kind of broad context suggested by the 'law jobs' theory, which in turn I tried to interpret and refine in order to defend it against standard critiques of 'functionalism'; while praising his use of deliberately vague terms in some contexts (e.g. trouble instead of dispute, law–government in place of law) I tried to clarify some of his concepts; I was not an unreserved admirer of his prose style and I have, in turn, been taken to task for not taking his verse or his ideas on aesthetics seriously enough. But I have not, I hope, been like Kipling's 'Disciple' who 'shall wound him worst of all'.[36] The indexes of my books are evidence of the extent to which I used Karl as my most regular reference point.

Other American interludes

I have spent about 25–30 per cent of my working life in the United States, first as a postgraduate student, then as a Visitor in the University of Chicago (twice), Yale, the University of Pennsylvania, The University of Virginia, Northwestern, Boston College, Boston University, Stanford and, since 1981, as a fairly regular visitor at the University of Miami Law School.[37] Between 1963 and 1971 I made several visits to the United States, all connected with my work on Llewellyn. Of course, there were other diversions, but only a few episodes are relevant to this narrative.

First meeting with Terry Anderson

In 1964 while teaching about problems of law in Africa to finance my work on the Llewellyn papers, I first encountered Terry Anderson, who was to become one of my two closest male friends. At the time he was a third-year law student. He had been in Llewellyn's Elements class which death had rudely interrupted – by then he was a convert and, because of this, a protégé of Soia Mentschikoff. Terry had recently been awarded a Fellowship to work in the Attorney-General's office in Malawi – then ruled by the dictatorial right-wing President Banda, who seemed to wear evening dress all the time – the exact opposite of Nyerere's open-necked Dar es Salaam. Terry had been given a 'dress allowance', a British term, and he wanted advice on how to spend it. Soia told him to consult Twining. We invited the Andersons to tea. The meeting was rather formal, Terry the student even wore a tie. My advice was: 'Buy a tux.' Terry misread this as advice from a snotty Englishman, rather than a sardonic Dar es Salaamite, but he followed the advice. It came in useful in Malawi and thereafter until he outgrew it. Later we became co-teachers, collaborators and close friends. The link was Karl and Soia rather than Africa. It represented a marriage of theory and practice of which Karl would surely have approved – Anderson the tough, relentless litigator and Twining the free-wheeling theorist. It was not only an intellectual marriage. In the early years I used to board at his house. We were so close that we might have been perceived to be an odd couple, but for Terry's widespread reputation as an energetic heterosexual. We have collaborated for nearly forty years and we are still friends.[38]

Yale: 1965

In October 1964 I accepted appointment as Professor of Jurisprudence at the Queen's University Belfast (Queen's). Getting itchy feet in Dar, I had already accepted a year's appointment as a Visiting Fellow at Yale Law School. Queen's generously allowed me to postpone my arrival in Belfast for six months (June–December 1965). In New Haven I nervously prepared for teaching at Queen's (did I really deserve a Chair?); otherwise my main project was working on my book on Llewellyn and during that period I conducted a number of amateurish interviews with some of Karl's contemporaries in Chicago, Washington DC, New York and California.

Corbin

By far the most worthwhile of these was two interviews with Arthur Corbin who had been Karl's teacher and 'father in the law'. Nearing 90, almost blind, quite deaf, chair-bound, he not only agreed to be questioned, but wrote a substantial note on his relationship with Karl and commented on a rough draft that I had prepared.[39]

I have written quite a lot about Corbin because not only was he one of the most important influences on Karl, but he was also largely responsible for transforming Yale Law School in a direction that might now be called 'Realist'.[40] He is particularly interesting as a precursor of American Legal Realism who wrote a major treatise. He pioneered an alternative, evolutionary approach to contract doctrine. 'Pared-down principles there must, of course, be . . . the law . . . but it seldom struck me that the ones I found in print were the ones.'[41] In his view, each fresh case tests all previous formulations of a rule or principle. His own treatise on Contract originally had 'tentative working rules' in the subtitle, but the publisher scratched it for commercial reasons. Treatises have to make confident statements. Corbin was the expositor who was the most subversive of blackletter exposition.[42]

At Yale I also encountered Harold Lasswell's 'science of politics' (*Who Gets What When and How?*) and Lasswell and McDougal's Law and Policy Science – an intriguing offshoot of Legal Realism. This was an odd mixture: a free-market version of the American Dream, modified utilitarianism, with 'dignity' as its core value, turned by McDougal into a doctrinaire, and in my view, muddled technocratic method, but quite stimulating. In New Haven I also recorded the childhood and adolescent memories and Dinka songs of my former student, Francis Deng.[43]

During this exciting, varied but angst-ridden period, I made friends with Charles Black (a civil liberties icon) and his family and heard a lot about *Brown v Board of Education* (1964) and *Griswold v Connecticut* (381 US 479 (1965), a forerunner of *Roe v Wade*) from colleagues who had been involved. I had extended contact with several leading members of faculty (including getting tax advice from Robert Bork – later famous for his rejection as nominee for the Supreme Court). I also got to know some younger scholars involved in the rather repetitive American version of Law and Development, several of whom became leading members of the critical legal studies movement (Abel, Felstiner, Trubek and Santos). The New Nations Program in Chicago had been less political.[44]

The Law in Context series

Perhaps the most significant episode during my stay at Yale was entering on a publishing venture.[45] Robert Stevens was my host at Yale. During my stay in New Haven, he and I persuaded Weidenfeld and Nicolson to try to move into law publishing as part of undermining the 'Expository Orthodoxy'. It is worth telling the story of its genesis.

By 1965 I was switching from reacting to the Doctrinal Tradition (hardly represented at Yale) to learning about and working out alternative approaches in respect of theory, scholarship and teaching. When I reached Yale in 1965 I was already committed to studying law 'in context'. When a Sudanese student asked 'why was the camel in a *zoo*?' the scales had fallen from my eyes – neither in this case, nor most of the other Torts cases we had studied did the facts fit Sudanese conditions (Chapter 5). In Dar es Salaam the mandate for UCD and the Law Faculty had been clear. We had to be contextual (Chapter 6).

I had got to know Robert Stevens when he was visiting Dar from Yale and he was instrumental in my invitation to New Haven. He was already an iconoclastic critic of the English Bar and English legal education who soon afterwards collaborated on two books with a Sociologist, Brian Abel-Smith.[46] He and I persuaded Weidenfeld and Nicolson to try to break the near-monopoly of Butterworths and Sweet and Maxwell over academic law publishing in UK by launching a series of 'counter-textbooks'. Our aim was 'to subvert and revolutionise' (sic) the prevailing orthodoxy in English legal education. George Weidenfeld was interested because he wished to expand into academic publishing and he had been advised by an economist (John Vaisey) that the law publishing scene was so dull and unadventurous that he could hardly fail to make a difference. Originally, Robert and I proposed a journal, as we were pessimistic about finding suitable authors for a book series. However, Weidenfeld's decided to go for books.

The series was largely Robert's idea. He had contacts with Weidenfeld's, and he had an even more jaundiced view of English academic law than I did. He and I were co-editors for thirty-one years, despite which, we remained close friends. He brought to the task a critical perspective on English legal culture, an

acute understanding of the strengths and limitations of American legal scholarship, a lack of inhibition – made easier by the Atlantic – a grasp of
economics, and a good historical sense.[47]

The most difficult problem turned out to be naming the series because two
other publishers had captured 'Law and Society' and 'Law in Society'. That was
one of the first signs of an intellectual awakening in English legal circles.[48]
Searching for an alternative, I extrapolated the phrase 'Law in Context' from
a student book called *Contract in Context* by Addison Mueller (1951), which
introduced the subject through a case study of the transactions and problems
of Mr Blandings trying to build his Dreamhouse.[49] Robert was sceptical, but
could offer no alternative, so the title was accepted *faute de mieux*. It has since
been adopted widely, perhaps because it is suitably vague as a label for broader
approaches.

The Law in Context series survives today with over fifty titles in print and
more out of print and still flourishing. It has been one of the most satisfying
activities of my academic life. Robert and I became founding co-editors in
1966; over fifty years on I am still a co-editor. This is the scholarly activity
which has given me the most satisfaction. It has been like being a midwife to
over a hundred babies.

Penn: 1971

A semester at the Penn Law School in 1971 gave me the space to finish KLRM.
It also gave me experience of teaching two full courses in an American Law
School, one on American Legal Realism and an interdisciplinary seminar on
Problems of East African Law.[50] The most significant episode was that I gave
a paper at Cornell Law School on Holmes's 'The Path of the Law' which was
published, after much reworking, in 1973 in the *Cornell Law Review* as
'The Bad Man Revisited'. For the next twenty-four years this was the text
which expounded the theoretical aspects of the concept of standpoint in legal
contexts. Then in 1997 I further developed the analysis at a symposium to
mark the centenary of the publication of the 'Path of the Law'. Although both
of these papers were ostensibly about Holmes, they were in essence vehicles for
developing a central aspect of my ideas (Chapter 10).[51]

And so to Belfast.

8

The Queen's University Belfast (1966–72)

Serendipity again

University College Dar es Salaam was mentored and helped by the Inter University Council based in London with one representative on the College Council. In August or September 1964, Professor Francis Newark, Dean of the Faculty of Law at the Queen's University Belfast, came to Dar for a Council meeting. As there was no hotel near the new campus, he was billeted *chez* Twinings. Our guest bedroom was my study. I thought Newark was a dry old stick, but we got on well enough. Apparently, he was impressed by my Jurisprudence library – which was quite good. A few weeks later, completely out of the blue, I received a letter from Newark inviting me to apply for the Chair of Jurisprudence at Queen's. Books do furnish a room!

I was taken completely by surprise. I had begun to think of moving on and was contemplating a research post at Lagos or a lectureship at Southampton whose Dean of Law, Arthur Philips, had worked in East Africa. With some hesitation – was this serious? Could I cope? Where exactly was Belfast? – I sent in an application to Queen's. Before flying to the UK for an interview, I learned that the University of Leicester had just advertised the founding Chair for a new School of Law. Having nothing to lose, I contacted the Registrar of Leicester asking for an appointment with the Vice-Chancellor. He said that the process had hardly begun as the closing date had not passed. His tone suggested that he thought that it was rather uppity for a youth from Dar es Salaam to make such an enquiry. I went to Queen's, was interviewed, and was offered the post on the spot. I hesitated and said I would need a week to decide as I had another possibility to explore. I then phoned the Registrar at Leicester and told him that I had been offered a Chair at Queen's. Reluctantly he arranged an interview with the Vice-Chancellor. I do not remember the details of that meeting very well. I may have lectured him on how to set up a law school – and when I told him that the amount they had budgeted for the law library was less than 25 per cent of what we had already spent on our library at Dar, he began to listen. The timing of the appointment process was wrong, so I accepted the post at Queen's. I hope that this helped the new Dean at Leicester.

I was told only a little about the background to the vacancy at Queen's on my first visit. The post had been vacant for some time since the resignation of Professor James Louis Montrose, who had been Dean since 1934. He was well-known as an advocate for liberal legal education and for numerous public activities in both Northern Ireland and England. He shared similar views on Jurisprudence and legal scholarship with his close friend, Julius Stone, and I found his intellectual legacy very helpful because it included the most enlightened LLB curriculum in the British Isles.

Nearly thirty years of Deanship, interrupted by war service in the RAF, ended in tragedy.[1] There was a formal annual election for the Dean. This had been uncontested since 1938, but in the early 1960s after some acrimonious in-fighting, Montrose was deposed by a vote of 4–3 by younger faculty members. He stood again and lost. He then took off on a series of visiting appointments, including Singapore (where he was Dean in 1965–6), Australia, and finally New Zealand, where he died of cancer in October 1966.

I learned later that 'the Montrose Affair' had been simmering for some time, but ironically came to a head when Montrose 'dictatorially' reinstated a student who had been rusticated by an Orwellian 'Progress Committee' for an off-campus incident. Montrose considered this to be none of the business of this committee. After a bitter fight that lasted over a year, Montrose resigned from Queen's. Newark reluctantly took over. The bitterness lingered on – so much so that a small Faculty had been divided into three Departments to keep the factions apart. I only learned when I arrived in Belfast for interview that the Association of University Teachers (AUT), of which Montrose had been a leading member, had urged a boycott of Queen's because of the 'Montrose Affair', but the rights and wrongs of this were rather obscure. I barely knew what the AUT was and I sympathised with Montrose. I did not withdraw and was offered the job. So I found myself not only Professor of Jurisprudence (which I felt was grand) but also Head of the Department of Law and Jurisprudence. Theory sceptics used to misquote Ulpian as having said that Jurisprudence was the knowledge of all things human and divine – except law.[2] So this was a comprehensive remit, except that there were also separate Departments of Private and Public Law.

Context

The background to the next seven years needs some explaining. Ireland in general, and Northern Ireland in particular, are complex and opaque societies. Having married a Dublin Protestant, I had already spent time in the South. Penelope had been brought up never to discuss either religion or politics on social occasions. She had barely crossed the border and was quite apprehensive about living there. As a Protestant she had expected to be quite at home but was disappointed. I had been intrigued and bewildered by Dublin culture, but that proved to be nothing compared to our bafflement in Belfast.

We arrived in Belfast in January 1966 having effectively been overseas for nearly ten years. We did not have TV in Dar and Khartoum and I had seen only a couple of the blockbuster movies and none of the avant garde ones for a decade. Mainly through the BBC World Service I had learned about the Cuban Missile crisis, the Kennedy Assassination, the Beatles, James Bond, Swinging London, drugs and Mary Quant. Ian Smith's Rhodesian UDI (11 November 1965) happened just before we arrived in Belfast and Claire Palley, the historian of Southern Rhodesian politics and constitutions, joined Queen's at almost the same time as I did.[3] Visits to the United States in 1963, 1964 and 1965 had put me in touch with American politics and culture, but as regards the UK and Europe I had a lot of catching up to do. From 1966 I vicariously experienced many other events beyond Belfast: for example, a majority Labour government in Westminster, responses to UDI, England winning the World Cup, the Aberfan disaster, the Nigerian Civil War, the Thalidomide Affair, de Gaulle's 1967 blocking of UK from the European Community, the Moon Landing and the Magic Roundabout were among happenings that engaged my attention. I was in Chicago in April 1968 when Martin Luther King was assassinated, visited New Haven during student disorders and was in Belfast during the student unrest in '1968', which really happened there in 1969.

Sectarian tensions were mounting in January 1966, but they were still fairly quiet. The main noise came from the Rev. Ian Paisley, whose ranting sermons and antics (including throwing snowballs at the Taoiseach on a visit to Belfast in 1968) were increasing media attention. Soon after we arrived, Penelope and I, out of curiosity, went to listen to one of his sermons. We were eyed with suspicion, but allowed in, and were quite shocked at what we heard. Our reaction to him was rather like British liberal reactions to Donald Trump fifty years later.

In Belfast we mostly lived in an expatriate cocoon. The Faculty was quite hierarchical and social contact with students was more limited than I was used to. The University was quite cosmopolitan[4] and its social life for us was largely expatriate, because most of the local middle class were very family-oriented and hardly ever entertained outsiders at home. When the Troubles became more serious we were even more isolated and our children complained that they were under house arrest. We had little contact with locals other than colleagues and the legal establishment, except that, after a year spent reading Social Studies at Queen's, Penelope did social work for two years on both sides of 'the Peace Line'.[5] We explored the beautiful countryside and the 'safe' bits of Belfast as tourists rather than residents. Penelope had relatives in Dublin, a city I came to love. For a time, we borrowed a small isolated cottage in the Mournes, with water, but not electricity or adequate heating. We liked it, but the children and the cats did not.

From this plethora of events and concerns I shall focus briefly on two which are particularly relevant as background to this period: sectarian conflict in

Northern Ireland and the changing legal scene in England. I was an appalled spectator of the former, but with a ringside seat; I was actively, if peripherally, involved in the latter.

The Troubles

We were truly outsiders except in one important respect: we had intimate vicarious access to the sectarian conflicts, mainly through three remarkable people. The first was John Graham, Penelope's first cousin, with whom we drank and supped a lot. He was correspondent for the *Financial Times*. From 1971 this included at the Europa, 'the most bombed hotel in Europe' where most of the press corps stayed. The second was Tom Hadden, son of a local doctor, who was in my department from 1969. He played a leading role in trying to bridge the sectarian divide, not least through founding and editing *Fortnight*, an influential non-sectarian political and cultural magazine of which Gerry Adams reportedly said: 'A month without *Fortnight* would be twice as long.'[6] The third was Kevin Boyle, a young lecturer in Criminal Law and Criminology with whom we became very close. He was a leading member of the civil rights movement, including being spokesman and informal legal adviser for the People's Democracy until he was ousted for being too moderate. Kevin remained a close friend until his death in 2010. I had overlapping academic interests with both Tom and Kevin in relation to socio-legal studies. I learned much from both about law in action in Northern Ireland, fact-based policy and, most important, a nuanced view of the intricate relations between law and politics. Simplistic mantras like 'All law is politics' just won't do.

I wrote an account of my relations with these three remarkable people, but I have reluctantly dropped it as being largely irrelevant to this memoir. Suffice to say that fed by these insiders I became obsessed by the conflict and local politics but, unlike some colleagues, I did not engage with them academically until towards the end of my stay. I pored over several newspapers, read *Fortnight* assiduously, and listened three or four times a day to the local radio, quite often hearing Kevin being interviewed. In Belfast I felt that each day the roofs were being lifted off particular houses in different parts of the city so that one could peek inside. This was in addition to my three involved informants, who were very close to the action. At such close quarters, as in Kenya, it was often difficult to distinguish politics from gossip. Although I had the access and the opportunity, I kept my distance academically, unlike my fellow expatriate colleagues, Harry Calvert and Claire Palley. Indeed, I did not really try to analyse Northern Ireland politics as a scholar – I felt that most of the participants, other than my friends, were deluded, dogmatic and crazy. I thought that the Protestant leaders in particular were votaries at the shrine of bigotry, chauvinism and intolerance. This was tribalism rather than nationalism as I understood it.

How all this affected my academic work is hard to say. The situation was a large part of the backdrop and my 'problem of belief' surfaced again (Chapters 2, 3 and 9). To me the leaders on both sides seemed irrational and unpersuadable. Penelope, usually apolitical, a Dublin Protestant, became quite a strong Nationalist sympathiser; our son Peter, born in Hatch St. Dublin, more mildly so (he still backs Ireland against England in the Six Nations competition). Karen and I could not identify with either side and felt alienated. Locals on both sides complained that we English did not understand them. They were right. I was quite well-informed, but mystified. I have never lived anywhere that I felt more of an expatriate than in Belfast.

Sectarian conflict, the resurgence of violence, the political and other responses, the role of Queen's in this situation, troops on the street, were in both the background and the foreground until we left in March 1972. Bloody Sunday occurred in January of that year, but its full significance took time to surface. Even in extreme conflict situations, such as this, life goes on: shopping, getting to work, children going to school, teaching and research and socialising at the University still happened. They were only occasionally interrupted by the Troubles. One became street-wise, comforted by maxims and myths such as Republicans get up late, so shop early; this cinema, that theatre, these pubs are not targets; if electricity is attacked that's the IRA; if water, the Loyalists and so on.

Outwardly we remained calm. I only realised my underlying tension on visits to England: at Woolworths in Leamington, I saw an unattended package and realised that *no one* else was paying it any attention – should I raise the alarm? One evening on the underground in London I felt the handle of my overnight case vibrating. I checked that it was mine, got off at the next station, put the case behind one pillar, hid behind another, crept forward and peeked – it was indeed vibrating. I should have emptied the station; instead, violating all instructions, I opened the case. My electric razor had turned itself on. I was bathed in sweat and ashamed. But many people love living in Ulster. In 1972 when students heard that I was leaving, a group of six or so came and grilled me: did I fish? No. Did I shoot? No. Did I play golf? No. Did I think that the countryside was beautiful? Yes. Did I walk? Yes. Why was I leaving? I had been offered an exciting job at Warwick. 'Ah. Then, it's not these pesky local bothers is it?' No. This was partly true, for the Warwick job was very much a positive; but Belfast was no place to bring up children, especially the schools segregated by religion, class and gender. We had reluctantly sent them to boarding school in England, where Peter suffered nightmares about us being blown up. Yet over half of Queen's law graduates opted to stay in Northern Ireland.

Life went on and much of my work was remote from the local 'bothers', but I did become intellectually and emotionally engaged with them. However, I approached these at a quite general level of principle, without much explicit reference to the specifics of Northern Ireland and this I felt was required in teaching. I remained fascinated, but uninvolved until, near the end of my stay,

I did publicly engage with issues about emergency powers and 'severe inter-rogation' and this sharpened my views on justice, human rights and utilitar-ianism (Chapter 9).

Legal change in England

I did, however, become involved quite actively in the changing legal scene in England, especially in relation to law reform and legal education and train-ing. This was a period of intellectual awakening and reform in legal circles, well caught by Gerald Gardiner and Andrew Martin's *Law Reform Now* (1963). That preceded Gardiner's period as a reforming Lord Chancellor (1964–70). During that period Law Commissions were established, Parliamentary Ombudsman Services were instituted, and the Ormrod Committee on Legal Education in England and Wales began work. Some academic lawyers, notably Michael Zander and Robert Stevens, broke with tradition by being openly critical of the legal establishment and its entrenched conservatism.[7] This was also the period of university expansion, greater focus on the social sciences, the creation of a first wave of new ('plate-glass') universities, and the Open University; the monopoly of law publishing by Sweet and Maxwell and Butterworth began to be eroded, and there was a general sense of intellectual excitement. We felt we were in the Yellow Submarine. With a few colleagues, I became involved with several of these developments both in Northern Ireland and in England. The Law in Context series, submissions to the English Law Commission and the Ormrod Committee, the Young Members' Group of the Society of Public Teachers of Law, the Statute Law Society and the Armitage Committee on Legal Education in Northern Ireland were the most salient ones. As we shall see, from quite early on I had long discussions with Geoffrey Wilson who became the Founding Professor of Law at the new University of Warwick (Chapter 12). In Belfast we had especially close relations with the First Parliamentary Draftsman at Stormont, Bill Leitch, who had outstanding skills and interesting ideas related to drafting and making legislation. A younger colleague, Abdul Paliwala, was seconded to his office half-time and became the first and probably the only Zanzibari ever to work in the Northern Ireland Civil Service. I was a founding member of the Statute Law Society and participated in two of its reports. I also had close contact with Sir Leslie (later Lord) Scarman the first Chairman of the Law Commission and law reform in both England and Northern Ireland was high on our agendas. Later I was a member of the Armitage Committee on Legal Education in Northern Ireland, which learned to avoid some of the mistakes made in the Ormrod process.[8] In all of these activities my African background and my experience of American Law Schools proved to be highly relevant. It was an exciting time to be an academic lawyer.

Teaching Jurisprudence at Queen's

Life goes on. Despite the Troubles and the ferment, most of my teaching and writing during this period had little to do with local issues. Indeed, under the Irish Universities Act 1908, I was required not to do or say anything 'calculated to offend the religious susceptibilities of [my] students'.[9] Hardly compatible with teaching Jurisprudence. The average ratio of each class was roughly 50+ per cent Protestant, 40+ per cent Catholic, the rest not local. I managed to navigate these difficulties, partly by some pedagogical tricks, but mainly by indirection. The assumptions I challenged were not obviously local. I sometimes got the whole class to hiss or clap together.

My main writing project was the book on Karl Llewellyn, which I submitted to Weidenfeld's in 1971 (Chapter 7); the second one, on interpretation of social and legal rules, was not finished until after I left Queen's; this was based on our first-year teaching and was similarly not closely related to local matters (Chapter 11). My relatively thin list of publications mainly dealt with Legal Education and Jurisprudence. The former were very much directed to the English debates, the latter were only subliminally influenced by my Northern Ireland experience.

Montrose's main legacy was a large number of loyal former students and a very progressive undergraduate Law degree: an innovative and enlightened curriculum for a four-year Honours Degree (few opted for the three-year Pass Degree), subjects that were ahead of their time such as Labour Law and Social Legislation, a requirement that every student had to study at least one or two subjects in depth (sadly lacking in the current English scene) and three compulsory theory subjects, labelled Juristic Technique, Legal Philosophy (half-course) and Advanced Jurisprudence. Rarely has a Professor of Jurisprudence had such an opportunity. I kept the labels and tried to continue the spirit of Montrose.

Montrose had left before his curriculum was implemented, so I had a virtually free hand in filling in the details. Between 1966 and 1972, I had several very able younger colleagues to help me, including Katherine O'Donovan, Nial Osborough, David Miers, Abdul Paliwala, Tom Hadden, Peter Fitzpatrick, all now well-known as academic lawyers, and Reg Weir (later a Lord Justice of Appeal in Northern Ireland). They were all near the start of their careers and I was the Professor, which meant boss in those days. I gave them each some space, but I was clearly the leader of a team.

It was at Queen's that I found my feet and my voice, without publishing much during that period. I incubated my ideas, largely through teaching, so it is worth concentrating on that. I designed Juristic Technique as a course on sources of law that combined theoretical ideas with the development of intellectual skills, especially skills of reading and reasoning about cases and statutes. Eventually this became a book, *How to Do Things with Rules* with David Miers, which had matured over ten years of teaching before it was first published in 1976 (Chapter 10).

The half course on Legal Philosophy was devoted to intensive study of a selection of set texts. The list was reviewed every year and colleagues could offer texts of their choice. One year I used to visit a Nationalist student who was interned without trial in Crumlin Road Gaol but allowed to continue his degree studies. On one visit I brought with me two of the set texts, Mill's *On Liberty*, and Engels's *The Holy Family*. Engels passed without question; but Mill was confiscated and only allowed in after a formal protest. In teaching this course I combined Collingwood's method of studying philosophical texts with Llewellyn's rationale for a course on Jurisprudence: the purpose is for each student to integrate their general beliefs about religion, politics, morals and society with their beliefs about law.[10] Reading was a personal as well as a disciplined matter: first set the text in context (historical) – especially the author's concerns: what was biting him? (At that time there were no women jurists recognised as canonical). Stage 2: analytical – what questions did the text address? Were they appropriate expressions of the concerns? Were they open to criticism as questions? What answers did the author suggest? What justification did he advance for his conclusions? In short, a neo-Collingwoodian reconstruction of the text. Stage 3: applied – so what? What are the implications and applications of this text – in relation to concrete issues or other thinkers? Stage 4: critique – do I agree with the questions? Do I agree with the answers? Do I agree with the reasons? A Llewellynesque exercise in self-definition of which, I think, Collingwood might have approved.[11]

My examination questions for this course tended to be personal: are you a utilitarian? Do you have any natural rights? Are you a positivist? The students well understood that I would not take Yes or No for an answer and that they had to argue for a position, after clarifying the meaning of the question. I continued to use this approach in my Jurisprudence teaching. Later, I broadened it to include how to read any kind of materials of law study, distilled in *The Reading Law Cookbook*, which consists almost entirely of questions.[12]

The first two courses (first and second year) were coherent and relatively easy to teach. I do not remember the students complaining that they were compulsory or 'too theoretical', perhaps because we gave them some freedom of choice within each of them. However, there was some student resistance to the final course called Advanced Jurisprudence (fourth year), which was also compulsory. Some of the resistance was understandably unintellectual or practitioner-oriented, but some was anti-intellectual, which was disappointing given the liberal ethos and traditions of Queen's. We tried a number of devices to counter this: at some sacrifice of coherence we gave students freedom to choose from a wide range of questions, sometimes four out of sixteen.[13] In mid-sessional exams I used to administer a 'Russian-style test' – at the start of the course I would hand out a two-page document with about thirty questions on them, telling them that at the mid-sessional we would draw ten questions out of a hat of which they would have to answer three; they enjoyed the hat, probably ran books on the odds of getting any particular questions (how many could they risk not preparing for?), and were led into focusing on significant questions.

Several colleagues contributed to the (Advanced) Jurisprudence course; I focused mainly on Bentham, American Legal Realism (my version of 'realism' came later) and empirical legal studies and the students were exposed to a range of other points of view. I used a similar approach when I moved to Warwick and UCL, but in both places at undergraduate level we were constrained by having only one compulsory course on Jurisprudence/Legal Theory in a three-year LLB.[14] I tried to cope with this by introducing sub-options and a compulsory essay for which each student could propose the topic which had to be approved. But I missed the space I had had at Queen's, so at UCL I concentrated more on postgraduate teaching.

My duties at Queen's were quite demanding in term-time, and I still kept up my African connections during vacations, mainly by external examining – extending my range to West Africa, Kenya, Uganda, Lesotho, Botswana and Swaziland. As Head of Department I had some administrative duties and, by virtue of that, was on several University bodies. However, largely thanks to the kindness of my two senior colleagues, Lee Sheridan and Francis Newark, I only had to serve as Dean for a bit more than a year. During my time at Queen's I continued to worry about justifying my appointment as Professor with a thin publishing record. I had been appointed on promise and I struggled to finish my book on Llewellyn (KLRM). So I was grateful for that relief.

Scholarship

At Queen's almost all of my teaching, thinking and writing fell within the sphere of Jurisprudence broadly conceived, but towards the applied end. Apart from KLRM my writing dealt with quite general ideas, but in a rather fragmented way: my inaugural lecture, 'Pericles and the Plumber', drew largely on American ideas to ground an argument about rethinking legal education in the UK;[15] in 1966 I tried to develop a rationale for the Law in Context series, partly through a critique of orthodox legal textbooks and 'the Expository Tradition';[16] 'Ernie and the Centipede' explored the idea of 'fact-based classification' of legal fields explicitly in relation to the newly formed English Law Commission's long-term strategy – how might 'the statute book' be organised in future?[17] The course on Juristic Technique and its child, *How to Do Things with Rules*, focused on the interpretation of social and legal rules and the continuities between them in a deliberately concrete way, exploring the tensions between generality and particularity largely through analysis of case studies drawn from several areas of social life in addition to law; much of my Jurisprudence teaching involved close reading of selected texts, not all of them 'philosophical'. In all of these activities I was theorising, but in a decidedly particularistic way. It was in contemplation of my move to Warwick that I first thought in a sustained way about Jurisprudence as a subject in order to confront the relationship between my professed subject and an institution dedicated programmatically to 'broadening the study of law from within'.[18] My underlying concern was what could a legal theorist offer to the Warwick enterprise? This found expression in my inaugural lecture at Warwick, 'Some Jobs for Jurisprudence' which was delivered late in 1973 and published as a more general statement about the national scene in academic law in 1974.[19] This was my first attempt to think about my conception of Jurisprudence, the place of Legal Philosophy within it, and theorising as an activity and its potential contribution to the health of Law as a discipline, anticipating the views set out above in Chapter 1. None of these activities fall clearly within 'Legal Philosophy', but they were all exercises in theorising. Accordingly, it is clear that most of my academic activities during the Queen's period were jurisprudential, whereas at Warwick I was mainly concerned with implementing the enterprise of broadening the study of law from within.

My two main projects during the next thirty years or so related to theorising first about Evidence and then, from the mid-1990s, about Globalisation and Law. Both can be broadly interpreted as middle-order theorising. During that period, which can be said to have begun with the appointment of Ronald Dworkin as Hart's successor in 1969, Jurisprudence generally became more abstract, morphing into self-styled 'Legal Philosophy', which grew away from my central concerns and, in my view, from the discipline of Law. Jurisprudence became a subject apart. This tendency began in Oxford and diffused quite widely through what might be termed a generation of Hart's intellectual grandchildren, most of whom were supervised or influenced by his three leading successors, Dworkin, Finnis and Raz. While respecting some of the work of individuals, I do not think that this development was generally good for the health of Law as a discipline. I kept in touch with these developments but did not participate much in what became the mainstream.[20]

Towards the end of my time at Queen's I became associated with the Bentham Project at UCL and unearthed two manuscripts on torture and prepared them for publication. About the same time, and not coincidentally, we formed a staff-student working party to contribute to public debates on emergency powers, interrogation techniques and associated matters. The aim was to try to analyse the issues with the 'relative detachment' appropriate to a university. These two activities are discussed in detail in the next chapter. Chapters 9–11 deal with theoretical ideas that were significantly developed during my time at Queen's: Normative Jurisprudence (Chapter 9), standpoint, questioning and legal reasoning (Chapter 10) and social and legal rules, how they are related and problems of interpreting and handling them (Chapter 11). The story of my move to Warwick is postponed until Chapter 12.

Four-year degrees

Apart from developing my own ideas without too much pressure to publish, perhaps the main lesson for me came from experiencing a four-year undergraduate degree in Law. At Warwick and UCL the first degree in Law (other than for mixed degrees) was only three years and I realised that many of their main constraints were due to the course being too short and pressures to overload the curriculum. Thereafter I was convinced that the Achilles Heel of legal education and training in England (but not Scotland and Northern Ireland) was the three-year undergraduate degree for 18-year-olds. For several years I chaired a working party on Four-Year Degrees in Law. At both Warwick and UCL I successfully pressed for a provision that allowed undergraduates to opt to take four years over the LLB, but this was a failure because very few availed themselves of the opportunity. However, most mixed degrees (e.g. Law and Sociology at Warwick) were for four years. In those days mandatory grants were available for four-year degrees, including means-tested maintenance grants, so the main obstacle was not at first economic. Today student debt exerts heavy pressures in the reverse direction. Queen's held on to the four-year degree until 1991-2 and Scottish universities, to their great credit, have retained four years for Honours. In England this was a cause that for the medium term seemed unwinnable, so I focused much of my energies at UCL on postgraduate legal education. But I remain convinced that so long as undergraduate legal education for 18-year-olds remains one of the shortest in the world, most of the problems and conflicts will continue unresolved: the creeping core, the overloaded curriculum, the struggle between balancing knowledge and skills, pressured career choices and the immaturity – intellectually, practically and professionally – of 21-year-old law graduates. Recent changes in university finance and the regulation of legal services have made matters even worse. We are now at the start of a period of serious rethinking about the economic base of tertiary education. There is little hope for undergraduate legal education in UK until four-year degrees become the norm.

9

Normative Jurisprudence

At his best, man is the noblest of all animals; separated from law and justice he is the worst.

(Aristotle)

There is no crueller tyranny than that which is perpetuated under the shield of law and in the name of justice.

(Montesquieu)

Technique without ideals is a menace; ideals without technique are a mess.

(Karl Llewellyn)

Introduction

The biggest impact that my experiences in Belfast had on my thinking as a jurist related to Normative Jurisprudence. Towards the end of my time there I became involved in public debates about emergency powers and torture and this linked closely with my growing interest in Jeremy Bentham's utilitarianism in relation to rights, justice and public policy. I have written extensively in this area recently, especially in my *General Jurisprudence* (2011),[1] but many of my ideas were forged in observing and reflecting on the conflicts in Northern Ireland, which is why this chapter belongs to the Belfast period. It outlines their development through the problem of belief, classical utilitarianism, Hart's fragile modified utilitarianism, to a position that is generally agnostic, quite sceptical about universalism and 'ideal theory', and much closer to the pragmatism of Amartya Sen and Yash Ghai on human rights and justice than to Rawlsian idealism or Dworkinian objectivism. I do not claim to have added much to these topics that is original or distinctive, except perhaps in relation to human rights scepticism,[2] but it is an important part of my intellectual journey.

Normative Jurisprudence

Understanding law involves concepts, values, facts and legal knowledge. Normative Jurisprudence is a rough label for that aspect that deals with values: questions about law and morality, justice, rights, legitimacy and so on.[3] One way of looking at it is as moral philosophy and meta-ethics applied to law. Normative jurisprudence now occupies a central place on the agenda of Anglo-

American jurisprudence as is illustrated by the attention given to Bentham, Dworkin, Finnis, Rawls, Raz and modern critical theory. Whether normative theories of reasoning and rationality, and questions of relativism or scepticism about them, are subsumed under Normative or Analytical jurisprudence is largely a matter of convenience.

I believe that Normative Jurisprudence is a central part of understanding law, but, as suggested above, my contribution has been modest.[4] There is a particular reason for this: I am personally a moderate sceptic or agnostic about values. I do not believe in universal moral or natural law principles; I have a quite pragmatic, mildly sceptical view of human rights and justice as ideas; I am not a strong relativist or atheist,[5] but nor am I an objectivist in morals. I think there is a strong element of ethnocentrism in most universalist positions. I have some principled moral and political commitments, but I do not claim that these are based on firm philosophical foundations. I am not a strong subjectivist in that I do have a working assumption that reflection, reasoned debate, conversation and negotiation can help to advance understanding and build working consensuses and reasonable accommodations up to a point. But I also accept that entrenched beliefs are not much susceptible to rational persuasion nor Habermasian dialogue. Belief pluralism is a fact that we have to live with. I want to try to understand the world as well as to change it. For such reasons I regret that so much legal scholarship is normative and opinionated.

This chapter gives a brief account of the development of my ideas in this area, in which I end up remarkably close to Herbert Hart, a modified utilitarian, a democratic liberal (in the John Stuart Mill sense) and a kind of legal positivist. But the roots of this are somewhat different from Hart's.

As recounted in Chapter 2, from an early age I had problems with beliefs, values and commitments. Although my revolt in the Boy Scouts was mischievous, lurking behind it was probably an instinctive resistance to being pressured into making a promise that I did not intend to keep. I had no objection to helping old ladies across the road or to doing a good deed every day, but staying clean in thought, word and deed was neither attractive nor feasible. Similarly, having opted for confirmation as less undesirable than boxing, we were in theory free to duck out of the ceremony until the day before, but having feebly expressed some of my doubts, I succumbed to the pressures to go ahead. I swore that I believed the Thirty-nine Articles of the Anglican Faith. But how could one swear to belief in those that one just did not understand or in those that one thought that one understood but did not agree with, or in those on which one was agnostic or even more doubtful? Like Bentham, I felt that I was being coerced into lying. Legalistic? Not really. Literalistic? Not by my lights.

Later, as an undergraduate, I kept returning to the fact of belief pluralism: we live in a context in which people believe many different things; the world contains many ideologies, religions, cosmologies, moralities; but for the accident of birth I could have been a Jew, a Buddhist, a Mormon, some sort of

Muslim or a militant atheist. Most people cannot be persuaded to change their beliefs. Belief pluralism is a social fact (Chapter 3). That was the starting point for my personal philosophy and approach to Normative Jurisprudence.

I puzzled – sometimes agonised – about belief and acceptance, belief and commitment, belief and action, leaps of faith, miracles, revelation, prayer, bowing to authority. This uncertainty seemed to be a psychological state as much as a tangle of philosophical puzzles. In time, I accepted agnosticism about religion and, more guardedly, about morality. I understood that in order to act and make choices, to decide what one thought was right, one needed certain working assumptions – some values for the time being, some planks or rafts to keep one afloat in a sea of uncertainty.[6] These agnostic concerns to some extent inhibited unwavering commitment to any particular ideology, ethic or cause. At Oxford I sampled various political clubs, stayed away from religious ones, was convinced by none and joined the Liberal Club, which I did not take seriously. I had some strong instincts – to preserve my autonomy, to resist authority and to go my own way – with occasional acts of visible non-conformity. Basically, I felt that I did not know and had to live with this. A rather intellectual version of a not atypical adolescence – also not very different from the young Bentham.

In studying Jurisprudence, I was suspicious of Natural Law; even Aquinas's subtle reconciliation of revelation and reason failed to persuade. How could one be sure about revelation? Was not reason another wobbly plank? The culture of legal education in Oxford in the 1950s was quite strongly positivist. Law as it is should be distinguished quite sharply from law as it ought to be. Our task was to learn what the law said and apply it. One should not let one's value preferences or political views influence one's interpretation of the law; one should master the law before one attempted to criticise it. Indeed, criticism was not really a proper activity for law students.

In Oxford, John Austin, and to a lesser extent Bentham, were one part of that culture, but it was Austin's positivist theory of law rather than his utilitarianism that one studied. Austin was preferred to Bentham. He was 'the Father of English Jurisprudence'. He dominated taught Jurisprudence, which was perceived as mainly analytical, though caps were casually doffed to some other 'schools': Historical Jurisprudence, Natural Law, Sociological Jurisprudence, Scandinavian (but not American) Realism. Law is a social phenomenon – what else? – but understanding law was knowing legal doctrine – the basic man-made concepts, principles and detailed rules of English and Roman law. Hart was my guru, and conceptual analysis became my starting point.

Herbert Hart had his own concerns about morality.[7] These became apparent to us in his debates with Lord Patrick Devlin about morality and the criminal law, especially in regard to prostitution and homosexuality in the wake of the Wolfenden Report (1957). Hart revived and refined John Stuart Mill's view in arguing that law should not prohibit or punish acts, even if they were perceived to be immoral, unless they involved harmful consequences to others or to the 'public interest'. He strengthened his case in his brilliant writings on punishment in which he struggled with Benthamite utilitarianism. He found consequentialism attractive, especially in relation to public morality: generally, the law should be concerned with the maximisation of utility, the greatest good of the greatest number. But some implications of pure utilitarianism went contrary to his deepest instincts: inflicting harm on the innocent; sacrificing the rights of the few to the interests of the many and other forms of unqualified majoritarianism. In all of these instances pure utilitarianism went against his intuitions and he felt the need to invoke some principles independent of utility to modify his utilitarianism. In extreme cases one might justify punishing the innocent, but only if no utilitarian considerations allowed an escape and one acknowledged that one was sacrificing an important principle independent of utility (e.g. punishing the innocent is unjust). Hart never found a satisfactory basis for his rather weak moral pluralism. Towards the end he acknowledged as much: '[W]e have not yet developed a theory of individual rights, comparable with utilitarian theory in clarity, detailed articulation and in appeal to practical men . . . So it is true on this subject as on others, that where Bentham fails to persuade, he still forces us to think.'[8]

I was attracted to Hart's debates with Devlin about the relationship between law and morals, his treatment of punishment and, not always consciously, by his underlying political liberalism in the English (not the American free-market) Millian sense. Hart was more a social democrat, committed to the welfare state, than a liberal democrat, but he stuck with the individual as the primary moral unit and with John Stuart Mill on the importance of autonomy. In nearly all of these matters I came close to Hart on this, with the exception that I was personally more concerned about ethnocentric tendencies in Western moralising and probably more attracted to aspects of communitarianism.

I mainly encountered philosophical issues in ethics via Hart, especially in relation to the justification of punishment. After studying them in more detail I was attracted to Benthamism, but worried by some of its implications. I took a whole course on Utilitarianism in Chicago (taught by J. B. Schneewind), from which I learned that Bentham's idea of pleasure could cover all human desires and satisfactions; that wealth was a dangerous proxy for these; that the felicific calculus was a metaphor and should not be interpreted literally in a mathematical way, as some maintained. Chicago economists' propensity to apply cost–benefit analysis to almost anything gave me pause. I also learned that most of the more trenchant criticisms of utilitarianism were focused on individual ethics rather than public morality; and that in the latter sphere Benthamism had been ably defended by A. J. Ayer against some of the main attacks.[9] That was helpful in underlining that both Jurisprudence and Bentham were mainly concerned with public morality rather than individual ethics. Later, when teaching about Bentham, I urged students to work out which version of utilitarianism they thought to be the least vulnerable before pitting that version against their own intuitions, beliefs and commitments. Moreover, even if they believed that they had some natural or moral rights, they should take serious account of Bentham's criticisms of the French Declarations of Rights.[10]

Torture

My interest in utilitarianism was brought into sharp focus by events in Northern Ireland. The revival of the Troubles from the mid-1960s and the British response raised important issues about interrogation techniques and emergency powers. In 1971 the Compton Report found that certain brutal techniques of interrogation, notably hooding, noise, deprivation of sleep and a diet of bread and water amounted to physical ill-treatment and were unacceptable. In 1972 the Parker Report confirmed that these techniques were illegal and they were discontinued for the time being.[11] Later in *Ireland v The United Kingdom* (1978) the European Court of Human Rights held that the 'Compton techniques' did not constitute torture but were nevertheless violations of Article 3 of the European Convention on Human Rights as constituting 'inhuman and degrading treatment'. These techniques, together with derogation of civil liberties, especially internment without trial, were publicly debated mainly in terms which had affinities with utility versus human rights.

Queen's had a strong tradition of not tolerating sectarian intolerance on campus. This stance was generally understood and respected both within and outside the University. However, universities are expected to contribute to their local community and to engage in appropriate ways with important issues of the time. In 1971–2 some students became increasingly critical of the alleged aloofness of Queen's. A standard response was: 'Get off the fence? – on which side?', given that local students divided approximately in a ratio of 50–55 per cent (Protestant) to 45–50 per cent (Catholic). But this was too glib. In the Law Faculty some of us formed a staff–student, non-sectarian, working party to contribute to public debate on contentious issues 'with relative detachment', starting with interrogation techniques and emergency powers.[12] We consciously applied academic values in our approach to the task and some people may have felt that this over-intellectualised fiercely contested political issues. This was an exercise in consensus politics. The process was illuminating, but I was ambivalent about some of its products. In particular, we produced a pamphlet on emergency powers which inevitably represented a balanced package of compromises.[13] I was dismayed when some Conservative MPs later selectively cherry-picked particular recommendations out of context. However, the exercise was a valuable experience for the participants and it did represent a strong public reaffirmation and application of the academic ethic to political issues.

Involvement in this working party increased my interest in these topics and I devoted a good deal of time to them both as a scholar and public intellectual, gradually getting dragged into the murky waters of the literature on torture. In 1971 I was invited to join the Bentham Committee, which was responsible for the editing and publication of Jeremy Bentham's manuscripts at University College London. There I found two unpublished manuscripts on torture dating from the mid-1770s to 1780. In the mid-twentieth century, most English moral philosophers had lost interest in torture, treating it as 'beyond the Pale', but these manuscripts were intellectually interesting as well as topical. With the help of Penelope, who did most of the editing, we prepared an article containing the two pieces together with a commentary.[14] Interestingly Bentham acknowledged at the start that, until he turned his attention to the subject, he would never have imagined that he would approve any practice that could properly be called 'torture'. Indeed, he had welcomed its abolition by several 'of the most absolute governments of Europe ... But in the course of a scrupulous examination a man learns to render himself proof against the delusive power of words, and to correct the first impressions of sentiment by the more extensive considerations of utility.'

Bentham reluctantly concluded that 'there are a very few cases in which, for a very particular purpose, Torture might be made use of with advantage'. He even argued that in some circumstances coercive torture could be more easily justified than punishment because the infliction of pain could be stopped the moment that the objective of the coercion was achieved (duration). Perhaps the strangest aspect of Bentham's account is his claim that 'The great objection against Torture is, that it is so liable to abuse.' That is not most people's answer to the question: 'What is wrong with torture?' Some may emphasise the extremity of pain, the denial of dignity, extreme coercion or the cumulation of bad consequences both direct and indirect. Bentham had two significant insights: torture is a vague and complex concept that covers a variety of practices of varying degrees of horror;[15] and as a practical matter the greatest evil is its institutionalisation and routinisation.

It is unnecessary to summarise Bentham's complex, insightful and shocking analysis here – it is readily available elsewhere. To be fair to him, he came to his main conclusion reluctantly, he laid down quite stringent conditions for the application of torture and he restricted the concept of torture to the infliction of bodily pain for the purpose of coercion – thereby excluding many of its current uses, such as incapacitating political opponents and terrorising the population. Moreover, he did not publish what he had written; perhaps he realised that his arguments, like the practice itself, could be readily abused and that he indulged in self-censorship.

However, I took responsibility for publishing the manuscript because, contrary to Bentham's rather complacent assumptions, far from being 'abolished' the practice of torture had become widespread, even routine, in many countries of the world in the twentieth century. Bentham's discussion of torture is easily criticised. His definition of torture is both too wide and too narrow: it is wide in that leaves out any requirement of extreme pain; but it is also too narrow for today in that it defines the purpose of torture in terms of coercing an individual to do or desist from doing something, typically to make a confession during interrogation. Despite setting down some stringent conditions for justified use, Bentham's account boils down to little more than cost–benefit analysis. He concludes that there may be situations where inflicting torture is the lesser of two evils so that its use may occasionally be justified.

Aware that Bentham might be cited out of context or misinterpreted, my commentary emphasised the extreme narrowness of his justification and supplemented his arguments against the practice. In particular, I argued that in addition to arguments based on principles independent of utility, even a utilitarian could support a general absolute legal prohibition on torture and analogous practices for the pragmatic reason that it would probably be, and still is, widely used beyond any colourable justification. Torture needs to be studied, analysed, reported and fought just because, even more than slavery, it has not been abolished as an institutionalised practice. It still flourishes in some countries.[16]

In addition to the article on Bentham, I attended a conference in Paris on Torture in 1973 and gave a paper to the Aristotelian Society in 1978,[17] urging philosophers to pay attention to the conceptual and philosophical issues involved. Both experiences were unpleasant. The Paris Conference, organised by Amnesty International, was the start of the campaign for a UN Convention on Torture. I was dismayed by the experience: horrendous reports not only of individual cases but of the extent of institutionalised torture; human rights activists wringing their hands helplessly; international lawyers thinking in terms of a twenty-year process (in fact the Convention came into effect in 1987, 'only' twelve years later). Amnesty itself dealt admirably with individual cases, but did not seem to have much interest in systematic research on the causes and means of combating torture nor a vision about how to prevent, preferably abolish, it in practice, not only in law.[18] At the meeting of the Aristotelian Society a well-known philosopher objected to having the subject debated at all. I insisted that there was a real-world problem with philosophical aspects, but I sympathised with the objector: even at that meeting some of the discussion seemed to me to trivialise the issues, so that I felt that we were fiddling while Rome burned. Bentham frequently gets cited out of context, without mention of his hesitations and strict conditions. Many arguments can be abused, especially the argument from the extreme case (e.g. the 'ticking bomb' scenario), which when invoked usually ignores the distinction between institutionalised torture and extreme one-off choices. The recent debased US debate since 9/11 over water-boarding and other practices amply illustrates the problem.[19]

After leaving Northern Ireland in 1972 I gradually escaped from studying torture, although like poverty, inequality, insecurity and even slavery the subject is always with us. I can no longer claim any special knowledge of torture and efforts to eradicate it. But my sense is that while a great deal of attention has been focused on law and individual cases at national, transnational, international and supranational levels, the literature is unbalanced and skewed away from some of the most important issues. For example, nearly all of the legal literature has been focused on international law or on the 'morality of torture'. Very little attention has been paid systematically to such questions as: under what conditions does torture flourish? Who is responsible and accountable for institutionalised torture? By what process does torture become routine? What is the link, if any, between torture and democracy? With a few exceptions, hardly any serious historical accounts of the phenomenon have been undertaken, but there is a lot of thinly disguised prurience about techniques and instruments of torture. One interesting exception is John Langbein's *Torture and the Law of Proof* (1977), which convincingly shows that changes in the Law of Evidence, especially in regard to confessions, contributed more to the decline of the practice in canon law than the exaggerated influence of enlightenment thinkers, such as Beccaria, who influenced Bentham. Sir Edward Coke complacently claimed that English law did not condone torture but, even now, 'visitors with strong stomachs' can ponder this as they queue for tickets ('no refunds if you faint') to the dungeons of Warwick Castle, complete with oubliette, interactive and participatory gimmicks and selfies ('What a Scream!').[20]

One of the very few exceptions to the lack of systematic analysis of institutionalised torture is work sponsored by the Association for the Prevention of Torture (APT). Founded in Geneva 1977, APT is an international non-governmental organisation focused on the prevention of torture and other acts of cruel, inhuman or degrading treatment. APT's strategy is based on the belief that prevention of torture is best achieved through three integrated elements: effective monitoring, legal and policy frameworks and ensuring determination and capability on the part of international and national actors. In 2011–12 it supported a four-year project on torture prevention led by Dr Richard Carver of Oxford Brookes University, the objective of which is 'to identify the key factors leading to a reduction in the risk of torture and other ill-treatment'.[21] This study, with a modest team, resulted in an excellent interim report to the Swiss-based APT, followed by a substantial book published in 2016, co-edited with Lisa Handley. Its starting-point was no more than a hypothesis:

> In recent decades, treaties have required states to adopt a series of preventive measures in order to reduce the risk of torture. These measures, originally inspired by common sense and practices that seemed to work, have not been systematically tested.[22]

Carver acknowledges that there is an extensive scholarly literature about torture in philosophy, psychology, medicine and law (especially international law and human rights). But nearly forty years after the Paris Conference, he found the literature still unbalanced:

A large body of work examines the physical and mental effects of torture and the treatment of torture victims. More pertinently for this study, an extensive literature describes the prohibition of torture in international law and the obligations that states incur in customary law, international humanitarian law, and human rights law, notably in the two international preventive treaties, the Convention against Torture and Other Cruel, Inhuman or Degrading Treatment or Punishment (UN Convention against Torture, UNCAT) and its Optional Protocol (the Optional Protocol to the Convention against Torture and other Cruel, Inhuman or Degrading Treatment or Punishment, OPCAT), as well as the European Convention for the Prevention of Torture and Inhuman or Degrading Treatment or Punishment (European Convention for the Prevention of Torture). Psychological research is relevant to this study in that it has revealed that human beings have a propensity to torture in certain conditions, *suggesting that rules and systems are the key to prevention. Social scientific and historical research into the causes of torture, and factors that may prevent or mitigate, has been rarer.*[23]

In 1984 Amnesty published a strategy for reducing the incidence of torture generally. Although this was based largely on anecdotal experience in a few countries rather than systematic research and analysis, the Carver Report and book suggest that by and large their prescriptions were sound. In the past thirty years the situation has improved substantially, mainly in countries whose governments actually want to try to tackle the problem.[24] Amnesty's twelve-point programme did correctly pinpoint measures that can work.[25] With the wisdom of hindsight they look like not much more than common-sense answers to unasked questions about the demography and distribution of institutionalised practices, such as where and when does torture take place? Who are the victims and who are the perpetrators? What are the incentives and deterrents for those responsible? And so on. One crucial change has been to switch the focus to police stations in the first forty-eight hours after arrest rather than in prisons over longer periods. Statistically, the main victims are the deprived, the homeless and persons suspected of petty crimes rather than 'terrorists' and members of transnational criminal organisations. Preventive measures in police stations can be effective, such as recording or videoing interviews, good record-keeping, rules excluding improperly obtained evidence, availability of lawyers, professionalisation of police training and discipline and greater transparency overall.

Returning to the subject in 2016, I have been surprised and pleased that Carver and Handley convincingly conclude that:

The message from our findings is one of cautious optimism. It is apparent that torture prevention can be effective and that the priorities set over the past three or four decades at international, regional and national levels have been broadly correct. When opportunities to torture are reduced, the incidence of torture falls; and if torturers are effectively investigated and prosecuted, it falls further. Monitoring can also be effective by identifying systemic problems and promoting reforms of law and practice. The lesson to be drawn is that, while some priorities may need to be reordered, patient application of these basic preventive measures is likely to yield results.[26]

Of course, there is still a huge problem, especially in countries with civil wars, extensive unrest, undisciplined security forces or repressive regimes. It is tragic that this kind of research was not undertaken twenty or thirty years earlier. On the whole academics seem to have contributed little in this period, except for moralising and formal legal measures. Insofar as 'the problem of torture' has attracted scholarly attention in the past thirty to forty years, from the point of view of prevention generally the wrong people have been barking up the wrong trees.[27]

The main reason that I have dwelt here on this distressing topic is that I think that the distortions in the academic literature on torture and its relative neglect of the central practical issue of its prevention echo similar distortions in Jurisprudence and the discipline of Law when attention has been focused on analytic truths and ethical puzzles to the neglect of empirical reality. We need an epidemiology of torture and an empirically informed discipline of law.

This is not to suggest that philosophers have nothing to contribute. Bentham's manuscripts illustrate some of the limitations of utilitarianism. Moral philosophers who argue that torture is always wrong and jurists who support an absolute prohibition in law (as I do) seek to justify their position within different frameworks – some consequentialist, some deontological, some appealing to intuition. Bentham's account is not an answer to the question: 'What is wrong with torture?' But it contains the seeds of two important insights: first, he was right in identifying its susceptibility to abuse, to its being used beyond any colourable justification; secondly, this illustrates an important distinction between individual infliction in an extreme case and torture as an institutionalised practice.

Today it is recognised that torture is used for many purposes. In his book on *Torture and Moral Integrity*, Matthew Kramer has produced a useful typology including placatory, intimidatory, extortionate, act-impelling, punitive, sadistic, discriminatory, humiliative, extravagantly reckless, incapacitative and edifying (including aversion therapy).[28]

This is illuminating, but one wishes that Kramer had not confined himself to justifying absolute moral prohibitions using mainly hypothetical examples, rather than turning his attention to the extent, causes and conditions for actual practices. He even criticises Shue for being as much concerned with empirical matters as analytic truth.[29] The problem of torture needs both. Conceptual analysis (e.g. of responsibility, accountability, transparency, inhuman, degrading cruel treatment) has its uses; but if conceptual and moral issues are treated as isolated from practical problems in the real world they tend to become irrelevant, when they are not, and can distract attention from the most acute and common practices.[30]

Today torture is still endemic in a majority of countries, almost always without any colourable justification or excuse. This suggests that the central 'problem of torture' is not about its justification in a narrow band of extreme cases, but about its prevention and – optimistically – its abolition as an institutionalised practice that is widespread, embedded and tolerated very widely. Like 'the peculiar institution' of slavery the main question about abolition is not whether, but how. Like slavery, it is so commonplace that political and moral opinion has been cauterised – routine torture is not news. Like slavery, laws at global, international, regional and local levels are of symbolic value, but often ineffectual. Like slavery, the mere passing of laws does not mean 'abolition' in fact and does not solve 'the problem'; unlike slavery, it has not yet been the subject of a really powerful movement that has captured the public's imagination. One special characteristic of the present picture is that most victims of torture worldwide are criminal suspects, not alleged terrorists or political opponents. Bodies like Amnesty and APT have done noble work, but their resources are tiny compared to the scale of the problems. Contrast the investment in other diseases such as cancer and dementia, and one can see the imbalance.

Human rights and justice

Of course, torture was not the only topic in Normative Jurisprudence that engaged my attention. Over the years I struggled with Bentham's vicious, but incisive, attacks on human, moral and natural rights.[31] For him rights are creatures of positive law; talk of non-legal rights is mischievous nonsense. On the whole, I think that human rights law and human rights movements have probably been a force for the good and I have supported Bills of Rights and other human rights instruments and activities, mainly for pragmatic reasons. But it is difficult to construct a stable philosophical basis for non-legal rights and some of the claims of human rights discourse seem to me to be overblown. I have so far ended in the intellectually unsatisfactory position that natural and human rights may not exist as moral rights, but the discourse of human rights – talking as if they do – can pragmatically be very useful, and sometimes effective, in holding governments to account. As my friend Yash Ghai argues, human rights talk provides a workable language and an armoury of arguments for debating and negotiating constitutional and other political settlements. It is useful to talk as if they exist.[32]

In teaching I have usually devoted quite a lot of attention to Justice. Again, agnosticism and hesitations about universalism and 'ideal theory' have inhibited any attempt to make a distinctive contribution in this area. Since 1971 John Rawls's *A Theory of Justice* dominated the landscape. It deserves respect and careful study, but it always left me uneasy. Like Hart and Amartya Sen, Rawls had initially been attracted by utilitarianism and had worked out his ideas in opposition to it. His arguments were very carefully crafted and challenging, but I was never really persuaded. When Rawls ventured beyond some American cultural diaspora and took up 'globalisation', I had no difficulty in finding *The Law of Peoples* naïve, parochial and of almost no practical interest.[33]

I have long been an admirer of Amartya Sen's writings on famines, the capabilities approach, gender and the human development index.[34] When he belatedly published *The Idea of Justice* in 2009, I found this more appealing than Rawls, but I still had reservations.[35] Llewellyn highlighted Edmond Cahn's *The Sense of Injustice* (1951), an intriguing work of armchair psychology, and for a time I flirted with the idea that there may be a near universal sense of injustice, but I did not find the empirical research very satisfactory.[36] I have found the writings of Singer and Pogge inspiring, but I have remained a relatively well-read agnostic. In teaching about distributive justice, I used a Llewellynesque nursery example: mother has one indivisible cake (or other unique good). Her six children put forward different claims that they were the one to have it: desire, merit, age, strength, timing, 'my turn', 'destroy it' and fair procedure. In class we played with degrees of desire and merit and others of Bentham's dimensions, but usually the discussion ended up with drawing lots as the fairest distribution. Pedagogically this worked rather well, but it is hardly ground-breaking. So, although I devoted much of my teaching to Normative Jurisprudence, I cannot claim to have had a very distinctive set of views: I am a modified utilitarian, a political liberal, and I prefer Amartya Sen's practical capabilities approach to justice to Rawlsian ideal theory.

10

Standpoint, questioning and 'thinking like a lawyer'

The choice of the point(s) of view from which the story is told is arguably the most important single decision that the novelist has to make, for it fundamentally affects the way readers will respond, emotionally and morally, to the fictional characters and their actions.

(David Lodge)[1]

But if we take the view of our friend the bad man we shall find that he does not care two straws for the axioms or deductions, but that he does want to know what the Massachusetts or English courts are likely to do in fact. I am much of his mind. The prophesies of what the court will do in fact, and nothing more pretentious, are what I mean by law.

(Oliver Wendell Holmes Jr)[2]

Standpoint

Jurisprudence is a questioning and reasoning activity. A useful starting point for almost any enquiry is: who is asking whom what question(s) in what context? This is one version of 'clarification of standpoint'. I latched on to the basic idea shortly after sitting my finals in Oxford in 1955. I have been using it ever since. This section sketches the story of its development. The concept will recur in several later chapters.

Professor Hart's lectures in 1954, in particular his inaugural lecture, started me thinking about questions and questioning and that led on to my interest in the idea of standpoint or point of view. Hart criticised 'what is . . . ? questions', such as What is art? What is justice? What is law? What is a right? He showed that they are often defective and need to be challenged before they can be sensibly answered. They can be defective, first, if it is not clear what they mean and, secondly, if interpreted in particular ways, they may be based on false or dubious assumptions.

The meaning of questions like 'What is art?' or 'What is law?' depends on who is asking the question in what context for what reason. It could be a foreigner unfamiliar with the English word, asking for a simple verbal equivalent in another language. In the case of the word 'law' this is not easy, because it is ambiguous, and in one of its primary meanings there is no distinction made in English between *lex/ius, droit/loi, recht/gesetz*. In some contexts that may not matter, but in others this opens up a Pandora's jar of questions.[3] Or the questioner may be seeking to clarify a possible ambiguity: whether in this context 'art' is being used only in the aesthetic sense or is referring to any kind of skill – as in the statement 'negotiation is an art'. But the questioner may be an art historian, whose field is Art. Why is she asking this question? Maybe she is setting an examination paper? Or maybe she is thinking how to stipulate the usage of the term in an article she is writing on art in Papua New Guinea in order to delineate the scope of her enquiry; or maybe she is asking: what is the nature or essence of art? A sensible response to this last question is to express scepticism about the assumptions behind it. Why assume that art has a nature or essence? Maybe she is deeply puzzled about philosophical questions underlying her field of specialisation – she is worrying over a concept that she has previously just taken for granted. It may be appropriate to ask her to frame the question more precisely. Is she asking which of two (or more) theories of art is the most convincing? Or is she, inappropriately, asking for a general definition of the word 'art'? Or maybe one can infer from her tone that she is dismissing all such theoretical questions and, following jesting Pilate, asking 'What is art?', but not staying for an answer. In short one needs to clarify the meaning of the question, the concerns behind it and the standpoint of the questioner. Since many questions in Analytical Jurisprudence had been posed in 'what is . . . ?' terms, Hart's challenge was immensely important in the subsequent development of the field.

Hart's inaugural lecture was seminal for me. However, over time I became increasingly dissatisfied with his narrow view of the agenda of Jurisprudence – was he focusing on the best questions? He had adopted the doctrinal assumptions of his predecessors and focused on much the same concepts, such as law, right, obligation, rule, but not on concepts needed for empirical enquiries, even though he viewed law as a social phenomenon.[4] He upgraded the methods of Analytical Jurisprudence, but stuck with its narrow agenda.[5]

I mentioned in the Preface that in July 1955 I picked up a battered copy of R. G. Collingwood's *An Autobiography* in a bookshop in Keswick and that it was an epiphany. It is surely a great work of literature, indeed of fiction. The key idea for me was that all History is the History of thought: to understand Aristotle's *Ethics*, or Nelson's decisions at Trafalgar, one needs to put oneself in the writer's or actor's shoes and try to understand their situation, concerns, role, concepts, information and perceptions in order reconstruct what they were thinking and what it meant.[6]

In a famous article on causation, Collingwood brought out another aspect: 'A car skids while cornering at a certain point, turns turtle, and bursts into flame. From the car-driver's point of view, the cause of the accident was cornering too fast, and the lesson is that one must drive more carefully. From the county surveyor's point of view, the cause was a defective road surface, and the lesson is that one must make skid-proof roads. From the motor-manufacturer's point of view, the cause was defective design, and the lesson is that one must place the centre of gravity lower.'[7]

This illustrates clearly that different kinds of specialists have different kinds of lenses: they bring concepts, questions and specialised knowledge from different professional or other backgrounds. The concept of lens is crucial in standpoint analysis in relation to both theoretical and practical questions.

Reading Collingwood was for me a huge step forward, but it did not dissolve all my puzzles. Soon after that, I read E. M. Forster's *Aspects of the Novel*, written in 1927.[8] Two related, seemingly contradictory, ideas struck me. First, Forster praised Percy Lubbock's *The Craft of Fiction* (1921) and quoted with approval his statement:

> The whole intricate question of method, in the craft of fiction, I take to be governed by the question of the point of view – the question of the relation in which the narrator stands to the story.[9]

I devoured Lubbock and most of the novels he discussed. The central ideas were distinctions between the impartial or partial onlooker and the omniscient author and seeing everything through the eyes of one or more participants. This developed Collingwood's idea of History by differentiating several different types of points of view. It had immediate resonance in relation to studying law.

However, and secondly, in the later parts of *Aspects of the Novel* Forster seemed to alter course. He sharply criticised Henry James for adhering too rigidly to a consistent standpoint – sacrificing humanity and life to aesthetic form. In particular, in *The Ambassadors* James constructed an aesthetically complete form – like an hourglass:

> [B]ut at what sacrifice! . . . the cost is a very short list of characters, – mainly one observer who tries to influence the action and the second-rate outsider – and these characters . . . are constructed on very stingy lines . . . Why so wanton with human beings?[10]

In short, James's aesthetic formalism cut out the messy reality of life. That was just how I felt about Law and the dominant tradition – only a little less dominant today – of doctrinal formalism, as I interpreted it then (Chapter 13). This emphasis on particularity of different viewpoints was intuitively appealing. When I defected from Hart – at least he thought so – to something called 'realism', standpoint and multiple perspectives became key concepts for me. But, of course, I stuck with his idea of internal points of view.

Whilst in Dar es Salaam in 1955 I studied several of Collingwood's more substantial works, especially *The Idea of History* and *The Principles of Art*. For a while I flirted with the idea of constructing a *novum organum* for Law along Collingwoodian lines, but I soon realised my own limitations and kept returning to just two specific ideas in *An Autobiography*: standpoint and the logic of question and answer.[11]

Differentiation of standpoint was already a powerful tool in both Analytical Jurisprudence and Philosophy.[12] For example, Bentham's distinction between the expositor and the censor was central to his thought. In an influential article John Rawls claimed to dissolve the long-standing battle between retributivists and utilitarians about the justification of punishment by assigning each theory to a different standpoint: utilitarians address the legislator's question: under what conditions should [state] punishment be justified? The retributivists answer the judge's question: should I punish this person? This led on to a controversial distinction between act- and rule-utilitarianism. Several other jurists used differentiation of standpoints to dissolve puzzlements and advance their ideas by showing that rather than disagreeing about shared questions, protagonists in long-running debates were addressing different questions.[13] This has great explanatory power, but is sometimes overused. As we shall see, clarification of standpoint also has other uses, for example in anchoring an enquiry at an early stage, in bringing to the surface how much legal discourse is participant-oriented, and raising related questions about roles.

From early on, I emphasised the importance of clarifying standpoint in teaching and developed it as a key intellectual tool in that context.[14] It brings out the extent to which academic law is a participant-oriented discipline. Law students are rarely asked to adopt the standpoint of observers rather than actors.[15] Rather they are asked to *pretend to be* different kinds of participant: Advise your client; What should we (the legislator) do? How should I (as appellate judge) decide this question of law? What is for me (advocate) the best theory of the case? This is obvious in role plays, such as moots and mock trials. But it is much more pervasive than that. And I noticed that in intellectual exercises students often shift standpoints without realising it. Nietzsche said that the commonest form of stupidity is forgetting what one is trying to do. For law students the commonest form of stupidity may be forgetting who they are pretending to be.

Clarification of standpoint can be quite simple or more or less complex, depending on the context and nature of the enquiry. In teaching, I have usually advised students to follow a simple three-step protocol at the start of any enquiry: who am I? At what stage in what process am I? What am I trying to do?

The first question is not an invitation to existential *angst*. For law students it is normally enough to select one of the standard functionaries, such as advocate (for one party) or judge. The second question specifies the situation and immediate context. If this is litigation, which law students are frequently asked to imagine, it is useful to begin with a simple linear model of the total process of litigation starting with a triggering event, such as a death, a minor road accident, or an incident in a pub. In simplified form the model outlines a typical series of decisions and events or stages in litigation involving different actors, including investigation, a decision to seek legal advice, the initial consultation followed by action (e.g. a solicitor's letter or an arrest), through to a decision to prosecute or sue or abandon the case, or to negotiate (plea bargain? settlement? mediation?), pre-trial decisions, preparation the night before trial, actions and decisions in court by judges and other participants, procedural decisions, decisions on the law, decisions on the facts, and then on to decisions on sanctions (punishment, damages or other remedies), decisions whether to appeal, other decisions in the appellate process, post-trial decisions (including parole, bankruptcy, revenge) and the end of the process or its revival or continuation as in a feud. This model illustrates the variety of actors at different stages of litigation or other dispute processes, with different roles, vantage points and aims, and information needs. It is linear, whereas in practice the sequence of decisions and events in disputes can vary considerably.[16]

Of course, legal actors are involved in other processes and transactions besides litigation: negotiating deals, drafting contracts, interviewing, checking title, attracting clients, inventing tax avoidance schemes, destroying evidence, money laundering and so on; again, each of these has more or less standard procedures and models, but in every case there may be special other considerations.

It is important to distinguish between using standpoint analysis for rational construction or reconstruction of purposive thinking and for psychological or otherwise empirical study of a person's point of view, including their attitudes, feelings, intuitions and so on. These might be crudely characterised as the 'right brain' and 'left brain' approaches.[17] Collingwood used standpoint in the first way and was criticised for being too rationalistic. To start with I used clarification of standpoint in much the same way, pragmatically as a useful intellectual device, like Collingwood, usually positing a rational actor thinking purposively, typically adopting a normative model of a standard role, rather than using standpoint as a tool for empirical study of actual actors or classes of actors. Later I started to reflect about the implications of the idea. In a series of papers, spread over many years, I elaborated the general approach, while still focusing more on the pragmatics than its philosophical implications.[18]

Theorising standpoint

Having been introduced to the idea of standpoint by Collingwood and Lubbock in 1955, I continued to use it in a rough and ready way in teaching and in trying to sort out disagreements and differences in legal theory. Then, while visiting the University of Pennsylvania for a semester in 1971, I began to develop the idea more systematically. I gave a course on American Legal Realism and we spent about two weeks focusing on Oliver Wendell Holmes's classic article 'The Path of the Law' (1897). This is the text that has been most used to suggest that Holmes, Llewellyn and other Realists advanced 'a prediction theory of law'. They did nothing of the sort.[19] I argued that the context was an address about legal education to law students at Boston University in which Holmes was urging intending practitioners to adopt a more realistic standpoint for them than those of appellate court judges and advocates, viz. 'The Bad Man' and his legal adviser, a counsellor more often in his office than in court. The weakness of the Langdellian case-method system has been that it makes students focus on the higher reaches of the system and wholly exceptional client problems. In hammering home his plea to students to be more realistic about legal practice Holmes resorted to rhetoric and epigrammatic statements, including a famous passage in which he introduced the amoral Bad Man who 'does not care two straws for the axioms or deductions'. He is only interested in what the courts of Massachusetts or English courts are likely to do in fact.

Severed from its context, this passage was widely treated as Holmes's definition, or even theory of law. In 1971 I drafted a paper which defended him from these unscholarly interpretations, but criticised him for being too court-centric, omitting the other decisions and events that a rational real bad man might be concerned to predict.[20] However the device suited Holmes's immediate purpose, which was to persuade students to adopt the standpoint of a typical office lawyer and to wash this standpoint in 'cynical acid' so as to distinguish legal and ethical questions. For Holmes's Bad Man also provides a powerful image for a positivist perspective, which sharply distinguishes between morality and law. The Bad Man is amoral, rather than immoral.[21]

This paper was mainly about the implications of 'The Path of the Law'. Switching to the standpoint of the Bad Man and his advisers does make prediction a central concern and presents legal rules as only one of many aids to prediction. But prediction of what? Not just what courts will do. For a more realistic approach one needs to go beyond Holmes, who focused on courts, and ask for a more detailed risk analysis for an individual citizen assessing a number of contingencies and options, such as how likely is it that they will be suspected, brought in, interrogated and so on?

Whilst in Philadelphia in 1971 I became interested in Erving Goffman's writings, especially *Asylums* (1961) and *Presentation of Self in Everyday Life* (1959). As he was in the Sociology Department, I contacted him and we met in a bar for a long conversation. He was encouraging, but the only detail that I remember is that he advised me to steer clear of abstract role theory and to keep things concrete. I suspect that he influenced me more profoundly through his writings.

Standpoint analysis became a central element in my approach especially in teaching interpretation of legal and social rules (Chapter 11), reading juristic texts (this chapter, below) and Evidence (Chapter 14). My 1971 essay contained the seeds of a more general analysis of standpoint, which I developed in several later papers and applied systematically in student books on rules and evidence.[22] These essays explored, inter alia, 'bottom-up' perspectives and total process models of litigation as useful thinking tools.

I am sometimes asked: what is your concept of standpoint? If that means, what factors do I take into account in clarifying standpoint, the answer is: it depends on the context. The term 'standpoint' is quite ambiguous and with several shades of meaning in different contexts.[23] It is often best kept quite vague at an abstract level. Terms such as vantage point, historical situation, immediate context, role, perspective and objectives sometimes need to be differentiated. Sometimes epistemology or ideology may be relevant. Often a general concept of standpoint suffices; sometimes it needs elaborate analysis, observing such distinctions or with reference to immediate concerns, available information, tactics, specialised lenses and so on. Collingwood's account of causation, quoted above, illustrates how different kinds of specialist have diverse kinds of lenses in practical as well as theoretical enquiries. They bring to bear concepts and questions and a stock of knowledge from their professional backgrounds. And there may well be other local or specific factors that influence the standpoint and judgement of an individual engineer or county surveyor or insurer about causation in a particular road accident.

In teaching I usually restricted the standpoint analysis to various standard characters, differentiated mostly by their roles: legislator, judge, jurist, advocate, adviser, investigator, party, user, witness, victim, offeree, and many others have stereotypical roles as actors in legal processes. They operate in different, but related, contexts with different objectives and resources. Standard standpoints, characterised mainly in terms of situation and role, have some explanatory power. They capture common ways of differentiating between classes of actors but can fall short on particularities. A historian trying to explain Nelson's decisions at Trafalgar (or that of each French and Spanish Admiral) could start with stereotypes, but very soon would need more data – about his vantage point, the information he had, his ideas about the enemy's intentions and capacity, the weather conditions and his own expertise, skills, temperament, strategy and objectives. In analysing the standpoint of a particular legal actor in a specific situation 'realistically' one may need to ask many detailed questions about their situation relevant to the particular enquiry.

It is worth emphasising that the same actor, such as a solicitor or prosecutor, in the same case may have different roles and aims at different stages even when representing the same client – initially the solicitor will typically adopt a pessimistic stance, advising caution; but if the case gets to court then the role of the advocate (who may or may not be the same person) is typically to win the case by appropriately forceful argument; yet again, in a plea in mitigation in a criminal case the situation, the roles of adjudicator and advocate and the relevant information are different and, for example, previously inadmissible evidence may now be used.

Sometimes students are asked to adopt the role of observer, or participant observer, rather than an actor. As with actors, there are many kinds of observer.[24] But these are not always easy to differentiate. This is nicely illustrated by the elusive role of the expositor. Even when writing a doctrinal essay or discussing a contested point of law, the student is often implicitly asked to adopt the role of expositor. But what exactly is that role? It is often remarked that learned authors of treatises or scholarly articles are participants in the legal system – they may influence judges and practitioners, they may even be cited as authorities, and they may shape the climate of opinion or help to change the law directly or indirectly or even through private legislation.[25] In short, expositors can have impact. They have the ambiguous role of participant-observers. On one view, there is no such thing as neutral or objective exposition of law. But many expositors claim to be legal scientists or at least relatively detached scholars (Chapter 13). Such considerations make the standpoint of expositor more problematic than it may seem at first sight.[26]

The role of the judge is similarly problematic, especially in appellate or otherwise hard cases. Most will agree with Bentham that in routine cases the judge should aspire to rectitude of decision; that is to say, apply the law correctly to facts proven to be true. But a great deal of Anglo-American academic literature is focused on cases where the law is unclear. What is the nature and extent of judicial discretion? If judges make law, are they involved in interstitial legislation? Can or should judges be guided by morality in hard cases? If so, whose morality? How can judicial discretion be reconciled with the Rule of Law? Is the judicial finder of fact like a historian? What is the significance of the maxim 'judges decide, historians only conclude'? How far are all of these questions over-generalised?[27]

Much intellectual effort has been invested in such issues about adjudication and there is little consensus at general or even local levels. That is obvious. Less obvious is the point that adopting the standpoint of an appellate judge to try to clarify other theoretical issues typically allows puzzlements about the judicial role to complicate and obscure puzzlements about other topics.[28]

I am also asked whether my approach to standpoint commits me to rejecting the idea of 'a view from nowhere'.[29] This raises profound and complex philosophical questions about objectivity, knowledge, freedom, the self and so on, to which I do not have ready answers. My interest and use of the idea of standpoint has been more pragmatic than philosophical. My response is that there is probably a tendency in that direction, but no necessary commitment, that I consider objectivity and subjectivity to be relative matters and that as a scholar I aspire to relative detachment.

One final observation: analysis of standpoint brings out the unrealism of much academic law: a few elementary statistics can show how rare contested trials and appeals on questions of law are in contrast to decisions at other stages of litigation or in non-litigious processes, yet the tendencies in academic law go in the reverse direction. Students are usually asked to pretend to be actors in the higher reaches of the system. It is much more fun to pretend to be a Supreme Court Justice, the Attorney-General or a Minister or a QC or a policy-maker than a magistrate, pupil barrister or legal executive, administrator or witness. Moots are admittedly easier to stage than mock trials, which also tend to be focused upon that wholly exceptional event, the contested trial. There are some justifications for treating jury trials or appeals to the Supreme

Court as paradigmatic, in terms of their visibility, importance and interest; but the main driver for emphasising these lofty roles is the doctrinal tradition of legal scholarship and education: the assumption that the study of doctrine is the be-all and end-all of academic law (Chapter 13).

Questions and questioning

> I keep six honest serving-men;
> (They taught me all I know)
> Their names are What and Where and When
> And How and Why and Who. (Kipling)[30]

Questions have taught me nearly all I know. I am inquisitive, have developed questioning skills in teaching, examining, interviewing, debating, problem-solving, inspecting and, of course, enquiring and thinking. A central aim of much of my activity in legal education has been directed to righting the imbalance between emphasis on know-what to the detriment of know-why and know-how (Chapter 16). Latterly I have started to ask questions about questions. Scattered throughout this book I have given examples of questions that I have asked or failed to ask. Even as a child questions intrigued and bothered me: I failed to ask my mother directly what my 'thing' was called and wasted a lot of time failing to find out; at school there were questions that put me on the spot ('Boxing or confirmation?'), and ones that troubled me (How many of the Thirty-nine Articles do I really believe?) (Chapter 2). We have seen that Herbert Hart was the first to teach me that questions may be ambiguous, based on false assumptions or otherwise open to criticism (Chapter 3). I learned from Collingwood that a question is often the attempted expression of an underlying concern or puzzlement and that [most] propositions can usefully be looked at as answers to questions; and that a question may be an indirect or misleading expression of an underlying concern. For example, in reading a text it may be useful to start by asking: what questions was she trying to ask? What was biting her? This idea leads on to clarifying standpoint: who is asking what question in what context, and why?[31]

In our academic culture students starting on a PhD are advised to clarify, refine and articulate with precision their 'research question' and 'sub-questions' before moving on to matters of method, hypotheses and the like. A carefully crafted research question can anchor an enquiry, but is open to revision. When reading a thesis, I regularly check early on whether the conclusions are answers to the original research question, which sometimes gets forgotten. If a thesis is conceptualised as an argument justifying one's conclusion(s), the ideal type should fit the model Question-Answers-Reasons (QAR). This is sound advice, provided the student does not get prematurely stuck into a corner with a narrow, sterile question or set of questions, or ones that she is not really interested in or competent to answer. Questions about standpoint and concerns can help the student bring to the surface what she really cares about or wants to know: what is biting her?

There is a large and diverse literature on questions and questioning. Much of it relates to practical advice on skilful questioning in particular kinds of context: how to ask questions in class or in police investigation and interrogation, or interviews on TV or for jobs and all sorts of other practical enquiries. In many of these the questioner knows or has a pretty good idea of the answer in advance – examiners are meant to do so and barristers are advised that in cross-examination one should never ask a question to which one does not know the answer. There are fascinating accounts of the skills of good questioners (such as David Frost in *Frost-Nixon*, or Jon Snow, or Sherlock Holmes). There are collections of notable cross-examinations as models for advocates, especially in America. One of my favourite passages in literature is the scene in Dostoyevsky's *Crime and Punishment* in which Porfiri Petrovitch interrogates Raskolnikov like a fly-fisher playing a trout.

In my role as teacher, examiner and inspector of institutions (mainly law schools) I became quite proficient at asking questions. But it was much later that I began to think and read about the theory and practice of effective questioning in different contexts. Much of it is to do with psychology, but there is also a fragmented philosophical literature, which I found rather disappointing.[32] One question that is open to criticism, but which still nags me is: what makes for good questions? Intellectually I know that there is no 'silver bullet' at such a general level and that on the whole the appropriateness of a question or line of questioning depends on context – that is, who is asking whom, about what, for what purpose, in what circumstances, with what resources and prior information? Some of the underlying concerns relate to creativity and invention, others to questioning tacit knowledge and working assumptions.[33] There is plenty of writing about specific types of questioning in, for example, cross-examination, medical diagnosis and social science investigation. I think that a few general things can be said. However, the fact is that I am a practitioner more than a theorist of questioning and an essay on 'good questions' must await another occasion.

In this book I have deliberately used questions as a device for stimulating interest and there are many more questions than answers. That, I think, is appropriate for a jurist's memoirs. However, I have borne in mind Morris Zapp's criticism of his colleagues in the Rummidge English Department:

> Their pathetic attempts at profundity were qualified out of existence and largely interrogative in mode. They liked to begin a paper with some formula like 'I want to raise some questions about so-and-so', and seemed to think they had done their intellectual duty merely by raising them. This manoeuvre drove Morris Zapp insane. Any damn fool, he maintained, could think of questions; it was *answers* that separated the men from the boys. If you couldn't answer your own questions it was either because you hadn't worked on them hard enough or because they weren't real questions. In either case you should keep your mouth

shut. One couldn't move in English studies these days without falling over unanswered questions which some damn fool had carelessly left lying about.[34]

'Thinking like a lawyer': 'legal method', 'skills' and 'legal reasoning'

The phrase 'thinking like a lawyer' became fashionable as a way of epitomising learning objectives of the Langdellian case-method approach in the United States. Restricted to case-law skills, this is easily criticised, for it assumes that all lawyers think, and that they think in the same way about the same matters. Taken literally these assumptions are clearly false, for legal practice is stratified, complex and diverse. Moreover, understanding law requires further stand-points and questions.

It should be clear by now that throughout my career I have been strongly committed to the values of liberal education in the English and Scottish traditions. Both the classical and the medieval seven liberal arts were all oriented to developing transferable intellectual skills.[35] I have also supported a switch within professional training from emphasis on legal knowledge to direct teaching and learning of specific professional skills and techniques, such as negotiation, advocacy and drafting, but that needs to be kept fairly distinct from developing general intellectual skills (Chapter 16).[36]

'Legal method'

As a teacher my central aim has been to teach students to think, actively, analytically and imaginatively. My teaching of 'Legal method', Juristic Technique, Evidence, Torts and even Jurisprudence (how to read a text, con-ceptual analysis, constructing arguments, questioning one's own assumptions and presuppositions[37]) have all been skills-oriented in accordance with the values of liberal traditions of learning. Despite my unhappy experience of Classics at school I did learn how to read, write, parse, translate and even compose passable light verse – all of which have stood me in good stead. It was tough and it was not fun. The mantra for most of my own courses has been: 'TOUGH, BUT FUN'. My undergraduate Law degree, despite its shortcom-ings, as well as teaching me how to write to deadlines, did develop some powers of analysis. So did my self-education in Philosophy.

'Skills'

As an educationist I have had to fight on four fronts: first, against rote learning and emphasis on coverage rather than depth; secondly, for balancing know-what, with know-how and know-why (knowledge, skills, understanding); thirdly, a rearguard action against the threat of imposition of more knowledge-based material onto already overloaded undergraduate curricula when professional training in England, especially for the Bar, moved to a greater emphasis on direct teaching of basic professional skills. Here, the central argument was that as academics 'we are in the skills business too'.[38] Fourthly, I then had to support this position against academic colleagues who thought that emphasis on skills was illiberal, 'instrumentalist' or banausic. My argument was that this was to conflate specific operational techniques (such as letter writing or conveyancing) with transferable intellectual skills. Liberal education in classics, history, literature and the humanities has been largely skills-based: historians do not just mug up facts, rather they learn how to do history and be historians; similar approaches are found in most studies in logic, rhetoric, literature and the pure and applied sciences. Such approaches are sometimes crudely instrumentalist, but that is neither necessary nor desirable.[39]

As a scholar I have traced the history of the American Skills Movement in legal education, placing Langdell, Llewellyn and Frank at the centre.[40] I told the story largely in terms of Langdell's switch from knowledge to case-law skills, which dominated elite American law schools to the 1940s and beyond. Llewellyn wrote that Langdellian skills were 'sharp and well-instilled, but the wherewithal for vision was not given'.[41] In 1944 Llewellyn himself chaired a Committee on Curriculum that advocated a broadening out from case-law skills to a list of six 'lawyering skills', which included drafting and appellate advocacy. In the late 1950s Irving Rutter, a pupil of Llewellyn's, produced an analytical model for a systematic approach under the title of 'A Jurisprudence of Lawyers' Operations'.[42] Such an approach, he suggested, should begin with a job analysis of what lawyers in fact do, breaking each kind of job down into operations, then transactions and then extending a skills analysis of each 'skill set' into a more specific set of techniques. Llewellyn, as we have seen, saw no inconsistency in emphasising skills with proclaiming that 'the best practical training, along with the best human training – is the study of law, within the professional school itself, as a liberal art'.[43] Later Rutter's approach was the basis of the McCrate Report on 'Fundamental Lawyering Skills' which was quite influential in the United States.[44] The main weakness of that report was its insistence on retaining the fiction that the American legal profession is homogeneous, monolithic and classless, which empirical studies have shown is just not the case. This false assumption underlies the ideas of 'basic skills' and 'core subjects'.[45]

My first public experience of 'the skills debate' was at the Commonwealth Law Conference in 1993. A distinguished Australian QC argued that 'skills can only be picked up in practice and that the function of law schools is to teach legal doctrine'.[46] This stimulated some sharp rejoinders. He had quoted a great classical scholar as authority for his argument. My modest contribution was to point out that classical education is itself largely a training in transferable intellectual skills. This conflation of intellectual skills and professional techniques has continued to bedevil discussions about 'legal method' and 'legal skills'.

There is no point in fighting old battles here and most of my somewhat repetitive writings in the area are easily accessible.[47] The war is not over, because bureaucracy, new technology and student apathy are among the forces that will generally push towards easier options than thinking for oneself. However, I do think that the time is ripe for rethinking our idea of 'legal method' in the current context. This is partly because the skills and competencies to be expected of future law graduates and lawyers of different kinds are expanding all the time and we do not have a coherent working theory for dealing with this.

To begin with, it is important to distinguish between the skills that an undergraduate law student needs and 'lawyering skills'. For example, some courses on 'Legal Method' deal with such matters as how to use a law library and other study skills.[48] Most emphasise skills in interpreting cases and statutes. Some have extended the idea to introduce even first-year undergraduates to basic 'lawyering skills' such as negotiation, advocacy and drafting. While not opposed to that idea in principle, I think that it is important to keep intellectual skills conceptually separate from study skills and professional techniques that are quite specific to particular kinds of practice. What legal practice involves ranges from sharply honed generic intellectual and problem-solving skills to specialised kinds of operation or to form-filling or box-ticking or adept use of scissors and paste.

If intellectual skills are to be at the centre of academic legal education then enough time needs to be allowed for direct study as well as reinforcement. This is especially the case if the idea of 'Legal Method' is expanded to include fact-handling as well as rule-handling, comparative method ('we are all comparatists now'),[49] basic numeracy and scientific literacy (science and scientific evidence are growing in importance) and some basics of semantics and conceptual analysis. Yet the more skills one tries to fit into a single module or course the lower will be the levels of competence attained. Otherwise 'first steps' will decline into 'learning about' a shift back from How? to What?, as happens in many courses on 'Legal Method'.

So how to approach rethinking 'Legal Method' as a subject? First, it is important to grasp some basic distinctions, many of which are standard in educational theory: affective/cognitive learning objectives; learning what, learning why, learning how (knowledge, theory, skills); learning about and learning how; intellectual skills, and specific practical techniques; mastering the basics, increasing competence and reinforcing it; learning through direct instruction, by picking it up, by controlled experience, learning by doing and reflecting on it ('experiential learning') and so on.

Some of these distinctions are contested or elusive: for example, there is controversy about how far 'skills' and 'knowledge' can or should be kept apart. As Herbert Simon pointed out in relation to 'problem-solving' it 'must, of course, be taught in the context of a rich environment of problems – mostly but not entirely drawn from the professional field in question – there is no such thing as expertness without knowledge'.[50] For me, that is mostly a matter of emphasis and it is important to bear in mind that in law most detailed knowledge is local.

Two of these distinctions relevant to the concept of 'legal method' are regularly conflated in legal education discourse. The first is between learning about and learning how. Books on 'Legal Method' quite often tell about the doctrine of precedent and the alleged rules of statutory interpretation, but do not encourage students to learn how to use the techniques of precedent in constructing a legal argument or how to read a statute or some particular part of it.[51]

A second set of distinctions that are sometimes glossed over is between learning the basics of a skill or skill-set, mastering it to a level of competence or excellence and reinforcing it through practice. One can read a manual on driving a car, one can do enough to pass a driving test, but one only becomes an excellent driver by repeated practice, with or without additional formal instruction. Courses on Legal Method and some of the skills courses at the vocational stage are only 'first steps' towards mastering the relevant skills. Our culture of legal education and training has, on the whole, not taken the idea of direct advanced skills training very seriously. The Bar in England has instituted post-qualification training in advocacy, but that is a long way behind some of the more specialised courses offered by the American National Institute of Trial Advocacy.

One of the most successful courses I have been involved in has been an access course, which focused only on 'legal method' and had no separate substantive law elements.[52] By learning how to read and use cases and statutes students in fact mastered many of the basic concepts and principles of Contract, Torts and Criminal Law, because the concrete material concerned these subjects.

In recent debates in England the idea of 'graduateness' has become quite fashionable, but it is also contested.[53] Insofar as this suggests that all graduates should have learned to read, write, analyse, argue, synthesise and communicate orally and in writing (and I would add have some basic numeracy) the idea of a liberal legal education is consistent with this. There remains a question whether there is anything unique or special about legal materials and about ways of thinking, using and arguing about them. This is a controversial area which can be usefully considered in relation to the topic which is conventionally referred to as 'legal reasoning'.

Reasoning in legal contexts

For my whole career I have been involved in thinking, reading, teaching and writing about reasoning in legal contexts. Over time this has resulted in broadening my focus in several directions. Starting conventionally with reasoning from authoritative sources (mainly cases and legislation) about disputed questions of domestic law, as they featured in reported cases of judicial decisions, each of these elements was extended gradually to other kinds of texts (e.g. policy documents, trial records), other kinds of questions (e.g. questions of fact, reasoning in sentencing), other kinds of actor (e.g. police, detectives, prosecutors, advocates, parole boards), other kinds of operations related to litigation (e.g. police investigations, settlement out of court, fact-finding, appeals, mental health orders), to non-litigious operations, and to foreign and transnational legal systems, and non-state normative orders. All of these activities and decisions can in principle involve reasoning.

My first step away from tradition was to shift the emphasis from 'learning about' to 'learning how'. In Khartoum I taught students how to read and use reported cases and statutes as part of my course on Introduction to Law. I did something similar in Dar es Salaam, where I also offered an extra-mural course on 'Clear Thinking' to the public at large – in fact about a dozen or so anglophone clerks and school teachers. Later in Warwick I offered a similar extra-mural course on 'Rule-handling'. In teaching I emphasised that practical reasoning in law is not so very different from ordinary 'common sense' practical reasoning and that this (especially informal logic) was the best starting point for both extra-mural and law students.

In Belfast the year-long course on 'Juristic Technique' gave us an unusually large amount of space to expand the subject. In the early years I interpreted my task fairly conventionally, except that I drew heavily on what I had learned in Chicago from Levi and Llewellyn. Statutory interpretation had been given much less attention than precedent in traditional courses; stimulated by two colleagues – David Miers and Abdul Paliwala – we placed much more emphasis on legislation, including drafting, processes of enactment and finding one's way around complex statutes.

The idea that there are close similarities and continuities between reasoning in legal contexts and ordinary practical reasoning became a central plank of my approach. It is easy to show that the English doctrine of precedent, the rules about admissibility of evidence, and the rules of statutory interpretation were only a small part of what is involved in arguing about interpreting cases and statutes, questions of fact and so on. For example, the doctrine of precedent is largely permissive, except that lower courts are bound by precedents from higher courts; however, there are several standard techniques for departing from an adverse upper court precedent.[54] On the other hand, there are conventions of respect for 'merely' persuasive precedents, from lower or cognate courts, and for precedents from some other jurisdictions – but the conventions are vague. In contrast with the anaemic doctrine, Karl Llewellyn constructed from a sample of state appellate cases an illustrative list of sixty-four 'Available, Impeccable Precedent Techniques' used by judges in handling prior precedents, both favourable and unfavourable, in justifying their own decisions.[55] Here practice is richer, more complex than and greatly outruns doctrine in sophistication and nuanced reasoning. The same applies to reasoning in interpretation of statutes where, except for a few very specific rules, the principles are more like warring ghosts than helpful guides. In short, precedents are more important than the doctrine of precedent; evidence is more important than the Law of Evidence; and handling statutes involves much more than understanding the principles and rules of statutory interpretation, which are not very useful in struggling with a complex statute. The doctrinal aspects may be a part of what is distinctive about legal reasoning and interpretation, but they are not the best place to begin.

It is also easy to show that the importance of such rules in practice is often greatly exaggerated, mainly by the force of the assumption that the best starting point is studying the doctrine. Often, in interpreting a particular provision, after clarification of standpoint, focusing on context or on the original perceived problem is a better next step than identifying the rules. Where the rules appear to be thin or ineffective or ghostly, important questions are worth addressing such as: what would we study if there were no rules – or very few? This line of thinking was developed in relation to the course on Juristic Technique and *How to Do Things with Rules* (Chapter 11). It was also important in my approach to Evidence (Chapter 14).

In this early development standpoint analysis took on an increasingly important role, as did a total process model of different kinds of litigation or dispute processing. In my teaching two distinctions became especially important. First, I have always emphasised direct learning of skills in contrast to colleagues who suggest that one develops these while learning substantive law. That Pick-it-up view conflates reinforcement and learning the basics. Secondly, the term 'legal method' in legal education often conflates learning about and learning how: it is one thing to study about how judges in particular cases or Lord Denning or Justice Cardozo reasoned; it is another to learn the basics of how to reason as judges or advocates do, let alone how to emulate great judges or advocates. An exercise in writing a judgment in the style of Lord Denning may combine the two, but this is asking a lot of beginning law students.[56]

The bias in traditional legal education, and even some legal-method books, has been on learning about rather than learning how. The main exception is role-playing in traditional moots, where students adopt the roles of advocates arguing 'moot points' (i.e. difficult questions of law) before a mock appellate court, sometimes composed of fellow law students or lecturers or even real judges. Moots can be excellent vehicles for preliminary training in appellate advocacy, but in my experience emphasis on etiquette, style of presentation, correct citation of authorities and thinking on one's feet often dilutes the core element of argument. The correct vocative in addressing judges, dress, body language, procedural matters, finding one's place in bulky volumes, handling interruptions, and other matters often distract attention from the core intellectual skills of constructing a valid, rational and cogent argument and presenting it persuasively.[57]

A third major step away from traditional approaches to 'legal reasoning' was to ask: in what kinds of operations do lawyers and other actors need to *reason*? The answer, of course is many. In the Preface to *How to Do Things with Rules* we summarised one answer as follows:

> Those who participate in legal processes and transactions, whether or not they are professionally qualified to practise law, are called upon to perform a variety of tasks. Professional legal practice encompasses such diverse activities as advising on the procedure of a particular course of action, collecting evidence, negotiating, advocacy, other kinds of spokesmanship, drafting statutes, regulations, contracts and other documents, predicting decisions of various types of courts, tribunals and officials, determining questions of fact, making and justifying decisions on questions of law, communicating information about legal rules, or devising improvements in the law.[58]

This overview of standard activities in which professional lawyers are involved ties up with Irving Rutter's 'Jurisprudence of Lawyers' Operations'.[59] The word 'Jurisprudence' in Rutter's title is significant. For the approach also points to a host of theoretical questions, both normative and descriptive. For example: can all these reasonings be subsumed under standard models of practical reasoning? In regard to each standard kind of operation, in what non-trivial respects does 'best practice' deviate from ordinary practical reasoning? Are there patterns of reasoning that are generalisable across different operations? For example, does reasoning in negotiation within litigation follow essentially the same pattern at every stage? How does reasoning in negotiation in civil cases differ from reasoning in plea bargaining (approved and not approved)? What are the uses and limitations of cost–benefit analysis in each of these operations? Does the Cautious Solicitor argue in the same way as the Bold Barrister and the Puzzled Judge? Some of these involve explicit reasoning and for all of them the reasons for the decision can in theory be rationally reconstructed.

In UCL in the mid-eighties I devised a module on 'Reason, Reasoning and Rationality in Legal Contexts' which was based on this kind of approach, but I was diverted to other matters and only offered it for two years with the result that I never developed it fully.[60] One of those diversions is relevant here. This was to focus on how to construct, refine and criticise arguments involving inference from evidence. With Terry Anderson and Dave Schum, I developed this in teaching and writing in courses called 'Evidence and Proof' and 'Analysis of Evidence'. Out of this came our version of 'Modified Wigmorean Analysis' (MWA) and a lot of theorising which is discussed in the chapter on Evidence (Chapter 14).[61]

For many years I have railed against the practice of treating the term 'legal reasoning' as being confined to reasoning about questions of law. This complaint has generally fallen on deaf ears, probably because this practice has deep roots in the doctrinal tradition and the quest for finding features that make law unique or special (Chapter 13). For example, some of the most rigorous discussions in Jurisprudence are concerned with whether 'legal reasoning' is a subset of moral reasoning or unique in important ways. This can be read as a sharply focused rerun of positivism versus anti-positivism debates. Recently I have completed the first draft of a paper provisionally titled 'Rethinking "Legal Reasoning": A Modest Proposal'.[62] This is a critique of the practice, suggesting that 'much of the standard literature is narrowly focused, decontextualised, susceptible to tunnel vision with severe imbalances in the attention accorded to different topics and the relations between them'. On the positive side it argues that focusing on the broader field of 'Reasoning in Legal Contexts' opens up new enquiries and some possibly surprising conclusions: for example, that reasoning about disputed questions of law and of fact in adjudication are much more similar than is commonly supposed in respect of structure, the uses of narrative,[63] and potentially shared concepts (e.g. relevance, weight, cogency, admissibility, coherence and logical consistency).[64]

I divided my critique of the traditional literature into two, reflecting the difference between mild and strong versions of legal realism (Chapter 13). The Modest Thesis argued in detail that it is obvious that decisions on questions of law potentially involving reasoning are made by different actors with multiple standpoints in a variety of contexts; that judges, lawyers and other actors also make other kinds of decision that involve a variety of kinds of reasoning; and that these other reasonings and how they relate to each other are jurisprudentially and practically important and have been largely neglected (reasoning from evidence being a partial exception). The Modest Thesis explicitly drew attention to this neglect and suggested some ways in which a broader approach to reasoning in legal contexts might be approached.

Of course, the Modest Thesis is not modest – hence the capitals – because it opens up a huge range of interrelated lines of enquiry. I also suggest that even the Modest Thesis has implications for our understandings of reasoning about questions of law: for example, that texts of such arguments, such as judgments in the Law Reports, take for granted certain conventions and standards governing law reporting; or more specifically, communication between counsel and the Bench may assume some unstated understandings shared by members of a particular legal community. Thus, many explicit legal arguments can only be explained by reference to tacit knowledge of various kinds that need to be brought to the surface; furthermore, much of such knowledge tends to be contextual and local, threatening the generality of bland decontextualised theoretical statements.[65] Thus even the Modest Thesis challenges very abstract accounts of 'legal reasoning'.

Conscious that many scholars wedded to the narrow view of 'legal reasoning' are likely to be resistant to even the Modest Thesis, in my preliminary paper I concluded:

> [S]tronger versions of the thesis of this paper challenge any suggestion that 'legal reasoning' can be understood divorced from any consideration of contextual factors. In short, decontextualised accounts of legal reasoning often distort, mislead, delude or deceive. This paper advances the Modest Thesis, but suggests that stronger versions can mount further powerful challenges to mainstream views of legal reasoning. That is my reply to those who shrug their shoulders and reply: There are of course many interesting questions about other reasonings in legal contexts, as this thesis suggests, but I am only interested in reasoning about questions of law.

This is still work in progress.[66]

Standpoint and putting texts to the question

> There was a young student from Ealing
> Who got on a bus to Darjeeling.
> The sign on the door
> Said 'Don't spit on the floor',
> So he lay back and spat on the ceiling.

This limerick has been my main vehicle for introducing the idea of standpoint. Most students remember it, but not all recall the point, which is mainly to bring out the difference between participants (on the bus) and observers (outside the limerick).[67] In teaching Evidence I have used original trial records extensively, especially Edith Thompson's stream of consciousness love letters, about which one student said: 'If you can analyse Edith's prose, you can analyse anything.' Over many years of teaching in the UCL Law Teachers' Programme I have only identified two students who claimed to have studied more than one trial record in their primary legal education, only one who had studied a limerick, and none who had analysed love letters. Is this the dead hand of the doctrinal tradition or is it that law teachers do not know how to use such wonderful materials in teaching?[68]

Broadening out from conventional teaching of 'legal method' has already been discussed in relation to the Newspaper Exercise and other materials of law study and more systematically differentiated methods of reading. The skills of reading as an intelligent law student should be added to the idea of 'thinking like a lawyer' as part of 'legal method'. But reading what? Much of orthodox 'legal method' teaching has been confined to conventional techniques for reading and using cases and statutes. It has emphasised only two types of text and a limited number of ways of reading them. The typical context was adjudication (not even litigation conceived as a total process) and the assumed standpoint has been that of a judge or a student studying reported cases. But why only two kinds of materials and these limited types of reading?[69]

Later in the Law Teachers' Programme at UCL I would ask the class: 'During your primary legal education, how many of you studied particular specimens of actual wills? Or complex commercial contracts? Or a major corporate merger? Or airline tickets (including the small print)? Or articles of incorporation? Or trial records? Or other formal legal documents?' The answers were usually none or one or two of one or two. Some had studied novels, films or plays, but were not sure why. Very few perceived newspapers or original documents as potential materials of law study. This, of course, was not a serious survey. But it does suggest some hypotheses for empirical testing in a given jurisdiction at a specified period:

(a) Law teachers rarely, if ever, use materials other than conventional ones (constitutions, treatises, statutes, reported cases, law journal articles) in teaching undergraduates or other primary legal education.

(b) Few law teachers teach systematic approaches to reading law reports for different purposes and from different standpoints; few teach systematic approaches to reading other potential materials of law study.

(c) Almost any text or artefact can be used to further sensible learning objectives for law students, if used reflectively and in a disciplined way.

During the 1980s, I tried to systematise the approach to reading any kind of text relevant to studying law, including cases, statutes, contracts, constitutions, trial records, policy documents, newspapers, and novels. After clarifying standpoint, the core of the approach is to ask three questions: What? Why? How? What is the genre, nature and provenance of this text? What are my objectives in reading it now? What method of reading is appropriate to these objectives? I condensed this into a twelve-page text, called *The Reading Law Cookbook*. It consists almost entirely of questions. I tried to persuade a publisher to take it, but he pointed out that even puffed out with some pictures it would need to sell thousands of copies to break even. I published it as an Appendix to *How to Do Things with Rules*, where like most appendices it seems to have passed largely unnoticed. A somewhat longer, wordier book, called *Reading Law*, is part of my unfinished agenda. I have kept putting off completing this, because I prefer the compactness of the *Cookbook*. Ability to put texts to the question should be a central part of 'Legal Method'.

11

Social and legal rules

[O]nly by one's going slightly taut
in the capriciousness of summer air,
is of the slightest bondage made aware?

(Robert Frost)[1]

Inky-fingered and dust in lung
over the parchment scholars pored,
gathering apples of legal dung,
heaping the gatherings on the board.
Sparrows that labored before the Lord,
Filling the tree to which they clung.
What would they do with the precious hoard?
'The rule is settled', the sirens sung.

(Karl Llewellyn)[2]

Normative pluralism

Ask yourself how many examples of rules, norms, laws, indicators, precepts, decrees, commands, guidelines, rules of thumb, standards, maxims and mantras you have encountered in the past twenty-four hours.[3] How many did you obey, observe, comply with, disregard, evade, avoid, flout or waive? To what extent were your responses to these semi-conscious or subconscious or as Robert Frost suggests?

Can one deny that rules in a broad sense are pervasive in all aspects of social life? When I ask my students to list all the examples of different rules and norms they have encountered in the past week even the lazy ones come up with at least a hundred. Their lists include moral, dietary and legal rules; the rules of sports and games – in England, the Laws of Cricket, the Rules of Association Football and the constitutive rules of chess; morning rituals, medical prescriptions and instructions, diet regimes; traffic laws, local driving etiquette, the University's parking regulations; IT protocols and algorithms; the rules of grammar, syntax and spelling; greetings, Facebook conventions; criteria of politically incorrect speech; insults and taboos; the internal governance of their law school. American students doing the newspaper exercise in 2012 (see Preface) may have encountered the American Constitution, the WTO and IMF, Florida state law, European Union Directives, Israeli law, Islamic banking practices, the rules of tennis, ritual mourning and funerals in Baghdad or Afghanistan, the Torture Convention and numerous examples of treaties, customs, conventions, folkways, mores and 'soft law'. They find codes, statutes, regulations and common law principles and rules in the law books and course materials they hump around; they notice how classes are rule-bound by tacit and express conventions in respect of time, dress, turn-taking, use of computers and the language of instruction . . . and so on through the day.

The students recognise that they have experienced extremes of *anomie* (rulelessness) and rule density; that rules and outcomes, rules and their reasons, rules and ideals are not always co-extensive; they cruise through nearly all of these, only occasionally pausing to think about them. They also realise that they have quite a rich vocabulary for talking about them. When I suggest an unfamiliar term – 'normative pluralism' – to describe this condition, they have little difficulty in grasping the basic idea, although I identify some conceptual difficulties. They agree that we all encounter normative pluralism every day of our lives.[4] We treat it as a social fact. For the most part we cope with it without thinking. Occasionally, it throws up acute dilemmas or obstacles, but on the whole we skilfully navigate our way through and round dozens of different kinds of rules as a routine form of multi-tasking. This morning you may have violated some norms of which you are unaware and noticed but disregarded some that you don't feel apply to you, such as fashions in tattoos or new conventions of spelling in text messages. Only if someone asks 'How do you manage?' are you in danger of paralysis, like the centipede who was asked how she co-ordinated her legs. We can live with normative pluralism so long as we don't ask too many questions about it.

These simple examples raise many questions in the general theory of norms. What are norms? Are the terms 'rules' and 'norms' synonymous?[5] Under what conditions is it true to say that a rule actually exists? Rules are generally assumed to be central to law, but how much do we understand about them? What counts as a norm? How many rules are there in The Sale of Goods Act, 1893? Is the whole Act, one law, one rule? Is each section a rule? Each clause? Each sub-clause? Do all norms or rules belong to some larger grouping – a system, order, code, muddle, agglomeration? Can one distinguish clearly between social norms and other kinds? Are legal rules just one species of the genus social norms? How do rules differ from empirical generalisations, habits, commands, predictions, patterns, models, routines, practices, customs, conventions? The general theory of norms transcends scientific, humanistic, and applied disciplines. It is not as well-developed as it should be because, as Frederick Schauer rightly says, it is found 'in varied literatures with too little intersection'.[6]

I will at least touch on several of these topics, but first let us start with some preliminary points: first, many of the long-standing puzzles in Jurisprudence are part of, or at least overlap with, puzzles in the general theory of norms.[7]

Secondly, this chapter is concerned with the place of rules in legal theory and the discipline of law: it emphasises the continuities between legal and other kinds of social norms, without drawing artificially sharp distinctions between them; it suggests that legal theory can draw on and contribute to the general theory of norms and can borrow from and lend insights to other disciplines.[8] Thirdly, terms like 'rule' and 'norm' have numerous shades of meaning; there are also many ways of categorising different types of norm/rule in different contexts (e.g. by source, by form, by the kind of activity they govern, by who they are for or who are their subjects). In this chapter I shall use 'norms' and 'rules' as synonyms and as broad generic terms referring to general prescriptions that fit the logical form 'If X, then Y' – if X happens then Y ought (should, must) (not), may (not), can (not) happen.[9]

Reprise

Aspects of these concerns have been touched on in earlier chapters, but in a fragmented way. They came together during my time in Belfast. To recap briefly on some of them: I have been fascinated by rules from childhood. At school I experienced the internal governance of a largely autonomous total institution, 'the House', as much a matter of politics and diplomacy as of authoritarian rule. Coping involved a quite subtle combination of learning a barbaric vocabulary, a few explicit rules and conventions, many tacit ones, a concept of 'House Spirit' and being attuned to expectations, power rivalries, privileges, hierarchy, bribes and coercion. Playing the conscientious objector in relation to the Boy Scout's oath was partly a frolic, but partly an instinctive resistance to being forced to lie; I suffered real angst in eventually swearing to the Thirty-nine Articles of the Anglican Faith as part of confirmation (Chapter 2).

At Oxford the focus was largely on doctrine.[10] I have told how I came to feel betrayed by *Salmond on Torts* and disgusted by the approach of the leading law crammers; then, inspired by R. G. Collingwood's *An Autobiography*, I developed my concept of standpoint (Chapters 3 and 10). So I learned early on that when approaching a legal topic, such as strict liability in Torts,[11] to start with the concerns or problems or 'mischiefs' that prompted the making of the rule, rather than with the rule itself and then to ask whether it was an adequate response to those concerns – whether, for example, it was under-inclusive or over-inclusive or badly expressed, and whether events after the making of the rule had changed the context significantly and, finally, who is considering or interpreting or assessing the rule(s) in what context, for what purposes?

It was at Chicago that I was first stimulated to focus seriously on the nature, making and interpretation of rules. I encountered mild forms of rule-scepticism and satirised its critics in a poem which won Llewellyn's Jurisprudence Poetry Competition for 1958:

> A young Chicago lawyer,
> Somewhat green, but sharp and frank,
> I'm trained to cook the figures
> Of a Union or a bank,
> And scramble through the brambles
> With the Cheyenne and his squaw,
> But what the facts do in court
> Is what I mean by LAW . . .
>
> The religion of the jurors
> (Kalvenistic, I suppose)
> The digestion of the judges
> (The Digest clearly shows
> That judges after breakfast
> Are much fuller than before)
> And what the facts DO in court
> Are what I mean by law.[12]

I have already explained how neither Llewellyn nor I can be sensibly interpreted as a strongly rule-sceptic; how in Khartoum and Dar I had had to struggle with both conceptual and practical problems concerning 'customary law'; and how at Yale in 1965 I became fascinated by Arthur Corbin's idea of rule-statements being 'tentative working rules', open to adjustment in each new situation. In writing KLRM I devoted a good deal of attention to Llewellyn's alleged rule-scepticism, his conception of rules in the Uniform Commercial Code and his unfinished book on *The Theory of Rules*, all of which have been touched on above (Chapter 7).

By the time I reached Belfast in 1966 I had quite a rich background of stimuli for thinking about rules, but these were far from being a coherent set of ideas. During my time at Queen's I co-taught a first-year course on Juristic Technique.[13] To start with, we followed tradition in focusing on the interpretation of reported cases and statutes. However, I soon began to deviate from standard approaches. I built on Llewellyn but went beyond him.[14]

The first step away from tradition was to reject the practice of treating the doctrine of precedent and the rules of statutory interpretation as the *starting point* for dealing with this area. If the focus was on cases and statutes as texts, and the course was about techniques of reading, one needed first to ask some Why? What? How? Questions. For example: who is interpreting what text in what context for what purposes by what means? The starting point is clarification of *standpoint*; the next step is to ask what kind of *texts* are these? How are they constructed? By whom? For what purposes? What don't they tell you? Then, what is involved in *interpretation* of any text? Is there anything special about *legal* interpretation of these texts? Where interpretation in legal contexts is *problematic*, why is this? What exactly is causing the difficulty? What resources and techniques are available to this interpreter in this context?

As soon as one has started to ponder such questions, a number of points become clear. First, there are many types of interpreter, with different roles, who confront varied kinds of texts in particular contexts for different purposes. For example, in interpreting a recent case, a solicitor advising a new client is in a different situation from a barrister using it as part of her argument in court or a judge having to determine which interpretation to adopt or a textbook writer using this case as a source for expounding the law. A law student writing an essay on the historical development of a legal topic or on Lord Denning's style of reasoning through cases is in a different position again from an academic writing a critical case note on a recent decision of the Court of Appeal. The text remains the same, but the appropriate ways to read and use it are different from each other, although they may overlap.

Secondly, if on examination one concludes that the doctrine of precedent and the rules of interpretation give only very limited guidance to legal interpreters, one is led to ask: are there shared characteristics of interpretation of legal and other kinds of texts such as the Bible, or a poem, or a play or a novel?[15]

Thirdly, there is an intimate link between reasoning and interpretation, as we saw in Chapter 10, and this raises a number of theoretical questions, such as what is the relationship between reasoning towards and justifying a decision? What is the relationship between standpoint and reasoning? What kinds of reasoning, other than about 'questions of law', typically occur in legal contexts and how are they related to each other? To what extent can all reasoning in interpretation in law be usefully treated as a subset of practical reasoning?

How to Do Things with Rules

In Belfast I collaborated in teaching Juristic Technique with several colleagues. With one of them, David Miers, I co-authored a book called *How to Do Things with Rules: A Primer of Interpretation* (*Rules*). First published in 1976, this was successful enough to go into four further editions.[16] This is the book which has given me most satisfaction as an author, partly because I enjoyed using it in teaching, partly because we invested a lot of effort in each new edition, not least to try to keep it fresh, and partly because it was both instructive and fun to work closely with David Miers.[17] I also think that theorising about rules in law and beyond is of great importance in many disciplines and that Law as a discipline has much to offer to a general theory of social rules as well as to Jurisprudence and legal practice (Chapter 20).

Rules is an introductory text, with first-year and pre-law students as the primary audience. This put severe constraints on what could be fitted into the book and how it has been perceived. The subtitle, *A Primer of Interpretation*, signals that it is introductory, concerned with both theory and skills, but limited to interpretation, mainly of legal rules and texts. For many years I have collected material and hoped to produce a second book, a cross-disciplinary monograph rather than an advanced text addressed to a wider audience, but this is still unfinished business (Chapter 20).

The Preface to *Rules* introduces the main themes:

All of us are confronted with rules every day of our lives. Most of us make, interpret and apply them, as well as rely on, submit to, avoid, evade and grouse about them; parents, umpires, teachers, members of committees, businessmen, accountants, trade unionists, administrators, logicians, and moralists are among those who through experience may develop some proficiency in handling rules. Lawyers and law students are specialists in rule-handling, but they do not have a monopoly of the art. A central theme of this book is that most of the basic skills of rule-handling are of very wide application and are not confined to law. There are certain specific techniques which have traditionally been viewed as 'legal', such as using a law library and handling cases and statutes. But these share the same foundations as rule-handling in general: they are only special in the sense that there are some additional considerations which apply to them and are either not found at all or are given less emphasis in other contexts.

The purpose of this book is to provide a relatively systematic introduction to one aspect of rule-handling: interpretation and application ... The juristic assumptions can be stated in simplified form as follows: specialists in law are characterised as much by their supposed mastery of certain kinds of skills as by their knowledge of what the law says. This is the core of the notion that law is essentially a practical art.[18]

Three important themes are central to the book: the continuities between legal rules and other kinds of social rules, factors that give rise to doubts in interpretation and the nature of interpretation as an activity.

Continuities between legal rules and other social rules

While the main focus of *Rules* is on reading, interpreting and using legal rules derived from English cases and legislation, a central thesis is that there are substantial continuities between legal rules and many other kinds of social rules, and that nearly all the factors that give rise to difficulties of interpretation are present in a great variety of types of social situation, and can cause dilemmas, frustration or perplexity in almost any kind of case, whether it is trivial or momentous, simple or complex, legal or non-legal. Chapter 1 of *Rules* contains a range of concrete examples taken from the Bible, literature, the nursery, cricket, interpersonal relationships, institutional relationships (schools, prisons, parks), as well as examples from anthropology, education and medical treatment. These largely precede conventional legal examples dealing with traffic, the protection of wildlife, bigamy cases, regulation and compliance, negligence, human rights, culminating with nine detailed passages dealing with standpoint and role, and an extensive case study relating to the creation and interpretation of a short statute.[19]

This anthology of concrete examples runs counter to the general practice of emphasising the unique or special characteristics of legal rules; rather it stresses the continuities involved in interpretation of various kinds of clearly legal rules, examples of borderline cases, and of social rules that are clearly not legal. The emphasis on problems and attempted solutions that are not peculiar to law is continued throughout, with interpretation of statutes and cases being treated as only having a few exceptional features, such as alleged rules for interpreting rules and some elaborate procedures for rule creation. There are rules about rules and even rules about rules about rules. Rule-handling is a basic human skill. This is a Llewellynesque continuation of the theme that the study of law is a humanistic discipline.

Diagnosis before prescription: the conditions of doubt

The second original feature of the book is a diagnostic model for puzzled interpreters (with almost any kind of standpoint) that presents an illustrative list of twenty-five 'conditions of doubt' that may singly or in combination be at the root of interpretive difficulties in particular cases with both legal and many other kinds of rules. The model gives examples of common conditions of doubt and is presented as an analytical tool that can be routinely used.

One of the examples we used most in *Rules* to introduce this idea was *The Case of the Legalistic Child*: Mother has made a rule that Johnny should not go into the larder without her permission. Her avowed aim is to stop Johnny eating between meals. Johnny shows that this rule is both over-inclusive and under-inclusive. First, he uses a broom to hook out a pot of jam from the larder; secondly, he sees the cat in the larder helping herself to some salmon; Johnny refuses to stop the cat, saying that he is not allowed in the larder. Johnny is involved in a number of further incidents all of which show how things can go wrong in problem-solving, rule-making, interpretation and enforcement.

Let us suppose that Father arrives home to find Mother distraught about these two incidents. Father believes in the Rule of Law and due process, so he cannot arbitrarily take Mother's side or punish Johnny. He has a dilemma. He is husband, and father, and called on to be an impartial adjudicator or arbitrator. He recognises that he has conflicting roles. He is not sure how to proceed. Believing in diagnosis before prescription, he first asks, what is my problem? And then, what problem was Mother trying to solve by making this foolish rule? She says it was to stop Johnny eating between meals. But why does Johnny do this persistently? There could be several reasons, but Father, an amateur psychologist, suspects that Johnny is craving for affection rather than snacks. So maybe he should just hug him; but that will upset Mother and Johnny might interpret this as rewarding him for being a clever Dick. Father thinks about the rule – clearly it is inadequate for its stated purpose, irrelevant to Johnny's emotional problem and over-inclusive with regard to the cat. But has Johnny broken the rule? Was using the broom constructive entry? That is a bit of a stretch, especially if we want to discourage Johnny's legalisms. In the end, Father indicates disapproval of Johnny's behaviour, acquits him and then gives both wife and son great big hugs.

Father's analysis could be pushed further, but some readers may think that he is being over-analytical already. Why not just give Johnny a clip over the ear? Well, why not in 2018? Father has been doing an exemplary analysis in diagnosing his problem. He has seemingly conflicting roles; Mother misdiagnosed the original problem and made things worse by poor rule-making; Johnny was pushing it with his interpretation, but deserves the benefit of the doubt on this occasion. For the future he should be discouraged from legalism, but he needs affection. So does Mother. Sometimes problems are best solved by hugs rather than rules.[20]

Johnny irritates some readers, but this example illustrates several points: that in interpreting rules we need to start with the initial concerns or a perceived problem; that it is important to differentiate standpoints and roles; that various other factors in the process from initial problem to stages of interpretation and enforcement can combine to create puzzlement and doubt; and that diagnosis before prescription is a good rule of thumb. The example also shows how doubts about rules can arise in seemingly simple domestic contexts as well as in complex official legal processes.

The list of conditions of doubt is divided into four rough stages: first, conditions arising before the creation of the rule, such as a misperception of the situation or problem to which the rule was a response ('the mischief'), or a lack of clear or coherent or consistent policy objectives, or the sheer complexity of the original situation or problem, or that the problem was not suitable for dealing with by rules.[21]

The second, or rule-making, stage may have led to incomplete, indeterminate or otherwise imperfect rules; for example, some are ambiguous or otherwise unclear through poor drafting, or the rule is under-inclusive or over-inclusive. Mother decreed that Johnny could not enter the larder without permission; this was under-inclusive and Johnny found more than one way round it to obtain and eat food between meals. Over-inclusiveness can prohibit innocuous or beneficial activities or cause other collateral damage, like bombing with drones.[22]

The third stage of diagnosis pinpoints events after the creation of the rule, such as changes in social context or values, new inventions, subsequent changes in other rules or just that strict application of the rule would lead to injustice in current circumstances.[23]

Finally, the fourth stage relates to special features of the present case: for instance, that it is right on the borderline (like Johnny's use of the broom or goal-line decisions in football) or there is doubt whether the procedure followed was fair or appropriate or that a decision in accordance with a clear rule would have bad consequences.

The conditions of doubt are many and various. The diagnostic model helps to answer the question: *Why* is this rule (or case) puzzling from this standpoint?

Unfortunately, many accounts of methods of interpretation omit this aspect. They start with the rules of precedent or statutory interpretation, or the general issue raised by the rule or case (e.g. 'the issue(s) of law')', or go straight to choosing one possible interpretation among two or more or to an intuitive or knee-jerk reaction. Often, they underestimate the wide range of conditions of doubt and the possibility of their combining. One key lies in the fallacy of The Way of the Baffled Medic – Prescribe First, Diagnose Later If at All – a common fault in rule-making as well as interpretation.

The chapter on conditions of doubt is the fulcrum of *Rules*. The first part of the book builds up to the conditions of doubt in relation to both routine and problematic readings of rules in fixed verbal form, rules not in fixed verbal form and of texts and situations. The diagnostic model is explained and illustrated in Chapter 6 and then is applied in detail to reading, using and interpreting legislation and cases in English municipal law and the European Union and the Council of Europe (The European Convention on Human Rights). The final chapter provides flexible protocols for approaching such materials.

The book concludes with an elementary introduction to basic aspects of reasoning about disputed questions of law and provides some elementary guidance on constructing such arguments. Overall, this is a much more systematic approach to interpretation of legal texts than we have found in the literature.[24]

Interpretation

A third theme is about the nature of interpretation, including analogies and differences between legal, literary and theological texts – a topic that I later developed in a number of other essays.[25] To make the subject manageable in this context we concentrate mainly on a quite narrow situation of a puzzled interpreter faced with a problem of determining the scope of a pre-existing rule before applying it to a particular situation or type of situation. To do this we follow the theological distinction between 'exegesis' (the strict linguistic interpretation of biblical texts) and hermeneutics (the search for the spiritual truth behind the texts). The puzzled interpreter's question is exegetical: does this case fall within the scope of this text? The answer may depend on attaching a precise meaning to particular words, even consulting a dictionary, or using a variety of aids to interpretation, including the purpose, spirit, rationale, context and other materials.

In other contexts, 'interpretation' is often used to cover both the scope of the words used and the broader or deeper meaning of the text – both the letter and the spirit. By taking a narrow sense of interpretation we skip round some of the tangled issues of interpretation in other disciplines, which would need to be canvassed in a more ambitious study of rules.[26] This enables us to take a more detached view of the tension between rigorous textual analysis and 'understanding' a rule in terms of meaning, intention, purpose and context and not to assume that the latter is always preferable to the former. That, too, depends on the context.

In *Rules* we flatly reject extreme versions of the indeterminacy of rules, viz. the idea that all rules are open to multiple interpretations. We distinguish between routine and problematic interpretations and define the latter as referring to situations where puzzlements or difficulties arise in interpreting or applying a particular rule or rules.

We are also critical of Dworkin's blanket admonition: 'make the text the best it can be'; that is fine for a conductor of Beethoven's Fifth or the producer of *Hamlet*, and can be applied to judges and authors of books in fairly typical contexts; but it leaves out many other kinds of interpretation, including interpretation to further one's own or one's client's interests (e.g. tax advisers and advocates), the cautious solicitor, the Bad Man and especially someone critical of the text. My favourite example is Dorfman and Mittelart's *How to Read Donald Duck: Imperialist Ideology and the Disney Comic*[27] in which two Marxists reveal Walt Disney's characters and texts – especially his early ones – as being racist, sexist, imperialist, fascist and almost any other kind of politically incorrect -ist as well as being bourgeois capitalist. This critique is hardly charitable, but it surely counts as an interpretation.

A special feature of *Rules* is the two substantial chapters on Legislation. They were mainly drafted by David Miers, who has become a leading expert on the subject in the UK.[28] Drawing on this insider knowledge, we have given more space to Legislation as a topic than to other sources of law because of the overriding amount, range and importance of legislation (including subordinate legislation) in the UK and the European Union.[29]

For that reason, we deal with Precedent after Legislation to emphasise the points that legislation (including subordinate legislation) is now by far the most important form of municipal law in England and Wales and most reported cases today involve the interpretation of statutes. Chapter 9 deals in depth with precedent, emphasising the richness of the *practice* of precedent in contrast with the poverty of the *doctrine* of precedent. The section on 'the ratio decidendi' is a robust analysis of what is involved in extracting propositions of law from cases by interpreters with different standpoints and explores briefly possible analogies between interpreting cases and biblical parables – another topic on which I have written at length elsewhere.[30]

Rules was designed as a flexible tool, from the teacher's point of view, with ample materials and exercises to choose from. It has been used as a general introduction to the study of law, an introduction to jurisprudence, in conversion courses for non-law graduates, in sixth forms, in extra-mural classes on clear thinking and as an introduction for civil law-trained lawyers to the supposedly peculiar ways of thought of common lawyers. It is particularly pleasing that pre-law students at A level and in access courses find it interesting and accessible. Its main aim is to be a practical introduction to common law method that combines theory and working through exercises and examples.

I have spent some time on *Rules* to illustrate how pervasive, important, varied and complex rules can be in most aspects of social life and how interpreting legal rules as a species of social rules can be helpful in bringing out the continuities of legal and other social rules rather than the special or unique characteristics of legal interpretation.[31]

12

Warwick (1972–82)

I had at the start to decide upon a generic term for the new universities – they will not be new for ever. None of the various caps so far tried have fitted. 'Greenfields' describes only a transient phase. 'Whitebrick', 'Whitestone', and 'Pinktile' hardly conjure up the grey or biscuit concrete massiveness of most of their buildings, and certainly not the black towers of Essex. 'Newbridge' is fine as far as the novelty goes, but where on earth are the bridges? Sir Edward Boyle more felicitously suggested 'Shakespeare'. But I have chosen to call them the Plateglass Universities. It is architecturally evocative; but more important, it is metaphorically accurate.

(Max Beloff)[1]

Take a Valium. Have a party. Go on a demo. Shoot a soldier. Make a bang. Bed a friend. That's your problem-solving system . . . But haven't we tried all that?

(Howard Kirk)[2]

I hate that phrase 'the real world.' Why is an aircraft factory more real than a university? Is it?

(Richard Hugo)[3]

Flashback: Geoffrey Wilson

I started in Belfast on the first of January 1966. Shortly after that I encountered Geoffrey Wilson, first in print and then in September at a conference on 'The Concept of a Law Degree' in Cambridge at which we immediately became allies and friends. At that event, Patrick McAuslan (ex-Dar, then at LSE, soon to be at Warwick) presented a sharply critical paper on the relationship between legal education and training in England. This was the first conference of the Young Members' Group (YMG) of the Society of Public Teachers' of Law (SPTL) which had been started by Tony Bradley of Trinity Hall, Cambridge – a future Dar es Salaamite.[4] For most of the next seven years or so Geoffrey Wilson was a key figure in my professional life and it was largely because of him that I moved to Warwick in 1972.

Wilson's 1966 article contained the following passage:

The time is ripe for a consideration of the part played by the law and lawyers in society and the influence that the developments in the social sciences and the increased interest in the social relations of law are having, or should have, on the administration of the law, the nature and scope of the lawyer's expertise and the scope of legal studies generally. Old views of the lawyer's role, of the proper location of the borders between judicial and legislative processes, between the courts and other dispute-settling procedures, between law and the social sciences are in the melting-pot. What is missing is a vigorous philosophy of law that will tie together the leading influences and motives behind the new developments and at the same time point the way to the future. In the United Kingdom in particular the opportunity is at last at hand to destroy once and for all the image of the English lawyer, academic as well as practitioner, as a rule-dominated conceptualist. One firm thrust and the dominance which the analytical positivists have enjoyed over the lawyer's view of his role and the scope of legal studies can be destroyed forever.[5]

Geoffrey read a draft of 'Pericles and the Plumber', my inaugural lecture at Queen's, which I delivered in January 1967.[6] This was very different in style from his polemic, but moving in the same direction. One difference between our pieces was that, although stimulated by American ideas, Geoffrey did not explicitly mention them to a Cambridge audience; whereas my lecture focused on what we might learn from the United States, but discreetly did not suggest that the UK could also learn from Dar es Salaam. Geoffrey's 1966 statement (he published several more) had some other nuanced differences. He was reacting against the specifically Cambridge version of doctrinalism and against the attitudes and pretensions of the English Bar as he perceived them. His main complaint was that the legal profession and its culture were out of touch with the realities of English society. He implied that legal education was narrow, rule-bound, insular, and unrealistic. In a later piece he compared the phrase 'English legal scholarship' to a 'disposable plastic cup ... Each adjective strengthens the message that one cannot expect much in terms of quality or long-term utility from it.'[7]

Geoffrey and I had overlapping, but significantly different backgrounds. He was four years older; his father had been a regular soldier, and he had moved through many schools as an Army child, before settling down and doing well at Peter Symonds' Grammar School in Winchester. From there he won an exhibition to Queens' College, Cambridge. After National Service, he went up to Cambridge in 1949. Both of us had wanted to read History, but read Law instead. Our motives were different. I bowed to parental pressure. According to one of his sons, conscious of his modest social background, Geoffrey chose Law because he felt that it would provide a more level playing field on which to compete with upper class 'peers'. He was soon recognised as an outstanding student. After a string of Firsts and prizes, he was immediately elected to a Research Fellowship at Queens' followed by a full Fellowship and University Lectureship in 1955.

Geoffrey spent a year at Yale and Berkeley in 1960–1, but our first experiences of the USA had been rather different: he was not a student there, he specialised in Constitutional Law, and he had a mixed reaction to American legal education. The cultures of Chicago and Yale law schools were not the same: Chicago was oriented towards leading Chicago and Wall Street Law Firms and economics and business; as I learned in 1965, Yale looked more towards Washington DC, the softer social sciences and public policy.

As a person, Geoffrey was highly intelligent, interested in music, fine art, ritual and bargain hunting. His home was like an untidy museum. He exhibited a striking mix of charm, scepticism and penetrating observation. My most vivid memory was that he asked good questions, especially in job interviews and in seminars, where his probing could be devastating. Some found him quite abrasive. I soon realised, that despite his polemical attacks on its approach to Law, he really loved Cambridge, including the rituals and privileges and – for him – a laid-back atmosphere. He wrote well, but only bothered to publish when he felt there was a good reason. Except for a quietly subversive casebook on Constitutional and Administrative Law, by 1966 he had not published much and was not under pressure to do so.[8] He loved teaching and was popular among undergraduates: he distributed doughnuts in lectures, lent prints to Queens' students and played a full role in College life.

About a year after we first met, Geoffrey was appointed to the Founding Chair of Law at the University of Warwick with a clear mandate to innovate. During the next phase we had many discussions about his plans. I have vivid memories of long walks in the Mountains of Mourne and a quite extensive correspondence. I could not join Warwick at the start as there was only one Chair. Anyway, Queen's had treated me generously, so I felt that I could hardly leave so soon after arriving. However, two of Geoffrey's original team, Patrick McAuslan and Sol Picciotto, were ex-Dar es Salaam, and so in the early years Geoffrey had to listen to a lot of 'In Dar es Salaam we . . . '.

It is difficult to assess how much Geoffrey and I influenced one another at this stage. We bounced ideas off each other and let our imaginations fly. I had had the experience of founding a new law school. We had different interpretations of American law school culture and American Legal Realism. He was strongly committed to undergraduate teaching, while I was already becoming more interested in postgraduate courses. I almost certainly tried, but failed, to persuade him of the advantages of a four-year honours degree, such as those at Queen's and Edinburgh. In those days such degrees attracted mandatory grants. The Warwick story might have been very different if I had succeeded on this issue.[9]

Geoffrey was just one of a number of British academic lawyers of our generation who rebelled against their initial legal education and sought to develop alternatives. His contribution was unique in that he seized the opportunity to establish a radically different law school in an innovative environment and to implement an exceptionally coherent view of what that institution should be. Appointed to Warwick two years after the university was founded, he had almost three years in which to develop an ethos, design a path-breaking undergraduate curriculum and recruit a lively team of like-minded younger colleagues from several countries.

In the early years Warwick was clearly 'Wilson's Law School'. It is known today for having pioneered a 'law in context' approach. Geoffrey's vision was more specific. The key ingredients were starting with real-life social and political problems rather than formal legal rules; freeing legal studies from insularity by emphasising foreign, European Community and international law, thereby anticipating concerns with 'globalisation'; and arguing that the discipline of law can offer distinctive lenses for understanding society. He insisted that Warwick was a Law school, not a cross-disciplinary 'cafeteria of Sunday supplement law'. Although cautious about collaboration with social scientists (he preferred 'two disciplines in one head'), he played a major role nationally in developing socio-legal studies in the UK.

Geoffrey's most striking and important departure was the initial under-graduate curriculum at Warwick. This emphasised transnational law and included several subjects not then normally studied by undergraduates. Some were classified by socially relevant categories rather than legal concepts: Housing, Planning, Companies, Labour Relations, Finance and Taxation, Family, Welfare, and Consumer Law.[10] When challenged about the number of compulsory subjects, his standard riposte was: 'How can anyone understand a capitalist society without having studied both Labour Law and Company Law?'[11] 'Anyone' included non-lawyers.

Geoffrey's and my ideas and approach were very similar. Rather than the vague rubric 'law in context', the early Warwick mantra was 'broadening the study of law from within' to which he gave a quite specific meaning. However, there were some differences, which in time became more pronounced. He considered himself to be reacting against rule-dominated positivism and the culture of the legal establishment; my central concern was the relationship between 'theory' and 'practice'. I had not entirely rejected 'positivism' in a fairly narrow sense. I still believed that it is often useful to distinguish law as it is from law as it ought to be and that conceptual analysis is important. Geoffrey leaned towards Roscoe Pound's sociological jurisprudence; my approach was more Llewellynesque – more particularistic, less schematic. Geoffrey favoured studying foreign legal systems on their own terms rather than from a comparative perspective; his focus was on Europe; mine was still on East Africa and, more generally, the Global South. I was prepared to concentrate on English laws and institutions in their own historical, social and political contexts; he was mostly concerned to study contemporary local social and political problems from essentially a Fabian point of view. At the time I found British political attitudes about Left and Right quite parochial and insular, and was more concerned with North–South relations, colonialism, neocolonialism, 'development' and diffusion of law. Geoffrey considered him-self to be both a public lawyer and an endlessly inquisitive, sometimes quirky, intellectual. He was often quite dismissive of 'theory' and of Jurisprudence (which was quite weak at Cambridge); I considered myself to be a theorist with some expertise in private law. These were mainly differences of emphasis, but there were also quite strong contrasts of personality. Nevertheless, we got on quite amicably until he abruptly stepped down from the Chairmanship and, reluctantly, I had to take over.

In 1973, already separated from his first wife, Geoffrey took up with a beautiful and intelligent younger woman. By then, such relationships were generally accepted – A. B. Weston's adventures in Dar had been much more spectacular. Unfortunately, Marcia was the current wife of a junior colleague and that was considered scandalous, not least by the partners of younger staff. My memory of the details is a blur. Geoffrey took leave of absence in February 1973, but did not officially resign the Chairmanship until 1974. Happily, the marriage was a success; they produced three talented sons and a close-knit, almost self-sufficient family. Geoffrey exchanged the role of paterfamilias of a lively group of younger colleagues to actual, engaged fatherhood. He stayed on at Warwick as Professor until he retired in 1997, but after 1973 played an increasingly marginal role in the development of the Law School.

Reluctant Chairman

I found myself holding the fort in an unsettled period, not only related to Geoffrey's personal life. At national level in 1973–4 there were major strikes, the fall-out from Bloody Sunday, increased IRA bombs, two General Elections, inflation, a recession, the three-day week, entry to the EEC, the oil crisis, apartheid, the Cold War and much else besides. Almost the only good news was that Warwick's most famous alumnus, Steve Heighway, scored for Liverpool when they won the 1974 FA Cup Final. Things were hardly less turbulent in Warwick University; there were hangovers from earlier troubles on campus[12] and some uncomfortable divisions within the Department.

Having to take over from Geoffrey at short notice was extremely inconvenient. I had just settled into my project on Evidence and had applied for a major research grant. I felt that I had done enough administration in Dar and Belfast. I was Acting Chair, then Chair of the Law School from February 1973 to September 1975 and again through 1977–8, a total of about thirty months. My friend and ally, Patrick McAuslan, took over from me in the interim on the understanding that I would serve another year on my return. During 1975–7 I was away from Warwick because I managed to get a major research grant for my work on Evidence and spent an academic year as a Visiting Fellow at Wolfson College Oxford, followed by visiting appointments at the University of Virginia and Northwestern University Law School.

Much of my energy as Chairman was devoted to keeping the Law School running, though not always smoothly, recruiting staff, fighting our corner at University level in a time of cuts and maintaining good public relations. On the whole the teaching went well, research less so. Some of my younger colleagues were more interested in micro-politics than serious research: there was even a suggestion that research and publication were 'careerist', an idea quite contrary to the University's and my own ethos. On the other hand, they were enthusiastic teachers and, I think, for students it was a very good time to be at Warwick.

Some saw committee work as a source of power, until I renamed all administrative tasks as 'chores' – perhaps my greatest achievement. That worked for most administration, except appointments, the most hotly contested sphere in my time. Formally, the appointments process was centralised at University level, usually with the Chairman and one other colleague serving on the Appointments Committee for lectureships and above. However, the Law School set up its own unofficial elected appointments committee, which drew up a long-list, interviewed candidates, and then sent a brief short-list up to the centre. This provided an opportunity for hotly contested elections, intrigue, cabals and an arena for debating conflicting views. It survived unnoticed by the University until a candidate sent a claim for travel expenses to the Registrar of the University rather than to the Law School, who used the visiting speakers' fund. The University declared the departmental appointments committee unconstitutional, but our committee still continued to operate underground for a time.

Later I used this as a fable to illustrate the idea of interposed norms – our elections were more 'real' than the University's Charter and Statutes, which were 'surface law'.[13] However, the power of the illegal body was also fictitious, for it soon became clear to me that for many colleagues their sense of power came from conducting interviews rather than influencing outcomes – so that after a day of subjecting candidates to tough questioning, the interviewers often failed to report on the interview. When the Chairman attended the University Committee, he treated the Law School's informal committee as purely advisory and not very forthcoming with its advice.

Soon after I took over as Chairman, I agreed to a demand from younger colleagues to hold a discussion on revising the curriculum. The proposal was made in terms of student choice, but they clearly also wanted to innovate. The outcome was that some of Wilson's preferred courses were made optional and some new ones were introduced. In my view this was inevitable because of the expansion of the School and colleagues wishing to design their own courses. However, I had the strong impression that Geoffrey blamed me for diluting his coherent vision of an undergraduate degree. I agree that something important was lost, but with an expanding institution such a specific ethos and limited curriculum were unsustainable. There would have been much less of a problem if we had had a four-year LLB. I would have been able to make the case for keeping Company and Labour Law compulsory and having some advanced options as well.

However, we did to some extent retain some fact-based classification of subjects – that is, that some traditional courses were redistributed on the basis of a non-legal or social rather than a legal category; for example, Land Use and

Housing Law and Housing Finance for Property, or Evidence and Proof for the Law of Evidence.[14] This raised questions about the recognition of the Warwick LLB for exemption from Part I of the Bar and Solicitors' examinations.[15] In dealing with the legal professions I chose diplomacy rather than confrontation. The first problem was that we did not have a course called 'Torts' – 'torticles' had been distributed among Civil Liberties (defamation), Land and Housing (trespass and nuisance) and Company Law (economic torts), Evidence and Proof (law of evidence) and a course on accidents.[16] Nor did we have a course on Equity and Trusts. Over a bottle of Claret I negotiated a deal with Robert Goff QC (later Lord Goff), whose lectures on defamation I had attended at Oxford.[17] He was representing both barristers and solicitors. He made it clear that he was not concerned with the quality of the Warwick degree, but rather with closer supervision of the then emerging polytechnic law schools. We both realised that this business of recognition of first degrees in Law was a charade – illustrated by the fact that, so far as I can tell, no proposal for a single honours degree in Law was ever rejected in the post-Ormrod period. Only mixed degrees (like Law and Politics) caused problems. Nevertheless, a great many academic lawyers experienced unnecessary angst or unwarranted idleness (no new courses) because of this requirement. Later recognition of degrees became a major political issue as the number of core subjects was quietly expanded. That conflict continues in 2017 with the Solicitors' Regulation Authority trying to impose what is in practice a pre-Warwick regime.[18]

This is not the place to try to reconstruct the early history of the Warwick Law School, which is attracting the attention of several legal historians. Here I shall confine attention to two topics: 'Warwickisation' (rethinkings of traditional fields), and some of my external activities during this period. 'Law in context' and 'R/realism' as ideas are dealt with in Chapter 13.

Rethinkings

Perhaps the most interesting aspect of Warwick for me was the injunction to every member of academic staff to rethink their subject in a broader way. This applied first to teaching and then more generally to research and scholarship. As Editor of the Law in Context series over time I recruited more than a dozen Warwick authors, including some who never completed their projects. Ten produced excellent books.[19] Three of them, Patrick Atiyah, Patrick McAuslan and Michael Chesterman, deserve attention here; in Chapter 14 I shall give an account of my own efforts to broaden the study of Evidence in Law.

Some years ago, I entered 'rethinking' as a keyword in the University of Miami Law Library catalogue and it came up with 138 books, of which 100 or so had the actual word in the title. The great majority of these had been published in the previous twenty years. There were, of course, many more articles. Any scholarly enquiry requires some rethinking, but these referred mainly to whole sub-disciplines, such as International Law or Comparative Law, or less extensive, but substantial, subjects such as Evidence or Negligence. Many of the titles implicitly promised a more or less radical approach. Such large-scale rethinkings can be responses to dissatisfaction with traditional or settled ways of thought or to perceived challenges from changing circumstances, as with 'globalisation', or to self-criticism or more complex combinations of factors. The titles often carry a suggestion of self-promotion.

It is worth examining some examples of specific rethinkings that I have experienced at close quarters which are directly relevant to the themes of this book. I have already described how Hart introduced 'the revolution in philosophy' into Jurisprudence. In Chicago, experience of an American law school brought to light some fundamental aspects of my dissatisfaction with my English legal education; in Khartoum, and more explicitly in Dar es Salaam, in the radically different contexts of two newly independent countries we had to reconsider almost everything we had learned about law. I will deal later with my thoughts about how globalisation challenges settled assumptions about particular topics and about Western traditions of academic law in general (Chapter 18) and I have illustrated some culture shocks. But there is something special about the programmatic approach adopted at Warwick, as illustrated by the work of these three colleagues.

Patrick Atiyah

The first in time was a book by Patrick Atiyah, who had been my colleague in Khartoum and was the first person I invited to contribute to the Law in Context series. I asked him to do a book on regulation or commercial law in practice; however, he said that he was bored with contract and commerce. He wanted to do a number on Torts. Remembering my 'betrayal' by *Salmond*, I accepted immediately. Within a relatively short time Patrick produced a book, *Accidents, Compensation and the Law* (1970),[20] that met all my complaints about *Salmond*. He critically analysed the common law action for negligence in the context of a total picture of accidents in society and an overview of different kinds of compensation system. Focusing mainly on negligence, he dealt with insurance, settlement out of court, the unpredictability of damage awards (he later wrote a book on *The Damages Lottery*)[21] – in short, all of the major omissions from *Salmond*. He demonstrated the incoherence and inconsistencies both within the Torts regime and in relation to other compensation regimes such as private insurance, criminal injuries compensation and social security benefits – so-called 'systems' based on different, often confused ideologies. The book was a highly critical account of the existing Torts regime in both design and practical operation and made quite radical proposals for reform. Nearly fifty years later the book is in its eighth edition (2013). Atiyah's proposals have not been implemented and, because (rather than in spite) of that, generations of students (by no means all) have been saved from the account of negligence that misled me as a student. This marvellous book did not replace the doctrinal texts, but placed them in a radically different framework and most later books have since acknowledged the relevance at least of these other factors.[22] *Accidents, Compensation and the Law* was published before I recruited Patrick to Warwick in 1973. There he devoted himself to a contextual history of contract, *The Rise and Fall of Freedom of Contract* (1979), which he had nearly completed before he moved to the Chair of English Law at Oxford in 1977.

Atiyah's method is interesting in contrast to traditional Torts textbooks. First, his *standpoint* was of a mildly Fabian legal scholar talking *about* the Torts system in general, rather than expounding its rules in detail. Secondly, it was critical, with a clear sense of underlying *political values and rationales*. Thirdly, it was concerned with the *actual operation* of the relevant law; fourthly, it substituted 'compensation for accidents' (not a doctrinal concept) for 'Torts' and 'Negligence' as *the organising concept* and this provided a basis for comparing different compensation regimes and showing up the injustices, incoherence and anomalies of the situation. Fifthly, he explained the situation largely in terms of a *history* of piecemeal growth without any coherent guiding principles or ideology. Finally, the book is explicitly addressed to law students to help them to *understand* the existing system; the explicit *critique and recommendations* were largely confined to a relatively short last chapter. Brilliantly edited and updated by Peter Cane since 1987, for me this is a model of excellence for a 'contextual' work. There is no ideal type for such works, but anyone wanting to rethink a doctrinal field can learn a great deal from it.[23]

The McAuslan legend

Patrick McAuslan and I were two of the three co-founders of the Law Faculty in Dar; we had jointly drafted the entry on Law in the prospectus for schools (Chapter 5); I think of that as the first 'law in context' manifesto; Patrick was also a founder member of Warwick Law School; he had arrived before me and had already occupied Land Law and Planning; Evidence was my second choice to Land; it is a good thing that Patrick got there first because he did a much better job than I could have done; he pioneered two highly original courses and later on became a leading consultant on land reform and urban planning in forty-two countries (his estimate), mainly in the Global South.[24]

Rather than try to describe how Patrick actually constructed his pioneering courses on Land Law and Land Use Planning, I have tried to reconstruct his approach as an ideal type. I have called this 'the McAuslan legend'.[25] The approach goes something like this. The first step is, like Atiyah, to choose a suitable organising category, preferably fact-based,[26] that is directly related to some social phenomenon or socio-political set of problems: for example, land or land use rather than Real Property, or Property or some other abstract legal concept. The second step is to construct a total picture of the social phenomena involved. In my version Patrick takes out a map of England and Wales and asks how much land is there and what are the main uses to which it is put? How are these distributed statistically and geographically (demographic realism)? Land use can be roughly categorised as industrial and commercial, agriculture, housing, transport, amenity (including sport), security (including the armed services), governance and administration. With regard to each use ask: Who are the main actors and legal persons affected? What are the main institutions and transactions involved in each type of land use? What gives rise to disputes? And so on. The third step is to acknowledge that though this construction of a total picture of land and its uses sets a broad context, it immediately reveals that for the purposes of designing a course or a student work, quite difficult selection is necessary.

Patrick decided to focus on two categories, one traditional (housing) and one almost completely undeveloped in legal education in UK at the time (problems of land use planning).[27] The choice of these two topics from a much wider field could be justified by their social importance, their interest, their practical value for intending practitioners and their link with tradition. Conventional Real Property courses focused very largely on housing, the 'house' typically a mansion called Blackacre, with a butler, footmen and six maids' bedrooms in attics upstairs. Warwick students would be expected to be familiar with the basic concepts, principles, rules and transactions of property law; housing is a good vehicle for studying these in context.

In this instance there is still room for some more demographic realism; for example, where are the houses and where are the people? The answers to these questions revealed some significant gaps in traditional treatments, in which almost no mention was made of the homeless, squatters, travellers ('gypsies') and council house tenants who, before Mrs Thatcher's reforms, constituted over 50 per cent of occupiers in England and Wales. No wonder that in the late 1960s there was felt to be something 'unreal' about Blackacre – like Downton Abbey without the downstairs. Each of these categories is associated with complex problems and legal responses, involving many fields of law – for instance, issues of discrimination in relation to public housing, which had been the tinder for reigniting the Troubles in Northern Ireland.[28]

Once again, this approach shows up the complexity of problems, the intermingling of different fields of law and acute issues of selection. Patrick had the luxury of two full compulsory courses spread over two years and he still had to make some hard choices about focus and educational objectives. Someone adopting exactly the same approach could have come up with a very different design for their course or a contextual book.[29]

Michael Chesterman

Michael Chesterman, an outstanding Australian lawyer, contributed two books to the Law in Context series. The first, *Charities, Trusts and Social*

Welfare, was an excellent social history of charity law; the second, now in its fifth edition with new editors, has become one of the most respected student books on Trusts, while maintaining a contextual approach with a commercial focus.[30] His standpoint and approach were different in each book, and different again from those of Atiyah and McAuslan.

These three examples show how flexible, yet related, contextual approaches can be and how they can be accepted as both scholarly and innovative at the same time. I shall deal in the next chapter with the meanings of 'law in context' and its relationship to R/realism and in Chapter 14 with my own attempts to rethink Evidence.

Outside Work

Nearly all academic lawyers undertake work beyond their formal duties.[31] A few are paid, most do a lot *pro bono* or for nominal amounts, as with external examining. During the 1970s I continued to serve as an external examiner in Africa and in English polytechnics, mainly to support these institutions. It was also a good way of networking and keeping plugged in to the gossip circuit. At various times I was involved locally in extra-mural teaching in Coventry, the Warwick District Community Relations Council (Chairman for two years), as the one agnostic on the Bishop of Coventry's Council for Social Responsibility (the most intellectual of these pursuits) and in various legal education and publishing activities, including a few consultancies. I attended conferences, was particularly active in the Society of Public Teachers of Law and the UK Association for Legal and Political Philosophy. I was also much involved in the Bentham Project, which will be discussed below.[32]

Warwick was still a 'new university' when I joined. It was an intellectually exciting place and politically riven. The first Vice-Chancellor, Jack Butterworth, had from the start favoured close links with industry; this was not favoured by those on the left and this led to conflicts described in Edward Thompson's polemic, *Warwick University Ltd*, published shortly before I arrived. Warwick has since been the most consistently highly rated of that generation of plate-glass universities; some of the credit for this must go to Butterworth, who made some brilliant appointments to founding chairs and let them get on with the job: Mathematics, English, Bio-Chemistry, History and Social History (who barely spoke to each other) and Economics were all outstanding and leaders in innovation. Particularly when Chairman, I was involved in various committees and working parties at University and other levels, some quite rewarding, some acrimonious, but rarely dull. All of this was a fairly typical set of undertakings for a middle-aged Law Professor, except that Warwick in the 1970s was an intellectually exciting place.

Despite all of these activities, I managed to do a fair amount of research and writing. At both Warwick and UCL it was sometimes suggested to me that I was spreading myself too thin both over outside activities and the range of topics I wrote about. This was partly true, but I can plead in mitigation that my intellectual interests were not as diverse as they seemed: Bentham was relevant to Jurisprudence, Evidence, and torture; I treated my work on Evidence as a case study of broadening any field and what is involved in a 'law in context' approach; the projects on law publishing and information were directed to strengthening the infrastructure of academic law and my writings in the area mostly linked legal education and scholarship with high- and middle-order theory. The crucial point was that I had one major project: from 1972 for all of my ten years at Warwick and well beyond that. Evidence was my priority. Bentham, Legal R/realism, contextual approaches, reasoning in legal contexts and comparative procedure (in which I dabbled) were all part of that project. Towards the end of my time at Warwick I published a number of 'foothill' essays, trying out my ideas on particular topics; several of these became an integral part of my three main books on the subject,[33] which will be discussed in the chapter on Evidence. All of these were published years after I left Warwick, but the groundwork had been done during my time there. I ranged widely but I was not a dilettante. The next two chapters deal with my project on Evidence (Chapter 13) and Legal Education (Chapter 14), one scholarly and one mainly activist. Both of these belong to the Warwick period, but also overlap with the next phase after I moved to UCL in 1983 (Chapter 14).

My time at Warwick was both very stimulating and quite stressful. I thought highly of both the University and the Law School. However, after 1980 I felt that my scholarly work was being interfered with by academic administration and politics and I feared that I might be pressured into being Chairman again for several more years. Early in 1982 Jeffrey Jowell, the Dean and Head of Department at UCL Faculty of Laws, sounded me out about my possible interest in being successor to Professor Lord Lloyd of Hampstead as Quain Professor of Jurisprudence. I hesitated because Laws at UCL had the reputation of being very traditional and rather complacent, although Jowell was trying hard to change that. Eventually, after the post was advertised, I applied, was interviewed and was made an offer, which I accepted after assurances that I would not be under pressure to be Dean for at least several years. I took up the post on 1 January 1983. The next phase (1983–99) is covered in Chapters 15–19.

13

Jurisprudence, law in context, realism and doctrine

Natives of all sorts and foreigners; men of business and men of pleasure; parlor men and backwoodsmen; farm-hunters and fame-hunters; heiress hunters, gold-hunters, buffalo-hunters, bee-hunters, happiness-hunters, truth-hunters, and still keener hunters after all these hunters . . . Fine ladies in slippers and mocassined squaws; Northern speculators and Eastern philosophers; English, Irish, Germans, Scotch, Danes . . . modish young Spanish Creoles, and old-fashioned French Jews; Mormons and papists . . . In short a piebald parliament, an Anarcharsis Cloots Congress of all kinds of that multiform pilgrim species, man.

(Herman Melville)[1]

Theorising Jurisprudence

Look at the indexes of panoramic Jurisprudence readers for students, such as Freeman and Lloyd's *Introduction to Jurisprudence*, and one can identify many of the characters in Herman Melville's evocation of a dockside crowd. It seems like Babel; small wonder that students are bemused. The aim of this chapter is to give an account of my first concerted attempt to develop a coherent conception of Jurisprudence as a field and as an activity and to examine the ideas of law in context, realism and legal doctrine in relation to this. Most of these ideas were formed while I was contemplating the move from Belfast to Warwick and after my arrival in 1972. My thinking on these issues has developed since then, but the basic ideas were formed in that period.

In the first twenty or so years of my career I was learning and teaching about various pockets of Jurisprudence without thinking much about the nature, scope and point of the field as a whole. I was theorising, but doing it rather than reflecting on it. I accepted Llewellyn's view of Jurisprudence as dealing with general questions about Law that includes 'any careful and sustained thinking about any phase of things legal, if the thinking seeks to reach beyond the practical solution of an immediate problem in hand'.[2] I quite liked Julius Stone's rough working classification of the subject matters into three parts for the purposes of presentation, which I now render as Analytical, Normative and Empirical. Even then, I realised that understanding legal phenomena and ideas involves concepts, values and facts and that any rough taxonomy of this vast, ill-defined field was in danger of treating 'schools' or 'isms' as competing rather than complementary approaches.

My working assumptions about Jurisprudence as a field developed slowly over time. The story can be summarised as follows: I was inspired by Hart's approach, but was never satisfied with his agenda.[3] What I took away from Llewellyn's course on 'Law in Our Society' was a broad view of theorising as an activity in which he emphasised a horse-sense view of Jurisprudence for 'the hundred thousand' rather than constructing a rigorous, abstract Philosophy of Law or a Science. What I liked best was the idea that the main aim of such a course was getting students to relate their beliefs and attitudes and working assumptions about law to their views about politics, morality and the cosmos, and to reflect on them critically in moving towards a working whole view of law and life. After that, in teaching Jurisprudence I tried to adopt Llewellyn's learning objectives, but used careful reading and conversing with original texts (exercises in self-definition) as the main means of achieving this. One's experiences in Khartoum and Dar es Salaam daily challenged parochial common law assumptions and, over time, some of the mainstream Western assumptions of academic law (Chapter 19), but not to the extent of abandoning either Hart or Llewellyn or my efforts to build bridges between them.[4] In Belfast, with a talented, but individualistic, team, in three courses we explored many juristic texts, issues and enclaves without trying to develop one overarching coherent view of the vast field and heritage. Rather I saw it as a house with many mansions or like Melville's evocation of a dockside crowd, a view that I presented satirically in 'The Great Juristic Bazaar'.[5]

Moving from Belfast to Warwick stimulated me to reflect on what mainstream Jurisprudence, and Llewellyn's particular take on it, might contribute to the Warwick project of 'broadening the study of law from within'. The outcome was 'Some Jobs for Jurisprudence', my inaugural lecture at Warwick.[6] It is worth pausing to consider this lecture as it was my first attempt to theorise my view of theory – that is, to think about and articulate my conception of Jurisprudence, the place of Legal Philosophy within it, theorising as an activity and its potential contributions to the health of Law as a discipline, largely anticipating the views set out in Chapter 1.

For my Warwick audience I had several aims: first, to reaffirm my commitment to the Law School's ethos – in particular, that it was a *Law school* committed to a broader approach across all legal fields;[7] secondly, to emphasise the open-endedness and fluidity of the aspiration to broaden the study of law from within: that it was not committed to any particular ideology (Warwick was perceived as very left-wing) and that we did not seek to replace one orthodoxy by another; rather that we should build bridges with neighbouring social sciences, but still retain links with mainstream Jurisprudence and Legal Philosophy; thirdly, to warn that Law is more participant-oriented than our neighbours in the social sciences and humanities with whom we hoped to establish links; and, finally, that the idea of 'law in context' does not involve denying the importance of exposition of doctrine or conceptual analysis.

I also wanted explicitly to address the question: what can Jurisprudence offer to the enterprise of broadening the study of law from within? In the published version this was expressed in terms of five functions of legal theorising: the conduit function,[8] high theory, the development of working theories for participants, theories of the middle order (in the Mertonian sense) and the synthesising function.[9] I suggested that the last three had been neglected.

This lecture was published over forty years ago. I had not reread it in full for about twenty years. When I did revisit it, it seemed rather a good statement of my present views.[10] Today I adopt a global perspective, I place more emphasis on non-state law and legal pluralism and critical examination of the working assumptions and presuppositions of oneself and others; my views on Evidence at the time were rudimentary;[11] but the ideas on the roles of theorising, the emphasis on standpoint and participant perspectives, the contrast between English and American reactions to 'formalism' and the interpretation of 'law in context' could all have been expressed very similarly in 2018. So were my reasons for promoting Law as a potentially great humanistic discipline.[12]

American Legal Realism (ALR) and law in context

This is a good place to say something about the term 'law in context' and its relationship to ALR. It has been applied to the series of that name, to the approach pioneered at Warwick, to a loosely labelled 'movement' and to my own general approach. These usages are all connected, but there are nuanced differences of meaning. It is not a field concept like 'Socio-legal Studies' or 'Sociology of Law' and it is broader than both. Rather it applies to a general approach or perspective in contrast to narrow doctrinal approaches.

We have seen that this term was our third choice of title for the series.[13] I rather liked it, largely because it was vague and open-ended, but not meaningless. It would have been foolish of the editors of a book series to give the term more precision. We wanted broader works than traditional, which went beyond purely expository or doctrinal works, but broader in what respects was left open.

As editors we did not have much difficulty in deciding whether a proposal was 'contextual' enough, though there were, of course, borderline cases. What we did learn was that authors – and others – interpreted 'law in context' in many ways. Some thought that just inserting or tacking on a bit of 'context' as a prelude to exposition was enough, but that was not what we intended. During the 1970s and 1980s there was a distinct tendency to equate a contextual approach with policy orientation. Much excellent reformist writing has been contextual, especially since evidence-based policy-making became fashionable. But much contextual work is descriptive, explanatory and interpretive without necessarily being prescriptive. Atiyah's *Accidents, Compensation and the Law* was regarded by some as radical, even extreme. But the core of the book was a fresh framework for looking at and contrasting different compensation systems.[14] Policy and reform have featured in many books in the series, but not usually as central. For quite a few they are marginal. 'Law in context' should not be equated with 'instrumentalism' or 'legal liberalism'; so far as ideology is concerned, both the term and the series are open-ended.

The catchphrase for Warwick's mission was 'broadening the study of law from within'. That is a bit more precise than 'law in context' and refers to an aim rather than an approach. I am not sure whether it was Geoffrey Wilson or I who coined that phrase. I thought 'within' caught Geoffrey's vision very nicely: Warwick was to be a law school; the staff would be almost entirely legally qualified, though some would have two or more disciplines in one head, and the graduates would get an LLB degree that would be recognised for professional exemption.

Of the three 'rethinkings discussed in Chapter 12, there is some affinity between the methods used by Atiyah and McAuslan, but Chesterman's approach was quite different. My strategy for rethinking Evidence, as we shall see (Chapter 14), was different again. I do not like being labelled, but 'law in context' is better than most: I advocate thinking in terms of 'total pictures', mainly to set a broad context; I think that judicial and other related decisions are best studied in the context of a total process model of litigation and that the approach applies beyond litigation and dispute-processing to all kinds of legal 'action'. Normally rules need to be interpreted, applied, studied and used with reference to context.[15] Whether the relevant 'context' is mainly historical, social, political or something else depends on the particular enquiry and its standpoint;[16] I am careful not to treat law as context, and to give doctrine its place; for me, 'law in context' as an approach challenges the idea that Law is an autonomous discipline or that there are pure forms of legal knowledge; I think that understanding law requires openness to other disciplines, but I am a jurist rather than a philosopher or a social scientist or historian; law is my primary discipline, as it is for most others who claim to use this approach.

In academic law a 'movement' is vaguer than a 'school' but more specific than a trend.[17] The Law in Context Movement has been similar to the American Realist Movement (ALR) in being centred on university law schools, in mainly involving a fresh generation of younger law teachers and in claiming to be in reaction against a dominant orthodoxy. As in America, there were a few individual scholars who had earlier advocated broader approaches to academic law.[18] However, in the UK in the 1960s the context and the intellectual climate were quite different from the United States in the heyday of ALR. The post-World War II welfare state, the end of Empire, the rapid expansion of higher education, a tradition of professional formation outside the universities, an academic milieu more hospitable to socialist and Marxist ideas and many other factors made up a contrasting background. Some of the advocates of broader approaches had studied in American law schools, but others, like myself, had returned from teaching in newly independent countries, where they had needed to confront problems of adapting or replacing English law in radically different political, economic and social conditions. It was natural for them to emphasise 'context'.

Intellectually, there were some significant differences between ALR and British contextual approaches. Both largely defined themselves in terms of a revolt against a caricatured 'formalism': in America the prevailing orthodoxy ('Langdellism') had been charged with three main weaknesses: a deluded emphasis on deductive logic, over-concentration on higher courts and a lack of empirical concern with the realities of the law in action. This resulted in a divergence between those who wished to develop more sceptical, policy-oriented approaches to case-method teaching and those who wished to develop the study of law as an empirical social science – two different enterprises. In the 1960s and 1970s the English version of 'formalism' was also criticised for being out of touch with the 'law in action' (both professional legal practice and the operation of law in society); it was also castigated for being narrowly focused, educationally illiberal and politically conservative. On my interpretation, in the UK different diagnoses prompted varied prescriptions: a more humanistic pedagogy, interdisciplinary co-operation, empirical research, progressive law reform and radical social-theoretical critiques.[19] If the central plank of legal realism is the importance of focusing on the law in action, the main proposition attributable to contextual approaches is that for most purposes in studying law the study of rules or doctrine alone is not enough.[20] What is enough is left open.

The label is vague, but not devoid of content. 'Law in context' is not a theory of or about law, nor is it a school or a branch of legal philosophy. It overlaps with 'realism' and has a loose historical connection with ALR. What is significant as 'context' itself depends on context. For example, in writing about a specific juristic text, the concerns and situation of the author are nearly always relevant; historical and cultural background are often important; the text may belong to some specific literary or scholarly genre; the text may be a contribution to a contemporary debate; and so on. What is significant depends on the enquiry. *Contexere* ('to weave') suggests interdisciplinary perspectives, but 'law in context' is broader than that; for example, it includes but goes beyond socio-legal studies which applies mainly to empirical research using social scientific methods.[21]

The idea of 'law in context' is not rooted in a particular or distinctive general theory of or about law. The term can be restricted to state or official law or can be used more broadly. It accommodates positivists and non-positivists, students of legal pluralism and advocates of liberal legal education and of enlightened vocational training. It can accommodate a wide range of political views, although it has a 'progressive' tendency. It is not an 'ism'.[22] Such an approach favours thinking in terms of total pictures and total processes, as is illustrated by Atiyah and McAuslan. Similarly, students of civil and criminal procedure set the detailed study of contested trials and appeals in the context of a total process model, emphasising the interrelationship between different stages in the process of litigation, the relative rarity of contested trials and successful appeals and the importance of settlement out of court, plea bargaining and other forms of dispute resolution.[23]

The Warwick Law School, the Law in Context series and the Sociology of Law have been viewed by some as left-wing. In the 1960s there were feeble jokes equating Sociology with socialism. Maybe there was a general leftward bias: Gil Boehringer, a Marxian (ex-Belfast and Dar es Salaam) was not far off the mark when he identified the ideological assumptions underlying law-in-context practices as 'Fabian Jurisprudence', implying that they were vague and contradictory.[24] However, 'law in context' is not an ideology or a political programme; it merely provides a flexible framework for diverse ways of breaking out from a narrow tradition. Several books in the Law in Context series could be interpreted as having right-wing or feminist or other political tendencies, but a particular political orientation is not a necessary element in a contextual approach. This lack of a clear ideological or political foundation has led to accusations that law in context, socio-legal studies and R/realism are 'atheoretical' or 'apolitical'. This misses the point. For me personally the underlying ideology is a liberal interpretation of the academic ethic. Those who think that the overall purpose of scholarship and education is *not* to understand the world, but *instead* to change it, clearly differ from this view, but even they can be accommodated in this broad movement.

During the past forty years 'law in context' has been largely absorbed into the mainstream of academic law in the UK and most other common law countries. It has become respectable. Today the most visible signs are in academic legal literature: in 2017 the Law in Context series, now published by Cambridge University Press, had over fifty titles in print, with more than fifty no longer in print; the *Journal of Law and Society* is well-established and has been joined by *Law in Context* (Australia), *The International Journal of Law in Context* (London) and others. 'Context' regularly appears in the titles of books and articles. Just because of its widespread acceptance, the central ideas are open to many different interpretations.

I have contrasted 'law in context' with ALR because, while there is a historical connection between the two 'movements', there are some important differences, not least in the stories and contexts of their development. The next section explains why I have recently emphasised the distinction between ALR as a historical phenomenon and 'legal realism' as a jurisprudential concept which, in order to elucidate it, needs to be detached from its historical and its purely American associations.

Realism and realism: taking realism seriously in legal theory

In my early writings I followed convention in treating ALR as a historical phenomenon identified with a few scattered individuals at a particular period in the story of elite American law schools. From the start I criticised attempts to reduce their ideas to a single 'ism', ignoring the diverse and quite original contributions of individuals.[25] I contested the suggestion that ALR only dealt with adjudicative decisions on questions of law in hard cases, but acknowledged that the bulk of subsequent interpretations and debates focused mainly on that peculiarly American preoccupation. In retrospect it seems not very surprising that in England ALR was not taken seriously as a contribution to Jurisprudence: C. K. Allen mocked it as 'Jazz Jurisprudence',[26] Hart misleadingly dismissed Realists as believing that 'talk of rules is a myth';[27] and not much attention was paid to issues such as whether the leaders of critical legal studies were the true heirs of ALR.[28] From the 1980s ALR faded away from many Jurisprudence reading-lists in UK; probably less so in the United States because it was widely regarded as the most distinctively American kind of Jurisprudence. It was recognised that ALR had been influential on the culture of American law schools and they are acknowledged as forerunners of the Law and Society Movement, Socio-legal Studies and other empirical approaches especially in the United States. But, as Schlegel has argued, Llewellyn was probably the only professed member of the Movement who developed Realist ideas as a form of Jurisprudence.

Recently there has been a revival of interest in ALR in the United States by selective and charitable reading of a few texts. Brian Leiter advanced an interesting reconstruction of ALR, linked to naturalism in Philosophy, interpreting it as a basis for a philosophically defensible position centred on 'the core thesis' that 'judges respond primarily to the stimulus of facts'.[29] Hanoch Dagan, a US-oriented Israeli, published an excellent book *Reconstructing American Legal Realism and Rethinking Private Law Theory* (2013). I have commented on both in detail elsewhere.[30] Here they are mainly interesting for trying to revive the idea of ALR as a kind of Jurisprudence. But, in my view, by using the historical ALR as their starting point they have undermined the significance of their respective theses.

Another significant development is the rise of a New Legal Realism (NLR), spearheaded by several scholars at Wisconsin, including Stewart Macaulay and Elizabeth Mertz, and now firmly established as a movement centred on an important journal, *Empirical Legal Studies*. NLR is presented by its leaders as primarily an activist movement concerned 'to integrate empirical legal studies in concrete ways into academic legal practice, especially law teaching and legal scholarship'. It is out to change what academic lawyers do and to foster empirical legal approaches rather than make any sustained contribution to Jurisprudence. It is admirably lively and varied and so difficult to generalise about. Wisely it has distanced itself from ALR: it is not confined to adjudication; it has expressed a tentative interest in 'globalisation' but so far from an almost entirely American viewpoint; it could be interpreted as a resurgence of the 'scientific' ALR wing, but without being puristic about methodology.[31] It is a welcome addition and stimulus to empirical legal studies.

What does it mean to be realistic about law and why is the idea important?

Stimulated by these American developments and in preparing the 'Afterword' for KLRM, I have begun rethinking the idea of legal realism as a juristic concept. What does it mean to be, or aspire to be, 'realistic' about law? Some of my recent writings have tried to address this question head-on at the level of theory, formulating the central idea as a single proposition:

> That knowledge and understanding of empirical dimensions of law and justice are relevant to (weak), an integral part of (moderate) necessary/essential (strong) to understanding law and legal phenomena.

This is a precept about appropriate perspectives for studying and talking about law, but on its own it is not a distinctive theory of law. It prescribes an important or necessary, but not a sufficient, condition for understanding law. Insofar as it offers some strong challenges to various kinds of legal dogmatics this version of realism demands attention.

Let us return to the epiphanic moment in 1955 when I felt that I had been betrayed by my favourite undergraduate textbook, *Salmond on Torts* (see above, Chapter 3). My complaint was not that it was merely incomplete or misleading but that it had led me to seriously *misunderstand* the law of negligence and personal injury claims. It had given me a false picture. It presented just decontextualised doctrine, only marginally relevant to the outcomes of claims and disputes in this area. Generalised, this claim is that doctrine on its own cannot be *understood*.[32] We can treat that as an example of strong realism.

First, the idea of 'legal realism' needs to be detached from its American roots. Concern about the realities of the law in action was never an American exclusive. This kind of 'realism' is not confined to the United States, nor is it focused mainly on adjudication, let alone appellate adjudication on questions of law. For most non-American jurists, legislation, regulation, compliance, enforcement and attitudes to law are as important an aspect of understanding law as high-level adjudication.

Secondly, even strong legal realism does not involve a denial of the importance of doctrine, nor of the possibility of clear or routine cases, nor of an internally consistent or coherent justificatory theory of Torts doctrine.[33] At a general level, it can provide a basis for criticising the *dominance* of doctrinalism within Western traditions of academic law; it challenges claims to *exclusivity* or *self-sufficiency* of strong versions of 'legal dogmatics' or 'legal science'; and it raises questions about what is involved in understanding a legal rule or principle or a doctrinal 'system'. But it is not inconsistent for a realist to accept that knowledge and understanding of legal doctrine is also a necessary but not a sufficient condition of understanding law and legal phenomena.

Thirdly, in this view legal realism is not a legal theory, nor a method, nor an approach, nor does it presuppose any particular concept of law. It only prescribes an important or necessary condition for understanding legal phenomena and ideas. It does suggest that any theory or view of, or approach to, law which ignores this prescription is probably defective. The claim that the law in action and context are important or necessary as part of understanding law does not necessarily imply a particular epistemology, even for non-cognitivists. In short, a plea for realism is a plea for *focus* on what actually happens in addition to what is meant to happen in the law in action and much else besides.[34]

Fourthly, focus on what? The idea of 'realism' is associated with a number of phrases, such as the law in action, how law works, the contrast between aspiration and reality, and between appearance and reality. Clearly the concept is both vague and philosophically problematic. But the idea of realism in law catches a central truth: in order to understand law, the study of doctrine alone is not enough. In other words, one has to be concerned with social facts, context, consequences and what actually happens in the 'real world'.

Fifthly, this formulation deliberately leaves open deep philosophical questions about 'reality', 'understanding' and 'legal knowledge'. This is the deliberately question-begging move. My personal view is that sensible answers to that kind of question depend on the context and conditions of a particular enquiry. Historically, it may have been a matter of chance that Llewellyn and Frank chose the word 'Realism' and 'Realistic', probably to differentiate the new movement from Pound's version of Sociological Jurisprudence. Fortunately, except for some necessary differentiations between American and Scandinavian brands, little attention has been focused on the concepts of reality/realism/the real.[35] We have not taken the label too seriously. Otherwise we might have been plunged into an abyss of metaphysics and epistemology about unreality, irrealism, magic realism, multiple realities, virtual reality and so on. Like Pontius Pilate, on the whole we have not stayed for an answer.

If we interpret a concern with being realistic about law in terms of some version of philosophical or social realism or naturalism, we are in trouble. However, a simple way round this morass is to beg these abstract questions until one has settled on a single proposition as a starting-point such as the one set out above. In this formulation the idea of realism leaves open questions about the nature of 'reality'. Here 'realism' is about *focus* not about epistemological aspects of what constitutes understanding law. I suggest that this 'ism' can be rendered as a necessary, but not on its own a sufficient, element of understanding law in general terms.

In this context 'weak legal realism' amounts to not much more than the assertion that Empirical Legal Studies are an important part of the study of Law at a general level.[36] 'Moderate legal realism' is critical of generally narrow approaches and of 'pure' or exclusive doctrinal studies, or their dominance, but acknowledges that in some contexts propositions of law and even chunks of doctrine may be comprehensible and adequate for particular purposes, for example, summarising the law as it is at the moment in a routine case.

Weak and moderate versions of realism are likely to be acceptable to most legal scholars in the common law tradition, possibly less so in purer or more exclusive enclaves of civil law traditions. 'Strong legal realism' is obviously more interesting theoretically. For this amounts to the proposition rules can only be ever understood 'in context'. This can be interpreted in several ways.

We have seen in discussing 'rule scepticism' that some believe that rules are fictions, or phantoms or not real.[37] I personally believe that rules are as real as beliefs or models or words, unlike ghosts or unicorns.[38] We can make, break, observe or otherwise experience them. But I agree that there are many difficult philosophical problems about their nature, taxonomy and under what conditions it is true to say that a rule exists. Similarly, I reject the idea of radical indeterminacy in respect of all social and legal rules, but I think that some of the kinds of scepticism in this area deserve to be taken seriously.[39]

Another kind of scepticism was, perhaps surprisingly, expressed by Ronald Dworkin, who emphasised that 'the idea of law as a set of discrete standards, which we might in principle individuate and count, seems to me a scholastic fiction'.[40] A similar idea is that all rules belong to a larger system or code or agglomeration which, in turn, may be hard or impossible to individuate as a discrete entity or unit.

Another different idea, is that no rule or body of rules can be understood independently of a broader context or sphere. Denis Galligan develops this interestingly in relation to the concept of 'social spheres' – that is, 'an area of activity in which participants share understandings and conventions about the activity, and which influence and guide the way they engage in the activity'.[41] He contrasts lecturing (which is loosely constrained) with the practice of psychiatry, which is more dense, 'with density expressing the relative power of social spheres in influencing their members'.[42]

A strong realist would emphasise such difficulties. Indeed, these examples are significant warnings about being over-confident about the existence, scope or rationale of rules without reference to 'context' in its many forms. I shall not pursue these hares here, but I shall touch on them again when considering the need for more sophisticated theorising about social norms (Chapter 20). Moderate realism suffices for my immediate purpose, which is to underline the challenges it poses to the doctrinal tradition, as I interpret it. In particular, the propositions that for most purposes of understanding law (i) the study of rules alone is not enough and (ii) that assuming that the concept of law should be restricted to rules or norms is subversive of that enterprise.

On a strong version of the realist thesis one cannot understand any legal phenomena if one does not take into account how they operate in fact.[43] It suggests that one cannot understand the law of Negligence if you ignore insurance, negotiated settlements, and the damages lottery, as Patrick Atiyah demonstrated. Doctrine without some reference to its context and operation is unreal; but realism about law has to include doctrine. They need each other.[44]

1 The author

2 The TANU Building

3 The First Fourteen

4 President Nyerere opening Dar Es Salaam University campus

6 H. L. A. Hart

5 Jeremy Bentham (the Auto-icon)

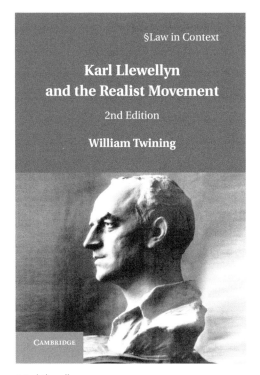

7 Karl Llewellyn

8 Soia Mentschikoff

9 Terry Anderson

10 John Henry Wigmore

11 Human Rights Southern Voices, Jordanstown 2008

12 Lowering the flag

Conversely, even strong and moderate realism are consistent with the idea that doctrine is also important: it too is generally a necessary, but not a sufficient, element of understanding law and legal phenomena. The relationship between this view of realism and doctrinalism is not simple. For example, a strong or moderate realist will reject the idea that legal dogmatics or legal science constitutes an autonomous discipline;[45] she will challenge the overall dominance of the doctrinal tradition within the discipline of law; some realists will reject the idea that law consists only of rules or doctrine and will emphasise the importance of institutions, processes, personnel and legal technology as part of understanding law in addition to rules and norms; and there is room for differences and disagreements about whether concepts such as officials, institutions or legal techniques can be elucidated without reference to rules or norms.

As interpreted here, even moderate realism has a contribution to make to Jurisprudence, not as a theory of or about law, nor as a rounded philosophy of law, nor as a rival or subverter of analytic, idealist or doctrinal approaches, but rather as one integral part of understanding law. In this view, legal realism is best treated as a hedgehog concept, that is that it stands for one Big Idea – the importance of the empirical dimensions of law and justice as part of understanding law. Once that proposition is accepted, the gates open to all of the foxy diversity, controversy, differing traditions and dilemmas and problems within empirical legal studies.

Doctrine

A central theme of my approach to understanding law has been that strong versions of the doctrinal tradition are too narrow, impoverished and abstracted from 'real life'. I have argued that in most contexts the study of rules alone is not enough; I have railed against blackletter textbooks; the Law in Context series was set up as a series of 'counter-textbooks'; I accept labels such as 'contextual' and 'realist', provided these labels are not treated as indicating a distinct 'theory of law'; and some of my writings about the 'expository orthodoxy' have been quite polemical. So it is not surprising that I should be perceived as an opponent of formalism and of doctrinal approaches. That is a mistake.

I shall argue here that as a critic of the expository or doctrinal tradition, I am a moderate. I have never been a rule-sceptic; I believe that rules and doctrine are a central part of understanding law; that doctrine and context are complementary; rather, one of my main concerns has been to build bridges between two traditions that have strayed apart. In short, my role is rather like Hans Sachs in *Die Maestersinger* (less the nationalism); I want my discipline to break free from a constricted tradition but not to jettison it.

In 1958 Herbert Hart launched a sharp critique of Dias and Hughes's textbook on *Jurisprudence* (1957).[46] Apart from some detailed criticisms, his main targets were the assumption that Jurisprudence is a subject susceptible to textbook treatment and that learning potted summaries of what other people had said rather than engaging directly with important issues and original texts was educationally deplorable. I was encouraged by this critique and, in 1966, in a memorandum for the Law in Context series I indulged in some youthful rhetoric against blackletter textbooks:

> As educational tools textbooks fly in the face of some of the fundamental values of university education and at the same time they are primitive as means of training effective practitioners; as works of scholarship they may be accurate but are rarely exhaustive; they are rarely sufficiently comprehensive to be efficient as works of reference; as works of intellect they are with [few] exceptions unimaginative; they have no pretensions to be works of art.[47]

The Law in Context series provided in an open-ended way a constructive alternative to the expository tradition without substituting one orthodoxy for another. In 1971 I returned to the fray. While commenting on the third edition of *Dias on Jurisprudence*, I extended Hart's critique to all textbooks, arguing that 'the textbook *style*, for any legal subject, is difficult to reconcile with the values of legal education'.[48] The core of these critiques was educational, an attack on rote learning in legal studies.

My article was quite strongly criticised in his Presidential address to the Society of Public Teachers of Law by Professor T. B. Smith of Edinburgh, who defended the expository tradition, using the great Scottish institutional writers, such as Stair, Kames and Erskine, as exemplars.[49] They took on whole systems of Private Law and Criminal Law in a way that was systematic, critical and designed to last.

I replied, reinforcing my criticisms of the English expository tradition mainly on educational grounds.[50] Of course, here Smith and I were at cross-purposes. A noted Scottish nationalist, he was drawing attention to leading expositors as great scholars who systematised Scots law. These treatises were significantly different from the genre of books that I was attacking and Smith was reminding us of the superiority of the Scottish tradition.[51] However, the two genres shared one feature: both were almost exclusively concerned with doctrine and, as a 'realist' and 'contextualist', I was arguing against that.

Over the past fifty years or so there has been an understandable tendency to contrast Socio-legal Studies, Sociology of Law and 'law in context' (three overlapping concepts)[52] with 'blackletter approaches' or 'doctrinal formalism'. Like American Legal Realism, law in context and Socio-legal Studies have sometimes been depicted as a reaction against formalism. Such polemics have often descended into caricature and selective critique.

In order to disentangle some important issues, it is useful to give a careful account of 'doctrine' and to differentiate it from 'law as rules' conceptions of law. If doctrine is equated with 'school rules' approaches or classic blackletter law, it offers targets that are too soft. Most leading expositors have assumed more refined conceptions of doctrine than the mere reporting or description of categorical precepts. Fortunately two respected jurists have provided richer interpretations.

In setting up a crude distinction between the 'doctrinal concept' and 'the sociological concept' of law,[53] Ronald Dworkin usefully included principles, concepts and distinctions in addition to rules in his idea of doctrine. This concept allows for forms of exposition that are rigorous and sophisticated. Dworkin explicitly denied that doctrine consists of rules and principles. Rather, his is a picture of propositions of law linked to their underlying rationales.[54] This suggests a more robust version of the tradition against which R/realism has reacted than 'law is rules' conceptions and labels such as formalism, legal dogmatics, blackletter law, the expository orthodoxy and the textbook tradition. Some clear weaknesses within the doctrinal tradition can be identified, which are not necessary parts of that tradition: the deductive model of legal reasoning; the slot-machine image of adjudication (mechanical jurisprudence); strong versions of the idea that exposition of doctrine can be 'scientific'; insistence on the study of doctrine as an autonomous discipline, purified of all non-legal elements; and the dominance of the expository tradition as the only worthwhile perspective and approach to understanding law. Here my concern is to integrate the best elements of doctrinal analysis with empirical and normative approaches as a more promising path to understanding legal phenomena and ideas.

Andrew Halpin has suggested an even 'richer notion' of legal doctrine that includes not only rule-formulations, but also principles, differentiated conceptions of interpretive roles and informed conceptions of the nature of legal materials, all of which are normally 'beneath the surface'.[55] This extension of the constituents of 'doctrine' captures the best practices of the leading treatise writers, especially in the American tradition, such as Story, Wigmore, Corbin, Gray and Scottish institutional writers.[56]

Insofar as accounts of doctrine approximate to Dworkin's or Halpin's conceptions, I accept that it is an essential part of understanding law. The best expositors set their interpretations of specific rules in the context of complex webs of concepts, distinctions, principles, rules and reasons. Many leading expositors in the common law tradition have in fact been successful practitioners with at least tacit knowledge of legal practices and sophisticated, though usually unstated, views on judicial roles and other relevant matters. This has prevented them from becoming too abstracted from local legal practice and 'the law in action'. In short, they were often implicit realists. Gray, Holmes and Corbin, all leading expositors, have also been recognised as predecessors of American Legal Realism. Such examples of links between doctrinalism and realistic perspectives supports the view that they can be complementary rather than rivals.[57]

The common law has not been receptive to strict ideas of 'legal science' and purer forms of exposition. There are several reasons for this: if one accepts the view of the development of common law as a form of custom mediated through practitioners and judges, even the systematisers like Blackstone and Coke did not really have a clear conception of system building; the importance of legislation as a source of law, allied to a strong tradition of legal positivism and an antipathy to natural law, meant that the predominant cast of mind was pragmatic and particularistic.

A clearer form of an ideal type of classical doctrinal exposition is to be found in the civilian tradition. For example, a recent article sets out to explain why socio-legal studies have achieved little recognition in French universities:[58]

> Law faculties in France remain dominated by doctrinal analysis ... [a] traditional notion of 'fundamental legal science that has its specific purpose of the systemization of norms' was in the charge of jurists rather than judges or legislators; and a distinct, autonomous legal science was supported by a centralised state framework for universities 'guaranteeing the institutional reproduction of disciplines within the university system.' Doctrinal scholarship is imagined as analogous to architecture rather than mere description. Empirical approaches were excluded from this tradition and socio-legal studies have not been recognised as a distinct field. Scholarly discourse on law has been clearly distinct from that of social science.

Most empirical legal research in France has taken place outside the law faculties.[59]

The common law may have had a debased or impure form of doctrinalism; or perhaps that is its strength. However, the English expository tradition is still perceived by its critics as 'formalistic'. Like other 'isms', 'formalism' is a crude term with many shades of meaning. For example, American Legal Realism has been interpreted as part of a broader 'revolt against formalism', exemplified by John Dewey in philosophy, Charles Beard in history, Thorstein Veblen in economics and Oliver Wendell Holmes in law. As Morton White explained, all of these figures 'were eager to come to grips with life, experience, process, growth, context, function'.[60] They reacted against over-emphasis on abstract logic, mathematics and 'scientism' in their respective disciplines. This is quite an illuminating way of setting American Legal Realism in the context of broader trends in the history of American thought. Unfortunately, 'formalism' is sometimes used as a vague general term of abuse. Recent scholarship by Summers, Tamanaha and others has shown that dismissing the predecessors of Legal Realism as 'formalists' involves caricature and over-simplification of history; that there were many strands of 'formalism'; and that formality in law can serve important functions that are worth preserving. For example, rituals and standard forms are important legal phenomena.[61]

If the tone of my early critiques of the expository orthodoxy was polemical, my views were always quite moderate. I have never held that doctrine is unimportant. I have not been sceptical about the existence or importance of rules and principles nor have I subscribed to strong versions of indeterminacy in regard to interpretation of doctrine or rules.[62] The 'law' in the term 'law in context' includes doctrine, but it also includes institutions, processes, structures, practices, personnel and craft traditions. It is sometimes reasonable to interpret 'context' as referring to any factors outside doctrine, although it is often unwise to draw a sharp distinction between law and context.

What are my main objections to the sophisticated ideal type of doctrinal formalism? First, I reject strong versions of autonomous disciplines. I do not think that understanding law can be advanced within the confines of a closed discipline. Law as a discipline is partly institutionalised in university law schools, but legal research, invention and education are not confined to them. For example, many judges and practitioners are genuine scholars. Other institutionalised disciplines contribute directly or indirectly to the enterprise of understanding legal phenomena and ideas. Law schools may have distinctive cultures, but not autonomous epistemologies.

A second objection is that sometimes, as is reported of French Law faculties today and which I frequently encountered in my career, adherents to the doctrinal tradition want to keep exposition of doctrine pure and exclusive. 'That's sociology, not law' was a common mantra of rejection of broader approaches. In the early years of the Law in Context series there were reports that some law librarians refused to order some titles in the series because they were not law books. Often exclusivity has been maintained in practice, without specific reference to other approaches. Blackletter texts survive. The central message of realism is that doctrine cannot be self-contained, treated in isolation as a thing in itself and for most practical and theoretical purposes the study of doctrine alone is not enough.

A third objection is that 'scientific' doctrinalism is hard to reconcile with legislation, regulation and modern styles of governance. Even in code countries, law-making tends to be reactive, ad hoc, messy, fragmented and particularistic. There is room for tidying up the statute book and the never-ending search for principle and for continual attempts to make statute law more systematic. However, Karl Llewellyn reported one German 'legal scientist' lamenting that the legislature could repeal his whole system, his life-work, overnight. That sounds like building sand castles at low tide.

The basic realist objection is against the dominance of, or an exclusive emphasis on, doctrinal studies, not on doctrinal studies as such. This dominance and the tendency to exclusivity have pervaded Western systems of academic law for at least two centuries. Doctrine is necessary, but not sufficient, for understanding law. This insufficiency is not merely incompleteness; it often involves distortion, as is illustrated by my complaint against *Salmond* (see above, Chapter 3).

Ironically, Hans Kelsen is viewed as the prime exemplar of 'formalism', yet his pure theory specified that legal knowledge could only be of formal structures of norms cleansed of all impurities. Moreover, Kelsen can be used to undermine any claim to purity or science by expositors, because impurities inevitably enter as soon as substantive rules of law are articulated. In short,

Kelsen's 'pure theory' is about form and structure, not substance, and so does not provide a theoretical basis for 'scientific' or 'pure' exposition of the content of legal norms.[63]

In many common law jurisdictions, the doctrinal tradition is no longer as dominant as it was. For example, in 2004 Fiona Cownie reported that a majority of English academic lawyers that she interviewed claimed to favour law in context.[64] Some of this may be lip-service, but contextual approaches have become part of the mainstream. Nevertheless, only a small part of the practices in the doctrinal traditions satisfy the rich conceptions of what is involved by Dworkin or Halpin. Even these exclude too much.

What is perhaps less apparent, but very significant, is how dominant the idea of law as doctrine or rules is among our canonical theorists. Almost all mainstream jurists of the nineteenth and twentieth centuries have been doctrinal theorists, advancing conceptions and theories of law that conceptualise law in terms of rules, principles and formal normative structures. Kelsen, Hart, Dworkin, Finnis and Raz are prime examples of jurists rooted in the doctrinal tradition. Debates between positivists and anti-positivists are mainly within that tradition. Whether intentionally or not, they have given theoretical respectability to a set of constricted and unrealistic practices.

One of my objections to the practices of most Analytical Legal Philosophers has been that they pay too little attention to non-doctrinal concepts – to those of talk about law as well as law talk (i.e. doctrine).[65] Even the leaders of the critical legal studies movement, such as Duncan Kennedy, focused on 'liberal legalism' as their main target, captured mainstream courses like Contract, and were uninterested or disdainful of more empirical approaches. Some student works on Jurisprudence range quite widely, but the jurists who are treated as mainstream nearly all fit *within* the doctrinal tradition.

For a time, I interpreted Hart's famous claim that *The Concept of Law* was 'an essay in descriptive sociology' as offering an 'olive branch' to the emerging field of socio-legal studies.[66] Of course, Hart was not doing Sociology, but making the point that sociologists (and other empirical scholars) need concepts as part of their enterprise of describing, explaining and interpreting social facts. Later Nicola Lacey, an eloquent ally in the cause of building bridges between Analytical Jurisprudence and Empirical Legal Studies, persuaded me that Hart shared Oxonian disdain for Sociology and really believed that armchair conceptual analysis could proceed independently of involvement with social reality.[67] His failure and that of his followers to analyse concepts such as institution, dispute, function, profession and lawyer partly followed from the view that these were not relevant to a Legal Philosophy which has been conceived in terms of doctrine.

14

Rethinking Evidence

The field of evidence is no other than the field of knowledge.

(Jeremy Bentham)[1]

The law has no mandamus on the logical faculty.

(James Bradley Thayer)[2]

In any inference task our evidence is always incomplete, rarely conclusive, and often imprecise or vague; it comes from sources that have any gradation of credibility.

(David Schum)[3]

The subject of Evidence deserves a more central place in the discipline of Law.

(William Twining)[4]

Evidence is important for all of us. Everyone deals with evidence and inferential reasoning every day of their lives, in every kind of work situation, in specialist areas, in academic and historical enquiries and as ordinary citizens in deciding whether to marry, in choosing package holidays, in shopping, in other everyday decisions and in listening to arguments or debating issues. The English system of administration of justice depends heavily on lay magistrates, jurors, tribunal members, umpires and referees and others to make decisions based on evidence. This assumes a general idea of 'cognitive competence' on the part of adult citizens – that is to say, that nearly all adult members of society can make rational judgements about questions of fact using ordinary practical inferential reasoning based on evidence.[5]

In recent years Evidence as a subject has become very topical. More or less simplistic forms of evidence-based medicine, evidence-based policy and evidence-based decision-making in many spheres of life are salient features of bureaucratisation and the audit society. If one applies the Newspaper Exercise to evidence it will be found to feature on every page and evidentiary concepts such as relevance, cogency, plausibility and rationality are an essential part of the discourse. Dope testing of athletes, the use of new technology in decision-making in sports, authentication of art works, problems of proving genocide, DNA, 'fake news' and the credibility of 'experts' are familiar themes. In popular culture, detective fiction has expanded its horizons to include forensic science (Patricia Cornwell), Forensic Anthropology (Kathy Reichs), scenes-of-crime officers (especially on television) and various forms of intelligence analysis. After 9/11, the starting point for post-mortems was a judgement that 'American intelligence agencies did not possess the analytic depth or the right methods accurately to assess [possible threats]'.[6]

Everyone is concerned with evidence; it is important in most spheres of life, especially decision-making, and it has special significance in contemporary public life. Moreover, Evidence is fascinating as a subject of study. Yet, paradoxically, within the discipline of Law it is widely perceived to be a narrow specialism, arcane, technical, esoteric, artificial and of diminishing importance. This perception fits much of the practice of Evidence scholarship, teaching and discourse. That is because that practice is based on a fundamental fallacy: that the Law of Evidence is co-extensive with the field of Evidence in Legal Contexts. This crude conflation is a clear example of the distorting influence of the doctrinal tradition. Evidence specialists, at least until recently, have focused almost exclusively on the Law of Evidence (mainly the rules of admissibility). Perceptions are further distorted by treating the contested jury trial as the paradigm situation of litigation and appellate courts, which have limited powers in Anglo-American law, as the main arena for the development of Evidence doctrine.

This chapter helps to explain this dire state of affairs through the story of my project on Rethinking Evidence, begun in 1972. Some progress has been made since then, but the project is unfinished as the battle is far from won. In particular I have had limited success in persuading *all* academic lawyers to 'take facts seriously' as part of their general intellectual equipment and different specialisms. It is worth summarising the case for this to change.[7]

Evidence, Proof and Fact-finding (EPF) is important for all academic lawyers, not just specialists, because:

1. Understanding evidence is an important part of understanding law.
   (a) EPF is important for legal theory because it raises a whole range of theoretical issues that are generally marginalised in the agenda of mainstream Jurisprudence.[8]
   (b) EPF should play an important role in the study of many specialised areas of law, e.g. how does one prove causation in conspiracy or genocide or disasters at sea.
2. EPF is important in legal practice, both in litigation and non-litigious business.
3. EPF is a good vehicle for developing some basic transferable intellectual skills. It should, inter alia, be treated as an important part of basic Legal Method.[9]
4. As the discipline of Law responds to 'globalisation', interesting new theoretical and practical issues arise in respect of transnational relations, comparison, generalisation, and hybridisation.[10]
5. The subject of Evidence is coming into its own as a distinct multidisciplinary field.[11]

Rethinking Evidence: the story of a project

Jeremy Bentham and the American Realist Jerome Frank originally stimulated my interest in Evidence, a subject that I had hardly encountered in my formal legal education. Moving to Warwick in 1972 committed me to rethinking the subject as my contribution to the Law School's mission 'of broadening the study of law from within'. For the next sixteen years or so the study of Evidence in legal contexts was my main project. Thereafter I continued to take an interest and to teach 'Analysis of evidence' until I gave up teaching in 2011.[12]

During the Warwick period I considered that what I was doing was responding to Jerome Frank's plea to take facts and fact-finding seriously.[13] He had plausibly argued that well over 90 per cent of legal practice was taken up with questions of fact,[14] but almost all academic attention was focused obsessively on questions of law in superior courts – a disease known as 'appellate court-itis'.[15] The disease persists today. The focus needs to be adjusted. Frank's thesis was correct, but he never worked out a satisfactory way of implementing it in his teaching or writing. Thus, the standard accounts of the subject of Evidence in Law have continued barely to reflect the actual problems and practices of lawyers and lower courts and tribunals, let alone broader conceptions of the field of Evidence in other legal contexts.

A second stimulus was the realisation that Jeremy Bentham had written more about adjective law (evidence and procedure) than about any other subject, but that he had been largely ignored by modern Evidence scholars.[16] A third interest was in some particular examples of alleged miscarriages of justice, including the Sacco-Vanzetti case, the tragedy of Edith Thompson and cases concerning atrocities associated with the IRA. A central question was: how can one analyse such allegations in a systematic way?[17]

My interest in Evidence started at roughly the same time as the development of 'the New Evidence Scholarship' in the United States. In the early years that movement was mainly concerned with issues about probabilities and proof, with quite sharp divisions between Baconians (inductivists) and Pascalians (who believe that all probabilistic reasoning is in principle mathematical) – with further divisions between Bayesians, frequentists and other schools of statistics. I joined in these debates, as I did in relation to later issues about the relationship between narrative and argument in legal fact-finding, but my main concerns were broader.[18]

The project on Evidence roughly divided into five phases which overlapped in time and subject matter.[19] First was the establishment of an ideal type of twentieth-century legal treatment of Evidence as an academic subject in order to make a critical assessment of its strengths and limitations. Second was a reconstruction of the intellectual history of Anglo-American approaches to the study of Evidence as a distinct field, from the publication of the first treatise in 1754 by Chief Baron Gilbert to the 1970s. Third was an analysis of the basic concepts of the Law of Evidence and of what Wigmore called the 'logic of proof' and of the relations between them.[20] Fourth was the consideration of the philosophical underpinnings of previous attempts to construct a general theory of evidence in legal contexts. Finally came the exploration of the role of evidence in other disciplines, in public life and in general culture and to consider the potential of Evidence as an integrated cross-disciplinary field.

A narrow orthodoxy within the doctrinal tradition

The first step was to construct an ideal type of orthodox Anglo-American approaches to the study of Evidence, to articulate their underlying assumptions, and to assess them critically. For example, the subject of Evidence in Law was treated as co-extensive with the Law of Evidence, mainly the rules governing admissibility; the contested jury trial (a wholly exceptional event)[21] was treated as the paradigm case for the application of the exclusionary rules; doctrine constituted the whole subject matter of Evidence; this was developed mainly in appellate courts, whereas most action was in lower courts and pretrial; in Jurisprudence the concept of 'legal reasoning' was limited to argumentation about questions of law (typically in 'hard cases') and reasoning about questions of fact was usually ignored or dismissed as mere common sense. This ideal type was narrowly conceived and easy to criticise. The real challenge was to construct a coherent conception of the subject of Evidence in Legal Contexts to replace that orthodoxy.

In 1972, shortly after I had joined Warwick, during a highly charged debate at the SPTL Annual Conference on reform of criminal evidence in England, I heard the leading Evidence scholar, Sir Rupert Cross, say: 'I am working for the day when my subject is abolished.' This provided a splendid foil for my work – for how could scholars *abolish* the subject of Evidence in law? What would one study about evidence if there were no rules? How much of Evidence doctrine consists of *rules*? What would be the place of the Law of Evidence within a broadened conception of the study of Evidence in Legal Contexts? What should we be studying about evidence or 'evidence plus' in addition to the rules? By what criteria might one judge what part of our heritage of evidence doctrine might be worth preserving or extending? And was not Evidence – narrowly conceived, riddled with technicality, relatively neglected as a subject of academic study in England and prone to cyclical, repetitive and deeply unsatisfying political debates – ripe for rethinking?

Early on I developed several main lines of criticism against the orthodox contemporary Anglo-American approach in the secondary literature and courses on Evidence. First, it was too narrow. Because it had focused almost exclusively on the rules of admissibility, it had almost systematically neglected a whole range of other questions, such as questions about the logic and psychology of proof and relations with other disciplines such as Forensic Science, Criminal Process and Statistics. Secondly, it was atheoretical: the leading theorists of Evidence had in recent years been largely ignored, and most discussions of evidentiary issues had proceeded without any articulated and coherent theoretical framework for describing, explaining or evaluating existing rules, practices and institutions. Almost all Evidence scholarship had assumed a rather naïve, common-sense empiricism, without much reference to epistemology or philosophical logic. It also failed to confront a variety of sceptical challenges to orthodox assumptions, ranging from Jerome Frank's fact-scepticism, through politico-ideological critiques, to various forms of epistemological relativism. It had proceeded in almost complete isolation from developments in relevant branches of Philosophy. Thirdly, insofar as orthodox academic discourse had moved beyond simple exposition, it had tended to be incoherent, for the conceptual framework of evidence doctrine did not provide an adequate framework for establishing links with other kinds of discourse. For instance, it did not easily accommodate questions about reasoning about probabilities in forensic contexts, a topic which had recently been given prominence in America and Australia from the late 1960s. Nor did it stimulate interest in the relationship between reasoning about questions of fact and law and other reasonings in legal contexts (Chapter 10).

Fourthly, bare exposition led to distortions and misperceptions of key evidentiary issues and phenomena. A weak version was that by concentrating on some issues to the neglect of others, a misleading impression is given of the subject as a whole. A stronger version is that such imbalances actually lead to misperceptions and error.[22] For example, nearly all of the existing literature on confessions treated retracted confessions as the norm; yet in practice retracted confessions represent only a small minority of all confessions, especially in jurisdictions that accept guilty pleas – rather different from mainstream civil law traditions. Typically, neither the scholarly literature nor public debate was based on a balanced and realistic total picture of the role of confessions in criminal process, such as the significance of confessing as an important stage en route to a guilty plea.[23] Evidence scholarship failed to give a systematic account of confessions in criminal process as *phenomena*. It provided no clear answers to such questions as who confesses to whom about what under what conditions, in what form and with what results? Yet how could one make sensible and informed judgments about the issues of policy relating to confessions and interrogation without at least tentative working answers to such questions?

These criticisms suggested some criteria which a broader approach to the study of evidence would need to satisfy in order to meet these objections, insofar as they are well-founded. In 1978 I summarised my response as follows:

> To meet the charge of narrowness, it would be necessary to identify at least the most important questions which ought to be tackled in a systematic and comprehensive approach to the study of evidence. This requires an adequate theoretical and conceptual framework.
>
> To meet the charge of incoherence, the relationships between the different lines of enquiry would need to be charted carefully and explicitly – there are, for

example, some puzzling questions about the connections between the logic and the psychology of proof, or again, between the study of evidence and proof on the one hand and of criminal and civil procedure on the other.

To meet the charges of theoretical naivety, important theoretical puzzles and disagreements would need to be identified and considered. It is not good enough to dismiss the sceptics, however exaggerated their views may be, by pretending that they do not exist or that what they say is irrelevant.

And to meet charges of distortion and misperception, it is important to paint as realistic a total picture as possible of the phenomena under consideration, so that particular issues can be set in the perspective of some reasonably balanced and realistic overview of the whole. That is part of what is meant by studying law in context.[24]

Some intellectual history

As I was historically inclined, the next question was: within the common law tradition has anyone tried to do this before? The answer was that for 200 years after the publication of the first treatise, Chief Baron Gilbert's *The Law of Evidence* (1754), there had been numerous attempts to develop a 'theory of evidence'; some of these were restricted to Evidence doctrine, but others had been quite broadly conceived. Rather than try to reinvent the wheel, I devoted some attention to intellectual history. The main exercise was to examine the assumptions underlying leading Anglo-American treatises on Evidence from 1754 to the 1970s, then to explain and construct a further ideal type of the assumptions underlying 'The Rationalist Tradition of Evidence Scholarship' to which the ideas of almost all common law specialist treatments had approximated. The tradition was heavily influenced by Bentham – especially the premise that the direct end of adjudication is rectitude of decision – that is, the correct application of rules to facts that were probably true. In short, the enterprise involves the pursuit of truth by rational means on the basis of inferential reasoning from evidence. Bentham argued that there should be no rules of evidence. This was considered too extreme, but the scope of the Law of Evidence narrowed considerably over time. Nevertheless, in the English and American academic traditions the assumption persisted that rules (or more broadly doctrine) constituted the subject matter of the discipline of Law and the Law of Evidence constituted the subject matter of Evidence in Legal Contexts.

The two outstanding figures in the Anglo-American tradition were Jeremy Bentham and John Henry Wigmore. I wrote a book about them (*Theories of Evidence: Bentham and Wigmore* (1985))[25] and used each as a reference point for developing my own ideas. Bentham inspired the model for the Rationalist Tradition. His proposals for reform were considered to be too radical, but almost every change over the next two centuries has moved in the direction that he indicated, but at a slower pace and in a piecemeal way which he would have condemned. Bentham also provided a foil for considering non-utilitarian and various sceptical perspectives.[26] It is relevant here to say something more about Thayer's conception of the Law of Evidence, Bentham's anti-nomian thesis and Wigmore's conception of 'the principles of proof'.

Thayer and Wigmore both emphasised the limited scope of the Law of Evidence. Their view can be expanded to an 'argument of exaggerated importance': what has to be proved (materiality) is prescribed by substantive law, not by evidentiary rules; there are almost no formal rules of quantum or priority or weight or relevance. Some doctrine, such as 'the best evidence rule', are little more than 'evidentiary ghosts'; the hearsay rules are a series of exceptions to exceptions to exceptions and, since the near-disappearance of the civil jury in common law jurisdictions (except the United States), it is nearing ghostdom in civil litigation; previously rigid rules have become discretionary guidelines; the surviving rules are often waived or ignored in practice, and many tribunals are 'guided but not bound' by them.[27]

Nevertheless, most evidence scholars, including myself, believe that some exclusionary rules, standards of proof and presumptions are worth fighting for. On the other hand, Bentham went further in attacking *all* peremptory rules of evidence, arguing that any binding rule of evidence was bound to be over-inclusive or under-inclusive because of the vast variety of combinations of circumstances involved in ordinary fact-finding. This 'anti-nomian thesis', although overstated, raises important issues in the theory of norms about rule-governed activities (Chapters 11 and 20).

Bentham's anti-nomian thesis sounds radical to common lawyers, but in nearly all other spheres of practical life we operate under a system of 'free proof' – that is, an absence of formal rules in regard to weight, credibility or quantum as well as admissibility.[28] Bentham's reason is instructive:

> To find infallible rules for evidence, rules which insure a just decision is, from the nature of things, absolutely impossible; but the human mind is too apt to establish rules which only increase the probabilities of a bad decision. All the service that an impartial investigator of the truth can perform in this respect is, to put the legislators and judges on their guard against such hasty rules.[29]

In an age of bureaucratisation, mechanisation and audit, this warning should still have resonance. The pressures to simplify, standardise and codify are greater than ever and some of the main instruments for this are formal rules, other formalisations and algorithms. For example, more extreme versions of evidence-based medicine have tended to move in the direction of rules and protocols of priority and weight (e.g. repeated clinical trials trump single laboratory studies which trump qualitative studies which trump patients' 'idiosyncratic opinions').[30] This approach resembles that of Chief Baron Gilbert (1754) (official documents under seal trump other official documents which trump unofficial documents which trump oral testimony). Bentham destroyed Gilbert's theory in the early nineteenth century.[31]

Interestingly, the two great expositors of the Law of Evidence confirmed this aspect of Bentham's thesis, arguing that key questions of relevance and weight could not and should not purportedly be governed by formal rules. As Thayer put it, 'the law has no mandamus on the logical faculty'.[32] Wigmore went so far as to say that a lawyer (invoking rules of weight) is committing 'moral treason'.[33]

However, Thayer and Wigmore acknowledged and supported the survival of some rules of evidence. Thayer's answer to the question 'what is the Law of Evidence?' was that the surviving rules are disparate exceptions to a principle of free proof (meaning the absence of formal rules). Wigmore followed this and acknowledged that the remaining rules were of diminishing importance.

Thayer's thesis raises the question: what is the nature, meaning, extent and justification of freedom of proof? His answer was in terms of ordinary inferential reasoning used in the practical decisions of everyday life. That is important, first, because it is accessible to ordinary adult citizens, who are thus competent to participate in adjudicative decisions based on evidence; and, secondly, because this is the best kind of reason available in most circumstances. In short, ordinary common-sense, practical reasoning is for the most part the best tool we have, despite its obvious frailties. That raises a host of theoretical issues.[34]

Thayer's conception of the Law of Evidence still underpins most of the Law of Evidence in the common law tradition. It is the basis of the American Federal Rules of Evidence and several other such codes. Sadly, most expositors and teachers focused on the exceptions – namely, the formal rules – and did not place enough emphasis on the idea that the key to understanding evidence in law is inferential reasoning or what Wigmore called 'the logic of proof'.

Wigmore built on and developed Thayer's ideas. He divided the subject of Evidence into two parts, The Principles of Proof and the Trial Rules, and argued that the former are anterior to and more important than the latter and have been marginalised in legal thought and that the neglect of the former has distorted perceptions of the latter. Wigmore made his name with his famous *A Treatise on the System of Evidence in Trials at Common Law* (1904), which is ostensibly about the rules and which dominated and indeed overshadowed American Evidence scholarship and practice for about fifty years. This still survives as *The New Wigmore*, but with some healthy competition.[35]

Unfortunately, Wigmore's attempt to develop The Principles of Proof was a flop. Presented in an idiosyncratic fashion, it was not taken seriously by either scholars or practitioners. First published in 1913 as *The Principles of Judicial Proof, as Given by Logic, Psychology and General Experience*, it seems that the publishers only agreed to publish two further editions to humour their star author and they insisted on renaming the third edition (1937) *The Science of Judicial Proof*, probably in order to suggest that it was a new book.[36]

The Law of Evidence

Thayer still provides the key to understanding the Law of Evidence in the United States and most common law countries. While arguing that lawyers tend to exaggerate the importance of exclusionary rules of evidence, I concluded that artificial rules of evidence can and do play an important, if narrow, role in reasoning about and deciding issues of fact in adjudication, litigation and more generally.[37] Ironically, having set out on a seemingly radical programme, I found myself reviving and defending some key aspects of the Anglo-American tradition that had been forgotten: Bentham's view of the ends of adjudication, Thayer's vision of the Law of Evidence as a series of disparate exceptions to a principle of free proof, Wigmore's chart method and several attempts mainly by American teachers to develop courses on fact-finding and the logic of proof. All of the latter went beyond conceiving of the subject of Evidence in Law solely or mainly in terms of rules. All died in infancy.[38]

The details of the surviving rules of evidence still remain the main focus of most courses and professional examinations on 'Evidence' in the United States and England and of most specialists in the field. I did not follow Bentham in arguing for the total abolition of formal rules. My position is that some of the exclusionary rules, principles and standards are very important, but they are only a small part of the subject and they need to be studied in the context of a broader conception of the field as a whole. In the early days of the project I taught selected topics in the Law of Evidence,[39] but later I left much of this to more interested colleagues. Terry Anderson integrated a shortened version of *Analysis of Evidence* into his course on The Law of Evidence with some success.[40] We used examples from doctrine in teaching Modified Wigmorean Analysis (see below), especially to illustrate the relationship between the logical aspects and the rules. In print I made specific criticisms of standard treatments of identification evidence, confessions and improperly obtained evidence, but a more comprehensive and detailed critique of one of the standard expository works might have been more convincing to traditional specialist colleagues. However, my main concern was to try to persuade all academic lawyers to 'take facts seriously' and to treat Evidence and Proof as central to the discipline of Law as rules, reasoning and legal methods – in other words, as transcending the main fields of substantive law. This advocacy seems to have been largely unsuccessful, probably because most academic lawyers perceive Evidence to be a highly technical, rather esoteric subject which is no concern of theirs, while many specialists felt that they were targets of my critique.[41] That case needs to be made again and again.[42]

Evidence and legal theory

Thayer and Wigmore provided the starting point for most of my subsequent work on Evidence. I built on their ideas and developed them in a number of ways. However, I deviated from them in some key respects: I broadened the focus from contested jury trials to a total process model of litigation and then to a consideration of evidence in other contexts. This flowed from my concern with standpoint and the idea that there are many kinds of participants in legal processes who are concerned with evidence in addition to judges and juries. They have different vantage points, roles, concerns, goals, skills and data. There are also different kinds of observers with analogous concerns, in particular various types of historians, especially those whose primary concern is what happened in particular past events (in short with historical fact-determination rather than explanation or generalisation).[43]

Another deviation from Thayer and Wigmore was to consider some alternatives to the epistemological and logical assumptions which were rooted in a particular cognitivist tradition of informal logic exemplified by Francis Bacon, John Stuart Mill and Stanley Jevons, and carried on in recent times by Stephen Toulmin, Jonathan Cohen and Douglas Walton. While often working within that tradition myself, I also considered some challenges to aspects of it exemplified by various philosophical sceptics, historiographers, probabilists (Pascalians, especially Bayesians), holists, narratologists and postmodernists.[44] This aspect of my work could be carried much further, but I concluded that Wigmore's assumptions were rooted in a robust tradition within which I could work for some specific purposes and which fits some models of 'best practice' for judicial and practitioners' practical reasoning. I shall not elaborate on this here.[45]

Some of the ideas that I had developed in relation to standpoint, process thinking, conceptual analysis and rationality were applied and refined in my studies of Evidence. I also used ideal types to help to dig out the stable but largely unarticulated working assumptions of Evidence scholars and to reveal the extraordinary degree of consensus underlying two centuries of Evidence scholarship which I labelled 'the Rationalist Tradition'.[46]

There is an intimate relationship between Evidence and Legal Theory. I have already indicated how the gravitational pull of doctrine both impoverished and distorted Evidence scholarship and marginalised the field within the discipline of Law. Similarly, analytical jurists have paid relatively little attention to the connections between Evidence and Legal Theory. Theorising about evidence in law inevitably involves philosophical questions about epistemology, epistemological scepticism, inferential reasoning, proof and probabilities that had generally fallen outside the sphere of mainstream Jurisprudence. The similarities and differences between historical and legal enquiries about particular past events were especially interesting. Less obvious was the role of narrative in relation to both types of question and the complex relations between narrative and argument in rational and other methods of persuasion.[47] One outcome is that relations between these various kinds of reasonings are not adequately explored.[48] Basic concepts in the subject of Evidence, such as relevance, materiality, probative force, probability, credibility and presumptions, have received rather uneven attention from analytical jurists. As we saw in Chapter 10, nearly all discussions of legal reasoning and interpretation concentrate on questions of law in hard cases, with little or no reference either to questions of fact and more generally to reasoning and rationality in other legal contexts such as investigation, negotiation and sanctioning.

Studying Evidence opened up for me a whole agenda of relatively neglected theoretical issues that belong to legal theory. These are not only interesting in themselves, but also can cast new light on traditional topics in Jurisprudence, such as the similarities and differences between types of reasoning; concepts such as cogency, weight and relevance in various contexts; varieties of scepticism; and many empirical questions in Psychology and Sociology.[49]

My inaugural lecture at UCL in 1983, about ten years into this project, was entitled 'Evidence and Legal Theory'.[50] This was an attempt to structure theoretical aspects of Evidence and Proof under the main 'jobs of Jurisprudence'.[51] I resisted the urge to call for a Brand New Theory of Evidence for the Modern Age, but suggested that one could map a number of related lines of enquiry under the organising concept of 'information in litigation' instead of 'judicial evidence'.[52] Later I developed some ideas about Evidence as a multidisciplinary field, involving many perspectives, specialisms and practical applications. With Philip Dawid, David Schum and others this was eventually developed into two further projects, including what seemed to be an ambitious programme at UCL that turned out not to be ambitious enough, as I shall relate in Chapter 20.

I have been criticised by Denis Galligan, among others, for producing what they see as unmanageable agendas:

> Twining seems to be suggesting [that] one is precluded from entering the arena without first mastering – in addition to the law and practice of evidence – the philosophy of knowledge and logic, moral and political theory, probability theory, psychology, ethnomethodology, and statistics – to name but a few pertinent disciplines. All of course are relevant to evidence, just as they are relevant to any area of social or legal enquiry; but it does not mean that all have to be merged into one . . . it is a mistake to think that broad generalisation of an interdisciplinary kind is a substitute for close analysis of a selective kind.[53]

This reaction is understandable. For some of the lines of enquiry I identified seem to be daunting. Galligan and I are in agreement that many disciplines are relevant to the study of evidence, that it is impossible for one individual to master many disciplines and especially that 'close analysis of a selective kind' is important – indeed, most of my work on Evidence has been on detailed topics. Furthermore, I am probably more of an anti-reductionist than Galligan.[54]

This criticism misses three vital points: first, most inferential reasoning in both legal and other contexts is based on 'common sense' in the absence of 'harder' evidence.[55] Secondly, scholarship and enquiry are largely collective enterprises pursued by teams, intellectual communities, allies and combatants who individually are variously equipped. Thirdly, rethinking a field or a sub-discipline, or something narrower is a never-ending task, more often than not collective but, as we have seen in Chapter 12, sometimes it can be significantly advanced by individuals. Such tasks are particularly important when, as in the case of Evidence in Legal Contexts, a field has become stuck in a narrow groove which not only leads to neglect of important questions but also distorts or impoverishes enquiries within that groove. Having devoted the better part of twenty years to 'rethinking' one legal 'field' as a case study of broadening our discipline, I may not have achieved much more than releasing some hares, most of which I have not been able to pursue very far or at all.

Teaching: tough, but fun

> Easy and Fun to Teach
> Tough but Fun to learn
> Most students are converts[56]

In collaboration with Terry Anderson, and later David Schum, Philip Dawid, Christopher Allen and others, I taught 'Wigmorean analysis' for over forty years and together we modified it in some significant respects. Although there were other aspects, especially to do with story-telling, we focused mainly on teaching our students to master some basic skills of constructing, reconstructing and criticising binary arguments based on evidence, especially mixed masses of evidence in complex cases.[57] The centre-piece was 'the chart method' which can be summarised as follows:

> Wigmore's 'chart method' is a specific set of techniques for analysing a complex body of evidence. In respect of a given case or disputed issue of fact, all of the data that are relevant and potentially usable in an argument for or against a particular conclusion ('the ultimate probandum') are analysed into simple propositions that are incorporated in a 'key list' of propositions. The relations between all the propositions on the key list are then represented in charted form using a prescribed set of symbols, so that the end-product is a chart or set of charts of a (typically complex) argument. The method is like chronological tables, indexes, stories, and other devices in that it is useful for 'marshalling' or 'managing' complex bodies of data so that they can be considered as a whole; it differs from these in that the organising principle is the logical relationships between propositions in an argument rather than time sequence, narrative coherence, source, alphabetical order, or other taxonomy.[58] The method is also useful for identifying strong or weak points in an argument and subjecting these key points to rigorous, detailed, 'microscopic' analysis.[59]

A partial illustration of the Chart Method

The illustration that follows assumes that the *ultimate probandum* is that 'X murdered Y' or, stated more formally, that '(A) Y is dead, (B) Y died as the result of an unlawful act, (C) it was X who committed the unlawful act that caused Y's death and (D) X intended (i) to commit the act and (ii) thereby to cause Y's death.' The coroner's report and observations at the scene satisfy all concerned that 'Y died at approximately 4:45 p.m. on 1 January in his house as the result of an unlawful act committed by another.' The following key list and chart analyse five testimonial assertions and related inferences that the analyst claims are relevant to the *penultimate probandum*: 'It was X who committed the unlawful act that caused Y's death.'

The key list

1. X was in Y's house at 4:45 p.m. on 1 January.
2. X entered Y's house at 4:30 p.m. on 1 January.
3. W_1 saw X enter Y's house at 4:30 p.m. on 1 January.
4. W_1: I saw X enter Y's house at 4:30 p.m. on 1 January as I was walking on the sidewalk across the street.
5. X left Y's house at 5:00 p.m. on 1 January.
6. W_3 saw X leave Y's house at 5:00 p.m. on 1 January.
7. W_3: I saw X leave Y's house at 5:00 p.m. on 1 January.
8. X was *not* at Y's house on 1 January.
9. X did not enter or leave Y's house on 1 January.
10. X: I never went to Y's house on 1 January.
11. X was at her office at 4:45 p.m. on 1 January.
12. X was working at her office from 9:00 a.m. to 5:00 p.m. on 1 January.
13. X: I was working at my office from 9:00 a.m. to 5:00 p.m. on 1 January.
14. A claimed eyewitness identification by a pedestrian walking on the other side of the street *is* doubtful.
15. It may be someone other than X whom W_1 saw enter Y's house.
16. The sun had set before 5:00 p.m. on 1 January.
17. A claimed eyewitness identification made after the sun has set is doubtful.
18. It may have been someone other than X whom W_3 saw leave Y's house.
19. W_2 saw X enter Y's house at 4:30 p.m. on 1 January.
20. W_2: I saw X enter Y's house at 4:30 p.m. on 1 January.
21. X's testimony should not be accepted.
22. X is lying about her actions and whereabouts on 1 January.
23. A person accused of a crime has a strong motive to fabricate testimony that might exonerate her.
24. X is the accused in this case.
25. X was probably not in her office on 1 January.
26. 1 January is New Year's Day and a legal holiday in this jurisdiction.
27. Few people go to their office and work all day on New Year's Day in this area.

The Chart

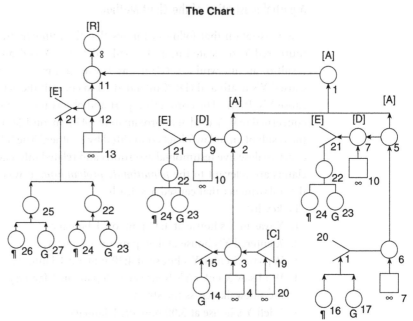

A = assertion; E = explanation; R = rival; and D = denial. Note that a defendant becomes a 'proponent' of rival and denial assertions, and thus the prosecutor may *use* the process of 'opponent's' explanation to undermine.

The Chart was constructed by Terry Anderson and is reproduced with his permission.

Over the years Anderson, Schum and I refined, simplified and extended Wigmore's rather ponderous approach in several ways and now refer to ours as 'Modified Wigmorean Analysis' (MWA).[60] There have been some misunderstandings about MWA. First, there is still a mistaken view that 'the chart method' or 'modified Wigmorean analysis' involves an unwieldy, over-elaborate, difficult, set of skills that is of limited use to practitioners.[61] This mistake is usually due to a confusion between the complexity of the method and the complexity of the evidence. The general idea is simple and quickly learned; like any technique, to apply it skilfully takes longer; it is mainly useful in dealing with complex mixed masses of evidence. With a simple protocol it can be applied easily to routine cases or to test whether a seemingly simple case is more complicated than appears on the surface.

On the basis of years of experience, we have shown that the approach is within the reach of undergraduate law students who can master the basics for simpler applications in two–three weeks (e.g. at the start of a traditional course on the Law of Evidence). One of MWA's most important uses is marshalling mixed masses of potential evidence into a structured argument. Most of our teaching has focused on quite impressive mastery of the basic approach in complex cases by third-year students or postgraduates in six–eight weeks.[62] Many of our former students have reported that they have found the approach of value in practice in both routine and complex cases. This is hardly surprising because the method is a semi-formalisation of best practice.

Secondly, this is another prime example of the continuing influence of the doctrinal tradition. The term 'legal method', along with 'legal reasoning' is typically restricted to argumentation and analysis of questions of law.[63] As Frank pointed out, in legal practice questions of fact and problems of fact-determination are far more common in adjudication for judges, jurors and others. That applies even more strongly to other events and decisions within a total process model of litigation and to practical decision-making in other contexts. By treating the Law of Evidence as co-extensive with the subject of Evidence in Law, scholars, teachers, trainers and even practitioners have almost completely marginalised what Wigmore called 'the Logic of Proof'. Symbolic of this neglect is the occasion when I found that a course on training detectives focused on the Law of Evidence, with instructors seriously opining that 'logic' was too 'academic' for them. But surely Sherlock Holmes is the patron saint of both investigators and evidence scholars.

By 1995–7 I had completed several books on Evidence and I was turning my attention to Globalisation and Law. My main ideas are to be found in *Rethinking Evidence* and *Analysis of Evidence*. Until 2012 I continued to teach Analysis of Evidence, mainly MWA, at both UCL and Miami, occasionally elsewhere. Dave Schum also taught it to students in several disciplines, including law. He also trained intelligence analysts. This is the kind of teaching that I have most enjoyed in my career and, on the whole, I think that I steadily improved. Co-teaching with a combative trial lawyer who was also a disciple of Llewellyn and a close friend was a constant pleasure.[64] Dave Schum and Philip Dawid added a multidisciplinary perspective.[65] Learning to master the basic techniques is tough, involving exercises on increasingly complex material. But it should also be fun. The raw material is very rich: not only alleged miscarriages of justice, other *causes célèbres*, but also texts taken from the Bible (Solomon and the Baby), literature, archaeology, intelligence analysis and so on. In addition, I have used other neglected materials of law study, such as limericks and love letters.[66] The students became very engaged with their major exercise, applying MWA to cases or historical puzzles of their choice; they participated in role plays, mock trials and story-telling, with the highlight being the annual Wigmore Days in the Anderson home in Miami and the Twining home in Iffley, when they presented their cases. In Miami, they were criticised and guided by 'alumni' of the course. They seemed to enjoy it. The most rewarding aspect was how skilled they became after a few weeks of drilling.[67]

15

Bentham's College (1983–99)

Introduction

I started full-time at UCL in January 1983, having taught for one day a week in the previous term.[1] By then we had bought and settled into a house in Iffley village, within the city limits of Oxford, and this has been our much-loved home ever since. As I write, I can look down to the Thames at Iffley Lock and in order to think I can sit in my chair or lie on my bed watching the river and the circling birds; or I can walk along the river south towards London or north-east towards the city or follow several other routes in the village. The decision to make our home in Oxford was a difficult one: I hate commuting, but I am not a Londoner by temperament. The family favoured Oxford. The overall result was that I involved myself less in the general London scene and wrote much more. In order to render my dues to the Faculty of Laws, UCL and the University of London, when I was doing full-time teaching I made a point of staying in London for at least three nights a week during term, mainly sleeping three blocks from the Faculty at the Penn Club, to which I was introduced by a Quaker friend. Those three and a half to four days per week were pressured; I did most of my research and writing in Oxford.

I have been a member of UCL for nearly thirty-five years. I still have a pigeon-hole.[2] I made many friends, only a few foes, enjoyed collegial 'Butler tours' to Russia, China, and Poland,[3] was stimulated by colleagues and students, was bored by committees, won a few battles, lost more and experienced many of the pleasures and pains of a fairly orthodox mid and late academic career. These are mostly peripheral to the narrative of the development of my thinking and writing, as I did most of that in the quiet of Iffley. This chapter focuses on the most relevant aspects: the institutional context, namely UCL, the Faculty of Laws, the Quain Chair of Jurisprudence and what I did, and did not do with it; my involvement with the inter-collegiate system of the University; the significance of my visits to Miami; and the relationship between my teaching and my writing between 1982 and 2000, the year that marks the start of my disengagement with UCL. This chapter is mainly about context. It provides some relevant background to the last four chapters on Legal Education, Globalisation, General Jurisprudence and 'R/retirement' (Chapters 17–20). To add a bit of colour

Chapter 16 evokes my contrasting relations with four jurists during the UCL period: two obsessives, Jeremy Bentham and Ronald Dworkin; a kindred spirit, Neil MacCormick; and my brother-in-Evidence, Terry Anderson.

Bentham's College

University College is often referred to as 'Bentham's College' and in recent years he has been used, sometimes overused, to symbolise the whole institution for public relations purposes. The myth that he was a Founder of UCL has been thoroughly debunked, for he was nearly 80, played very little part in its planning, and was quite critical of the 'aristocratic' approach of two of its founders, Henry Brougham and Thomas Campbell. He probably never even set foot on the site. In a picture painted in 1922 by Henry Tonks, a large JB is in the foreground, inspecting the plans with the architect, with three smaller Founders lurking in the background. The picture, which hangs in the Flaxman gallery, has been criticised for its lack of historical accuracy and its even greater lack of artistic merit. However, interpreting Benthamiana is a tricky business: JB is known as 'the spiritual founder' of UCL, even though spirit in the religious sense was not part of his vocabulary. This is quite appropriate, for the central planks of UCL's ethos are clearly Benthamite: religious tolerance, educational opportunity, freedom of speech and enquiry, useful knowledge and innovation were and still are among its cardinal values. Much of this ethos is explicit in his writings on education, especially *Chrestomathia* (1816).[4]

A second reason for calling UCL 'Bentham's College' is his continuing material presence in public – the famous or notorious Auto-icon constructed from JB's skeleton, his original clothes (now 'refurbished'), his walking-stick and some memorabilia, with a head of wax based on his death mask.[5] Anyone can today visit Mr Bentham during working hours in his cupboard in the South Cloister of UCL and giggle, stare in awe or even consult him. I will not retell the story or debunk the myths surrounding this remarkable phenomenon. I have written and spoken about it enough.[6] I have often used the Auto-icon in teaching (what does it mean; is this where utilitarianism leads us?), emphasising its ambiguity (is this vanity, arrogance, a joke or does it have a serious message?) and its subtle mockery of treating bodies as people or sacred objects rather than material things.

On a visit to UCL, Mary Robinson, ex-President of the Irish Republic (and an ex-law teacher), spoke about 'Imaginative Possessions', a phrase she borrowed from W. B. Yeats.[7] For England she instanced the common law, the English language and the place of land in our literature as formative influences on national identity; for Ireland she gave as examples the great potato famine, Seamus Heaney's 'two-mindedness' (both British and Irish), and the nested identity of being at once Irish and European – all examples of the point that nationalism can be outward looking and empathetic. Tonks's picture, the Auto-icon, and the massive collection of JB's manuscripts are imaginative possessions that form a central part of UCL's identity. JB feared ghosts, although he 'knew' that they were non-existent; one sometimes feels that the College has been possessed by the spirit of the Auto-icon, which invites frivolity, jokes and japes while sending out some sardonic, cryptic messages.[8] For Bentham was a serious, wide-ranging, highly original, and, up to a point, influential figure. He has also been excoriated and mocked. Recent revisionist scholarship suggests that he was more profound, more subtle and more conflicted than his widespread image as a mechanistic Gradgrind or shallow cost–benefit analyst suggests. Foucault made the idea of the Panopticon prison infamous, deservedly so in my view; but Bentham has been defended at a higher level of abstraction as a pioneer of openness and transparency, especially in relation to democratic theory. For him publicity was the main element that distinguishes representative democracy from despotism, because in the former 'some *eventual faculty of effective resistance*, and consequent change in government, is purposely left, or rather given, to the people'.[9] I shall discuss my own ambivalence towards JB below. Suffice to say here that UCL does have good reason to be proud of its association with Bentham and his followers, especially in its emphasis on tolerance, reason, transnationalism and engagement with real world problems and issues.

The Faculty of Laws

There have been some excellent histories of the University of London and of UCL.[10] Apart from a very useful article by John Baker (1976), the Faculty of Laws has not been so well-served.[11] There is room for more, especially covering the period of expansion since the 1970s. Institutions of learning need to be careful about making grand historical claims. UCL was indeed the first university institution to offer an undergraduate degree in English Law (1826) but by 1900 it had produced only 135 graduates with LLBs; UCL could also claim to have admitted the first woman law student to its courses (1873) and the first woman law graduate (1917) – different names and persons. Much more significant was the choice of the basic approach to law teaching. There were perhaps three models on offer: a School of Legislation based on Bentham's radical ideas; the first Professor of English Law, Andrew Amos, a rising practising barrister and devoted teacher, is said to have brought 'the fire and thunder of actual litigation' to the classroom; and John Austin, a shy, ascetic, abstract, positivist thinker, who was the first Professor of Jurisprudence.

Bentham was discarded; Amos did not last long. Sadly Austin's lectures failed for lack of a sufficient audience, so his principal legacy was The *Province of Jurisprudence Determined*, which he viewed as 'merely prefatory' to the full course of lectures which he never constructed. Austin was a disciple of Bentham and a committed utilitarian. It seems probable that if he had completed his plan he would also have dealt with 'The Art of Legislation' (what Bentham called 'Censorial Jurisprudence'), based on utility but in a more conservative form than Bentham. On its own Austin's *Province* was treated as presenting 'General Jurisprudence' as an abstract analytical science limited to the clarification of 'principles, notions and distinctions' which were a necessary part of all mature legal systems. If Austin had been a better speaker and had kept his audience both his legacy and English legal scholarship might have been very different. His idea of determining the essence or nature of positive law and of abstract analysis of what later became known as 'fundamental legal conceptions' provided the main basis for a dry, rigorous doctrinal tradition, based on a conservative version of positivism, isolated from both critique and the law in action.[12]

The extraordinary displacement of Bentham by followers of John Austin was a profound historical mistake: Bentham's Censor would have put the pedestrian Expositor in his place – a fairly lowly one, not the core of legal scholarship and understanding. It is true that Bentham's writings have to be selected carefully to be suitable fare for students, but as the excellent post-graduate course on 'Bentham and the Utilitarian Tradition' at UCL has shown, some of his texts make fine material for vigorous dialectical conversations with a range of opponents, critics and successors; indeed, I cannot remember having contributed to a more rigorous, enjoyable and coherent course. It sounds narrow, but Bentham ranged very widely while always coming back to a central point. His idea of a School of Legislation could perhaps have been improved by some fire and thunder, and more room could have been made for skills in handling basic concepts and detailed rules than he allowed; in time history, context, practicality and engagement with contemporary issues would have found their place in accordance with the general UCL ethos.

Alas, the dead hand of Austin's successors prevailed and the mainstream UCL tradition in Law became a strong form of doctrinal positivism (black-letter law) backed by a rigorous uncritical version of Analytical Jurisprudence. Legend has it that Georg Schwarzenberger, a distinguished Professor of International Law, used to say when addressing first-year students: 'This is not a Faculty of Justice; this is not a Faculty of Law; this is *The* Faculty of Laws.' Of course, there were individuals who deviated from this view, but nevertheless the core of the tradition was that students studied *leges* rather than *ius*.

In 1906–8 UCL, King's and the newly formed LSE agreed to pool many of their teaching resources under the umbrella of the University of London. The inter-collegiate system lasted in various forms until the mid-1960s at under-graduate level and until the late 1990s at postgraduate level. This mitigated the influence of Austinianism, made it possible to build up a strong full-time faculty and catered for a variety of constituencies: full-time and part-time undergraduates; the External system and a path-breaking, expansive, and eventually anarchic, postgraduate programme. I have told the detailed story elsewhere.[13]

In 1982 Jeffrey Jowell (now Sir), South African-born, ex-Oxford, LSE and Harvard, anti-apartheid activist, public law scholar and public intellectual, became Dean of the Faculty. From the outset he was concerned to move UCL Laws in the direction of more liberal, pluralistic, socially aware and reform-minded approaches. He recruited some sympathetic 'heavies' as professors: Bob Hepple (later Sir), a fellow South African and anti-apartheid activist (one of Mandela's lawyers in the Rivonia trial) and an influential Labour Law and Torts specialist;[14] Malcolm Grant (now Sir) who, like Patrick McAuslan, specialised in Planning Law as well as Land Law, with similar views and who later became a dynamic, inevitably controversial, President and Provost of UCL; and myself from the supposedly radical Warwick Law School. Later we were joined by, among others, Hazel Genn, a leading socio-legal scholar and public figure (Dean 2008–17 and now a Dame). It was an uphill task, because the tradition was well-entrenched and many colleagues had grown up in it. However, it is fair to say that over time UCL Laws became much more pluralistic and empirically oriented, thanks in large part to Jowell's leadership and appointments.

I did not try to 'Warwickise' UCL Laws, but I did introduce an element of coursework assessment, the idea of options within a course, some ideas about ways of introducing students to the study of law and a different conception of Jurisprudence. I also tried to contribute to a cosmopolitan culture, which started with the expanding postgraduate programme and filtered down to the undergraduates when English and French, English and Spanish, English and Italian and English and German Law degrees were introduced, accompanied by cadres of lively students from Continental Europe.[15] I did introduce an opt-in provision for a non-specialist four-year LLB but, as at Warwick, this failed miserably because of lack of uptake and lack of enthusiasm on the part of colleagues. For the Sesquicentennial Celebrations of the University of London in 1986 I wrote a quite light-hearted piece called '1836 and All That: Laws in London 1836–1986'.[16] There were three serious themes: that the scale and style of university legal education in England has been largely demand-led; that the most successful periods in the history of Law in London until 1986 had been when the various Law departments and faculties of the University had co-operated by pooling their resources in 'the inter-collegiate system' which flourished at undergraduate level from 1908 to about 1965 and continued in the massive LLM, involving five law schools, eighty different courses (at least on paper in 1987), nearly 500 students in 1987 and over 1,000 not much later.[17] I wrote a prose-poem in praise of the intercollegiate LLM which I later spent six months trying to save in 1993–4, but which inanely disintegrated around the Millennium, resulting in unnecessary conflict, much duplication and the withering away of many specialist options. I also praised the provision of opportunities to study for London Law degrees externally which continues today as part of 'the University of London International Programme', with the undergraduate LLB and a Certificate in Common Law still intercollegiate. This had not been a good vehicle for academic innovation. For most of its history the External LLB and LLM were not exciting intellectually, but their social history is magnificent, with many prisoners, including British prisoners of war, interned African nationalists and many others from many spheres and countries, obtaining Law degrees by distance learning.

The Quain Chair of Jurisprudence

The Chair of Jurisprudence at UCL was one of the two founding Chairs of UCL Laws. Jurisprudence and Legal Theory (*sic*) is still a compulsory subject within the LLB,[18] whereas it has become optional at Queen's Belfast and in many English and Welsh universities, but remains compulsory in leading Scottish law schools. At the end of the nineteenth century under the will of a former Professor of Anatomy, Richard Quain, four chairs were endowed in his memory and that of his brother, Sir John, a barrister and judge. By the time I took up appointment as Quain Professor of Jurisprudence the only discernible benefit for me was an annual Quain dinner for which the food (but I think not the drink) was paid for from the diminished Quain Fund. It looks as if the Quain family got a bargain. I was not much impressed by the title, nor were my children who called me the Quaint Professor; but other people were – to an extraordinary extent. When I joined UCL in 1983, I thought that Warwick was the better law school and that I was coming down in the world; but others (not only at UCL) seemed to be hugely impressed by the title and, more rationally, by the prestige of UCL; some were surprised at my appointment, because there may well have been better-regarded candidates. My five predecessors included two knights and one lord, who had all earned their honours by public service of various kinds. They were all scholars and public intellectuals. John Austin was an influential jurist, but Sir John MacDonnell, Sir Sheldon Amos and Lord (Denis) Lloyd are mainly remembered, if at all, as men of affairs rather than for their contributions to Jurisprudence. One is not remembered. Another exception was Glanville Williams, the leading criminal law scholar of his generation, who probably did much of the groundwork for his major books while at UCL, but published most of them after he moved to Cambridge in 1955.[19] Nearly all of them in their different ways could be called middle-order theorists, because they were concerned with the contemporary relevance of their work to genuinely practical issues. I was happy to follow in their footsteps, for that is how I see myself.

In 1983 the Quain Professor was still Professor of Jurisprudence for the whole University of London, not just UCL. This meant that it included responsibility for co-ordinating the teaching of theory courses in the intercollegiate LLM and in the External LLB, as well at all levels in UCL.[20] I also tried to build a legal theory community by initiating a University-wide seminar the organisation of which circulated around the six Law Schools until, about year six, it came to a halt at Birkbeck where it stayed. Even in 1983 there were signs that the

University might fragment into a series of independent institutions, as the larger ones – UCL, Imperial, King's, LSE and Queen Mary and Westfield – were already the size of middling universities and were expanding. From the start I was committed to preserving the University of London despite its rather heavy central bureaucracy, because there were distinct advantages in co-operation rather than competition, and Senate House protected smaller institutions such as SOAS, Royal Holloway, Goldsmith's College and a number of other valuable units, including the Senate Institutes of which the Institute of Advanced Legal Studies (IALS) was one. Accordingly, I devoted myself to University affairs as much as UCL ones. In 1993–4, I was seconded to Senate House (Graham Greene's 'Ministry of Fear') for six months to try to salvage the inter-collegiate LLM which was in danger of being scandalously underfunded.[21]

One of my first actions as Quain Professor was to review the curriculum for the 'theory courses' in the LLB, the LLM and the External LLB. Each presented different problems. Unfortunately, in the UCL, LLB Jurisprudence was in the final year. Some students resented having to take a compulsory course on 'theory' and were apprehensive because it seemed very different from what they were used to. There were several challenges: ensuring teamwork and individual space for a quite varied collection of colleagues eager to teach theory;[22] to try to help professionally oriented students to understand why theory was relevant to them and to learn to think in more abstract ways than they were used to; and to try to get Jurisprudence moved to the second year where it belongs, so that it can feed off and feed into other courses and help to give some coherence to the undergraduate degree. My theoretically oriented colleagues were an outstanding, talented, individualistic bunch, but hardly a team. We decided to do nearly all of the teaching by seminars, but to have one lecture a week in the LLB course as a supplement. This was my best opportunity to use the Quain Chair as a platform or pulpit for my views, but my colleagues wanted to participate, so the programme of lectures also became a compromise. Nearly all of my successors have seen the Quain Chair more as a platform than a job.

In contrast with these eager teachers the undergraduates seemed to me collectively to present a sullen, even hostile front to the course, at least in October. Although not all were destined for legal practice, UCL Laws' student culture appeared to be dominated by those who had secured training places in city solicitors' firms or aspired to do so. What was the relevance of 'theory' to them? Some were anti-intellectual, more were just unintellectual, some just wanted to do what was necessary to get a good class of degree. Most had gained a place at UCL because they were very good examinees. For them one difficulty was that they were used to substantive law courses examined by three-hour unseen exams and Jurisprudence was different in several ways. Later in the year it became clear that some were or had become genuinely interested.

My attempted solution to these twin problems of teachers' enthusiasms and student resistance was to introduce a considerable amount of choice within the Jurisprudence course: Part I was a general introduction to the field. We each took one or two seminar groups. I insisted that students should be exposed to reading original texts but gave some flexibility to the teachers to choose what texts to use beyond Hart's *The Concept of Law*, some Bentham and some Dworkin. Following Hart's example,[23] I extended the number of questions in the exam from four out of nine to three out of twelve (with some alternatives within a question). We divided Part II of the course into a series of options: three weeks on a 'Major work' (popularly known as 'big book') chosen from four or five texts, with a compulsory question on the exam for each book. In some years I used *The Cheyenne Way*, or Jeremy Waldron's *Nonsense Upon Stilts* (attacks on natural rights by Bentham, Burke and Marx), and once, not very successfully, Plato's *Gorgias*. My stated rationale was that anyone graduating with a Law degree from UCL should at least have read one whole book; many recognised that this made a valid point about our curriculum and practices. Then six weeks was devoted to a special topic, again from four or five options, each supervised by a different colleague, to be assessed by a substantial essay (maximum 8,000 words) counting for 25 per cent of the mark. Thus, my colleagues had some scope for choice in the first part and two lots of quite open choices in the second part. In the beginning, for the students, choice within a course was revolutionary, or at least novel, as was writing a substantial essay for assessment. They worried inordinately about these choices. By the start of term two the resistance was dissipated for most, although for some even the thought of an assessed essay was worrying. But it worked. Over the years I was repeatedly surprised and pleased in May at how the resistant students I had met in October could produce such excellent work.[24]

In my view, legal theory belongs in every year in different forms, but in a three-year degree the main Jurisprudence course should be in the second year, building on and illuminating 'bread and butter courses'.[25] I soon managed to capture some territory by organising the first-year undergraduate introduction course and to introduce at least some general perspectives and basic skills for beginning law students.[26] I emphasised that they had all experienced law, that mastering the jargon was no more difficult than learning a hundred words before going on holiday to Italy or Spain, and that far from being dry, esoteric and mysterious, Law is an exciting, important, humanistic discipline.[27] That course was attenuated because teachers of first-year subjects were raring to go and resisted allowing the introductory bit to last more than two or three weeks. And, of course, the first week was usually Freshers' week, so the audience for inspirational teaching was mainly composed of hung-over, homesick, bewildered teenagers.

At postgraduate level I had more scope. Candidates for the LLM were allowed to claim that they had specialised if they took three out of their four courses in one subject group. We created a Legal Theory Group: UCL took the main responsibility for Jurisprudence; LSE took on a new course on Law and Social Theory; we recognised a few other courses as being members of the group and over time we added Alternative Dispute Resolution, 'Jeremy Bentham and the Utilitarian Tradition' and my half-course on Evidence and Proof. I took responsibility for the Jurisprudence course and, as in the LLB, I introduced 'special topics' from which students could choose, to start with mine being 'Reason, Reasoning and Rationality in Legal Contexts?', which nearly became my next major project.[28] I also regularly taught Evidence and Proof, often with help from Christopher Allen and Professor Philip Dawid from Statistics.

The PhD degree was also awarded by the University of London. I did not take on many doctoral students, partly because until recently PhDs were rare in Law – the situation has now changed – but also because I did not approve of the way it was structured in London at the time: no postgraduate community; no methods courses; uneven supervision – with the result that most doctoral students were lonely long-distance runners focusing for three years or more of their lives on a single narrow question with very little support. On two occasions at conferences I floated a paper motion that the PhD in Law as practised in England was 'inhuman and degrading treatment' in violation of Article 3 of the European Convention on Human Rights. It was never put to a vote, but many colleagues acknowledged the point. Today the practice has greatly improved and if I had started now I would have recruited many more doctoral students.

The External LLB also had a Jurisprudence course. Soon after taking up the post, I convened a meeting of theory teachers in the University of London to discuss it. If I remember right about fifteen people turned up and expressed strongly conflicting views, illustrating the pluralism of Legal Theory in London. It soon came clear that there would be no consensus. So, as chairman, I asked for a volunteer to design the syllabus. Only Stephen Guest offered to help and he took it over and organised it for years. He did a very good job in his own way, but I soon regretted that I had not taken it on myself as it would have been a good opportunity to design a course that reflected my view of Jurisprudence and was suited to distance learning. At the time I felt that I had my hands full with the internal courses.[29]

Postgraduate affairs

In 1988 during yet another period of financial austerity, UCL introduced a Draconian policy of suspending students whose fees had not been paid. I was postgraduate adviser to two Ugandan students who were on government scholarships. This was just after the Amin and Obote periods, the civil war with the Lord's Resistance Army had begun, Uganda was in turmoil and it was hardly surprising that the government was behind with scholarship payments.

After two warnings the Registrar suspended these two students (along with others) without a hearing. I was outraged. After unavailing attempts to appeal and an acerbic correspondence with the administration, I decided to take stronger action. This was the period when fees for overseas students were becoming an important income stream. I had been doing a lot in helping to recruit overseas students for UCL (the Law Teachers' Programme was part of this – Chapter 17); I picked up the relevant files and stormed down to the Dean's office and plonked them on his desk, saying (well, not quite shouting) that I could not recommend UCL to overseas applicants when it treated students like this and so I would no longer recruit for the College. The Dean, Jeffrey Jowell, backed me; probably his only other option was to order me to continue to carry out my duties or face dismissal, even though my recruitment activities were mainly voluntary. After a delay the suspensions of the Ugandan pair were terminated, but they had lost a year. There were matters of principle involved and other students were affected, so I insisted that an adhoc committee be set up at College level. That was done reluctantly and ineffectually. I am not usually confrontational, but I was so angry that I was prepared to leave UCL. Jeffrey was sympathetic, but surprised at the strength of my reaction. This, I think, was not really because I had been born in Uganda, but rather because an injustice was being done to 'my' students.

There were several outcomes of this episode: the students were reinstated and helped from a hardship fund, but they had lost a year. I had made some enemies in the central administration, but maybe the procedures were softened; a committee was set up, but their first meeting was delayed until the autumn; I was not invited to meet them and in the end they did not seem to take the matter seriously. Most significant, I was persuaded to take on the position of Postgraduate Tutor in Laws, in charge of the whole postgraduate programme including admissions, staff–student relations and curriculum development. I have never enjoyed administration so much.

I took over from Andrew Lewis, who had done a sympathetic job in a rather formal way. I was surprised to find how much power and discretion were vested in this position. I insisted on the establishment of a Postgraduate Committee with student representatives to give authority to important decisions. I also persuaded Jeffrey Jowell that I needed a deputy. Alison Clarke joined me and was wonderful with the students. With Lorely Teulon as the efficient administrator our three-person team set about improving the whole system. I was popular with the postgrads from the start, perhaps because of my support for the Ugandans. My aim was to strengthen the academic programme, improve the facilities and generally integrate the postgraduates into the life of the institution.

As a symbolic act I cased Bentham House from basement to roof garden examining the pictures in the 'circulation areas'. Almost all were portraits or photographs. I reported that they depicted only two categories of person: single, mostly ageing (though not all white) males (famous alumni and distinguished professors) and groups of undergraduates, also nearly all male. There was not a single picture of even one postgraduate student. This was not because they were less photogenic; rather they were invisible in most respects: undergraduates were supposed to be represented on the Faculty Board, but they were not; the Student Law Society was really for 'weenies', as we used to call them in Chicago; there was no special physical place for postgrads in Bentham House, so they gravitated to IALS which housed the postgraduate law library and most rarely came to the Faculty. There were other ways that they were on their own. Some colleagues chose not to involve themselves in postgraduate teaching on the grounds that the standards were lower because entry was not competitive and they saw postgrads as both inferior and peripheral. In fact, the normal entry standard for the LLM was an Upper Second, many of the students were mature with varied experiences of life, including legal practice, most were motivated to learn – why else do postgraduate work? On the other hand, undergraduate admissions favoured 18-year-olds who were good examinees, who had been institutionalised for life (except for a few who were 'mature' (over 23) or had taken gap years). Sometimes their main motivation seemed to be to get through the hoops as quickly as possible to complete a *rite de passage* in order to join the legal establishment. This is, of course, unfair to many intelligent and interesting individuals. It was not the students' fault; rather it is the structural weakness of a system of three-year Law degrees for 18–21-year-olds (the shortest in the world), with an over-burdened curriculum largely dictated by practitioners, who would pressure these children to make premature career choices and swot up masses of doctrine only to tell them later that History graduates were favoured by the best firms because they had uncluttered minds.[30]

In 1993–94 I was seconded to Senate House for six months to undertake a review of the vast and unwieldy intercollegiate LLM as part of efforts to save the University of London from disintegrating through underfunding and resulting potential scandals.[31] By then the programme had over 1,500 students and virtually no central administration. This turned out to be less of a poisoned chalice than I had expected, because teachers of innovative, recondite or less populated subjects knew that the opportunity to teach them would probably disappear if each College offered its own LLM. They were proved right. With the help of Lee Sheridan, my former colleague from Belfast, we imposed some order and improved the resources. The intercollegiate degree survived for a few years. It was an ungainly beast, uneven in quality but adventurous intellectually and it pioneered some significant new developments. However intercollegiate rivalry eventually trumped innovation and specialist enclaves, and the LLM was foolishly replaced by several more narrowly focused programmes that largely replicated each other.

Research and writing

UCL is a great centre of scholarship, including innovative and cross-disciplinary work. I found both the Faculty and the College very supportive in this regard.

Splitting my time between London and Iffley, interspersed with a fair amount of travel at particular seasons, made for efficiency in managing my time and priorities. I prepared my teaching, taught and administered in London for a hectic four days a week from October to March; weekends and most of April to September were devoted to library research, thinking, conversing and writing mainly in Oxford at a more stately pace.

My research, writing and publication from 1982 to 2000 divides into four main areas. First, having spent ten years at Warwick doing the groundwork on Evidence, without publishing much, nearly all my main publications in that field came out in the first ten years at UCL. I continued to be active in the field for much longer, but the main books (*Rethinking Evidence, Analysis of Evidence, Theories of Evidence: Bentham and Wigmore*) belong to that period (see above Chapter 14). In 1983 I became Chairman of the Commonwealth Legal Education Association (CLEA) for almost a decade and during the same period I also published a lot on legal education and its infrastructures, but these were more 'activist' projects, as described in Chapter 17. My 1994 Hamlyn Lectures, *Blackstone's Tower*, was the most scholarly of my writings about legal education. After that I wrote little on the subject until a brief revival of interest in the aftermath of the Legal Education and Training Review (LETR) of 2013. Similarly, my main writings on Bentham date from my time as Chairman of the Bentham Committee (1982–2000) and most were explanatory or celebratory, rather than original contributions to Bentham scholarship. Globalisation and Law became my first priority as I wound down my work on Evidence in the mid-1990s (Chapters 18 and 19). Similarly, my main research and reading for that project was in the 1990s, but the three main books belong to the period of 'R/retirement'.

Evidence, Legal Education, Globalisation, Bentham – 'Why is a Professor of Jurisprudence writing about these topics rather than contributing to contemporary debates within Legal Philosophy?' someone might ask. Indeed, some did. The simple answer is that I am not that kind of jurist. *Rethinking Evidence* was always conceived as a case study illustrating what may be involved in 'broadening the study of Law from within'. That surely is a theoretical enquiry. The central question of my Globalisation and Law project was: what might be the implications of 'globalisation' for Law as a discipline and for Jurisprudence as its theoretical part? The mission of the discipline of Law is to advance understanding of its subject matters, viz. legal ideas and phenomena. Except perhaps for some of my more polemical papers on legal education, the great bulk of my work was theoretical in this sense. I was doing my job.

I still have a pigeon-hole at UCL, but for health reasons I visit it rarely. What I have enjoyed most of all about UCL has been its cosmopolitan ambiance. By the mid-1990s there were postgraduates from over sixty countries, lively undergraduates and postgraduates from Continental Europe, intending law teachers from several parts of Africa, post-apartheid South Africans, Bangalore graduates, and later even a few North Americans and Latin Americans had joined the long-standing flow of Greek shipping lawyers. It reminded me of the passage from Herman Melville's *The Confidence Man* that I had used to symbolise the Great Juristic Bazaar.[32] I loved the atmosphere and the vitality and I am confident that the spirit of JB, the Citizen of the World, takes maximum pleasure from it.

American interludes II (Miami 1971–2011)

When we get to Miami what we'll do is get some sort of job, you know; cause hell, I ain't no kind of hustler. I mean there must be an easier way of making a living than that.

(Rats to Joe, in *Midnight Cowboy* (1969))

My relationship with Florida, with the University of Miami Law School, and my close friend and collaborator, Terry Anderson, started in 1978. But it really belongs to the UCL period and the early years of retirement and fits in well here.

I first went to Florida in 1971 to visit Soia Mentschikoff with some last questions about KLRM. I was stressed about the book. I had recently seen *Midnight Cowboy* (the movie), in which, after exploring low-life New York with a Texan hustler called Ratso (Dustin Hoffman), Joe accompanies him on a Greyhound bus from New York to Miami. The film ends with Joe cradling the dead Ratso in his arms as they arrive at their destination. In 1971 I boarded a Greyhound Bus in Philadelphia. For the length of Florida, which seemed very long indeed, I kept looking sideways at my soporific companion to make sure that he was still alive.

This was the start of my forty-year association with Coral Gables, first as a private guest of Soia and later as a frequent Visiting Professor at the University of Miami Law School (hereafter UM). From 1969 Soia regularly taught for a semester at the Law School. She said she liked it because 'they have sand in their shoes'. However, she accepted appointment as Dean in 1974; it became Soia's School and continued to be so for some time after her retirement in 1983 and even her death in 1985.

On another short visit in 1978 I gave a Faculty seminar on Wigmore's chart method and after being quizzed on my Llewellyn book, I was invited to be a Visiting Professor. I was not able to accept until 1981 when I came for a few weeks to co-teach a seminar on 'Dispute Resolution' with the Dean. This meant that she attended the first and last sessions. After covering *The Cheyenne Way* and several anthropological case studies I introduced them to Wigmore's chart method, including analysing Edith Thompson's deathly letters to her lover. At the end we held the first, and most festive ever, Wigmore Day on Soia's boat dock outside her home; the students put on a Bywaters and Thompson show with 1920s music, as well as analysing some of the evidence. Throughout Soia lounged on a deckchair in a baseball cap, intervening only once to ask of Edith's letters 'Who said these were LOVE letters?'[33]

By 1981 Terry Anderson and I had agreed to collaborate on a book on Analysis of Evidence.[34] Since then we have continued as collaborators, co-teachers and close friends despite his contempt for deadlines. Terry deserves a section to himself in the next chapter, but before that I must say something of my relationship with the Law School.

From 1978 until 2011 I had an open invitation to be a Visiting Professor in the UM Law School. Initially I could only get away during UCL long vacations (the hurricane season), but then after 'early retirement' in most years I was able to go for the whole spring semester (January to May the best time of year) thereby missing the worst of the English winter. One should remember that Montesquieu as jurist emphasised the importance of climate in legal culture. Usually I taught Analysis of Evidence and a seminar; I could fill a whole book with accounts of experiences (including Hurricane Andrew, the build up to the Iraq War and 9/11), Florida pastimes (Penelope volunteered in two wonderful botanic gardens and we both frequented the Biltmore Hotel's famous swimming pool) and some memorable and warm friendships – far too many to do justice to here. Instead I shall focus on how my teaching, research and writing were enhanced by this arrangement.

These visits were enormously productive from my point of view. My globalisation seminar fertilised, broadened and advanced my work in the area (Chapters 18 and 19). Much the same applies to the Evidence courses, both on my own and especially co-teaching with Terry Anderson. The Library was excellent and easy to use and the support from librarians, Faculty assistants and others was tremendous; I took advantage of free photocopying. American law teachers do not realise how lucky they are in having this kind of support until they visit institutions in other countries. If I had chosen to, I could have made my job much easier than hustling, as Ratso suggested. Rather, having no administrative duties or micro-political diversions, I seized the opportunity to read, research, converse and write in optimal conditions.

For me the intellectual hub of the Law School was the programme of almost weekly Faculty seminars at which visiting speakers were challenged and colleagues, especially younger ones, were treated only a bit more gently. Papers were usually circulated in advance and, whatever the topic, were read carefully and questions prepared by a core of those who turned up regularly. Speakers were usually allocated about fifteen minutes, but by convention they could be interrupted at any time. On my first presentation I was thrown by an early intervention.[35] I tried to follow the example of those colleagues who prepared assiduously every week, because I felt that this was collegiality at its best. It took time, but it was doubly rewarding. On almost every visit I volunteered to present a paper to a Faculty seminar and at some workshop or conference; in addition to having my early drafts mauled by Terry, I was free to ask for comments from individual colleagues who nearly always complied.[36] I have not kept count, but I reckon that over twenty of my subsequent publications went through the Miami mill. This practice is widespread in academic law, but this was the best version that I have ever encountered. So, thank you.

There was one downside to being a perpetual Visitor. I did not feel that I belonged and some colleagues were unsure how to treat me. Was I a perennial guest? Or a full member? Or an intriguing foreigner? Or just a hanger on? For the most part this uncertain status did not bother me. However, I sometimes felt critical of local practices or conventions, but thought that expressing my views, however diplomatically, would be considered out of place. Opinions on intellectual issues, yes; but on conventions and policies, not my business. The most important example was that I felt that the Law School was missing opportunities to become a, perhaps even the, national centre of research and education about Latin American and/or Caribbean legal affairs. Miami was often talked of as 'the capital of Latin America', economically and culturally, as well as for cruises and shopping. The Law School had a few individual scholars interested in Latin American or other regional studies, but this was not an institutional priority. Early on, I asked why there were no courses taught in Spanish and no Law School cricket team. The response was that the Association of American Law Schools (or the American Bar Association) would not allow the first and that cricket was not known in Miami. Both excuses were untrue.[37] Some twenty years later a single course in Spanish was introduced to great fanfare and no objections. I had good contacts in the Caribbean and offered to do a tour to establish some links, but this was shrugged off as a boondoggle (hustling?).

As I interpret it, Soia Mentschikoff transformed a modest, but well-regarded local professional school into a national one and encouraged an outward-looking perspective, but the orientation was international and European rather than regional. By the time Soia died *US News and Report* law school rankings had only just begun (1983) and were not yet taken seriously. With the steady growth in influence of such indicators over time the highly controversial 'rankings game' came to the fore. When I first encountered these phenomena in the 1980s I was first amused, then highly critical.[38] Eventually what really shocked me was how seriously they were taken by nearly all the relevant 'stakeholders' – parents, students, alumni, administrators, funders, others, especially journalists and, reluctantly, even academics. The story is a long, complicated and, to my mind, tragic one. To put the matter very simply: the UM Law School might have tried to become a great centre of regional legal studies; instead it opted into the national league table model, struggling to hold its place in the second division with significant economic disadvantages compared to both publicly funded and well-endowed Ivy League institutions. Their competitive advantage was, and still is, location, location, location.

If I had become a tenured faculty member of a US law school, even if half-time, I would have felt obliged to commit to fighting to persuade my institution to break out of the stranglehold of the 'football league model',[39] by which the law schools have been squeezed into conforming to one set of aims and one set of criteria. American friends tell me that I would have lost and that the game would have been hopeless, not least for a foreigner.[40] They could be right. In the event I did not try at all hard to get such a position, because we preferred the UK as a place to live.[41]

16

Four contrasting relationships (Bentham, Dworkin, MacCormick, Anderson)

Over thirty-five years in both London and Miami I naturally acquired many friends, significant colleagues, outstanding students and splendid support from librarians and other staff. Not many overt critics, because the main technique of those from whom I differed most was Ignoring. That sometimes irritated me but, on the whole, I was pleased because I had plenty of sounding-boards and those with whom I had the most profound differences about the nature and roles of Jurisprudence tended not to move off their own confined territory. During the UCL period there were four people who were always present, sometimes in the foreground, more often just there as an important part of my intellectual milieu. Ambivalence marks my relations with Bentham; a sharp divide was apparent between Ronald Dworkin's and my ideas; and with Neil MacCormick, a kindred spirit, I enjoyed a close friendship; as co-author, co-teacher, sounding-board and friend my relationship with Terry Anderson was even closer.[1] These, including JB, are all contemporaries, in contrast with Hart, Collingwood and Llewellyn.

Sparring with JB

> I am the very model of an ambivalent Benthamist – viewing him with awe, but treating him variously as inspiration, formidable opponent, useful sounding-board, and as a crackpot.
>
> (William Twining)[2]

I am a jurist rather than a specialist Bentham scholar. My first encounter with JB was through Herbert Hart's inaugural lecture at Oxford in 1954. In 2017 I still keep up with the Bentham Project website. During the interim I have gained an intimate knowledge of a few of his extensive texts, probably about 10 per cent of over a million words. I even tried my hand at editing, but wisely decided that this was not my métier. I have regularly taught about him at undergraduate and postgraduate levels, focusing mainly on the principle of utility, fallacies, fictions and evidence. The Bentham Committee was established in 1959 to oversee the production of the scholarly edition of his *Collected Works*. I joined the Committee in 1971, became Vice-Chairman from 1976 to 1982 (while Hart was Chairman), and Chair from 1982 to 2000.

I have written and spoken about many aspects of Bentham's ideas but, except as an administrator and a rather ineffectual fund-raiser, my contributions to specialised Bentham Scholarship have been limited. I edited, published and commented on two manuscripts on torture;[3] I wrote extensively about his writings on Evidence and Jurisprudence; I used *Anarchical Fallacies*[4] as a launching-pad for exploring various forms of scepticism about human rights;[5] and in the 1980s and 1990s I gave several public lectures on Bentham and his ideas, especially in 1998, when celebrating the one hundred and fiftieth anniversary of his birth. The second General Editor, John Dinwiddy, tragically died young and I edited a collection of his main writings on Bentham.[6] Some of my writings involved explaining some of Bentham's main ideas and eccentricities to non-specialist audiences rather than contributing much to specialised Bentham scholarship, except sometimes to place him in some broader contexts.

My relationship to Bentham – the man, the Auto-icon, his manuscripts and his ideas – is a bit of a puzzle. A friend called it 'affectionate ambivalence'. I can understand Herbert Hart being mystified by my fascination with both Bentham and Llewellyn, two rather unlikely thought-mates. I can try to give a partial explanation. I have huge respect for Bentham – his unremitting rationality, his acuity, his foresight, his range, his originality, those of his values that are embodied in UCL's mission statements, his constant movement from generality to detailed particularity and back, the relentless application of his general ideas to so many different issues and his integrity, even his foibles. But I am not a Benthamite. I have always been deeply ambivalent about him, rather less so about Llewellyn. Like Hart, I am an insecure modified utilitarian and I very much agree with Hart's summing up: '[W]here Bentham fails to persuade, he still forces us to think.'[7] In commenting on the torture manuscripts and his attacks on non-legal rights, I have explicitly distanced myself from some of his positions. I do not think that the main thing that is wrong with torture is its susceptibility to abuse; I do not accept that all talk about non-legal rights is mischievous nonsense – human rights discourse and human rights law can be useful and have sometimes probably had good consequences – but I agree with most of Bentham's criticisms of loose rights-talk and I am not comfortable with ideas about inalienable, universal or absolute human rights.[8] Digging deeper, for me one of the attractions of Bentham is that there are crucial tensions in his thought and he struggled with these.[9] Was he an act-utilitarian or a rule-utilitarian – or does he undermine this distinction, which is, after all, a modern construction? Did he think that judges should be bound by rules in his ideal codes or should there always be some consequentialist leeway in judging in the particular circumstances of a case?[10] Did he really believe that there should be no peremptory rules of evidence or procedure? He supported the French Revolution in the early days (he was made an honorary Citizen of France) but he attacked very sharply the revolutionaries' manifestos – especially the Declarations of 1791–5. Was he in favour of their values, but shocked by their discourse or was there a deeper ambiguity in his thought? It is reasonably clear the Bentham was a radical rather than a revolutionary, usually giving a high priority to security, but there is room for different interpretations of his positions in this area. When security, subsistence, equality and abundance (the principles subordinate to utility) compete can one literally *calculate* what is the best course of action? Or is that just a metaphor? And how does liberty fit in? His ideas on democracy and constitutionalism provoke different interpretations. There are several quite illuminating debates within Bentham scholarship and there are always the possibilities that he changed his mind or that some of his central ideas are not coherent or even consistent.[11]

The first task of Bentham scholarship has been to establish, as far as is feasible, 'authoritative' texts (Bentham himself loathed authority). Begun modestly in 1959 and living a hand-to-mouth existence until recently, the Bentham Project had by June 2018 published thirty-three substantial volumes of *The Collected Works* (out of a projected eighty) and had done preparatory work on many more. It is more than half-way there, and it has an encouraging momentum. If Bentham had 'belonged' to France or Germany the project would have been state-funded and finished by now. Of course, Bentham studies will never be completed. Secondly, the publication of the *Collected Works* and the evolution of a transnational Bentham community has led to another kind of scholarship – revisionist interpretations and debates. Bentham himself sometimes distinguished between his 'arcane' and 'popular' writings; for example, *An Introduction to the Principles of Morals and Legislation*, perhaps the most studied utilitarian text of all, is much cruder and more easily criticised than his more arcane writings on utility. These are now accessible online, although not all are yet edited. A new, more complex, and for some less unattractive, Bentham is beginning to emerge, but we are some years off a fully reconstituted arcane version.[12] Thirdly, a comprehensive contextual narrative of Bentham's intellectual development has yet to be written. The historical and textual terrains are vast, sweeping across modern boundaries between disciplines, and a good deal has yet to be explored in detail. The challenges of Bentham scholarship are different from those confronting the Shakespeare industry, but hardly less daunting.[13]

I have often held imaginary conversations with the Auto-icon, sometimes standing in front of it/him, sometimes on buses or aeroplanes, sometimes lying in bed asking: 'What would you have thought about this, JB?' A quick look at the index in the Bowring edition or more expansive ones produced for the *Collected Works* may turn up some explicit references to his published works and now many more can be consulted online. But, using one's imagination, it is also fun to ask: 'What might JB have thought about this?' For example, it is interesting to extrapolate (not merely speculate) plausible answers to such questions as: 'What would JB have thought of using drones to bomb suspected terrorist targets with the risk of causing collateral damage?' (a simple risk analysis?) or 'How would JB have reacted to Brexit or Facebook or President Trump's use of Twitter?' There have been several Bentham blogs and many mentions of him in other ones and JB himself has made some contributions.

Blogs tend to invite frivolity or vituperation, or alternative facts. They are used mainly for public relations purposes. JB would have enjoyed the gimmickry, he was, after all, quite nerdy, but he would almost certainly have been horrified by casual or deliberate disregard for truth. On the other hand, one can easily imagine his delight at 'Transcribe Bentham', the prize-winning scholarly crowd-sourcing initiative by the Project that has resulted in volunteers transcribing Bentham's manuscripts with over 20,000 pages by May 2018. This surely ticks many of the boxes of Bentham's springs of pleasure: vanity, gadgetry, cost-saving/economy, popular participation and, crucially important, publicity.[14]

For me the completion of the Bentham Project has been a cause. At my interview for the UCL Chair in 1982 I said that the completion of the Project during my lifetime was my main intellectual ambition. That bold aspiration will not be realised, but it may have helped to secure the job. At least we can claim to have kept the Project afloat in a period when it might well have foundered for lack of funds.

Passing each other by: Ronald Dworkin

During the UCL period another omnipresence, booming rather than brooding, was Ronald Dworkin, who was almost my exact contemporary. Born in Rhode Island in 1931 he came to Oxford as a Rhodes Scholar in 1953. We both sat for the final examination for the BA in Jurisprudence in 1955. Herbert Hart was so impressed by Dworkin's paper in Jurisprudence that he purloined the script.[15] He gave me an A, but did not steal mine. Dworkin's script was the first frontal assault on Hart who became so obsessed with this relentless critique that he never paid much attention to other critics, especially more socially oriented jurists.

When Hart stepped down from the Corpus Chair of Jurisprudence in 1968 he encouraged and helped Dworkin (then at Yale, but still relatively unknown) to become his successor.[16] Dworkin was brilliant, forceful and egocentric. He was a good debater, but I found it almost impossible to argue with him except on his own terms.[17] For a number of years, while he was still at Oxford, we invited him to UCL to confront our undergraduate and postgraduate students. We primed them well, he handled the students gently, and it was good theatre. But the debate never strayed from Dworkin's home territory – law as an argumentative practice grounded in basic principles of morality.

Almost the first time I encountered Ronnie was at a seminar in Nuffield College Oxford shortly after his appointment to the Chair of Jurisprudence in 1969. He began unexpectedly by saying that the central question in Jurisprudence is: 'Who is the Top Banana?' Brushing aside the impious thought that this is an example of a question-expecting-the-answer-'ME', one can infer that his answer to this ambiguous question was, and still is for his followers, political morality. All of his writings flow from that premise. Reasoning about and interpreting legal doctrine is a set of argumentative practices based on moral principles and located in the superior courts of the United States and perhaps some other common law countries. The ideal judge, to whose approach all judges should aspire, is Hercules.[18]

Despite his American accent, Hercules' approach is general, but his application is particular, because the premises of a correct legal argument depend on the underlying ideology of a particular system:

> If a judge accepts the settled practices of his system – if he accepts, that is, the autonomy provided by its distinctive constitutive and regulative rules – he must, according to the doctrine of political responsibility, accept some general political theory that justifies these practices.[19]

This is an important idea, fraught with difficulties, and the subject of much controversy. This ideal type may be one powerful model of how common law judges faced with difficult questions of law should reason. I find it useful, but it is not the only model; it is not an accurate description of how common law judges in fact reason in hard cases, but some approximation to it; it is not an adequate account of the position and roles of common law appellate judges, which are much more complex than this model suggests; it takes almost no account of the different situations, historical contexts, roles and problems of upper court judges elsewhere in the common law world, let alone 'judges' (however conceptualised) in other traditions;[20] it equates law with legal doctrine; and it dismisses all other kinds of theoretical enquiry as philosophically uninteresting and not of practical importance.[21]

Dworkin, with typical *chutzpah*, claimed that his was the best theory of law. But is it a theory of law? It is not even adequate as a theory of appellate adjudication, still less of adjudication, still less of law. If it is a theory, it is an aspirational theory of what constitutes valid argumentation on questions of law in hard cases in some particular institutional contexts. It claims to be 'practical', but practical for whom? It does not claim to be realistic. It does not claim to give historical explanations of how particular traditions or institutions came to be. Nor does it make much allowance for different institutional structures and conventions in different legal traditions, cultures and municipal legal systems. Political morality is the Top Banana and understanding law involves looking through that lens alone.[22]

Dworkin's main achievement was to highlight and develop a kind of normative theorising which is different from classical Natural Law. That is an important contribution. Some of Dworkin's specific ideas were stimulating, even when wrong-headed: for example, the One Right Answer thesis, the idea of doctrinal integrity, the sharp, but in my view unstable, distinction between principle and policy.[23] He revived debates about positivism, which soon became repetitive and sterile; he helped to distract Herbert Hart from engaging seriously with empirical and contextual legal studies;[24] he fortified the tendency to treat abstract legal philosophy (positivist and anti-positivist) as co-

extensive with Jurisprudence or as the only intellectually respectable part of
it.[25] Most surprising of all, he implied that there are no 'philosophically'
interesting questions about understanding law other than moral ones.[26]
Everything else is subordinate, parasitical or of inferior interest to the Top
Banana. This is an impoverished vision of the discipline of Law and of
Jurisprudence as its theoretical part. And, of course, like most other canonical
jurists, Dworkin roots his conception of law and the agenda of Jurisprudence
firmly in the doctrinal tradition of substantive law.[27] The Achilles heel of
Dworkin's Empire was making a distorted view of adjudication central to his
vision of law.[28] This criticism sounds rather harsh, but it is, for the most part,
not disrespectful – we were just two different kinds of inhabitant within the
broad landscape of political liberalism.

In my personal view Dworkin was better as a performer than he was as
a scholarly writer; his intense/marathon Legal Philosophy colloquia at NYU
and UCL were perhaps his greatest achievements; he contributed some splendid polemical articles to the *New York Review of Books*. His books sold well,
and he was much-cited, but his style was rather convoluted and he often
appeared to be restating the same basic argument in different terms. For me,
he seemed impressive as a moral philosopher, though I did not agree with him,
but much less persuasive as a jurist: a hedgehog who claimed to know one Big
Thing and replayed it constantly with subtle, barely discernible variations.
From the standpoint of a jurist considering the health of the discipline of Law,
and of Jurisprudence as its theoretical part, his contribution is at best just one
limited, and not entirely convincing, part of what is involved in understanding
law, especially in an era of accelerated 'globalisation'.

My professional and personal relations with Ronnie can be dealt with quite
briefly. As jurists we were obviously different kinds of animal. We were continually passing each other by physically as well as intellectually: he taught in
Oxford and lived in London; I lived in Oxford and taught in London. I was
usually in Miami when he held his colloquia in UCL; when I was at UCL, he
was at NYU. Face to face we were civil; I encouraged his performances at UCL;
intellectually he ignored me.[29] I was generally more relieved rather than
irritated by this. We just had different agendas and styles. Once over a drink
he said something to the effect: 'You know, Bill, I think we have different
conceptions of the great issues of the age.' That was clearly true. For him this
meant, very largely, American political issues about race, inequality, abortion,
euthanasia and other questions that had divided the US Supreme Court. His
philosophical concerns were with equality and justice; his juristic focus was
almost entirely on adjudication on questions of law. I do not think in terms of
'great issues of the age' and my concerns have been more with colonialism and
decolonisation, nationalism, ethnocentrism, world poverty, terrorism and the
survival of humankind. My juristic agenda is also quite different. After a few
attempts to take him on I stopped trying. He was a poor listener, a non-reader,
and very skilful at switching a discussion or debate onto his own ground.

However, I did pay attention to Ronnie – how could one avoid it? – and I learned some things from him.[30]

Neil MacCormick: a kindred spirit and friend

While my relations with Ronnie Dworkin were incompatible intellectually and distant socially, Neil MacCormick and I developed an intellectual affinity and a warm friendship. I have written about the personal side at length elsewhere.[31] Here I shall concentrate on our intellectual similarities and differences and the role this relationship played in my intellectual development.

Our backgrounds were significantly different. His family were committed Scottish Nationalists. His father had helped to found both the National Party of Scotland in 1928 and its successor, the Scottish National Party (SNP, 1934). Neil was active in national politics from early on, ran in hopeless seats in Westminster elections and then was elected and served with enthusiasm as a SNP Member of the European Parliament for five years (1999–2005). He had a degree in Philosophy and Literature from Glasgow before reading Law at Oxford. His education, culture, enthusiasms and accent were nearly all Scottish; he wore a kilt and played his bagpipes on festive occasions; we shared a taste for single malts. I would like to say that we had similar personalities, as he was widely admired and indeed loved, combining intelligence, hard work, energy, panache, a love of teaching, talking and writing, and a great *joie de vivre*; but that would be to claim too much.

We were both influenced by Hart, Neil more than I. After my return to UK in 1966 our career paths were similar except, having been elected to the Regius Chair of the Law of Nature and the Law of Nations in Edinburgh aged 31, he retained this as his base until retirement and afterwards. My first memory of him was of two young Professors of Jurisprudence playing frisbee in the grounds of Belfast Castle at a conference on Constitutional Law in 1972, shortly before I moved to Warwick. We immediately bonded. Thereafter we kept in close touch as best we could at academic events, commenting on each other's drafts, seeking advice and staying at each other's homes when we examined each other's students.

Our views converged on many matters: we both were committed to liberal education,[32] to stimulating our students to think and to a conception of understanding law that encompassed concepts, values, facts and rational discourse, combined with some emotional intelligence. I sympathised with his political commitments and learned from him the difference between 'the dark side of nationalism' and the empathetic kind that is the basis for recognition 'as equally legitimate (because the same in kind) the love others bear for their own'.[33] Neil was more a philosopher than I ever was. We seemingly had different conceptions of 'legal philosophy': I confined the concept to the most abstract kinds of thinking and argued that Legal Philosophy was only one part of legal theorising; Neil had a Scottish view of 'philosophy' that rejected any sharp divide between theory and practice, the general and the particular or the abstract and the concrete. When President of the SPTL in 1984 he criticised some 'legal philosophers' as inviting the criticism 'that they lack any real interest in real law'.[34] Our only jointly co-authored paper showed that we had similar views on education; on the what, why and how of teaching Jurisprudence; on theorising as an activity; and on many other points.[35] Neil, in collaboration with Ota Weinberger, developed an institutional theory of law, which was the starting point of his ambitious quartet on *Law, State and Practical Reason* (1999–2008), completed not long before he died in April 2009. He acknowledged that his institutional approach was quite close to Llewellyn's law jobs theory.[36] Finally, although Neil's focus was firmly on the European Union/Community, he acknowledged the significance of globalisation and gave me valuable encouragement in pursuing that project.

There were naturally some matters on which we differed. Two are quite significant and stimulated me to clarify my own position.[37] First, in his later work Neil called himself a 'post-positivist'. He claimed that he had moved away from Hart's positivism and much closer to Dworkin's rejection of any sharp distinction between law and morality. It is true that in the first edition of his excellent book *H. L. A. Hart* (1981) MacCormick defended his mentor against Dworkin's criticisms, and that in the second edition (2008) he was more critical of Hart and seemed to be moving towards Dworkin.[38] Indeed, in *Rhetoric and the Rule of Law* he came close to Dworkin's thesis that there is a right answer to almost every disputed question of law, even in hard cases. In my view, Neil exaggerated the significance of the change. On the one hand, when he returned to Edinburgh he rediscovered his roots in the tradition of the Scottish Enlightenment, especially Smith, Stair and Hume. That tradition just does not fit most versions of the positivist/anti-positivist dichotomy. On the other hand, while in Oxford he could adopt the posture of a detached observer, but I have argued that his seeming change of view represented a gradual shift from that standpoint towards a greater emphasis on participant standpoints, reflecting his much greater involvement in activist affairs in his later years.[39] Neil once told me that often when shaving, he looked in the mirror and asked himself: 'Am I really a positivist?' The question clearly bugged him for a long time. If I had stood near him while he was shaving, I would have commented: 'Silly question.' If, as I believe, the positivist/anti-positivist divide is an obfuscating fog, his re-labelling himself is not very significant except when it obscures the point that he returned to his roots in neo-Kantianism and the Scottish intellectual tradition.

A second difference was that I failed to persuade Neil to take seriously the thesis that the mainstream literature on 'legal reasoning' is not only unduly narrowly focused, but also misleading about the place and role of practical reason in law. In the second edition of *Legal Reasoning and Legal Theory* he made a small concession to me by including a brief discussion of issues of fact.[40] Not long before his death he wrote some preliminary sketches on coherence which might well have led him to explore the relationship between narrative and argument in practical reason in greater depth. But he did not live to complete this. In my view this is significant because there is a hint of a lurking doctrinalism in his work on reasoning which fits uneasily with his institutional theory of law.

Neil did not live to engage with Amartya Sen's *The Idea of Justice* (2009), but I am confident that he would have sympathised with Sen's critique of 'ideal theory', exemplified by Rawls, in contrast with the Scottish emphasis on practical reason that engages with 'real world' issues. The central question of his last book, *Practical Reason in Law and Morality* (2009), was: 'Can reason be practical?' MacCormick's unequivocal response was: 'Most certainly it can!'[41]

Terry Anderson

In my faculty seminar in Miami in 1978, I was rash enough to claim that I was the only person other than John Henry Wigmore himself to try to teach his chart method more than once.[42] There was a growl from the end of the table, which sounded something like this: 'Not true. I have been doing this for years and I am doing it HERE AND NOW.'[43] This was Terry Anderson whom I had met briefly in Chicago in 1964. We joined forces and soon agreed to collaborate on a set of teaching materials based on our courses in Miami and England. I thought that we could toss this off in a few months; seventeen years later in 1991, it was published as a book, with a second substantially revised edition in 2005 (with David Schum as the third author) – a total period of twenty-seven years of collaboration on one project.[44] 1978 was the start of a special relationship which is still continuing.

Our collaboration broadened out to include co-teaching (mainly Analysis of Evidence, but also Elements on two occasions), sharing his house and an apartment in his bachelor days, being the two anglophone members of a team studying Dutch Criminal Procedure in the Netherlands in 1994–5, much dining out and drinking and nearly thirty years of hotly contested ping-pong – on which more later. From 1978 until now nearly everything that we have written on Evidence has been as co-authors, or contributing linked papers to a joint project, or at least having drafts rigorously and ruthlessly commented on by each other, often after lengthy discussion.

Of course, we are unlikely twins, not only in respect of height and appearance. Terry is a stocky mid-Westerner; a pragmatic, relentless litigator who is at heart a romantic and an idealist. I am taller, an English intellectual, an unrepentant theorist with a tendency to sit on the fence, and quite sceptical to boot. We had different teaching styles. Our cultural tastes – especially in literature – barely overlap, though Terry did convert me to John Grisham, Robert Parker and other crime writers. I liked Elmore Leonard, but Terry did not. On one occasion I tried to sum up our relationship:

The contrast in our table tennis styles epitomize our differences: Terry played a steady game with a persistent straight bat until he saw an opportunity where he [could] ruthlessly, like a good advocate, go for the jugular; I favored swerve and spin and nifty placement, with an occasional wild smash. We are both intensely competitive, but gentlemanly about lets and scoring. Over the years neither has dominated the other for very long – and on our kitchen table in Wassenaar – our only level playing field, but a bit small – we successfully played co-operative ping pong trying to extend the length of each rally.[45]

To some, the most unlikely aspect of our bond is this lengthy collaboration between a pragmatic, competitive American litigator and [someone perceived as] an Oxford 'legal philosopher'.

The key is, of course, we were both students of Llewellyn and Mentschikoff, both of whom rejected any sharp distinction between theory and practice – as did we. Because of that background we complemented each other, mostly sang from the same hymn sheet, and learned a lot from the experience.

Perhaps the most fruitful period of collaboration was our months together at the Netherlands Institute for Advanced Study in 1994–5. Freed from administration, teaching, litigation, and other distractions, Terry went Dutch. He learned the language fanatically, he cycled long distances, and he suffered and administered repeated culture shocks:[46] he was amazed to find that there were no juries in the Netherlands, that judges intervened actively and defence lawyers were frustratingly passive, that almost all serious criminal convictions were reviewed by an appellate court, mainly through a dossier that included prior convictions and depositions translated into legalese and so on. In November 1994, when it seemed that the whole local population were glued to their television sets following the O. J. Simpson trial, Terry administered culture shock by giving (well-attended) public lectures in which he tried to explain American criminal process while correctly predicting that O. J. would be acquitted. The Dutch found this incredible. Terry spent some weeks 'doing a Wigmore' on the inaugural lecture of Mark Geller, Professor of Assyriology at UCL.[47] The NIAS year also turned Terry into a comparative lawyer and led to his developing an 'audit model' which brilliantly explained how the Dutch system of criminal procedure was different, but not necessarily inferior to, the American adversarial system.[48]

A highlight of our relationship was the *Alcee Hastings* case in which one of the first ever black Federal Judges was indicted in 1981, and later impeached, on charges of conspiracy to solicit and accept a bribe.[49] Terry represented him *pro bono* for over a decade, often as the sole lawyer, with only some voluntary help from friends.[50] I was part of his legal team in the proceedings in the Senate in 1989, so that the only major case I was involved in was the impeachment of a Federal Judge who, having been acquitted by a jury and nearly absolved by the Senate Impeachment Trial Committee that studied the evidence, was convicted by a clear majority by those Senators who had not. Even the Chair of the Senate Committee, Senator Jeff Bingaman (D-NM), voted for his acquittal. Unusually Hastings was not disqualified from holding federal office (nor was he disbarred in Florida) and shortly after his conviction he was elected to the House of Representatives in 1993 and has been subsequently re-elected ever since. Alcee Hastings's character and story are almost as remarkable as his case.

I cannot go into detail about this epic here. There were multiple proceedings for over a decade. There were complex issues of Constitutional Law, Procedure, Criminal Law as well as extremely strongly contested issues of fact; there were political and racial undertones especially in the pursuit of impeachment after a jury acquittal and unresolved questions about the standard of proof in impeachment proceedings – I personally suspect that many Senators voted for conviction on the basis of 'Caesar's wife' concerns; and I remain convinced that this was an extraordinary miscarriage of justice.

During my visits to Miami I was able to observe Terry at close quarters working as a litigator, drafting and compiling reams of documents, discussing strategy, making tactical decisions, presenting arguments and never losing sight of the political and personal dimensions of the case, even when arguing abstruse questions of constitutional doctrine. I expected him to be single-minded, dogged, precise, thorough and craftsman-like. He was all of these things and more. He often seemed obsessive, but rarely skewed in his judgement. But I have never witnessed such relentless commitment, driven in part by a sense of injustice and in part by a concern to do his best as a lawyer. Karl Llewellyn would have been proud of him.

17

Legal Education

Look at me – I had no legal education

(Lord D)

If law be not a science, a university will best consult its own dignity in declining to teach it

(Christopher Columbus Langdell, 1870)

A great and noble occupation

(Henry Goudy, first President of the Society of Public Teachers of Law, 1909–10)

Introduction

The early years of my life in legal education were measured out with attitudes of members of the legal establishment who did not think I had a proper job. 'Look at me – I had no legal education' was the refrain of mid-twentieth-century Law Lords beginning with D – Lords Denning, Devlin and Diplock.[1] Other sneers were more direct. Nevertheless, Legal Education as a field of study and debate has taken up a great deal of my energies as a student, teacher, scholar, administrator, policy-maker and agitator. This was partly because I was interested in Africa and education and higher education before I was ever interested in law.

I have written extensively, probably too much, and quite critically about Legal Education as a field and legal education as a set of ideas, institutions and practices[2] as much as an activist as a scholar. Educational themes have pervaded earlier chapters. Most of my writings up to 1994 are collected in two books. *Law in Context: Enlarging a Discipline* (1997) brings together seventeen essays that advance the cause of broadening the study of law both generally and in specific ways (e.g. in respect of liberal education, access, skills and contextual approaches). *Blackstone's Tower* (1994) is a more coherent book which focuses on the history, traditions and prospects of English law schools as institutions. It makes the case for academic law realising its potential as part of the humanities and social sciences and making a greater contribution to general culture.

This chapter is mainly a gloss on these two books, highlighting their background and providing links with passages that might be still worth reading. I do this because since 1994, the world has changed, higher education and legal education are changing in response to many challenges, and my own ideas have developed, in some respects quite radically. For about twenty years after 1994 my attention was focused elsewhere, especially on Evidence and Globalisation, and I only performed or advised about educational matters in response to invitations. I still stand by much of what I said in my earlier writings, but perhaps I left too many of the working assumptions underpinning the unsatisfactory debates and literature unchallenged.

I became more actively reinvolved after the publication of the Legal Education and Training Review (LETR) in 2013.[3] In the final chapter (Chapter 20), the section on 'Rethinking Legal Education' marks a quite significant late shift in my views on how we might reframe thinking and talk about Legal Education as a field of reflection, research and policy as we enter an era of rapid, possibly revolutionary, changes in information technology, legal services, higher education and education generally. This is still unfinished business.

In order to simplify a complex and potentially repetitive narrative, in this chapter I concentrate on four episodes which are important to my story and for which I can accept some responsibility. The first is my inaugural lecture in Belfast in 1967; the second, a report on *Legal Education in a Changing World* (New York, 1975); the third, a conference on 'Legal education for non-lawyers', in Australia in 1977; the fourth, my involvement with two professional associations and a programme for intending law teachers.

Pericles and the Plumber

My first expansive statement about the field was in my inaugural lecture at Belfast in 1967. The full title was: 'Pericles and the Plumber: Prolegomena to a Working Theory of Lawyer Education' (hereafter 'Pericles').[4] The focus was on the role of university law schools in preparation for legal practice, but the central argument followed Llewellyn in his 1960 lecture on 'The Study of Law as a Liberal Art':

> The truth is, therefore, that the best *practical* training a University can give to any lawyer who is not by choice or by unendowment doomed to be a hack or a shyster – the best *practical* training, along with the best human training, is the study of law, within the professional law school itself, as a liberal art.[5]

'Pericles' was delivered in Belfast in January 1967. It was my first public attempt to challenge the prevailing orthodoxy in the UK. It has sometimes been read as sales talk about the superiority of American law schools. I deliberately focused on the United States because it was not diplomatic to suggest that Dar es Salaam had much to teach UK law schools. I have not changed my ideas on the value of liberal education in law, but my argument in this lecture has often been misunderstood as saying that institutions had to choose between two ideal types, whereas my argument was that neither the image of the enlightened statesman nor of the competent jobbing plumber is suitable for guiding decisions about lawyer education. The tensions between these aspirations continue.[6]

Since then the contexts, legal practice and formal legal education have expanded, diversified and changed significantly and my own ideas have developed. We are entering a period of even greater change. I still believe that Law is potentially an excellent vehicle for liberal education and that a liberal education is important for intending practitioners; but in advocating that American ideas should be taken seriously in the UK, I now think that I underestimated the differences in respect of funding, the higher education systems, legal culture, the organisation of legal services and the politics of legal education.[7] A few American ideas have been borrowed and adapted, such as law school clinics and books of cases and materials, but by and large this has proved to be an indigestible transplant.[8] However, the prestige of American law schools has provided a useful foil for critique of our own arrangements.

The International Legal Center, 1971–75: almost a global perspective

Membership of an International Legal Center (ILC) Committee in New York 1970–5 was a game-changer for me. We eventually produced a report entitled *Legal Education in a Changing World* (1975).[9] This was one of two committees set up by the ILC, to consider the future of legal education and research, mainly in the 'South', from a global perspective. The Committee was funded by the Ford Foundation and met over five years in New York. The Chairman, Professor Jorge Avendano, was from Peru and members were drawn from five continents. They transcended common law/civil law, North/South, practitioner/academic divides, but some individuals were much more active than others. The proceedings were in English, and the final report came to be dominated by some Anglo-American common law attitudes and ideas.[10] We were supplied with an enormous amount of qualitative information and opinions, but statistics and other hard data were very difficult to come by. Although our perspective was 'global', many countries were not covered – for example, the Soviet bloc and parts of Asia. This was during the Cultural Revolution and the report that we received on the People's Republic of China was succinct: 'There is no legal education in China.'[11]

Despite these limitations, the process was highly instructive and the Committee produced a forceful, sophisticated, succinct, forward-looking report that has stood the test of time.[12] During the next twenty years I used this as a starting-point and framework for analysing legal education policy and for several specific projects.[13]

Our remit covered the whole world, but this was before talk of 'globalisation' became fashionable. Our information was patchy, and our focus was almost entirely on national provision. The culture of law schools is to some extent transnational, mainly within legal traditions or families, but it is also much influenced by local factors. One of the strengths of the ILC Report was that it recognised that particularities of history, culture and tradition, especially higher education structures and finance, providers of legal services, ideology and distribution of power and privilege can all affect local patterns especially where there are conflicting interests. While advancing bold general ideas, it emphasised the importance of local context and held back from making specific general recommendations. It nevertheless provided a coherent framework for analysing and considering systems of legal education at regional, national and lower levels and pointing out possibilities. This served as a quite good preparation for my later work on globalisation. We adopted a global perspective, but our coverage of countries and regions was uneven.

One major lesson of the ILC exercise was that if one is talking transnationally or comparatively, it is imperative to think in terms of national 'systems' (or other large units) of legal education in order to consider the diverse ways in which learning about law takes place in different local contexts. Some smaller countries have a single national law school, but in many countries formal legal education is quite dispersed between various kinds of institutions in different sectors. For example, a project on the records of legal education in Greater London in the late 1990s identified well over a hundred institutions that were doing a substantial amount of law teaching. These included university and polytechnic law schools, the Judicial Studies Board, the Inns of Court School of Law, business schools, police colleges, paralegal organisations and private crammers, as well as provision for A level law and numerous adult education programmes.[14]

In order to spell out a bold vision of the potential role of mainly Western-influenced university law schools in 'the world' the ILC Committee had to move away from the idea of 'legal education' as something taking place almost entirely in universities, but it nevertheless focused almost entirely on institutions with almost nothing about informal learning about law. While recognising the diversity of providers of formal legal education, it emphasised a key role for university law schools, suggesting that they should be the fulcrum of a national system, concerned for the health of the system as whole.[15]

Law teachers as educators

The ILC Report argued that full-time academic lawyers should play a major role within a national system of legal education:

> The single most important resource in any national system of legal education is the law teacher ... The full-time scholar-teacher of law may need to be better equipped as a professional in three respects: as a lawyer, as a researcher and as an educator.[16]

Over the years I have used this passage as a starting point for analysing the roles and careers of law teachers, in particular arguing that they should view themselves as professional educators as well as scholars and lawyers.[17] The argument runs that collectively the academic legal profession and its representatives are and should be the main locus of educational expertise within their national system of legal education and training. This includes pedagogy, educational theory, knowledge of the higher education system, its history and funding, comparison with other jurisdictions and with professional formation in other occupations – matters outside the remit of most practising lawyers and judges. The important point here is that, insofar as law teachers collectively and individually take themselves seriously as educators and are taken seriously as legal education professionals with a near-monopoly of expertise, that expertise should extend to all important aspects of the national situation in their own country, not least in respect of all aspects of professional formation and development from cradle to grave. This may sound more demanding than it is.[18] In fact, there have been advances in recent years: some policy is more evidence-based, the literature is more sophisticated and sustained research mainly by academic lawyers is now quite well-developed. In England and Wales some significant moves have been taken in this direction, largely without fanfare, over the last forty years or so. Since the 1990s a great deal of the work for reviews of professional legal education and training has in fact been done by academic lawyers, including several Professors of Legal Education. This is especially clear in the case of the LETR report, for whom the four lead authors of the review could claim just these kinds of expertise.[19] But there is a long way to go if an academic legal community is to take much of the responsibility for the health of their national system of 'legal education'.

Scepticism about taking education seriously is still quite widespread. For example, it took a long struggle for Legal Education research to be recognised as worthy of recognition in research assessment exercises in UK. This attitude is outdated because both the literature of legal education and educational technology are unrecognisably more sophisticated than they were even ten years ago. Neuroscience promises important fresh insights. And the educational context is much more complicated than it used to be.

There is, of course, a widely held and not entirely implausible view that teachers are born, not made – or, at least, that good teaching is as much a matter of personality as expertise. There seems to be an equally widely held view among law teachers that specialists in education have little or nothing to teach legal educators and that Legal Education is not a respectable subject of study and research.[20] In my view, on the whole the professionalisation of education is to be welcomed, but some of the scepticism behind resistance to these developments is healthy.[21] Yes, we should take educational theory seriously, but the most fashionable kind of educational theory at present is, in my view, too intimately bound up with bureaucratisation and managerialism. Moreover, familiarity with educational theory and pedagogical technique is not a substitute for being competent in and enthusiastic about one's subject.

Two organisations and a programme

During the period 1976 to 1993 many of my legal education activities took place under the auspices of two organisations: The Society of Public Teachers of Law (1976–9) and the Commonwealth Legal Education Association (1983–93). I also instigated and taught on the Law Teachers' Programme at UCL (1984–present). These warrant some brief comments.

SPTL

Raymond Cocks and Fiona Cownie have produced an excellent history of the Society of Public Teachers of Law (SPTL), including the story of its expansion and transition from a gentlemen's social club to a learned society and professional association.[22] It is now called the Society of Legal Scholars and by 2016 it had more than 3,000 members. I was actively involved for a relatively short period (1974–9) during this transition and this section is just a gloss on Cocks and Cownie's account.

In 1966 during the Society's annual conference a Young Members Group was formed and in the coming years it provided a lively arena for discussing Legal Education.[23] Having already taught for seven years, I was too 'old' to join, but I participated in some of their activities and for several years undertook a number of projects to do with academic law publishing and localising legal literature in small jurisdictions.[24] Because of these activities I was made Chair of the SPTL Publishing Committee in 1974. Thus, I was associated with both youthful agitators and a prosaic-sounding professional project.

Election to the posts of Vice-President and President of the SPTL operated on the principle of Buggins' Turn. After a year each Vice-President was elected President, the main duties of whom were to host the annual conference, a largely social event, and to chair Council meetings. When in 1977 the Young Members' Group (YMG) nominated me out of the blue for Vice-President, older members, including myself, were taken by surprise. Some were alarmed. I was too old to be Young, but much too young to be Buggins. But for the fact that I was chair of one quite active SPTL Committee there might well have been a contested election (unprecedented) as it was clearly not my turn. Of course, the main weakness of the Buggins principle is that being President is seen as an honorific rather than as a job; there is little continuity and less leadership. Along with voluntary membership, this has been the weakness of the Incorporated Law Society of England and Wales and many other legal associations.

I took my nomination by the YMG to mean that my remit was to shake up the Society and to treat being an officer as a job. I only had two years. My plan was to make the SPTL into a learned society and a professional organisation. I thought that this would involve some quite radical changes: first, amalgamation of the SPTL and the Association of Law Teachers (ALT), which mainly catered for law teachers in polytechnics and further education, by extending membership of the former beyond full-time university teachers;[25] secondly, since nearly all law teachers are specialists, to expand and strengthen the specialist groups and make them the main arenas for scholarly discussions and initiatives; thirdly, to turn the Society's journal, *Journal of the Society of Public Teachers of Law* (JSPTL), into a genuinely scholarly publication, to change its name and siphon off papers about legal education to the ALT's journal, *The Law Teacher*, thereby strengthening both; fourthly, generally to help to bolster the infrastructure of academic law by continuing the law publishing project, starting an SPTL Law Series and exploring subsidies for some legal publications, such as specialised monographs; and, finally, to set up a working party on four-year undergraduate degrees in Law.

In his speech at the Annual Conference Dinner, my successor, John Smith of Nottingham, famously remarked: 'Last year was the year of Twining; this year has been the year of untwining.' This was witty and half-true. There were several disappointments: merger with the ALT failed narrowly to secure the required two-thirds majority; the specialist groups developed slowly, most mainly restructuring their meetings as special sessions at the Annual Conference – I had wanted much more. The SPTL Law series did not last long and subsidies for publication barely happened in face of the view that 'too much is already published';[26] and, most grievous blow to the Young Members, their motion to substitute a hop for the formal Annual Dinner was defeated.[27]

However, my term was not a total failure: two journals were strengthened; law teachers were better informed about publishing;[28] the Conference at Warwick was intellectually lively and included a coach trip to Stratford to see *Othello*, which included a particularly vicious Iago; this delighted both a leading 'Crit' and Myres McDougal a vociferous 'anti-crit' for different reasons, so that both of my Guests of Honour were happy. Imagine my pleasure when in 2002 the SPTL changed its name to the Society of Legal Scholars (SLS). Still a weakness today is the fact that membership of the SLS is still individual and optional, rather than institutional as it is for the Association of American Law Schools where almost all full-time scholar-teachers of law are automatically members by virtue of their affiliation. Such a move would greatly strengthen SLS as a representative body and pressure group.

Perhaps the most significant achievement was to set up a Committee on Four-Year Degrees, which I chaired. At the time, thanks to a quirk in public finances, the Department of Education and Science was unable to prevent students who opted for four-year undergraduate degrees from obtaining mandatory local authority grants. Ever since my time in Belfast I had decided that the standard three-year LLB at 18+ is the Achilles heel of English legal education.[29] We did stimulate a few such degrees (mainly mixed, e.g. Law and Politics, and English and Foreign Law ones)[30] and we kept the Committee going for a long time. Eventually we faded away without a formal report, because we did not want to give central government a clear target to attack. This was twenty years before the Labour government's Teaching and Higher Education Act 1998, which radically changed the financing of higher education.

CLEA

In 1983 at the Commonwealth Law Conference in Hong Kong I accepted nomination as Chairman of the Commonwealth Legal Education Association (CLEA) and continued in office as Chairman, then as Executive Chairman (with Yash Ghai as President), until 1993.

Despite the political ambiguities and ambivalences associated with that anomaly 'the British Commonwealth', I did not have many qualms about accepting. CLEA had been formed in 1971 at the Commonwealth Law Conference in New Delhi by Lakshmi Singhvi, who later became Indian High Commissioner to the UK. It was a professional association, essentially a subsection of the Commonwealth Lawyers' Association (CLA), initially only concerned with organising a legal education section of Commonwealth Law Conferences, including a Commonwealth Moot Competition. Over time it took on a life of its own.

CLEA was funded by the Commonwealth Foundation and provided with administrative support by the Commonwealth Secretariat.[31] In fact, CLEA's main function was networking, which it did rather well, partly because the legal establishments of member states found the conferences and specialist groups to be congenial and one interacted with Chief Justices, law officers, judges and leading practitioners from nearly fifty countries; it was a great arena for professional exchanges, testing the waters and, of course, gossip. During my involvement I attended events in Ocho Rios, Auckland, Nicosia, Kuala Lumpur, Colombo, Nairobi, the Isle of Man and Kwazulu Natal. It was very enjoyable and instructive.

CLEA was expanding. Under the leadership of Neil Gold, it was involved in a series of law teaching clinics, based on Canadian models, in various countries. At first the role of Chairman was little more than helping to plan and host one section of Commonwealth Law Conferences, which met with increasing frequency (first every four years, then three, then biennially). We also held an annual event at Cumberland Lodge in Windsor Great Park, mainly for overseas law students and teachers who happened to be in the country. In addition, I was personally involved in a series of projects, including topics as varied as preservation of legal records, access to legal education and legal professions, law publishing and legal information in small jurisdictions, skills development, training the trainers, law in multilingual societies, human rights education, law for non-lawyers and several other matters relevant to the infrastructure of legal education and training and scholarship.[32]

So far as I was concerned, I contributed some and learned a great deal. Like the ILC experience, it proved to be a staging point en route to my project on globalisation. One important lesson was that both of these activities had limited horizons. They were quintessentially anglophone and common law oriented, although ILC was officially crossing Western legal divides and CLEA did devote some attention to Islamic law, customary law and hybrid legal systems (Mauritius, Sri Lanka and Canada).[33] One lesson I learned was that the post-independence histories of former Dutch, French, German, Italian and Iberian dependencies were significantly different from each other and that extrapolating beyond the common law 'world' was very risky. I became conscious of my own ignorance, but nevertheless remained ignorant. This contributed to my view that many purported patterns and understandings of law in the world as a whole were sub-global, tied up with language, migration and other legacies of empire in addition to economics.[34]

LTP

Finally, at UCL since 1984 we have run an optional programme for present and intending law teachers from among our postgraduates, the Law Teachers' Programme (LTP). This has proved to be much more popular than we first expected and is still running. I still do some sessions each year. Interestingly, in an era which emphasises student-centred learning I find myself in a constant tug-of-war with the class: what they want (or think they want) is almost entirely limited to classroom pedagogical techniques (how to lecture, how to handle power-point etc.). I use my power and authority as teacher to insist on two themes: that it is no use rushing into the how of law teaching before you have given some thought to the what and the why – not only general educational theory and debates about the possible objectives of legal education, but also about the peculiar contexts within which learning about law takes place: the odd history and culture of law schools as institutions and the other contexts such as law firms, barristers' chambers and (formerly boozy) half days of continuing professional development. The LTP is quite different from the general short courses offered for early career academics at university level, which are abstracted from particular disciplinary cultures and usually concentrate mainly on pedagogy. There seems to be hardly any overlap between what we attempted in the UCL Law Teachers' Programme and, for instance, induction courses for new university staff or the more substantial Certificate of Learning and Teaching in Higher Education (CLTHE). The former emphasises the distinctiveness of the context, history and traditional assumptions of *legal* education, the latter general educational theory and pedagogical techniques, without much distinction between disciplines within a rather bureaucratic set of assumptions about universities. At various places they converge, and no doubt complement each other, but the style of the LTP has been quite different.

Law for non-lawyers

In the late 1970s I developed an interest in what is vaguely known as 'law for non-lawyers', an umbrella term encompassing street law, legal awareness, legal literacy, law days, legal consciousness, legal studies, service teaching, law in schools and, more recently, Public Understanding of Law (PUL).[35] These broadly related activities and studies also overlap with research into law and popular culture, knowledge and opinion about law, and human rights education. The main stimulus for my sporadic interest was a conference at Newcastle (New South Wales) in 1977 on 'Law for Non-lawyers'.[36] This brought home to me how much had already been going on, especially in the United States and Australia, under various labels, mainly outside university law schools. It also stimulated me to think about law as a part of 'general culture', a theme that I later developed in *Blackstone's Tower*.

My own paper, 'Legal Education for All', was a slim affair, starting with a satire on the idea that in order to learn anything you need a course in it, suggesting that after the Kerry Packer shake-up all cricketers need a legal education and this could be not less than a four-year degree programme, given the range of fields of law involved.[37] The main point was to link the subject of the conference to several areas that were neglected in conventional discussions of legal education, but which had been highlighted in the ILC Report.[38]

The 'commentator' for this rather fragmented paper was Gil Boehringer, then at Macquarie, a Marxian humanist, whom I knew quite well.[39] His comments did not directly address my paper, which he probably had not seen. Rather he used the occasion to criticise 'Law in Context' as 'Neo-Fabian Jurisprudence', which he said broadened the study of law without attaining depth. Warwick was broad, he suggested, but Macquarie was deep:

> [U]ntil our students developed the intellectual habit of deep enquiry of structured analysis asking what law is, what it does, how, why, when loaded conceptions of legality emerge and change, we will not have fulfilled our pedagogical task, nor I would argue our social duty.

It was a surprise to find a critique of 'law in context' surfacing at this conference, but by linking his remarks to citizenship and democracy Boehringer made them seem both relevant and challenging. I was not and never have been attracted to Marxism, and as an educator I have categorised my approach as embodying the basic values of the liberal tradition of education, but we seemed to agree on a number of points, such as the pervasiveness of law, that all academic legal education should be conceived as a part of general education, that students should be taught to think for themselves and to ask critical questions and that teaching law to non-lawyers in an intellectually exciting way is crucial. I mention this here, because Boehringer's comments stimulated me to think that law for non-lawyers could be as important as university legal education and that somehow this was a better starting point for developing a rounded perspective on Legal Education as a field and as a subject. Ruminating on this provided an important clue to why I was so dissatisfied with how conversations and battles about 'legal education' were conducted – a topic that I shall return to in the last chapter.

18

Globalisation and Law

William Twining,
'The Ship',
Station Rd,
Phoenix,
Nr. Vacoas,
Mauritius,
Indian Ocean,
The Southern Hemisphere,
The World,
The Universe etc., etc.

Introduction

This common childish conceit suggests two things about how we think. First, that it is easy to depict our world in terms of concentric circles neatly organised in a single hierarchy – local, provincial, national, regional, global and so on. However, usually things are more complex than that. Secondly, a child may think that the centre of the universe is where one happens to be. But maybe there is no centre of our universe or our world. The literature on globalisation frequently falls into both traps.

I started to focus on the implications of so-called 'globalisation' for law about 1990. However, panoramic views were part of my upbringing. My colonial childhood, World War II, adolescent stamp collecting (British Empire, Stanley Gibbons World catalogue), my father's Gibbonian tendency to set his particular thoughts in the context of world history and Llewellyn's concern 'to see it whole' all predisposed me to think in terms of 'total pictures' and 'whole views'.

In my early lectures in Khartoum in 1958–9 I set the Sudan Legal System in the context of a crude map of the state legal systems of the world to introduce some thoughts about colonialism, legal traditions and pluralism (Chapter 5). My Khartoum map was in effect a map of three imperialisms, British (common law), Continental European (civil law) and Soviet/Marxist (the USSR and Eastern Europe). It was rather vague about China. It served its purpose but I was left with a niggling doubt about the very idea of mapping law.

In Khartoum and Dar es Salaam in the 1960s, newly independent countries felt quite 'central' in that they were visited by World Leaders, foreign investors and many other visiting 'firemen'; they were a centre of attention in international relations, not least because of the Cold War, but at that time one did not think consciously in terms of 'globalisation'. In Chicago in 1964, through Soia Mentschikoff, I was involved in the Council for the Study of Mankind, an early multidisciplinary forum that went beyond the perspectives of international law and international relations. There I met a number of academics, some already famous, who were well ahead of their time. I remember lengthy conversations with a Roman Catholic priest, Father Thomas Davitt, who was trying to prove empirically (largely through ethnographic literature) that there are universal human values. I was not persuaded.[1]

In the late 1960s and early 1970s most of my own work was focused on specific matters such as Evidence, Anglo-American Jurisprudence, and responses to conflict in Northern Ireland. However, in addition to the International Legal Centre (ILC) projects on Legal Education and Research, in the 1970s and 1980s I became increasingly engaged in a range of activities with several Commonwealth institutions – the Commonwealth Lawyers Association (CLA), the Commonwealth Secretariat, the Commonwealth Human Rights Initiative (CHRI) and especially the Commonwealth Legal Education Association (CLEA), of which I was an officer from 1983 to 1993.[2] These were almost entirely anglophone and a confusing mixture of neocolonial, anti-colonial, and post-colonial attitudes and practices, but they did move one in the direction of thinking 'globally'.

In 1985 I was made to reflect on the parochial tendencies of my own discipline. During a week-long colloquium on Law and Anthropology in Milan and Bellagio several well-known anthropologists, including Elizabeth Colson and Philip Gulliver, disavowed both the anthropological present and the idea of 'tribes' as self-contained, isolated units. Some had moved sharply in the direction of setting quite particular studies in the context of World History or international trade.[3] In Italy, after a couple of days, I caught out American *anthropologists* talking about 'this country' as if they were back in USA. This experience set me thinking about ethnocentrism as a powerful tendency in academic law, if looked at from a global perspective. ILC and CLEA (Chapter 17) stimulated us to adopt broad geographical perspectives, but not yet, at least consciously, to think in terms of 'globalisation' as a set of processes that seemed to be affecting almost everything. Perhaps a more important stimulus in this respect was engaging critically with ideas about 'Law and Development'.

Law and Development

I have been interested in, concerned about and to some extent involved professionally with Eastern Africa and more generally with 'the Global South' all of my life. Colonialism, anti-colonialism, neocolonialism and post-colonialism have been part of the backdrop from which I never completely escaped. I have sometimes listed 'Law and Development' as one of my interests, but I have always been uncomfortable with the label.[4]

In Chapter 11 of *General Jurisprudence* I summarised the reasons for this at length, most of which need not be repeated here.[5] I did not think of my professional activities in Khartoum and Dar es Salaam – teaching, research, writing, law reporting, preservation of legal records and so on – as contributions to 'development'.[6] The same applies to most of my later involvements – examining, consulting and advising on legal education[7] or my period as an officer of the Commonwealth Legal Education Association (1983–93).[8] These were standard activities for an English academic lawyer; other than that, they were related to 'the Global South'. There are two major exceptions to this that are directly relevant to my globalisation project. First my criticisms of 'Law and Development' theorising anticipated much of my later scepticism about globalisation theory. Secondly, I was involved in a few consultancies which were explicitly related to structural adjustment.

The idea of 'Law and Development' became remarkably influential in anglophone legal academic circles in the post-Independence period. It was a construction of American lawyers, mainly academics, and their funders.[9] It was probably at Yale in 1964–5 that I first heard the question 'What is the role of law in development?' To me it seemed a strange juxtaposition.[10] This reaction probably reflected the views of most English lawyers and non-lawyers interested in Africa at the time. Their working assumption was that social order is a precondition of development, but beyond that law is no more than a technical body of rules and a flexible instrument for implementing particular policies. In *General Jurisprudence* I characterised this view as 'the law and order model', one of five theories of the role of law in development, all of which I criticised as being simplistic and over-generalised. Later I adopted the same approach in treating grand theories of globalisation as dangerously reductionist.

In the late 1990s I was involved in three consultancies, one in Tanzania and two in Uganda. All were explicitly linked to 'structural adjustment', about which I was deeply suspicious. I had also been wary about foreign consultants, who often seemed arrogant, overpaid and insensitive to local particularities. However, in 1994 I agreed to lead a team on legal education and training in Tanzania, which was part of an ambitious project dealing with Financial Management and Legal sectors (FILMUP) as a whole and jointly funded by a number of foreign governments and agencies.[11] I accepted because this involved funders co-operating rather than competing, thinking of the legal sector as a whole was a definite advance and I had some local knowledge (though outdated) and, as important, good contacts with former students. In the event, we had a strong team, excellent support and I was rather pleased with the outcome. This led me to accept two similar assignments in Uganda in the period 1995–2000, with rather mixed results and after that I decided to refuse further invitations.[12] A detailed account of these fascinating, challenging and, for me, instructive experiences must await another occasion. I used what I learned about Tanzania and Uganda in this period as detailed reference points when thinking about globalisation. But I was ambivalent about all three. Suffice to say here that I thought it rather an extravagant way of furthering my legal education.

Globalisation and Law Project (1990–present)

When 'globalisation' came into vogue in British academic circles in the 1970s, I was predisposed to take an interest. But it was only in about 1990 that I started a specific project on 'Globalisation and Law'. By then enthusiastic, sometimes frenetic, globalisers had invaded several adjacent disciplines, but Law seemed to have been left behind. As a start, I consciously revived my African interests. The countries of Eastern Africa, including Rwanda, Ethiopia and Sudan were experiencing a terrible period in most of their histories. They became, along with the UK, the USA and parts of Continental Europe, my main templates for testing general theories and generalisations about law in a period of accelerated interdependence.

Keeping in touch with this region impelled a rather pessimistic view of their prospects and, indeed, of human nature. It was hard to sustain one's earlier optimism, for they included, among others, the civil war in the Sudan, the effects of the oil crisis of 1973, Amin's and Obote's Uganda, Mengistu's Ethiopia, Moi's Kenya, the Rwandan genocide, famines and the 'dirty war' with the Lord's Resistance Army in Uganda. The rise of corruption and the intransigence of poverty in otherwise stable Tanzania were also part of a backdrop which hardly stimulated optimism about 'progress' or 'development'. They contributed to my tendency to be sceptical of most talk about 'globalisation'. Nevertheless, I hung on to a residue of faith in sincere versions of long-term aspirations for democracy, human rights, the Rule of Law, and good governance and in law as a potential instrument for good as well as for repression, anarchy and corruption. Like Robert Frost, I believe the world will end in either fire or ice, but I still think that it is worth soldiering on to mitigate suffering until that happens.

'Globalisation' and 'global'

There is a key semantic problem relating to the areas, fields or phenomena to which the term 'globalisation' refers. This has two aspects: first, among the many definitions and stipulations, two have quite settled but different usages. For many it is an ideological term, referring to 'economic globalisation', or the domination of the imagined world economy by the forces of capitalism and free-market ideology or whatever the Anti-Globalisation Movement has been against – which is many things. This is an explicitly political usage pioneered by Marx.[13] For Santos the world is an arena for hegemonic and counter-hegemonic struggles;[14] and the term is used in similar ways by many others.

This ideological usage predominates in political debates and in the media. For my purposes, this is too narrow.

Rather, if one conceives of 'globalisation' as a large fragmented horde of processes that tend to make human beings increasingly interdependent, it covers many phenomena in addition to economic ones: climate, pandemics, war, alliances, regional unions, trading blocs, scientific advances, cultural spread, migration, language, inventions such as mobile phones, telecommunications and so on. These spheres of interdependence are interrelated in complex ways; economics is an aspect of most of them, but it is too simple to subsume them under economic relations, and even more reductionist to treat them as consequences of capitalism or American hegemony.

Secondly, adapting Theresa May on Brexit: 'Most "Global" is not global.' My concerns and research are not limited to phenomena that are strictly worldwide, or even widespread – they relate to all kinds of social, political, economic, cultural and legal relations and their intensification. Pare away the hype and many of us are interested in significant transnational or cross-border processes – even down to relations between two or three units (e.g. countries, states, nations, multinational corporations, international sports federations, groups, extended families). Geographical or historical or linguistic or Internet proximity will tend to make such relations more intense and more frequent than genuinely or nearly global ones. The important point is that some of the most significant transnational patterns for law are *sub-global* – legal traditions, empires, diasporas, language, trade relations, conflicts, regional and other agreements, alliances, spheres of influence and so on. No empire, language, religion, diaspora, war, pandemic or legal tradition has yet covered the whole world.[15]

G-words like 'global' pose real dilemmas: they can mean genuinely worldwide, widespread or transnational; often the first is too narrow, the second is too vague and the third is too expansive. The term 'globalisation' interpreted literally is often much too narrow for our purposes. Yet 'transnationalisation' is awkward and places too much emphasis on national borders. Globalisation studies are now a recognised field. 'Global law' is best treated as no more than shorthand for 'Globalisation and Law', a field concept with almost no actual laws as referents.[16] Globalisation used loosely as an analytic concept tends to expand or limit the idea of 'global' indiscriminately.

Globalisation theory

In the early 1990s I canvassed the general cross-disciplinary literature on 'globalisation' quite extensively. I found it disappointing. Much of it was excitable, exaggerated, repetitive, over-abstract and highly speculative. There was a built-in tendency to over-generalisation. In early 1995, trying to bring some order into my rather haphazard reading, I tapped the words 'global' and 'globalisation' into a union library catalogue in Boston. After I had found over 250 books with one of those two words in the title I stopped. The vast majority dated from 1980. Many were cross-disciplinary and difficult to classify. There were hardly any focusing on law. There was a prominent movement called World Peace Through World Law and there were a few twentieth-century legal classics, especially after 1945, the most impressive of which was Philip Jessup's influential *Transnational Law* (1956); there was a vast literature on specialised transnational fields, such as Public International Law, but almost nothing that suited my purposes. For me the first major book ostensibly about globalisation and law was *Toward a New Common Sense* (1995)[17] by a Portuguese legal sociologist, Boaventura de Sousa Santos. At first this book seemed like a strange, learned, polemical, casserole or *caldeirada*.[18] It claimed to be 'post-modernist' and 'counter-hegemonic'. Fascinated, I buried my teeth into it, used it selectively in teaching and made it into a key reference point. About five years later I wrote a long discursive essay on it, trying to settle some of my own ambivalences about 'post-modernism' and macro-theorising.[19]

The general literature continued to proliferate. Amid a plethora of semantic disputes, wild surmises, economists' predictions and repetitious controversies I did discern a degree of consensus about a few important points: in brief, that globalisation has a very long history, but the processes had intensified and become more complex since World War II; that these processes are not one-way or unilinear; that in the past boundaries, borders and jurisdictions have tended to be treated as firm lines which justified treating nation-states, societies and 'tribes' as if they were self-contained, decontextualised units; that 'international' (a term coined by Bentham and used indiscriminately today) eclipses the many other kinds of cross-border relations that transcend simple geographical divisions; that transnational relations involve many other kinds of actors besides sovereign states, including multinational corporations, international financial institutions (IFIs) and other 'official' international organisations, non-governmental organisations, state agencies (such as USAID), voluntary associations, nations and peoples without states, large-scale migrations, social movements and even genuinely global groupings; and that processes of globalisation challenge conventional assumptions, concepts, agendas, priorities and theories in almost every discipline in the social sciences and humanities. There also seemed to be broad agreement that centralised world government was unlikely to be either feasible or desirable in the foreseeable future.

In the 1990s my first exploration of the general globalisation literature drew me towards the camp of 'globalisation sceptics', like Paul Hirst and Grahame Thompson. I was particularly resistant to grand theories of globalisation.[20] Recently, I was pleased to find a critical essay by William Robinson (2007), which, without claiming to be comprehensive, usefully categorised globalisation theory into five genres and pronounced a post-mortem on each, suggesting that by 2000 they had all run their course.[21] This expressed what I had long sensed. The main reason is that, outside a given context, 'globalisation' means little more than increased interdependence or interaction. Interdependence is a relative matter. These phenomena take so many forms at so many levels that they cannot be satisfactorily reduced to a single comprehensive theory or squeezed into a single framework. Globalisation theory can be analogous to a reductionist theory of everything, of little use even as an aspiration. However, 'Globalisation' now is established as a broad field concept. It usefully covers most studies of the complex processes of increasing interdependence. Beyond that it is almost systematically misused.

Globababble

At least these forays provided some starting points for studying the implications of globalisation for the study of law. Unfortunately, however, there is no consensus about the vocabulary of globalisation and associated concepts. One difficulty, as we have seen, is that 'global' is radically ambiguous: it is used loosely to refer to genuinely worldwide or fairly widespread or merely any transnational phenomena.[22] One can perhaps justify some sporting examples of 'World' competitions as referring to the best teams or individuals on the planet at particular sports, but the increasing popularity and influence of global, regional and national 'league tables' damn the metaphor. There are now so many 'world class' universities and other institutions that this currency is now inflated without any criteria of scope, quality or meaning. In Law we already have 'global law schools' (teaching the laws of every state legal system and Islamic law?); global law firms (serving many, most, all countries?); global lawyers (what do they know? How many are there? Whom do they serve?) and Global Law degrees (studying what?).

The phrase 'global law' has become entrenched in the titles of institutions, courses and even theories. Some leading theorists have justifiably attached this label to their own ideas: for example, Raphael Domingo clearly uses the term to refer only to an aspirational body of law confined to issues affecting all human beings. This is genuinely worldwide, but quite limited in scope.[23] For Neil Walker 'global law' refers to an 'intimated' body of concepts, principles and rules that may in time achieve the status of a (nearly) worldwide body of law;[24] and Benoît Frydman argues that international indicators and standards are becoming a new form of global law.[25] Others equate the term with expanded 'international law'; some, including myself, wish to confine its use to a very vague, ill-defined focus of attention, which includes many sub-global and transnational phenomena – in short a broad, vague and ambiguous field concept with almost no analytical purchase.

An intellectual lag

I found the general theorising on globalisation quite unhelpful. However, at less abstract levels there was an enormously rich and dynamic literature in many disciplines, and nearly all of my relevant reading on middle-order topics such as diffusion, pluralism, poverty, migration and development was cross-disciplinary. Generally, I found this literature uneven and eclectic, but much of it more advanced than in Law. For example, in relation to 'hard data', there were numerous international agency studies and highly developed global and regional statistics in such areas as economics, poverty, agriculture, education, health and population, whereas in the early 1990s there were almost no statistics related to law as such, apart from bits and pieces regarding, for example, children, family and crime. In the 1970s one ambitious project at Stanford (SLADE)[26] started to pioneer statistical comparative law, but was aborted for lack of funds. There was clearly an intellectual lag between Law and some adjacent disciplines.

Since then, largely because of the activities of the World Bank, OECD, UNDP, the European Union and other such agencies, it has been suggested that Law has experienced a numerical turn.[27] Like it or not we are now involved in Big Data, league tables and transnational indicators and most such global and sub-global statistics and indicators relating to law need to be scrutinised carefully, especially in relation to concepts, over-simplification and dubious evidence.[28]

Strategy

Over time I developed a four-pronged strategy for what became my main project for the next twenty years. First, to survey the general literature on 'globalisation'; secondly, to revisit my own Anglo-American tradition of Jurisprudence critically from a global perspective; thirdly, to concretise and ground the project through detailed case studies and some middle range theorising about a number of topics that appeared particularly relevant to the field of Globalisation and Law;[29] and fourthly, to draw some provisional general conclusions about the implications of adopting a global perspective on law. Out of my research and teaching in due course emerged three books: *Globalisation and Legal Theory: Exploratory Essays* (1999/2000) (GLT) which was indeed, exploratory; ten years later, the largest volume *General Jurisprudence: Understanding Law from a Global Perspective* (2009) (GJP), and then *Globalisation and Legal Scholarship* (2011) (GLS), which offered guidance to individual academic lawyers on how to think about the implications of globalisation for their own work.

Teaching and learning about Globalisation and Law

As with other projects, I used my teaching as a vehicle for developing my ideas and setting them in broad frameworks. From the mid-1990s the main vehicle for developing my ideas was a seminar on 'Globalisation and Law' mainly in Miami.[30] I started with a variant on 'the Newspaper exercise' (Preface) asking each student to mark all references to foreign and transnational law in a single weekday's edition of the *Miami Herald* or the *New York Times*. They found examples of transnational relations and laws and foreign law throughout, including on the sports, arts and financial pages. This had the desired effect in making them realise that they could not sensibly focus only on 'American law', that they had already encountered foreign law in many contexts and that how law is conceived and practised in the USA 'ain't necessarily so' elsewhere.[31] For each student the main task was making two presentations to the class, one relating to a substantial term paper on a topic of their choice, mainly fairly specific topics or case studies.[32] Supervising more than a hundred papers over a dozen or so years taught me a lot. Besides expanding my general knowledge, the course stimulated me to develop my own ideas in four specific ways: (a) 'g-words'; (b) mapping law; (c) macro-historical perspectives; and (d) standpoint again.

'g-words'

We first considered 'globalisation' from the perspectives of several disciplines, a fairly elementary introduction to the general literature and its debased vocabulary. Incensed by globababble I banned students from using any 'g-words' in the classroom – especially global law, global lawyers, Global Law degrees and global legal pluralism – unless there was a precise and clear justification, even though the course was called 'Globalization and Law'. The students got the message and had very little difficulty in complying. I made a second exception to my ban. From time to time the class was asked to adopt 'a global perspective' and to imagine total pictures of legal phenomena in the world as a whole – especially to set a context for more particular enquiries.

Mapping law

> 'Other maps are such shapes, with their islands and capes!
> But we have our brave Captain to thank'
> (So the crew would protest) 'that he has bought us the best –
> A perfect and absolute blank!'
> (Lewis Carroll, 'The Hunting of the Snark')[33]

For one group exercise we set out to construct imaginary maps of all 'legal phenomena' in the world which they thought significant and to explore the difficulties of doing this. The main purpose was to depict their variety and complexity. Before moving on to mental 'mapping', we started with traditional physical mapping – that is, depicting the distribution and scale of units such as state legal systems, imperial transplants and impositions, and legal traditions over space and time. Rather than stipulate a general definition of law, we first discussed which legal orders and other phenomena from a number of candidates they would include in their maps: for example, if one started with a standard map of members of the United Nations (sovereign states) this seemed straightforward, but uninformative and uninteresting – hardly better than the Bellman's map. Did this not leave out a great deal? For example, would one omit from a historical atlas of law in the world all mention of religious law, legal traditions, customary law, human rights, European Union law, Public International law or Native American law? What about *lex mercatoria*, which was often said to apply to many transnational commercial transactions, sometimes involving millions or even billions of dollars, but the very existence of which has been doubted by some on the ground that it has no authoritative source and no agreed content? Or what about *ius humanitatis* – the claim that all areas of land and sea that have not been appropriated by any particular state are held in trust for mankind as a whole – including most of the oceans and seabed, and large parts of Antarctica and the Arctic?[34] What of the law of nomads who indiscriminately wander over state boundaries? Or the Romani peoples who have their own legal language and can now communicate transnationally by email? In short, could one have a sensible, inclusive and relevant picture of law in the world if one only included state law? In this context, most would agree that we need some concept of 'non-state law' that is relevant to serious discussion of the implications of globalisation for our subject.[35]

That was only a start. How, for example, to map Islamic law?[36] If every devout Muslim carries the *shari'a* within them, one would probably find the phenomenon in most countries and moving around. Does it make sense to ask: *where* is Islamic law? Indeed, does it make sense to map law in spatial terms? – a question now canvassed in the emerging field of Law and Geography which has developed beyond my horizons.[37] And what about history? Can one 'map' legal traditions in terms of time and space? Is not most law traditional? Could one imagine a great historical world atlas which dealt with legal phenomena across both time and space?[38] How would one get the required data? What if there is little or no surviving evidence of some past legal orders or of hidden or tacit ones? Could we construct maps of our ignorance, or of injustice or distributions of power? Can a map be apolitical? There was plenty to discuss, not only in terms of physical cartography, but also in terms of mental maps. For mapping is a metaphor used in many disciplines. We started with a classic paper by Santos,[39] dabbled a bit in modern cartography and admired Edward Tufte's captivating suggestions for visualising ideas and information.[40] I concluded that even quite traditional maps still raise interesting questions in this context.[41]

The mapping exercise illustrates the near-ubiquity of normative and legal orders co-existing in the same time-space contexts and a map of legal traditions illustrates how laws, legal traditions and legal devices have interacted throughout history. This brings to the fore three topics: normative and legal pluralism; diffusion/reception/transplantation; and legal traditions. Each topic illustrates the importance and complexities of sub-global patterns for constructing overviews of law in the world.[42] Maps of empires go some way to explaining the importance of colonialism and imperialism in spreading law, but maps of diasporas, religion, technological innovation, language spread, trade patterns and wars can also serve to illustrate the complexities of diffusion. They all underline the point that, from this perspective, most significant patterns do not fit neat geometrical metaphors: concentric circles, vertical hierarchies, horizontals or diagonals; nor geological analogies, strata, layers or levels. Our heritage of law is much messier than that.

Of course, there is a limit to the value of traditional mapping, especially of ideas. For one thing traditional maps tend to be static, but the subject matters of our discipline are not. Another important lesson is that for physical mapping one can map *practices* (given adequate data) and one can infer beliefs, norms and attitudes behind the practices – people behaving, interacting, disputing, worshipping, fighting wars, travelling, migrating, writing, carving, cooking and so on. It is less easy to map abstract ideas, but law consists of ideas as well as practices. One can try to map where Islamic law has been practised on a significant scale, but how can one map Islamic law as ideas? And, the realist question again. Can one really understand Islamic law without information about the practices? With modern technology one could extend the exercise in several directions, but one would still need to be clear about the concepts.[43]

If the main purpose of mapping law from a global perspective is to set a context for particular enquiries, then rough brushstrokes, not too much detail and vague boundaries may be adequate. Are there other purposes? There might be – is that not like asking what are the uses and limitations of a good atlas of world history?

Macro-historical perspectives

I insisted that the students set their term-papers in appropriate historical contexts, but at the time I found no short historical overview that would serve as a satisfactory introduction to the course. It is plausible that World History or World Systems Theory might provide a good organising framework, or at least a starting point, for the study of Globalisation and Law.[44] Early in my project in the 1990s, I revisited some of these works, but decided that none was suitable as a starting point. Nevertheless, I stayed with the idea that a historical perspective is essential for approaching this field. Hence the idea of a historical atlas.[45]

I am too much of a particularist and a contextualist to feel at ease with 'World History' as a field. Insofar as it seeks to identify broad patterns it is useful as a source of bold hypotheses, provided it uses concepts which travel well and which can be tested in relation to particular times and places. But the genre is too susceptible to over-simplification, inadequate conceptualisation, reductionist tendencies and generalisations that go far beyond the available data. Fortunately, in 2000 the first edition of Patrick Glenn's *Legal Traditions of the World* was published in time for me to draw on it. This can be read as a welcome revival of the bold tradition of Historical Jurisprudence, best exemplified by Maine.[46] Perhaps inevitably, Glenn's book was subject to quite a number of particular criticisms, but it was soon recognised as a major contribution to Jurisprudence as well as Comparative Law.[47] Its strengths are that it adopts a genuinely global historical perspective; it is centred on a sophisticated concept of tradition as the transmission of ideas (hence narrower than and distinct from 'culture', which often covers practices and attitudes as well as ideas); by treating 'tradition' as the core concept it puts history at the heart of Comparative Law; it presents a sustained argument informed by social theory; and it addresses a wide range of topics and issues that have hardly had any attention in orthodox Comparative Law, including some contemporary topics that have hardly featured in orthodox texts, at least until recently.[48] Although Glenn sensibly denied that he was advancing a general theory of tradition, his analysis provides a usable concept with significant explanatory power.

As 'World History' becomes more conceptually sophisticated and better-informed, it promises to be a key driver of the study of 'Globalisation and Law'. It can already serve to counterbalance ahistorical approaches to the field and even the extravagances of globalisation theory. But it promises more than that.

Standpoint again

In thinking about the implications of globalisation it pays to start with a specific standpoint. In my Miami course neither globalisation theory nor legal theory provided a satisfactory way in for practically oriented students who were likely to be involved in specific, immediate, largely local problems in practising law in Florida or elsewhere. A broad overview of law in the world was sufficient to make them aware of potential transnational dimensions and their complexities. A more fruitful approach was to start by imagining the standpoints of a variety of individual institutions, actors and observers, including law firms, teachers, judges and scholars in specified contexts, and to get them to clarify their situation and standpoint before asking: how much of my/our work has or is likely to have transnational dimensions?

'Globalisation' touches everyone, but it affects individuals, institutions and groups in very many ways. To ask what are the implications of globalisation in the abstract is not susceptible of a general answer, because it depends on who is asking the question, in what context, for what purposes and in relation to what aspects of increased interaction or interdependence. It is usually better to begin by clarifying the context, situation, role and purposes and only then ask 'What are the implications of globalisation *for me* (or us) – for this paper, my course, my sub-discipline, this case, my job?' For some the answer might be very little; for others it might involve some radical rethinking. Some will see the challenges as an unwelcome threat to their established ways; others may welcome these challenges. Many will be somewhere in between. For example, an English teacher of Family Law in 2017 may come up with quite different answers from her neighbour who teaches Torts or Contract or Constitutional Law, and this will be quite different again from a conveyancing practitioner in Barnstaple or the Attorney-General of Tanzania or a US Supreme Court Justice contemplating how far it is proper for her to take into account developments outside the United States. They are in different situations and their answers will depend in large part on the criteria of relevance suggested by a clarification of their standpoint. This theme became the basis for my Montesquieu Lecture at Tilburg on 'Globalisation and Legal Scholarship',[49] which, like this book, is addressed to all academic lawyers.

Out of this course and my more focused research emerged three books and many articles, some of which were absorbed into the books. I will revisit *Globalisation and Legal Scholarship* in the next chapter. Here I deal briefly with the two other volumes that represent my most substantial writings in this area so far.

Globalisation and Legal Theory (2000)

For my project the literature from other disciplines was too extensive to be manageable except as background or for specific enquiries. I found our Western traditions had been too narrow to be a good starting point for exploring the implications of 'globalisation' for the discipline of Law. Our Western heritage has, at least until recently, been largely mono-jurisdictional, doctrinal and ignorant of other traditions and cultures. The second prong of my strategy was to revisit in detail an area in which I had some expertise, the Anglo-American tradition of Jurisprudence. I set out to study in depth some intellectual antecedents of my project within my own tradition, once again asking the question: 'Done before?'

Rather to my surprise I found that several canonical Anglo-US thinkers were more relevant to understanding law from a global perspective than I had expected. By and large they were state-centric, mono-jurisdictional, rooted in doctrinalism, uninterested in other traditions and cultures, with a tendency to ethnocentrism, paradoxically reflected in a tendency to universalism in ethics. With the exception of some American jurists, such as Pound and Llewellyn, they were generally not empirically oriented.

Nevertheless, they had some ideas worth preserving, and their limitations provided useful foils for a younger generation of revisionist thinkers.[50] Some relevant neglected texts were being rediscovered such as Kant's *Perpetual Peace* (1795) and Bentham's essay on 'Place and Time in Legislation'.[51] Over ten years I wrote a series of exploratory essays from this perspective, dealing mainly with individual jurists in the Anglo-American tradition, including Bentham, Austin, Holland, Buckland, Hart, Dworkin, Holmes, Rawls,

Llewellyn, Santos and Haack. A selection of these essays was republished in *Globalisation and Legal Theory* (1999/2000).

Focusing on one part of the vast heritage of legal theory had some rewards. First, some of the members of the canon were generalists: Bentham promoted Universal Jurisprudence; Austin the General Jurisprudence of 'maturer' systems; Holland (1906) conceived of Jurisprudence as a 'science', like Geology. There followed a period of emphasis on 'particular jurisprudence' that I experienced in Oxford as an undergraduate on the cusp of the change-over from Goodhart to Hart in the 1950s (Chapter 3). Particular Jurisprudence was mainly focused on basic concepts of English (or common law) claim-rights, obligations, persons, possession and so on until Herbert Hart reconnected the subject to abstract analytical philosophy under the rubric of 'General Jurisprudence' to which he gave a new meaning.[52] Hart launched a general descriptive jurisprudence. Although neither he nor his followers did much describing, they can claim to have provided some quite sophisticated tools for description. Ronald Dworkin, despite never breaking free from American obsessions with appellate adjudication, provided powerful tools and arguments for viewing law as essentially a moral and argumentative enterprise in some local contexts. Finnis's *Natural Law and Natural Rights* (2011 [1980]) still stands as a nuanced and cogent exposition of one version of Natural Law. I included Holmes in my explorations because, despite being nearly All-American (his correspondence with Laski and Pollock extends his range to London), he provided the launching-pad for standpoint analysis and bottom-up perspectives in Jurisprudence (Chapter 10). Each of these posed questions about the geographical reach of their ideas. I tried to show how Llewellyn's version of legal realism helps to fill a gap in our juristic heritage and I argued that in some contexts his law jobs theory, suitably refined, can provide one reasonably inclusive organising framework for constructing a broad overview of legal phenomena in the world as a whole while illustrating the variety and complexity of these phenomena.[53]

In *Globalisation and Legal Theory* I concluded that there is a good deal to build on and react to in the legacies of the Anglo-American tradition of legal theorising supplemented by some Continental European classics and revivals.[54] Moreover, there was a new generation of thinkers who were breaking away, including some disciples who had jumped on the shoulders of their guru, modifying him or stabbing him in the back: Pogge on Rawls; Tamanaha on Hart; Singer on Bentham; and maybe Twining on Hart and Llewellyn. Not all followed Kipling's conclusion:

> But his own disciple
> Shall wound Him worst of all.[55]

For example, Peter Singer, a formidable philosopher and an accomplished populariser, is a clear follower of classical Benthamite utilitarianism. He has applied his practical ethics to issues of world poverty, famine, and human rights as well as giving an elegant analysis of many global issues in his lectures on *One World*.[56] This in turn has provoked significant responses, for example by Onora O'Neill, and has linked juristic concerns to the developing field of International Ethics. John Rawls belatedly tried to extend his theory of justice to the world stage.[57] I am among those who found this thoroughly unconvincing, but at least it stimulated important critiques, not least from former followers, including Thomas Pogge and Amartya Sen. Patrick Glenn launched a new version of Historical Jurisprudence and *Grands Systèmes* theory, based on more sophisticated conceptions of tradition and of world history. Santos did something similar with Marx and Weber. Martha Nussbaum collaborated with Amartya Sen in developing the capabilities approach and led a movement to introduce feminist concerns into 'Development'.[58] More controversially, Brian Tamanaha, starting from Hartian positivist premises and legal realism, has tried to construct an ambitious general social theory of law as part of a genuinely global jurisprudence. His first efforts, especially his criteria for identification of law (the labelling test), diverted attention from his important contribution to elucidating less abstract concepts, drawing on social science and his own interests in law and development.[59] Since then he has argued powerfully for a 'Third Pillar' of Legal Theory, representing a socio-historical version of realism, which I shall touch on in Chapter 20.[60] These are just a few contemporaries within the Anglo-American tradition who have advanced the study of law and justice from a global perspective on the backs of their predecessors.

Globalisation and Legal Theory, while emphasising some clear continuities in our tradition, was more subversive than it looked.

General Jurisprudence (2009)

During the first decade of the Millennium I published a series of specific studies on diffusion, pluralism, 'surface law', rethinking Comparative Law and, most important, a piece called 'Have Concepts, Will Travel' which urged analytical jurists to switch their attention to constructing and elucidating concepts that could 'travel well' across legal traditions and cultures, or even jurisdictions such as England and France.[61] I will deal with these topics in the next chapter along with different usages of the of the term 'General Jurisprudence'. These were precursors to my most substantial contribution to theorising about Globalisation and Law, *General Jurisprudence: Understanding Law from a Global Perspective* (2009). This book is divided into two parts, broadly representing high- and middle-order theory respectively. Part A is a relatively systematic statement of my approach to Jurisprudence presented in a form that could be used as an introduction to the general field in the context of globalisation. Set in the context of a reaffirmation of a liberal view of the mission of academic disciplines,[62] it begins with a restatement of my view of Jurisprudence as the theoretical part of the discipline of Law.[63] In this view, any relatively abstract questions and ideas about law are 'theoretical' and therefore part of Jurisprudence. I had developed most of these views before I took up the study of Globalisation and Law as a subject.[64]

Chapters 2–4 are mainly about Analytical Jurisprudence.[65] Chapters 5–7 are about Normative Jurisprudence, especially utilitarianism, justice and human rights (the only really original sections were about human rights scepticism). Chapter 6 on 'Empirical Dimensions of Law and Justice' takes a fresh look at the transnationalisation of such enquiries and considered, rather cautiously, the idea of an 'Empirical Science of Law'.

Part B of the book consists of more detailed consideration of less abstract topics that was aimed to concretise the general ideas in Part A in more specific contexts and to illustrate the importance of middle-order theorising. Some of the relevant topics are discussed in the next chapter. They include chapters on diffusion, surface law, Law and Development, the idea of 'non-state law'[66] and a study of four 'Southern Voices' in relation to human rights. I shall deal with all of these under the rubric of middle-order theorising.[67] Finally, there is a concluding chapter mainly oriented to the future.

Since 2008, when I finished *General Jurisprudence*, I have continued to think and write within the broad field of 'Globalisation and Law'. *Globalisation and Legal Scholarship* (discussed above) applied my general approach to provide guidance to individual scholars. All of these added at least incrementally to my project, which still continues at a stately pace. Since then I have published essays on realism, normative and legal pluralism, and several other topics.[68]

Conclusion

Globalisation is not one thing; law is not one thing. Almost everyone involved with law needs to take globalisation seriously, but in different degrees, in different ways, in different contexts. Accordingly, most explorations of the implications of globalisation for law are appropriately approached at quite specific levels or at least through middle-range lenses rather than via general theories of law, despite the strong magnetic pull of universalism and Grand Theory.[69] That is why in my own work in this area I have focused on topics such as diffusion, Comparative Law and normative and legal pluralism, which will be considered in the next chapter. Broad working total pictures of law in the world from a global perspective can be useful for setting a context for more particular enquiries because such mental maps provide a broad sense of scale, distribution and proximities across space and time – what I call 'demographic realism'. But they need to signal complexity. A really good historical world atlas of law would have its uses, but also considerable limitations. For these reasons, I am reluctant to give general answers to the question: 'What are the implications of globalisation for law and its study?'[70]

19

General Jurisprudence

'Prolific misunderstanding' is a typical, perhaps a necessary feature in the process of appropriating another civilization.

(Franz Wieacker)[1]

Introduction

Since the early 1990s I have used the term 'General Jurisprudence' to refer to the heritage and activity of theorising from a global perspective.[2] This is not a new *kind* of Jurisprudence. Rather it is an extension of focus from municipal legal systems and classic International Law ('The Westphalian Duo') to include a wide range of transnational, supranational and other ideas and phenomena.

The term 'General Jurisprudence' is ambiguous and has a long and varied history.[3] In the English analytical tradition, 'general' referred to extension in point of space or time: Bentham, for example, distinguished between universal and local jurisprudence and equated 'general' with universal; Austin distinguished between the general theory of law common to maturer systems (General Jurisprudence) and the theory of law underlying a particular legal system (Particular Jurisprudence). 'General', contrasted with 'particular', often meant more than one – that is, covering or transcending two or more legal traditions, cultures, stages of development or even jurisdictions.[4]

My use of the term 'General Jurisprudence' is quite close to the English nineteenth-century usage, but is not confined to 'maturer systems'. This usage was current in Oxford when I was a student.[5] In my view, Jurisprudence is a synonym for legal theory; a theoretical question is one posed at a relatively high level of abstraction; 'General Jurisprudence' covers theoretical questions that transcend borders of time and space, legal traditions and cultures, legal families, even different jurisdictions at varied levels of abstraction. In this context, 'general' can be contrasted with 'particular' legal systems or traditions; it can also be contrasted with global and universal, indicating that it covers many intermediate geographical levels between genuinely worldwide and relatively local. That takes pressure off the overused 'global'. The key point is that in this usage 'general' transcends particular legal orders.[6]

Some commentators have asked: is General Jurisprudence (in my usage) possible?[7] If the question means 'will it be possible to achieve a fully integrated overarching *theory of law* or at least to move towards one?', my answer is that I do not know, but I am sceptical (Chapters 1 and 20). Applied to General Jurisprudence as an *activity*, the answer is: 'Yes – many people are doing it.' That is, many people are struggling with issues that cross boundaries of nation states, legal traditions and other disciplines at fairly general levels of abstraction from Neil Walker's and Rafael Domingo's ambitious attempts to theorise 'global law', through my more or less abstract ones to guide numerous particular theoretical studies and 'rethinkings'.[8]

In the context of my project on 'Globalisation and Law', I extended my ideas on Jurisprudence as a field, but did not change them substantially (Chapter 13). I still think it useful to think of the field in terms of heritage, ideology and activity, emphasising the latter. I still think that as an activity legal theorising can make several kinds of contributions to the health of our discipline.[9] Three of these have been particularly significant in my globalisation project. First, our stock of concepts for dealing with transnational and supranational phenomena is underdeveloped; we need more concepts that travel well. Secondly, middle-order theorising has a very important role to play in making sense of the implications of globalisation for understanding law: most significant transnational patterns are sub-global and many topics and fields such as pluralism, diffusion, human rights, international economic and financial law, regional regimes, cyber law and Comparative Law have become more salient in response to globalisation. This kind of theorising provides a crucial bridge between Legal Philosophy and specialised particular studies. Thirdly, because accelerated globalisation has presented radical challenges to some mainstream working assumptions of Western academic law and to the way certain key topics and transnational fields have been conceived and treated, there is a need for more self-critical legal studies. The next sections illustrate these themes.

Rethinkings

One of the most important tasks of theorising is the articulation and critical appraisal of the presuppositions and working assumptions and concepts of legal discourse generally and of more specialised areas. This is particularly useful when a sub-discipline or a specialist subject needs re-examination in the context of a changed situation or perspective. We have already seen some examples of such exercises in Chapters 12 and 13.

As the processes of globalisation impact on and give greater prominence to transnational fields, there is a corresponding need to subject their assumptions and discourses to critical scrutiny. There has already been much introspection and some more radical rethinking in sub-disciplines, especially in older transnational fields.[10] But the pattern has been uneven. As part of my globalisation project I developed a critical method by constructing ideal types of conventional conceptions of particular fields and topics and suggesting that one of the implications of globalisation is to challenge some elements in these ideal types. This section reports on three such exercises in ascending order of scope; the first is a critique of my first ever published article, which was on reception/diffusion of law; the second took selected writings on Comparative Law by leading members of the first generation of post-World War II comparatists and criticised some of their working assumptions; the third, more boldly and perhaps idiosyncratically, identified and challenged some mainstream assumptions of Western Legal Traditions of academic law about their discipline. Globalisation not only has implications for our detailed understanding of particular subjects, it also suggests possible challenges to the standard assumptions with which we approach them.

It is important to emphasise two preliminary points. First, these ideal types were intended to represent some scholars' working assumptions about their enterprise, not their actual practices which are generally more diverse, richer and often more sophisticated. Scholars often act better than they say. Secondly, my constructions are quite subjective and impressionistic. If one accepts the method, one can, of course, choose to construct different, perhaps more evidence-based, ideal types.

Diffusion/Reception/Transplants

I believe I have shown that massive successful borrowing is commonplace in law. Indeed, ... I have indicated that borrowing is usually the major factor in legal change. Legal borrowing I would equate with the notion of legal transplants. I find it difficult to imagine that anyone would deny that legal borrowing is of enormous importance in legal development. Likewise I find it hard to imagine that anyone would believe that the borrowed rule would operate in exactly the way it did in its other home.

(Alan Watson)[11]

No transportation without transformation

(Bruno Latour)[12]

In this context 'diffusion'[13] refers to the processes and outcomes of legal phenomena spreading between and among legal orders, including but not confined to municipal (i.e. state) legal systems. It is important because many of the uniformities and patterns that are observable transnationally or cross-culturally may be explicable in whole or in part by 'diffusion'. Furthermore, diffusion concepts may help to differentiate superficial similarities from genuine ones. Sociological scholarship suggests that there are very few examples of simple diffusion without adaptation; however, Alan Watson has argued that this may not apply so much to large-scale transplantations of laws and ideas which survive as surface law largely unresponsive to local social, political or economic conditions.[14]

While at Stanford in 1999–2000, I revived my interest in 'reception' and guided by a colleague, David Snow (best-known for his work on social movements), I plunged into parts of the sociological literature.[15] I was surprised by three things. First, although they had a shared history in early anthropology, this was another example of two bodies of literature (Law and Sociology) talking past each other; it was a case of mutual deafness – for example, a recent sociological literature survey barely mentioned law.[16] Secondly, the sociological literature was vast and quite sophisticated. Thirdly, it depicted a perspective that I had not imagined in my earlier work. Consequently, I set about some self-criticism.

In adopting the method of internal critique, I tried to show that much of the previous legal literature on legal transplants/reception up to that time, which contained some excellent studies, has been based on some simplistic assumptions.[17] Using my very first published article on 'Some Aspects of Reception', published in the *Sudan Law Journal and Reports* for 1957, I demonstrated that my account was based on a naïve model of reception that postulates a paradigm case with the following characteristic assumptions:

> [A] *bipolar* relationship between *two countries* involving a *direct one-way* transfer of *legal rules or institutions* through the agency of *governments* involving *formal enactment or adoption* at a particular moment of time (*a reception date*) *without major change* ... [I]t is commonly assumed that the standard case involves *transfer from an advanced (parent) civil or common law system to a less developed one*, in order to bring about *technological change* ('to modernise') by *filling in gaps or replacing* prior local law.[18]

Using concepts from Everett Rogers' *Diffusion of Innovations*,[19] the standard textbook on the subject (itself showing signs of age), I was able to show that none of these elements is necessary or even characteristic of actual processes of diffusion of law, broadly conceived. In short, these processes are much more diverse and complex than the 'naïve model' suggests. This complexity was best illustrated not by setting up a contrapuntal model, but rather by indicating possible deviations from each of the elements in the paradigm case. Here this is relevant not only because of the importance of diffusion as a subject, but also because a similar method can be used to explore how adopting a global perspective may challenge standard assumptions in the orthodox or mainstream literature on a particular topic (see Table 1).[20]

Table 1: Diffusion: a standard case and some variants

	Standard case	Some variants
a. Source–destination	Bipolar single exporter to single importer	Single exporter to multiple destinations Single importer from multiple sources Multiple sources to multiple destinations etc.
b. Level	Municipal legal system–municipal legal system	Cross-level transfers Horizontal transfers at other levels (e.g. regional, sub-state, non-state transnational)
c. Pathways	Direct one-way transfer	Complex paths Reciprocal influence Re-export
d. Formal/informal	Formal enactment or adoption	Informal, semi-formal or mixed
e. Objects	Legal rules and concepts Institutions	Any legal phenomena or ideas, including ideology, theories, personnel, 'mentality', methods, structures, practices (official, private practitioners', educational etc.) literary genres, documentary forms, symbols, rituals etc.
f. Agency	Government–government	Commercial and other non-governmental organizations Armies Individuals and groups: e.g. colonists, missionaries, merchants, slaves, refugees, believers etc. who 'bring law with them' Writers, teachers, activists, lobbyists
g. Timing	One or more specific reception dates	Continuing, typically lengthy process
h. Power and prestige	Parent civil or common law less developed	
i. Change in object	Unchanged Minor adjustments	'No transportation without transformation'
j. Relation to pre-existing law	Blank slate Fill vacuum, gaps Replace entirely	Struggle, resistance Layering Assimilation Surface law
k. Technical/ideological/cultural	Technical	Ideology, culture and technology
l. Impact	'It works'	Performance measures Empirical research Enforcement

The Country and Western tradition of micro-comparative law

> [S]ciences which have to busy themselves with their own methodology are sick sciences.
>
> (Gustav Radbruch)[21]

> If there is 'a sick science' in Radbruch's sense today it is not comparative law but rather legal science as a whole ... and comparative law can cure it.
>
> (Zweigert and Kötz)[22]

In a study conducted in the mid-1990s,[23] I used a similar approach to the one used in 'The Rationalist Tradition of Evidence Scholarship' to identify the underlying assumptions about a single field, Comparative Law.[24] I analysed what leading comparative lawyers had *said* about their subject in the period 1945–90, emphasising that in practice comparative work was very much richer and broader. This analysis resulted in an ideal type of mainstream conceptualisations of the field, which I labelled 'The Country and Western Tradition' (see Table 2). The purpose

Table 2: The Country and Western model of Comparative Law, 1945–1990[*]

(i) The primary subject matter is the positive laws and 'official' legal systems of nation states (*municipal legal systems*).

(ii) It focuses almost exclusively on *Western capitalist societies* in Europe and the United States, with little or no detailed consideration of 'the East' (former and surviving socialist countries, including China), the 'South' (poorer countries) and richer countries of the Pacific Basin.[**]

(iii) It is concerned mainly with the similarities and differences between *common law and civil law,* as exemplified by 'parent' traditions or systems, notably France and Germany for civil law, England and the United States for common law.

(iv) It focuses almost entirely on *legal doctrine.*

(v) It focuses in practice largely on *private law,* especially the law of obligations, which is often treated as representing 'the core' of a legal system or tradition.

(vi) The concern is with *description and analysis* rather than evaluation and prescription, except that one of the main uses of 'legislative comparative law' is typically claimed to be the lessons to be learned from foreign solutions to 'shared problems' – a claim that is theoretically problematic.[***]

[*]   GLT, 184–9.

[**]   During the period of the Cold War, a major exception to (ii) was Soviet or Socialist law, which was treated as belonging to 'Comparative Law' in a way in which African, Indian, Islamic and Hindu law were not.

[***]   On 'functionalist' comparative law, see E. Örücü and D. Nelken (eds.), *Comparative Law: A Handbook* (2007), *passim.*

was to show that the *focus* of mainstream micro-comparative law had been narrow in several respects. In a period of agonised introspection internal critics (e.g. Watson, Ewald and Legrand)[25] had raised important questions about the philosophical underpinnings, the methods, the purposes and the biases of Comparative Law, but they worked *within* the confines of the same tradition, largely restricted to municipal law (especially private law) of modern Western states, mainly comparing common law and civil law. The result was that large areas of existing scholarly concern, including religious law, African law, Human Rights and 'Law and Development', were not treated as belonging to 'Comparative Law', and that nearly all supra-state, sub-state, and non-state law was similarly ignored. There was some justification for this in the pioneering days after World War II, when a relatively new subject had to establish its relevance, its respectability and its utility within mainstream academic law, but this artificially narrow model does not seem appropriate in an era of globalisation.

After about 1990 the field of Comparative Law expanded to include a much wider range of legal fields (e.g. constitutionalism, human rights, responses to terrorism), comparisons at supra-state levels (e.g. comparative international law, regional human rights regimes), cross-level comparison (e.g. tribunals at different levels of ordering), comparison within legal traditions (e.g. comparative common law and civil law) and interactions between state and non-state law and even countries.[26] In the same period, multiple perspectives have been brought to bear – economic analysis, difference theory, critical legal theory, feminism, for example – and, as legal scholarship has generally become more transnational, the claim has been made that 'we are all comparatists now'.[27] There is a paradox here: all academic lawyers and law students have to make explicit or implicit comparisons, but to win one's spurs as a comparative lawyer requires a ten-year apprenticeship. For non-specialists the best that can be hoped for are some elementary warnings about the pitfalls of comparison as part of legal method.[28] This example illustrates how the approach advocated here can be applied to critical examination of any specialised field as it is conceived and practised in a particular time and place. Of course, this is quite common in 'rethinking' a field from the point of view of a fresh perspective, such as feminism, economic analysis or deconstruction.

Comparison is a stage on the way to generalisation. Comparative Law is crucial to the development of our discipline and Comparative Law theory needs developing. When Conrad Zweigert, a leading comparatist of the late twentieth century, urged his colleagues just to get on with the job,[29] that was possibly sensible advice to comparatists twenty years ago. In recent times comparative law has been highly introspective largely because of 'globalisation'. On the whole it has not been well served by theory, but that is changing. Far from being sick, it is now potentially the most important engine for transnationalisation of our discipline. It should be near the top of the agenda for General Jurisprudence in the next phase.

Western traditions of academic law: challenging some mainstream assumptions

A rather bolder use of this kind of critical approach was to construct some ideal types of mainstream assumptions of Western academic law which appear to be under challenge if one takes globalisation seriously. One example of such a template reads as follows:

(a) that law consists of two principal kinds of ordering: municipal state law and public international law (classically conceived as ordering the relations between states) ('the Westphalian duo')

(b) that nation-states, societies, and legal systems are very largely closed, self-contained entities that can be studied in isolation

(c) that modern law and modern jurisprudence are secular, now largely independent of their historical-cultural roots in the Judaeo-Christian traditions

(d) that modern state law is primarily rational-bureaucratic and instrumental, performing certain functions and serving as a means for achieving particular social ends

(e) that law is best understood through 'top-down' perspectives of rulers, officials, legislators and elites with the points of view of users, consumers, victims and other subjects being at best marginal

(f) that the main subject matters of the discipline of law are ideas and norms rather than the empirical study of social facts

(g) that modern state law is almost exclusively a Northern (European/Anglo-American) creation, diffused through most of the world via colonialism, imperialism, trade and latter-day post-colonial influences

(h) that the study of non-Western legal traditions is a marginal and unimportant part of Western academic law

(i) that the fundamental values underlying modern law are universal, although the philosophical foundations are diverse.[30]

This suggests that during the twentieth century, and before, 'Western academic legal culture has tended to be state-oriented, secular, positivist, "top-down", Northo-centric, unempirical and universalist in respect of morals.'[31] This template comes with a health warning. It is an ideal type of some tendencies in Western academic law. On its own it is almost a caricature. As generalisations, each of these propositions is subject to numerous exceptions, could be phrased differently and could be added to. The main claim is that insofar as these are common working assumptions or presuppositions of much contemporary legal discourse, each is subject to challenge by tendencies of 'globalisation' in some contexts. The use of this list is to raise some questions in regard to each proposition in a given context: is this being assumed here? If so does it hold good for this enquiry from a global perspective? Or have I been making this assumption here? Do I need to revise, modify, qualify or reject it from this standpoint?

This particular list and the formulation of each proposition is derived from my own reflections and interpretations about the challenges of adopting a global perspective. The list and the particular formulations can be revised or substituted by anyone who disputes them. It is only illustrative of a method of thinking critically about one's intellectual heritage, however one perceives it. All it does is suggest at a very general level a test for a critical approach to the question: 'What might be the implications of globalisation for me?'

Normative and legal pluralism

I have written a good deal about the literature on this complex subject, but my general position is simple.[32] First, there is no serious debate about the existence of state legal pluralism – that is to say, many states recognise bodies of religious and/or customary law as part of the state legal system. For example, when I was in the Sudan the official laws consisted of the Constitution, local legislation, with common law doctrine as a residual law imported under the formula 'justice, equity and good conscience'. They also recognised Muslim Law and Customary Law for limited purposes. What different sectors of the population treated as 'their law' was much wider than that, but not all of it was recognised as part of state law. For example, what Francis Deng reported as Dinka law was very much wider than the limited parts incorporated into Sudan state law.[33] There were a number of practical problems and controversial issues associated with state legal pluralism, such as how customary law could be proved and interpreted.

Secondly, normative pluralism is a social fact. That is to say, all human beings experience a wide range of different kinds of norms, rules and prescriptions every day of their lives. When I asked my students how many rules they had encountered in the previous forty-eight hours very few listed less than a hundred.[34]

Thirdly, in my view legal pluralism is also a social fact if one is using a broad conception of law. That is to say, more than one legal order can, and often does, co-exist in the same time/space context. Such orders may have little contact with each other or they may be related and interact in complex ways, sometimes in conflict, sometimes peacefully co-existing or influencing or complementing each other. Interlegality,[35] as Santos calls it, can be difficult to ascertain or describe and is often quite complex, as is inter-normativity: what is the relationship between our household's routines, the traffic laws, conventions of courtesy and a supermarket's regimes when you go shopping? Standpoint is important here: the main evidence that normative pluralism exists is that we all *experience* it; a legal system through its officials or jurists may deny that most kinds of social norms exist as state law. But those same officials cannot honestly deny the existence of such social norms, because they too experience them as officials as well as subjects. Some may be relevant to decisions they make. If their conception of law is restricted to their own legal system and the species of order of which it is a class, then they can deny that this is a situation of legal pluralism. That is a top-down view. From the standpoint of those subject to social norms, whether or not they are 'law' is very often not important. But a British Muslim who considers UK law and *shari'a* both as law is in a situation of legal pluralism.[36]

Fourthly, a lot of the controversy surrounding legal pluralism can be interpreted as the surfacing in a particular context of the familiar issues surrounding conceptions of law. This seems to have distracted attention from a range of other puzzlements about pluralism, interlegality, individuation of norms and normative orders, and general normative theory. I have dealt with these matters at length elsewhere.[37]

In my Miami seminar we spent at least two weeks on normative and legal pluralism as a topic. Having persuaded the class that they all had experience of normative pluralism and that anyone who denied this would be akin to a flat-earther, each student would present two case studies of examples of potential for legal pluralism. Santos's account of a *favela* in Rio (*Pasagarda*) contrasted nicely with the Common Law Movement in the USA (the 'legal system' of disaffected militias) because both largely defined themselves against 'asphalt law' (i.e. state law); the Otieno case in Kenya in which the widow of an 'urbanised' Nairobi lawyer contested burial rights with her husband's clan; and *Sudan Government v Balla el Balla Baleila*, in which the question arose whether cattle-owning nomads could claim reasonable provocation as a defence when they killed the driver of a train that had killed hundreds of their cows (held: that the standard was the reasonable Baggara tribesman).[38] These last two cases illustrated that 'state legal pluralism' is alive and well in countries that recognise aspects of custom and religion as part of state law.

It is especially revealing to consider 'pluralism' from bottom-up perspectives – for example, whether Muslims in Bradford were bound by the *fatwa* to kill Salman Rushdie because of passages in his novel, *The Satanic Verses*; or the dilemmas of a British Muslim woman engaged to a British Muslim man about the best order in which to take wedding ceremonies (should they register a civil marriage first or simultaneously?), whether to have a prenuptial agreement (and if so, in what form) and whom to consult in what order from among family, peers, an imam, a solicitor or a local advice bureau?[39] We only discussed problems of theorising 'pluralism' after we had considered such concrete cases in detail and, on the whole, we found most of the theoretical literature unhelpful.

Analytical Jurisprudence from a global perspective

I am mainly an analytical jurist. I have summarised my main ideas about the subject elsewhere:[40] in particular, that the English tradition of Analytical Jurisprudence is one among several European traditions; that concepts are important for analytical, normative, empirical and legal enquiries; and that analytical jurists in the British tradition have very largely confined their attention to doctrinal concepts and reasoning about questions of law, leaving vast swathes of legally relevant concepts unexplored if one adopts a broader conception of Law as a discipline.[41] This has been only partly mitigated by drawing on concepts from neighbouring disciplines as I did in my work on diffusion.

In 'Have Concepts: Will Travel' (2001)[42] I urged analytical jurists to turn their attention to constructing and elucidating concepts that could 'travel well' across legal traditions and cultures, or even jurisdictions such as England and France. The gist of the argument was that, because of their history, Western traditions of academic law had produced very few such concepts in regard either to law talk or talk about law. The latter could to some extent draw on concepts developed in neighbouring disciplines, but emerging forms of transnational law (including transnational, and – allegedly 'global' – standards and indicators) need new concepts and terms for their articulation, although we cannot expect a comprehensive legal Esperanto.

A simple example of a concept not travelling well is that of a judge: in press reports of a recent 'league table' of the gender balance in European judiciaries[43] England and Wales were placed near the bottom in respect of the number of women 'judges' compared to men; France was much higher up. Who counted as a 'judge' in this context was not reported in the press. In the original report it was limited to professionally qualified persons, but sitting on which tribunals was not specified. If lay magistrates had been included, the table would have been different, because rather more than 50 per cent of lay magistrates in England and Wales are women. They deal with approximately 90 per cent of criminal cases, the nearest equivalents of which are largely dealt with by professionally trained persons in nearly all the other OECD countries. The point is not just a semantic one; rather it is that the arrangements in respect of who is responsible for criminal adjudication are quite different in England from, for instance, our neighbour France. They are not comparable in such terms; there is no satisfactory concept that can help make the comparison. League tables, indicators and many transnational statistics are full of such false, dubious or otherwise misleading comparisons. The concept of judge does not travel well in this context.

This is a large subject with a huge and difficult agenda. In the appendices of *General Jurisprudence*, I included illustrative mini-studies of some concepts that need refining in transnational legal discourse to be used in making comparisons and generalisations.[44] The problem is familiar to anyone who does comparative work. Within Comparative Law there has been a good deal of literature struggling with doctrinal concepts, but this is very uneven in its reach. There is very little on concepts needed in making valid empirical comparisons and generalisations. Some other disciplines are more advanced and sometimes usable concepts can be borrowed (with care) for legal research.

But one of the implications of taking globalisation seriously is the great need for usable concepts for making comparisons and generalisations.

If one looks on concepts pragmatically as thinking tools, as Bentham, Dewey and Llewellyn all did, it is clear that empirical legal studies need appropriate and usable tools for interpretation, description and explanation of legal phenomena. They are needed for transnational statistics. At first sight this looks like a job for experts in conceptual elucidation and construction. However, many of these contexts are held or assumed not to be 'philosophically interesting' and so are beneath the radar of Analytical Legal Philosophers. While one can agree that some of the practical conceptual problems can be solved by careful crafting or stipulation for a given context, others need more skilful construction backed by understanding of the relevant facts, values and conceptual networks. Many of these problems are jurisprudentially interesting, whether or not they are philosophically interesting.[45]

Bridging analytical, normative and empirical divides

I have devoted much energy to trying to build bridges between the different intellectual traditions of Analytical Jurisprudence and Empirical Legal Studies.[46] Reconciling what I learned from Hart and Llewellyn was a start;[47] inviting analytical jurists to extend their focus beyond the doctrinal concepts of law talk to include basic concepts of talk about law, such as institution, dispute and social rule; or to help in crafting concepts that travel well across legal traditions and legal systems; or to provide help in refining concepts needed for the appropriate formulation of hypotheses, transnational comparisons and increasingly influential indicators. Conversely, I have tried to persuade socio-legal scholars and human rights theorists not to dismiss Analytical Jurisprudence as merely emanations of formalism or positivism.[48] I have criticised as 'silo thinking' the tendency to treat Analytical, Normative and Empirical Jurisprudence as semi-autonomous domains (Chapters 1 and 13). At less abstract levels I have emphasised that understanding Evidence, Comparative Law, reasoning in legal contexts or torture involves paying attention to concepts, values and facts as well as doctrine; and that being realistic is a necessary (or at least a very important) but not a sufficient element in understanding law (Chapter 13).

Of course, I have not been alone in these efforts. Among contemporaries, Brian Leiter has tried to 'naturalise' Jurisprudence by challenging sharp distinctions between analytical and empirical perspectives;[49] Nicola Lacey has shown how understanding criminal responsibility or doctrinal concepts of causation need to be understood in their historical, institutional and procedural contexts;[50] Harold Berman and others have argued for integrated forms of Jurisprudence;[51] Neil MacCormick's approach to Jurisprudence was in part driven by a sustained concern to bridge analytical, normative and empirical dimensions of law and justice;[52] and Brian Tamanaha's latest attempt to fight for recognition of social-historical perspectives as a 'third pillar' of Jurisprudence is an ally in the same cause.[53] At more particular and applied levels many legal scholars have explicitly adopted a 'law in context' approach, interpreting it in many ways.

In some quarters such approaches have met with sustained, largely quiet, resistance. To take three examples: those who are committed to strong versions of a 'scientific' approach to legal doctrine; analytical jurists who try to divine the essential nature of law through conceptual analysis or explanation or who hold that this kind of analysis can be done best, or at all, without direct concern for social or historical 'reality'; and those, like Ronald Dworkin, who maintain that understanding law is essentially a moral rather than an empirically grounded enterprise.[54]

This is not the place to revisit these old battles. But it is worth commenting briefly on their main strategies of defence: one is ignoring – that is, not responding to their critics; another is to take refuge in some strong version of the idea of autonomous disciplines; a third is to invoke a somewhat indivi-dualistic interpretation of freedom of enquiry: 'I pursue questions that interest me; you are free to pursue ones that interest you.' While the freedom of the individual scholar to seek the truth in her own way is an important strand in our academic tradition, this should not preclude intellectual challenges to their enterprise nor should it silence those who think that there are important collective interests in the health of scientific and other academic enterprises and that, especially in respect of institutionalised education, there are some responsibilities that extend beyond individual preoccupations or enthusiasms or hobbies.[55]

This book is concerned with the health of the institutionalised discipline of law, with particular reference to how the discipline and its many constituent sub-disciplines and enterprises is responding and might respond to its present situation and future challenges especially in respect of globalisation. To talk of the health of a discipline could raise several philosophical hares, but what is meant by 'health' in this context is quite simple: it is the point that one's conception of a discipline and how it is in fact practised are both susceptible to criticism and rational debate, here in terms of its mission in advancing and disseminating knowledge and understandings of its subject matters. The discussions of 'rethinkings' of various sub-disciplines and topics have been from the standpoint of someone who feels that the present situation is unsatisfactory; for example, to criticise the working assumptions and practices of the 'doctrinal tradition' when it has been exclusive or too dominant in legal scholarship or legal education. There are numerous other suggestions in preceding chapters.[56]

The central point is that we as jurists in the second decade of the twentieth century are in a different situation from our predecessors and those in other traditions and places. So much has changed: globalisation in its many forms; the world economy (if there is just one); the impact of new technologies; the threats of climate change; the repetitious debates and posturing of older ideologies; and the rise of polarised fundamentalisms, religious, economic or political. We have to construct new agendas and equipment for legal theory, including new concepts, new hypotheses, models and generalisations, refreshed ideas or more plausible ways of dealing with belief pluralism as an intransigent fact.

20

'R/retirement'

Introduction

This book has been a narrative of the development of my thoughts and the contexts of my various writings – contributions to the ever-moving bookshelf. Like Collingwood I do not anticipate writing much more, but unlike him I feel that I have had my say. So rather than finish with a grand finale, this chapter touches on a productive and enjoyable retirement, points to some unfinished agendas or business and clarifies some of my latest views.

Retirement, retirement, 'retirement', 'Retirement', 'R/retirement' – there are many distinctions within a process that is not unilinear. What the bureaucrats call 'human resources' may have recorded me as having Retired three or four times. After 1989 I was paid officially half-time, received a niggardly pension, but worked full-time. Later in Miami, from the late 1990s until 2011, I regularly taught a full load (a course and a seminar) from January to April (the spring – a Montesquieuite choice). For this I was paid quite well. In fact, 'R/retiring' was a slow process of disengaging from administration, academic politics, public performances and teaching. The result was that I wrote more, but at a measured pace.

'I am going to Madagascar in November', I remarked to a colleague early on in this process. He reacted with shock: '*November*?' he asked, without mentioning Madagascar. From then on, I realised that I could control my own agenda, although still susceptible to deadlines and other commitments. Twice I gave myself a sabbatical from 'R/retirement': no deadlines for six months. It required careful planning, but it was a liberation and a revelation. I had time to read and to have leisurely conversations. No report was required at the end. I began to offer free advice to 'kids' of 60, then 70, as a 'R/retirement' counsellor: for example, if you want to avoid having to write obituaries and to contribute to *festschrifts*, die young.

In my fifties I thought that I would officially retire at 65 and that any years I would survive beyond 70 should be regarded as bonus. Recently, looking back I realised that since having shed nearly all of my institutional commitments, I had written almost as much as in the whole of the rest of my career. Several of these are among my most substantial writings; some are my last words on a subject. A bonus. As Holmes suggests, old age is a good time for jurists.

The process of disengagement was gradual, but September 1999 provides a convenient marker: on my sixty-fifth birthday I was just starting a year's sabbatical at the Center for Advanced Behavioral Studies at Stanford, the social scientists' Nirvana. One philosopher, one novelist and myself (the only jurist) were the outsiders among forty-five Fellows, mainly behavioural scientists, with a leavening of anthropologists and historians. In addition to getting on with our own work, almost our only duty was to mingle with the other Fellows, which I did with pleasure and ethnographic interest.[1] Some of the social scientists had difficulty with disengaging from supervising graduate students and preparing grant applications. The three soloists were free from these burdens. The result was a delightful and very productive academic year, exploring California, making friends, conversing and reading as much as writing. This year was a watershed in two main ways: I became immersed in interdisciplinarity and I began to think more expansively.

In the late 1950s Trevor Rutter had said that I would become an essayist rather than a novelist or a scholar-statesman.[2] He was right. Early on I recognised that I had no talent for fiction, despite an aptitude for embellishing true anecdotes. By 1999 I had published or nearly completed four collections of essays: *Rethinking Evidence*, subtitled *Exploratory Essays* (1st edn, 1990); *Law In Context*, subtitled *Enlarging a Discipline* (1997); *The Great Juristic Bazaar*, subtitled *Jurists' Texts and Lawyers' Stories* (2002); and *Globalisation and Legal Theory* (2000), which could also be interpreted as a book of exploratory essays. Even *Karl Llewellyn and the Realist Movement* can be read as a series of studies of selected texts put in the context of Llewellyn's career, prefaced by a narrative story of the development of three East Coast law schools: Harvard, Columbia and Yale.

Since 1999, most of my work has centred on four main themes: Evidence as a multidisciplinary field, Legal Education, Globalisation and Law and General Jurisprudence. I have already dealt with the main works in earlier chapters.[3] Here I shall concentrate on some unfinished business and try briefly to clarify my latest general positions or postures. I shall finish by suggesting some ways in which Jurisprudence, as I conceive it, can help our discipline and its constituent sub-disciplines to adjust to accelerating globalisation and come nearer to fulfilling its potential as a central part of the humanities and social sciences.

Unfinished business

There is no end to scholarship and thinking. Like most scholars I have abandoned projects, unfinished business and some twinkles in the eye, including lines of enquiry that only others could carry out. My list of these is shorter and less intellectually ambitious than Collingwood's. *An Autobiography* was published in 1939 when he was 50. He realistically expected to die young and he set out his extraordinary unfinished agenda. He in fact died aged 53. Some of his most important works were published posthumously. I am 84, I expect to die old, and my own unfinished agenda is more modest. I have already touched on some aspects of these in Chapters 10 and 14. Recently I have revived a project on law in multilingual societies that I failed to get off the ground in the 1980s and which I hope will begin again at Warwick with the more focused title of 'Linguistic Diversity and Social Injustice';[4] plans are developing for follow-up activities on *Human Rights: Southern Voices*, also at Warwick;[5] I have continued to pursue my life-long interest in archives by involvement in an ongoing project on *Legal Records at Risk*[6] and some family archives, but this is more an avocation and a hobby.[7] Some others are less noteworthy,[8] but there are three that may be of more general interest that I shall deal with briefly. The first is a sequel to *How to Do Things with Rules* (*Rules*); the second is a continuation of the UCL Evidence Programme, which I still consider is unfinished business; and the third is an expansion of the field of 'legal reasoning'.

General theory of norms and social rules

Throughout my career – or longer, if one includes symptoms of incipient legalism during my teens – I have been interested in rules from many different angles.[9] This is hardly surprising, given their pervasiveness in everyday life, their prominence in the doctrinal tradition and the central place ideas about rules had in the work of both Hart and Llewellyn and their successors. Three themes were especially prominent in my early teaching and writing in this area. First, unease with the equation of law with rules and doctrine. My first inter-pretations of R/realism centred on the theme 'for most purposes the study of rules alone is not enough' – hence the importance of context, institutions, processes, power, impact and the relations between rules and actual practices (Chapter 13). Secondly, directly influenced by Llewellyn, I was more impressed by the continuities between interpreting legal and social rules than the few distinctive features of legal interpretation such as the doctrinal aspects of reading and using precedents and legislation. Here distinctions between legal and non-legal should not bear much weight, except in some quite specific contexts, for instance where a practical issue turns on the meaning of 'law' (e.g. who is an expert on Dinka law?).[10] The ideal type of conditions of doubt in interpretation applies to social and moral rules; in legal contexts there may be some additional considerations, mainly connected with the complexity of modern state law. A third theme, illustrated by *The Case of the Legalistic Child*, concerned *attitudes to rules* in relation to culture, individual psychology and especially the different standpoints and roles not only of professional participants in the context of rule-making, interpretation and application but also of subjects of rules as users, 'bad men', victims, witnesses and so on.

These three themes all find a place in *How to Do Things with Rules*, but as authors we were constrained by the fact that this book was both conceived and perceived as an introductory text for beginning law students – a primer of interpretation. The form constrained development of major theses and only a few colleagues have treated it as a serious contribution to scholarship or theory. However, we felt that some of the content was quite original and there were useful insights and intimations of others which could be further developed. Without being presumptuous I think that *Rules* contains the seeds of questions that could engage twenty dissertations.

Our heritage of this kind of theorising includes important contributions from moral philosophy, logic, speech act theory, sociology, game theory, economics, decision theory and jurisprudence, among others, to say nothing of artificial intelligence and neuroscience.[11] Despite brave efforts by David Lewis, Joseph Raz, Frederick Schauer and others, we are long way from having a settled framework of basic concepts let alone a fully integrated overarching general theory of norms. There is no agreed vocabulary, no settled taxonomy of types of rules or norms, and an uneven body of theorising about a bewildering range of issues.

Frustrated by the constraints of the textbook form, I had hoped to write a second book about rules in general. For many years I collected books, photocopies, examples, cases, clippings, ideas, cartoons and quotations as they cropped up. My improbable library includes manuals of etiquette and advocacy, encyclopaedias of sports and games, manuals for businessmen that one finds in airport bookstalls, guides to parenting and books with titles such as *Watching the English: The Hidden Rules of English Behaviour*[12] as well as standard academic works.[13] Material from some of these have been infiltrated into the five successive editions of *Rules*. In the late 1970s with a social psychologist, Sally Lloyd-Bostock, I started a project on 'legalism' which came to nothing as our interests diverged. I have toyed with the idea of an ethnographic study of the attitudes and behaviour of law examiners in relation to examination rules, marking standards and decisions; *The Examiners' Meeting* could be rendered in the same style as *Yes, Minister*.[14] I have written extensively on realism and doctrinal approaches, and on particular topics such as normative and legal pluralism; transplantation of law (what exactly is diffused? Doctrine, concepts, wigs, architecture, ideology?); Bentham's anti-nomian thesis regarding adjective law (evidence and procedure) (Chapter 14); and many other topics. Recently in Oxford I have followed the series of interdisciplinary seminars on 'Legalism' involving historians, jurists and anthropologists that has so far resulted in three substantial volumes;[15] and I have spent a lot of time on the nature, scope, limitations and functions of the Law of Evidence, bearing in mind both Thayer's dictum that 'the Law has no mandamus on the logical faculty' and Wigmore's irritated outburst that to talk of rules of credibility or weight was akin to moral treason.[16]

As noted above, I had hoped to produce a second book on rules, a cross-disciplinary monograph addressed to a wider audience. I did not get very far with the project because I have been daunted by the enormity of the task. Even if one confined one's attention to social rules as one species of a much broader genus, it transcends many disciplines and contexts, it is beset with philosophical and conceptual puzzles and it involves many lines of enquiry that lead in different directions. Not only are ideas of rules and norms relevant to all humanities and social sciences, but other disciplines as varied as Linguistics, Neuroscience and Computing would need to be involved.

It is now too late for me to set out on a major project on my own or as part of a team. But I can indicate some potential lines of enquiry that could help to form the basis for a multidisciplinary field, perhaps encompassing study of the theory and practice of social norms. This would probably be even broader than the ambitious UCL programme on Evidence.[17] One person on their own could not even sketch the outlines of what a genuinely multidisciplinary field on the study of social norms might encompass.

However, I am able to start answering the question: what might the discipline of law offer to such an enterprise? First, there is a sophisticated body of theoretical literature, ranging from the technological (e.g. on drafting, plain language, regulation) to general contributions to philosophical theory (e.g. Raz, Schauer); debates, some akin to theology, about formalism, literalism, constructivism, liberal interpretation and original intent; legal, sociological and managerial work on regulation and compliance; and so on. Law may not be merely a matter of rules, but all those professionally connected with law have to be at least aware of the basics of rule-handling. Secondly, the legal literature explores a rich array of concepts and distinctions on the nature of norms, types of norms and differences between norms and cognate concepts. Ordinary language exhibits some nuanced distinctions, for example between rules, principles, guidelines, standards and maxims; my shorter *Collins Thesaurus* lists eighteen synonyms of 'rule' (n.) in its main entry and several more in later sections. *Rules* adds others and discusses difficulties of classifying rules and explores distinctions between rules, commands, habits, predictions and values; we have been rightly criticised for not paying enough attention to standards;[18] Ronald Dworkin stimulated a rich debate about principles and related concepts; there is a growing literature on 'soft law' and nudging; Frederick Schauer illuminates the concept of 'rules of thumb'; technical works on legislative drafting, for example, extend the vocabulary; and there is some excellent literature on legislation.[19]

Thirdly, law provides a cornucopia of primary sources, texts and concrete real-life and imagined examples (e.g. hypothetical cases in moots, mock trials and examinations) from statute law, law reports, trial records and other actual cases. As mentioned before, one of the strengths of Law a discipline is that much of the raw material for legal scholarship comes unsolicited from the real world rather than from artificial examples dreamed up by academics. Here reality often outruns imagination.

Fourthly, the discipline of Law can offer material on a wide range of topics that might be worth pursuing in developing a multidisciplinary field centred on social norms in general. Even the compressed chapter in *Rules*, grandly entitled 'Of Rules in General', deals with rules and cognate concepts, rules and values, rules and results, difficulties of classifying rules, the relationship between rules, systems, orders, codes and other agglomerations (Does every rule belong to a system? Is English law systematic? What counts as a code?), and different meanings of interpretation and application. That is just a start.

Reasoning in legal contexts[20]

In 1983–4, when I took up my post at UCL, I designed a mini-course called 'Reason, Rationality and Reasoning in Legal Contexts'. This was an eight-week optional module within the LLM Jurisprudence course. It was a by-product of my Evidence project. It started with the combination of two ideas: first that lawyers (and other relevant actors) do not reason only about questions of law – much of my Evidence project concerned reasoning about issues of fact and problems of fact-determination; secondly, that adjudication is best studied in the context of a total process model of litigation broadly conceived.[21] Each actor would have a specific standpoint which changes as the process moves on. Many of these decisions or choices are typically not on pure questions of law or fact: for example, prosecutors have to decide whether or not to prosecute and on what basis; defendants in criminal cases have to decide whether or not to plead guilty, possibly after a bargain, or whether to appeal against conviction or sentence on what grounds; Parole Boards have to decide whether a prisoner is likely to be a continuing risk to the community. In real life judges of different kinds have to make diverse kinds of decisions as part of their jobs – for example, on admissibility of evidence, procedure, sentencing or costs or damages. Only for appellate judges (and a few others, such as legislative drafters) are questions of law generally paramount. Some actors can frame the issues themselves; some, including judges, must often take the issue(s) as framed by others.[22] Many of the decisions taken by actors in litigation are more or less routine, but all in theory involve reasoning towards and/or justifying each decision. In principle these are 'rational' and subject to rational reconstruction. It is obvious that even standard operations in litigation include many kinds of decision which may involve various, but often related, kinds of reasoning. And, of course, lawyers and other actors have to reason in many other kinds of non-litigious context. This is one area where the doctrinal tradition has impoverished legal theory and legal scholarship by almost entirely confining the term 'legal reasoning' and their attention to questions of law, typically in 'hard' – that is, exceptional – cases.

The imbalances of attention and of understanding in this area are clearly evidenced by the massive literature in both common law and civil law traditions about reasoning and argumentation about questions of law. This

literature pays scant regard to the fragility of the distinction between questions
of fact and law and the ways in which institutional contexts and conceptions of
role influence how issues are framed and processed, how cases are treated as
'worth appealing' and numerous other contextual factors. When I took this up
in the 1980s the literature on other aspects of reasoning in legal contexts was at
best patchy. There were some interesting studies on such matters as decisions
to prosecute, negotiation in civil and criminal processes, and pleas in mitigation, but nothing comparable in terms of extent or sophistication to the work
on questions of law. Scholarship has since developed significantly in most of
these areas, but largely disconnected from the jurisprudential literature about
'legal reasoning'. Much the same applies to the lively debates on probabilities
and proof which began in the late 1970s Moreover, there has been almost
nothing systematic about the similarities, differences and interconnections
between these different kinds of decisions and reasonings.

There is a host of interesting questions that can be posed not only in relation
to what constitutes a valid, cogent or persuasive argument in each kind of
context, but also how these various lawyers' (and others') reasonings relate to
each other. For example, can all reasonings be subsumed under a single general
normative model of 'practical reasoning'? Do binary questions of law, questions of fact and cognate others have structural similarities?[23] Why are they
thought to be different given the elusiveness of distinctions between law and
fact? There are also many empirical questions about how actors in fact 'reason'
in these different contexts, how they articulate such reasonings, and where do
rhetoric, storytelling and chance fit into this broader picture.[24]

My LLM module started modestly by exploring standard models and practices relating to investigation, decisions to prosecute, plea bargaining, settlement in civil litigation, mediation and adjudicative decisions on fact, law,
procedure and sentencing. Students were asked to do case studies on selected
operations. Although this worked quite well in opening up horizons, it soon
became clear to me that this field could not be dealt with satisfactorily in
a single module, even if I were competent to teach it. I had already done some
preliminary work on police investigation, decisions to prosecute, judicial and
jury fact-finding and probabilities and proof, and I had written in an elementary way about 'legal reasoning' in the conventional sense.[25] But it was obvious
that to deal with this properly would involve a major commitment and
substantial help from several fields. I reluctantly decided instead to continue
to concentrate on Evidence, Proof and Fact-finding and launched a full course
under that label. This involved a sharp focus on inferential reasoning from
evidence in various contexts, but did not spread out to the larger subject.

If I had not decided to take up 'Globalisation and Law' in the 1990s I might
have committed myself to 'Reasoning in Legal Contexts'. In the event I did
little more than deepen my study of evidential reasoning and involve Philip
Dawid, Professor of Statistics at UCL, an open-minded Bayesian, in teaching
and thinking about probabilities and proof in litigation, as well as evidence-

based policy and law-making. He later led the UCL Evidence Programme discussed in the next section. I sometimes regret not having made a greater commitment to these broader aspects of reasoning in law, as the neglect of this area is a prime example of the influence of the dominance of narrow doctrinal traditions. How can one understand reasoning about questions of law in isolation from other kinds of practical reasoning in adjacent institutional and procedural contexts?

Evidence II

From early on it was obvious that rethinking Evidence in legal contexts would involve cross-disciplinary work. In the early days for me this mainly involved probability theory (including inductive logic)[26] and historiography.[27] In the late 1970s and early 1980s I was a consultant on Law and Psychology to the Oxford Centre for Socio-legal Studies, working with Sally Lloyd-Bostock, a social psychologist who organised an excellent series of workshops involving various kinds of practitioners as well as academics from several disciplines.[28] Psychological studies of eyewitness identification were prominent at that stage.[29] To start with Terry Anderson and I concentrated on modifying Wigmore's 'Principles of proof'; as with history, the focus was on evidence of particular past events. Then in about 1980 we encountered David Schum and under his influence we broadened our range to include more disciplines and an extension to current and future-directed enquiries.

Dave Schum became the third member of a tripartite partnership that has now lasted nearly fifty years. As a social psychologist and statistician at Rice University he had encountered Wigmore's *Science* (1937) by chance and had used the 'chart method' in training intelligence analysts for the CIA. This led to a brilliant two-volume work on *Evidence and Inference for Intelligence Analysts* (1987). This was probably considered too daunting by the intelligence community and failed to attract attention beyond it. However, Schum persisted and in 1994 produced another major work, *Evidential Foundations of Probabilistic Reasoning* (1994) in which he synthesised basic ideas about evidence and inference from several more disciplines, including Logic, Philosophy, Semiotics, Artificial Intelligence and Psychology as the basis of a multidisciplinary 'substance blind' approach not confined to theoretical enquiries. Schum pointed out that accountants, actuaries, air traffic controllers and other practitioners on through the alphabet all have to make decisions on the basis of drawing inferences from evidence.

Schum's *tour de force* came out just before Terry Anderson and I were Research Fellows at the Netherlands Institute for Advanced Study (NIAS) in Wassenaar in 1994–5. Our group project related to the Netherlands Criminal Justice System, but we set up an extra multidisciplinary group from the other Fellows to explore methodological problems relating to evidence, inference, and interpretation. I formulated the following hypothesis as a starting point:

Notwithstanding differences in (i) the objectives of our particular enquiries; (ii) the nature and extent of available source material; (iii) the culture of our respective disciplines (including their histories, conventions, states of development etc.; (iv) national backgrounds; and (v) other contextual factors, all of our projects involve, as part of their enterprise, drawing inferences from evidence to test hypotheses and justify conclusions, and the logic of this kind of enquiry is governed by the same principles.[30]

This became known as 'Twining's hypothesis', but the project was based on Schum's approach. Towards the end of the year we invited Dave Schum to come over to Wassenaar to lead the final session and, in due course, an edited volume of papers from the project was published, with an overview and commentary by Schum.[31]

Since the 1990s evidence has become especially newsworthy.[32] Now in the Trump era, Fake News, viral rumours and disparaging of experts have continued the trend.[33] Today one can apply the Newspaper Exercise to news items involving talk about evidence and one is likely to find them on every page. Such developments were probably a major stimulus to the Leverhulme Foundation in 2002 to invite bids for a £1 million grant for a project on Evidence. Philip Dawid led the initiative to invite expressions of interest within UCL. Academics from over twenty departments responded and a multidisciplinary proposal, along with one from LSE, secured the grant (enhanced by the Economic and Social Research Council), which seemed enormous to those in the Humanities and some Social Sciences who were not accustomed to such expansive funding. Ably led by Philip Dawid, with participants from nearly twenty disciplines, the project struggled valiantly with the intransigent problems of multidisciplinary work.[34] The project culminated in a major conference held at the British Academy in 2007 and a substantial volume which describes and evaluates the project in 2011.[35]

I was a bit disappointed at the outcome of the project. The main reason, in my view, was that four years was too short a period for establishing an essentially new field. In fact, there seemed to be a reasonable chance of getting further funding, but Philip Dawid understandably wanted to step down and no one involved was prepared to take on the demanding role of co-ordinating a second phase. Several of us tried to revive the project, but except for a multidisciplinary seminar in the Graduate School at UCL, it eventually fizzled out. In my view there is a lot to build on from these initial projects, but if something like this programme were to revive, it would have to be more sharply focused and based on a clear consensus about the aims, methods and working assumptions.[36]

Since 2009 there have been many other developments in the field. Perhaps the most significant one has been a project sponsored by the Royal Statistical Society's Working Group on Statistics and the Law involving forensic scientists, lawyers and expert witnesses. This has produced four very useful guides for practitioners.[37]

Human Rights: Southern Voices

In 2005 I started on a more promising project. As a legal theorist adopting a global perspective I was concerned about the parochialism or insularity of the mainstream heritage of most Western Jurisprudence and the accompanying dangers of ethnocentrism and Eurocentric universalism in its practices. For example, the indexes of even the more expansive student books hardly contained the names of any 'Southern' jurists. The central question was: what steps might be taken towards trying to open up our Western practices in thinking, talking, debating, and teaching about theoretical questions concerning law in an era of globalisation?

I canvassed options about where to start. These included stimulating a series of book-length studies of non-Western jurists;[38] a project to facilitate translations of texts inaccessible to linguistically deprived anglophones; and encouraging the establishment of more academic posts devoted to relevant subjects. I decided to start with a modest plan to try to make a few specific jurists and texts better known in the anglophone West.[39]

After considering a range of candidates I cut my list to four individuals whom I respected, whose background was already familiar and whom I knew personally as colleagues and friends. I called this the 'my chums project'. Although I am not a specialist in human rights, the four I chose from a shortlist of seven or eight also had the great advantage that all were activists and writers about human rights, yet each of them, despite some striking similarities, had a distinctive approach to the subject.

After some preliminary research, I started with a public lecture in Alberta in 2005. The following is the abstract for that occasion:

In the context of 'globalization', Western jurisprudence has largely ignored non-Western viewpoints, interests, and traditions. This article takes a modest step towards de-parochializing our juristic canon by introducing writings about human rights of four 'Southern' jurists: Francis Deng (Southern Sudan), Abdullahi An-Na'im (Sudan), Yash Ghai (Kenya), and Upendra Baxi (India). All were trained in the common law and have published extensively in English, so their work is readily accessible, but their perspectives show some striking differences. Deng argues that traditional values of the Dinka of the Southern Sudan are basically compatible with the values underlying the international human rights regime. For An-Na'im, a 'modernist' interpretation of Islam is mostly reconcilable with international human rights, but acceptance of such ideas depends far more on conversations within Islam than on cross-cultural dialogue or external efforts. Ghai questions claims to universal human rights; however, from his materialist stance and his experience of postcolonial constitution-making, human rights discourse can provide a framework for negotiating constitutional settlements in multi-ethnic societies. Baxi argues that as human rights discourse is professionalized or hijacked by powerful groups, it risks losing touch with the suffering and needs of the poor and the oppressed, who are the main authors of human rights. They make a fascinating study in contrasts. But, although they differ, they do not disagree on most fundamentals; rather they complement each other.[40]

In recent years their ideas seem to have converged in some significant ways. First, all four are acutely aware that we live in a world characterised by a diversity of beliefs and culture. So far as I can tell, each of them would opt for what Patrick Glenn calls 'sustainable diversity' rather than some bland homogenisation in which one size is made to fit all.[41] Secondly, that they accept pluralism (of beliefs, cultures, traditions) as an intractable social fact raises issues that are fashionably discussed in terms of universalism versus cultural relativism, especially in relation to human rights. My sense is that all four are impatient about such debates. Each steers a path between strong versions of universalism and particularism. All four reject strong cultural relativism.[42] None of them treats the fact of pluralism of beliefs as a ground for abdicating moral commitments or refusing to criticise particular cultural practices. On ethical universalism, their positions are somewhat different: all four are politically committed to fighting for the basic values embodied in the Universal Declaration of Human Rights. An-Na'im comes close to espousing a religion-based form of ethical universalism; Deng emphasises human dignity as a basic value, but seems to use international human rights documents as consensual working premises rather than as embodying a single set of universal moral precepts; Ghai and Baxi pragmatically plugged into human rights discourse quite late in their careers, because it was so dominant in the spheres in which they operated. Ghai sees it as a historically contingent workable framework for negotiating constitutional and political settlements and developing constitutions through genuinely democratic constitutive processes, but he emphasises material interests rather than cultural differences as the main recurrent basis of conflict. Baxi also treats human rights as a form of discourse and emphasises its potential for abuse and obfuscation, passionately arguing for it to be allowed to be the medium for expressing 'voices of suffering', especially of the half of the world that is deprived of food, water, health, education and other necessities for a life worth living.

The lecture in Alberta went well. From this I learned that the topic could be made interesting and intelligible to people who were both geographically and intellectually remote from it. However, a single lecture, published in an excellent, but obscure, Canadian journal, would not do much to further the cause of making these authors and texts better known. If their voices were to be heard they had to speak directly to the intended primary audience, Western jurists and specialists in human rights. So I designed a book that was intended to be a model for similar projects. It was in a form that would make it usable in teaching as a resource or as a text. The ingredients were a substantial selection of key texts by each of the four; an introduction to the project as a whole; a short biographical and contextual introduction to each text; and a concluding chapter which, rather than criticising or analysing each text in detail, suggested how they related to each other and to the broader context of mainstream Western human rights literature. It also outlined some preliminary thoughts as to how this project might be extended.[43]

As editor I had several advantages. I knew each of the four thinkers personally and where they were coming from. I interviewed three of them and sent some questions to the fourth. I had a research grant for the project. We managed to bring all of them together at a symposium in Belfast in June 2008 when they exchanged views and discussed some issues about the project: what was meant by 'Southern' and 'voice' in this context. They all agreed that they were not *representing* anybody, that they were cultural hybrids, but that they were all concerned with 'Southern' interests and points of view and had extensive experience of dealing with actual problems on the ground. Some of these advantages will not be easily repeated and this model cannot be followed exactly. However, I am convinced that the contextual material and the grouping of several individuals together added to the value of the book.

What might be the next step in the project? I was well aware of the strict limitations of this first effort. The primary audience was Western. Secondly, the voices were all male; they were common law trained jurists of the immediate post-Independence generation (born 1938–46) from former British dependencies, writing in English, about human rights for anglophone audiences.[44] Each of these elements could be varied. I tried to stimulate some friends and colleagues to take up the challenge.[45] Of course, the possibilities are endless, for in addition to replicating my model, one could proceed along different paths by changing just one of the aspects that limited the initial project: why confine the audience to anglophone jurists and human rights lawyers? Why only texts written in English? What about earlier and more recent generations? And so on. Whatever project emerges out of Warwick will, of course, be modest compared to the possibilities, but it will be a useful next step and I hope that others will follow suit.

Rethinking Legal Education

> One of the central claims of the first edition of this book, was that the legal world would change more in the next twenty years than it has in the past two centuries. Three years on, I believe we are on course.
>
> (Richard Susskind)[46]

After completing *Blackstone's Tower* and collecting some of my essays on academic law (scholarship, education and training, legal theorising and reading legal texts) in *Law in Context: Enlarging a Discipline* (1997), I decided to turn my attention elsewhere and for about fifteen years I did not treat this as one of my interests. However, I was sometimes invited as an 'expert' to air my views. This was a conscious decision because I felt that there was something seriously unsatisfactory with the predominant modes of thinking, writing and debating about the general area, but I was not able to diagnose my dissatisfaction. I was not confident that I knew what I was talking about – or that anyone else did at the policy level. After the publication of the Legal Education and Training Review (LETR) Report I rather hesitantly reinvolved myself in the area mainly as an activist rather than scholar.[47] The report was in some important respects an improvement on its predecessors in England and Wales: it adopted an evidence-based approach to legal education policy in the context of the regulatory changes following the Legal Services Act of 2007; it was well-researched and more educationally sophisticated than all prior reports; the main groundwork was done by four academic lawyers who were specialists in the field; and there was quite widespread consultation. However, I was left with the same niggling sense of dissatisfaction not only about the report and its aftermath which were naturally constrained by narrow terms of reference, but also by the general discourse in the field as a whole. Since about 2016 I have begun to develop ideas about how the whole field of 'Legal Education' or 'Legal Education and Training' or 'Learning about law' might be reframed to provide a basis for thinking, research and policy-making in the coming years which promise or threaten to be a period of quite rapid change.

Before I temporarily 'retired' from the field I had taken a few steps in the direction of a radical rethinking. During the 1990s, as I began to think about 'globalisation', I used the device of a mythical report on 'Legal Education in Xanadu' in several papers to challenge some conventional ways of thinking about the field. Building on the ILC Report, I used the following working assumptions and hypotheses as a starting point for looking at the field from a global perspective:

In (almost) all societies:

Almost everyone receives some legal education.

That process lasts from cradle to grave.

The amount of informal legal education (i.e. outside educational programmes) greatly exceeds the amount of formal legal education, even for career lawyers.

The actual and potential demand for formal legal education almost invariably exceeds the supply.

Most formal legal education is delivered in institutions other than university law schools.

Within most countries, specialised institutions called 'law schools' can be quite varied.[48]

In the 1990s I used these propositions in papers with titles such as 'What Are Law Schools For?' or 'Recent Trends in Legal Education in the Commonwealth' and I followed the ILC Report in urging readers to think in terms of 'national systems of legal education'. I still stand by most of my detailed arguments, but rereading these after a break of nearly fifteen years a dose of self-criticism has pinpointed one major flaw in my own thinking since 'Pericles and the Plumber'. This was that in most of the discourse about 'legal education' we have paid lip-service to the twin ideas of life-long learning and switching attention from teaching to learning. Instead we had focused on institutions, teachers and courses in ways that side-lined these ideas and was inconsistent with my own hypotheses.[49] Even the term 'legal education' carries strong associations with

Table 3

	Primary School Model	Professional model	Friedman model
Who learns?	'Law students'	Law professionals (for whom law is a major part of work)	Everyone
When do they learn?	Age 18–25	Lifelong	Cradle to grave ('lifelong learning')
Where do they learn?	University and/or professional Law schools	University +, work, self-study, (life)	Home, workplace, disputes etc.*
What do they learn?	• Know what: 'core subjects' • Know how: (intellectual skills (some); basic professional techniques) • Know why (some theory; liberal legal education)	Application of law, informed by theory, etc.	Practically relevant (e.g. driving rules; consumer law; divorce law) or serendipitous matters, e.g. via the media.
How do they learn?	Formal study	Formal +	informally (plus some formal)**

* Cf. Santos's 'structural places': Householdplace, Workplace, Marketplace, Communityplace, Citizenplace, Worldplace. B. de Sousa Santos, *Toward a New Common Sense* (1995), 417.

** Informally by direct experience (regular/ episodic); indirect/vicarious experience; foreground observation; 'general culture' (e.g. TV, other media; oral tradition).

formal learning; 'Law *for* non-lawyers' is a give-away – *we* do it for *them*. The fact is that formal education and teaching is a very small part of learning about law, even for career lawyers, judges and legal scholars.

Adopting a perspective that focuses on learning rather than teaching and lifelong learning about law rather than formal legal education (in the sense of learning that takes place in specialised institutions and structured courses) has enormous implications that need to be worked out in detail.[50] This can be illustrated by contrasting three models of 'Legal Education' or 'Learning about law as a field'.

In a very preliminary way one can chart some of the implications in terms of three simplistic ideal types: (a) the 'primary school model' which has dominated nearly all legal discourse, research and debate until recently;[51] (b) the professional lawyer model, including 'the reflective practitioner', who learns by 'experience', Continuing Professional Development (CPD) and many informal and formal processes in very many different contexts; (c) the Lawrence Friedman model of Western societies as one vast school of law, involving all human beings (and other legal persons).[52] See Table 3.

These ideal types can be refined and expanded, but even in this crude form they illustrate some of the implications of taking lifelong learning rather than institutional provision seriously.

First, the part and the whole. Both the first two models can be subsumed under the third. This shows what a small part of the total picture of learning about law the first two models cover. We have seen already that in most talk of 'legal education' a vast proportion of institutions that provide substantial instruction about law fall beyond the radar.[53] Similarly, nearly all the leading reports on legal education and training have an extraordinarily narrow focus, but command a great deal of the attention of legal educators. They only deal with one small part of the whole of formal legal education. For instance, the following aspects are barely mentioned in the LETR Report: scholarship, postgraduate studies, public understanding of law, law in schools, human rights education, judicial studies, legal and multidisciplinary inputs into other kinds of professional formation (e.g. police training, forensic science, medicine, engineering, IT). Nearly all of these were outside LETR's remit, but decisions on professional legal education and training will have repercussions in other sectors. Changes in initial professional formation of providers of legal services (plus enhanced CPD) should not unduly influence developments of other aspects of the total sphere, especially at primary level and more generally in respect of legal education research.

Less obvious is what tends to be omitted because of the limited concerns of such reports. For example, differences with regard to function and priorities between different sectors can be seen by contrasting the LETR assumptions with those of elite law schools in England and Wales:

> Regulation of professional formation is rightly concerned *with basic day one competence* rather than *excellence* and perceived *necessary* requirements of competence rather than *desirable* characteristics of many practitioners such as numeracy, social science awareness, fact skills, command of languages, acquaintance with foreign legal traditions, implications of transnationalisation of law, and specialisms. That is natural for regulation, but narrow for the total system of LET. *The mission of university law schools is much broader* than provision of primary legal education (to intending practitioners and others), especially in *relation to scholarship, specialisation, advanced study, inter-disciplinary* work. *Regulation* of professional competence should *encourage rather than undermine* that mission.[54]

Thirdly, insofar as discussions and research focus on teaching and institutions (on formal education in a narrow sense), this leaves out nearly all informal learning, including the elusive category of learning by experience. Yet for nearly all those who follow law-related careers probably only a small proportion of their time will have been spent on 'formal' legal education. So far as I know, we do not have figures for this (I would guess a mean of four–five years, except for academics). For teachers, research about teaching is much easier and more satisfying than research about learning and, in this regard, we need much more help from professional educators and from other disciplines, such as Management and Medicine, where learning by experience appears to have had much more attention.

This is work in progress and one of my current projects is to explore further the implications of making use of the Friedman model in thinking about the field. For example, although academic lawyers interested in legal education have picked up some of the specialised concepts of education theory, there is a need for much more refined conceptual analysis in this area. Empirical research into life-long learning by lawyers opens up another Pandora's jar, where again we need help from professional educationists who seem to have generally steered clear of Law so far.[55] Another topic is the relationship between legal awareness/public understanding and formal legal education. When I have written about it I have generally treated it as a quite separate field. But the connections may be much closer than we have assumed. For example, DIY lawyering, law and the media and the changes in legal service provision are all relevant to understanding how individuals, corporations and groups learn about law, including about misinformation and information lags.[56]

This leads on to one more point to underline how radical rethinking of all aspects of learning about law is badly needed. We are already in a period of very rapid change in information technology, education, higher education (including finance), legal services and other aspects of the contexts of learning about law. Educationists are saying that it is virtually impossible to predict what education in schools will be like in ten years' time. The same applies to learning about law, so that much of our received wisdom and knowledge is likely to be superseded even in respect of the most studied aspects of formal legal education. Thinking about my own work, I have to confront how much of that will be worth attention in a few years' time. I am confident I would stick to the basic values of liberal education. But beyond that, watch this space.[57]

Some clarifications

Complaints about being misunderstood or misrepresented are wearisome for most readers. Nearly all jurists are prone to become victims of labelling, because commentators want to 'place' them in a school, or movement, or 'ism' or some other kind of pigeon-hole, as if each thinker should only be remembered for one thought. Rather than complain about misinterpretations of my work I shall try to clarify two potential points of misunderstanding in relation to this book. First, why do I focus on Law as a discipline when I emphasise the importance of other disciplines in understanding legal ideas and phenomena? Secondly, I address some confusions about the idea of 'a theory of law'.[58]

Why focus on Law as a discipline?

In many of my writings I have focused on the discipline of Law conceived as the study of institutions, ideas (including doctrine), practices and texts the mission of which is to advance and disseminate knowledge and understandings of its subject matters, whatever these happen to be at a given time and place. This does not mean that I believe in the autonomy of disciplines in an epistemological sense – in some characteristic forms of knowledge or understandings or methods that are severable from other forms. Some colleagues do. Rather I have emphasised the idea of Law as a discipline because historically and ethnographically in the West in modern times Law schools, the Law teaching profession, Law libraries and Law students have in fact been institutionalised in distinctive ways and have often been relatively isolated from other institutionalised academic disciplines which also tend to have more or less distinctive tribes and territories.[59] Anglo-American law schools have provided the main context for this narrative – including the history, economics, culture, politics, activities, trends, fashions, and controversies which characterise them, allowing for significant diversity among times, places, and traditions.

By choosing to focus much of my work, including this book, on the health of Law as a discipline, I have sometimes attracted criticism for seemingly isolating it from other adjacent disciplines and thereby reinforcing the tendency to 'silo' vision of strong departmental systems of knowledge organisation.[60] But I do not subscribe to any strong versions of the autonomy of disciplines nor to sharp distinctions between different schools, traditions or domains of Jurisprudence. Moreover, as a field concept the discipline of Law has no firm boundaries; it varies by time and place and specialisation, and often substantially overlaps with other fields. For example, study of Rawls's theory of Justice does not 'belong' to Philosophy or Political Theory or Jurisprudence – it is an important focus of attention in all of them, with many shared questions and a largely shared heritage of literature. And the scope of the discipline is constantly changing as is illustrated by the elusive referent of 'Law' in such phrases as 'Harvard Law School' (Chapter 1).

However, this explanation is not enough on its own. The question remains: if the aim is understanding legal phenomena and ideas, why focus attention on a single discipline? For this book, the answer is simple: it is a narrative of the development of my thought. I identify as a jurist, not as a philosopher or social scientist or historian. The primary audience is academic lawyers especially those whose institutional context is anglophone law schools. Nearly all of their students are law students; they claim to contribute to legal scholarship, legal theory or specialist legal sub-disciplines, and to the general health of their discipline. Their primary language is English and, for most of them, their professional formation has been in the common law tradition. Like me, they generally identify as scholar-teachers of law. Such factors are to do with our educational backgrounds, the institutional contexts and cultures in which we operate, our job descriptions, our professional identities and much else besides. I personally do not think it helpful to treat 'legal knowledge' as a specific epistemological form; some colleagues do. Even if I did acknowledge the distinctiveness and relative autonomy of strong versions of legal science or doctrinalism, the whole thrust of this narrative has been that understanding law requires multiple lenses, that our discipline needs to be open and outward-looking and that many enquiries directed to understanding law are best conducted by other kinds of specialist in other kinds of institution: for example, 'legalism' in behaviour or attitudes raises questions for psychologists and neuroscientists as much as it does for jurists or historians or anthropologists. I regret that so little of Socio-Legal Studies takes place outside law schools and that in England (more than the United States) nearly all psychological research about law takes place in law schools rather than Psychology departments;[61] and that some historians have tended to shy away from considering law from internal points of view, perhaps because it seems very 'technical' or because they have not been sufficiently aware of the significance of legal ideas and phenomena for their enquiries.

Symptomatic of some imbalances in the overall landscape of our discipline is the proliferation of 'Law and . . . ' fashions and movements, especially when the main initiative comes from lawyers. It is easy to satirise some of the practices by substituting 'by' for 'and' in this context: Economics by lawyers may be no more harmful than Economics by economists; Literature by lawyers may be harmless, even if it contributes little to the other discipline or literature itself;[62] Psychology or Psychiatry by lawyers may be as dangerous as surgery by lawyers. Sociology by lawyers and 'law in context' have both been criticised by sociologists of law, notably Roger Cotterrell and Simon Roberts (themselves both law teachers), for not breaking away from narrow lawyerly mindsets;[63] I am not qualified to assess to what extent Philosophy by lawyers has contributed much to Philosophy, but I can acknowledge that a significant number of philosophers have contributed significantly to legal understandings, especially when they have equipped themselves with adequate local knowledge. There are, of course, some individuals who have what Geoffrey Wilson called 'two disciplines in one head' and there are a few who teach in two departments, but for the most part academic lawyers are firmly rooted and embraced by their institutional context, the law school. And, as I argued in Chapter 16, academic lawyers are collectively responsible for the health of their discipline. None of this is inconsistent with believing that understanding law is a multidisciplinary enterprise.

Theories of law

> Make me no boundless love:
> Move me from case to case.

> (Anon)

In earlier chapters we have seen that my conception of Jurisprudence rejects any idea that it is a one-question subject or that it can be healthily abstracted from ordinary legal scholarship or that theories are the only or even the main products of the activity of theorising or that jurists should only be concerned with philosophically interesting questions or that doctrine can be interpreted without reference to context or that Jurisprudence or Law as field concepts have clear boundaries or can be treated as autonomous or self-contained (Chapter 1). Against this background, I wish to restate my position on theories of law to clear away some misconceptions.

The terms 'a theory of law' or 'theories of law' are ambiguous. They are greatly overused. If what is meant is a general definition of the word 'law', I share with many others the view that this is a futile enterprise, because the word has so many meanings and associations in so many different contexts. Even an attempt to provide a simple translation from French or German into English runs into difficulties, because our language does not distinguish between *ius* and *lex, droit* and *loi*, or *rechts* and *gesetze*.

If what it means, as it does explicitly for some, is the enterprise of trying to discover, divine, construct or impose the essence or true nature or core of law or a concept of law that fits all existing and possible legal systems,[64] I am not sure what kind of quest this is and I am sceptical of its value or feasibility in any of its standard versions.[65] I doubt that law has an essence or nature or core; if it does, how would one know if the quest had been successful? I am equally sceptical of the utility of such an outcome. How would it contribute to the health of our discipline? When is law a good organising concept? Can understanding law be reduced to a single perspective and one set of answers to one set of questions? Would not a single overarching conception of law artificially limit enquiry?[66] If, as seems to be assumed by some, the sole or main aim of Jurisprudence/Legal Theory/Philosophy of Law is directed towards that ultimate goal of Jurisprudence, what are the implications for less abstract enquiries within our discipline? A change of label?[67]

Like John Gardner, Ronald Dworkin's successor at Oxford, I do not have nor do I aspire to such a theory.[68] I am an anti-reductionist. For me juristic enquiries are concerned with a wide variety of questions relevant to understanding the varied, complex and fluid subject matters of our discipline from a variety of standpoints and perspectives. One suspects that an elementary conflation is sometimes being made between understanding the concept of law and understanding all of the ideas and phenomena subsumed under such a concept.

If the term 'theory of law' means a summary of the (main) ideas of an individual jurist restated or condensed as a coherent whole (his or her answers to his or her questions or to some shared ones), some thinkers are more susceptible to such treatment than others.[69] This is one task of intellectual history which takes many forms and is full of pitfalls. The most common ones, observable in introductory textbooks, tend to be the result of over-simplification: jurists tend to have more than one idea, resist neat pigeonholing, may change their minds, or contradict themselves or be open to different interpretations and so on.[70]

Some writers assume that defining 'law' is a necessary or the best *starting point* for any law-related enquiry. Others assume that all middle-order theorising is *dependent* on such a theory. Or that not searching for the one is unambitious.[71] But it seems strange that an obsessive one-question enquiry should be considered more ambitious than the endless search for better understandings of the immensely complex, plural and ever-changing phenomena that are the subject matters of our discipline. Even if the Holy Grail were found, it would boil few cabbages.

Related to these practices is the tendency to use 'law' as an organising concept for the study of a particular enquiry or project. We need organising concepts for providing indications of the parameters and focus of a particular enquiry or project or other intellectual enterprise. Sometimes 'law' may be adequate for such a purpose, but this needs to be approached with caution. Organising concepts are sometimes expected to organise too much. The adequacy of a particular organising concept (or framework of concepts) depends on the particular enterprise. What does it include or exclude or treat as a grey area? Is 'law' over-inclusive or under-inclusive for this purpose? Could a more specific category be more suitable? What is the concept expected to organise in this context? Is the choice of law (or related terms such as 'legal') being influenced by one of the assumptions made in the last paragraph or by the magnetic pull of Grand Theory? Or is it just a lazy choice?[72] For example, some writers on 'legal pluralism' insist that the first question is where a boundary between 'legal' and 'non-legal' is to be drawn.[73] In my view, that has had the effect of quite unnecessarily dragging the whole debate about the concept of law into an already confused scene.[74] In this context I usually adopt a broad concept of non-state law in order to make the point that 'normative pluralism' of various kinds is experienced by everyone and broadly understood, and that this is a topic about which clarification of standpoint is a better place to start for many, but not all, enquiries because the topic looks very different from the points of view of rule makers, enforcers, investors and other subjects, users and victims (Chapter 10).

Assuming that Jurisprudence is a one-question subject (Chapter 1),[75] some commentators, including allies, attribute to me 'a theory of law' or berate me for claiming not have one or for not making it explicit. I repeat: I do not have a general theory of law nor do I aspire to one. I do not subscribe to a general definition of law outside a specified context or contexts. Despite such denials and repeated assertions that I use several concepts of law, depending on context, these attributions have continued.[76] Chapter 4 of *General Jurisprudence*, has provided a salient target. There I suggested that a refined version of Llewellyn's law-jobs theory (which was a theory about groups rather than law) might be a useful starting point for the specific exercise of constructing a 'total picture' of significant legal phenomena from a global perspective. But I made it clear that such an overview would assume a working concept of law and was not intended as a path towards a general theory of law.[77] Maybe when commentators make such attributions they are succumbing to the gravitational pull of Grand Theory.

In a lecture focusing mainly on my book *General Jurisprudence*, Denis Galligan posed the question: why does Twining not make more use of social theory in developing the idea of General Jurisprudence rather than starting with Analytical Jurisprudence?[78] In fact I started with a classic conception of the mission of disciplines rather than Analytical Jurisprudence and Galligan attributed to me a view of Jurisprudence that I do not hold.[79] However, the first half of the question is a good one, and it has also been raised by others. A brief answer is that, as with World History, I have been resistant to macro-social theory and for similar reasons. I have read a good deal of Marx, Weber and Durkheim, and of more recent writers such as Selznick, Cotterrell and Santos, and I have learned a lot from them. Like Galligan, I particularly admire Max Weber. I have been influenced by him indirectly through Hart, Llewellyn and Galligan himself, especially on such matters as *verstehen* and the internal point of view, which is one source of my thinking about standpoint. I have drawn directly from Weber in respect of some of his particular ideas, such as bureaucracy, legal elites (*honoratiores*), science as vocation[80] and, above all, ideal types as a tool which I use regularly.[81] However, I have not been comfortable with Weber's more macroscopic ideas, in particular modernity and the distinction between formal legal rationality and substantively rational (and irrational) legal thought. To subsume my ideas about understanding law and legal phenomena under a purely or mainly Weberian framework would have been almost like submitting to another iron cage. However, I could well have discussed Weber more extensively in *General Jurisprudence*.

In considering the current state of our discipline I have found many examples of what Daniel Dennett called 'greedy reductionism':[82] for example, a tendency to leap from the local to the global (epitomised in the term 'glocalisation') without considering intermediate levels, such as regions or more messy sub-global patterns; reducing Legal Philosophy to the pursuit of an emaciated Holy Grail; the increasing use of indicators, league tables and other ratings; claiming universality for moral principles and human rights, while ignorant of other belief systems and cultures; leaping from the bottom rung to the top rung of ladders of abstraction without touching the intermediate ones; and making empirical generalisations about law in the world as a whole without adequate concepts, evidence or other data.

Here, let me set up two ideal types of conceptions of jurisprudential enquiries (there are many others). Let us call the one to which I approximate – the Marco Polo pole. One can set up as a contrapuntal ideal type the Kublai Khan pole, namely the view that the primary objective of legal theory is to construct general theories of law – or at least to control the world of law intellectually. In a wonderful passage, they are contemplating a chessboard. The great Khan is concerned to reduce his empire to order so as to try to actually control it. He is a systematiser, a reductionist. For Polo a single square in a chessboard is a launching point for a potentially endless enquiry:

> By disembodying his conquests to reduce them to the essential, Kublai has arrived at the extreme operation: the definitive conquest, of which the empire's multiform treasures were only illusory envelopes. It was reduced to a square of planed wood. [signifying nothingness].[83]
>
> Then Marco Polo spoke: 'Your chessboard, sire, is inlaid with two woods: ebony and maple. The square on which your enlightened gaze is fixed was cut from the ring of a trunk that grew in a year of drought: you see how its fibers are arranged? Here a barely hinted knot can be made out: a bud tried to burgeon on a premature spring day, but the night's frost forced it to desist . . . '
>
> (Calvino)

And Polo goes onto talk about 'ebony forests, rafts laden with logs that come down the rivers, of dock, of women at the windows . . .'[84]

In this context Marco Polo and Kublai Khan are ideal types. It is unlikely that any legal scholar or jurist conforms exactly to either model, but most tend to gravitate towards one or other pole along a continuum. I tend towards the Marco Polo pole, but that does not mean that I reject all simplifying tools such as models, hypotheses, organising concepts or provocative propositions; I think that Occam's razor can be a useful heuristic as a rule of thumb; in short I am a moderate particularist.[85] Katherine Hume suggests that the exchanges between Polo and Kublai Khan can be treated as a dialogue within a single composite mind.[86] That captures one of the basic tensions within the discipline of Law.

Envoi

> Don't ask where the rest of the book is. It is a shrill cry that comes from an undefined spot among the shelves. All books continue in the beyond.
>
> (Calvino)

I belong to a generation that grew up in the shadow of a 'World War', a 'Cold War', and a putative End of Empire. Wars civil, international and transnational have multiplied; there are now new perceived threats from climate change, nuclear proliferation, terrorism, angry populism and potential new Cold Wars; inequality grows. However, there has been some good news, even for pessimists. Poverty has decreased in some places; nuclear war has been averted; medicine is advancing; struggles for gender equality have gained momentum and so on.[87] In this book I have tried to tell a story about my thoughts and writings as a mid-Atlantic jurist, who has never fully disengaged from the postcolonial hangover, nor the romance of the Serengeti, and the Mountains of the Moon; nor adolescent agnosticism, the spell of Oxford, the grounded horse sense of Llewellyn and Mentschikoff, nor the love of books and the urge to write.

After an unenthusiastic start I became an enthusiast for my discipline. Among its great strengths are its reach; its vitality; its responsiveness; its rich heritage of accessible primary sources; its close links with the daily practice of lawyers, judges, law-makers, deviants, victims and good citizens; and the fact that it is continually stimulated by practical issues and real as well as imagined problems.

In 1990 I was able to write: 'During the past 30 years the discipline of Law in the Commonwealth has been undergoing an unprecedented period of expansion, experimentation and development. It has been transformed from a small-scale, low prestige subject into an unrecognisably more sophisticated, pluralist and ambitious enterprise.'[88] That trend has continued since then. From my perch in Iffley I daily see the many ways in which law and Law in Oxford, in Town and Gown and the media, differ radically from what they were like in the early 1950s. This has been repeated nationally and transnationally. Our discipline is much larger in scale, more professional, much wider in its reach, more cosmopolitan, more varied than it was then. There is momentum towards achieving a fair gender balance even in law. One can expect even greater changes in the next twenty years.

In Chapter 1 I indicated that I believe that Law as a discipline is potentially an important, lively and fascinating subject but that it is not fully realising that potential. I went on to repeat that from a global perspective in the twentieth century some mainstream working assumptions of Western traditions of academic law have often tended to be 'state-oriented, secular, positivist, "top-down", Northo-centric, unempirical, and universalist in respect of morals' (Chapter 18).[89] That is not as negative or as pessimistic as it might sound. Some of these tendencies can be rationally defended as suitable for their time or as still worth preserving. If one reads Law catalogues or prospectuses or Internet search engines, or attends 'Global Law Weeks' and the like, one cannot but be impressed by the liveliness, the diversity and the enthusiasm of the next two generations. Unlike their predecessors in the UK, they will be IT savvy and most of them will have doctorates. They seem better-equipped than we were to cope with the problems they will face.

Despite undoubted advances, in my view there are two main reasons why as a discipline, Law is not yet fulfilling its potential: it has not escaped from some of the limitations of the past and it is already faced with daunting challenges which are accelerating.

I have emphasised three constraining aspects of our legacy from the past: the almost exclusive focus on municipal law of single countries and traditions; the dominance of narrow forms of doctrinalism; and the uneven, largely parochial, focus of mainstream legal theorising.

Throughout the twentieth century, and before, with the exception of Roman Law, most legal scholarship was mono-jurisdictional. Transnational legal relations were mainly conceived in terms of relations between sovereign nation states. Comparative Law, Legal History, the study of other legal traditions and systems have been peripheral. The major Western traditions have not been well-equipped to deal with the challenges of accelerated globalisation. There is a need for improved tools and greater theoretical sophistication for dealing with comparison and generalisation across legal systems, cultures and traditions. Legal statistics largely driven by crude indicators are in their infancy. The dominance and narrow exclusiveness of strong versions of the Western doctrinal tradition have been mitigated, but the study and development of doctrine has yet to be fully integrated with broader, often cross-disciplinary, approaches. Mainstream legal scholarship and research has burgeoned in the last twenty years and although somewhat uneven and serendipitous in its coverage it has generally shown itself quite responsive to changing conditions and context, as is illustrated in the UK by the extensive involvement of academic lawyers in the Brexit process.

This book is mainly about Jurisprudence and the roles of theorising in maintaining the health of our discipline in challenging circumstances. As a many-layered activity it has a lot to offer in this situation. Thanks to Hart and his successors the subject came alive in the 1950s and has been through a very energetic period. It has attracted a great deal of talent. The dominance of the analytical tradition has resulted in some distortions. The rough division of the area into analytical, normative and empirical has encouraged a tendency to silo thinking. Law and Social Theory and other aspects of Philosophy – such as epistemology, logic, aesthetics cognitive theory and practical reasoning – have been relatively neglected. Development has been stunted by a narrow focus: Legal Philosophy has yet to take transnationalisation and globalisation seriously enough; it has not broken away from the stranglehold of constricted doctrinal assumptions to encompass talk about law as well as law talk and a much wider range of concepts;[90] it can challenge entrenched assumptions that need rethinking; and switch attention from essentialising the concept of law to contributing to the understanding of legal phenomena and ideas. And it can re-establish close relations with front-line legal and other scholarship of all kinds.

After a recent talk about globalisation and law to a multinational audience of young jurists the most interesting feedback was that my criticisms of bad practices seemed justified, but I was too cautious and left them with no positive guidance about how to respond. This was fair comment for that occasion. How might I have met this criticism on the day? Break away from the stranglehold of doctrinal assumptions to encompass explanation of talk about law as well as law talk and a much wider range of concepts; take transnationalisation and globalisation more seriously; challenge entrenched assumptions from a global perspective and test them for ethnocentrism; be very cautious about generalising across borders and traditions, but craft bold hypotheses and theses; look on all 'global' generalisations about law and nearly all universal prescriptions with a sceptical eye; theorise Comparative Law and help to make it more central; nurture closer regular relations with frontline legal scholarship; and beware of the gravitational pull of Grand Theory. Always remember that our discipline has a long history but its institutionalisation is still relatively young and immature.[91] Be clear about your values and commitments but take belief pluralism seriously; remember Llewellyn's dictum that technique without values is a menace; values without technique are a mess. Trip lightly up and down ladders of abstraction. Be careful of fashions, but keep an eye on developments in Neuroscience, Cognitive Psychology and Human Biology especially in relation to education, evidence and the general theory of norms.

'Give every man thine ear, but few thy voice.' These generalities are a bit too Polonius-like for my taste. To me they seem like common sense or at least horse sense. However, I hope that in this book one can find some more specific constructive suggestions: for example, empirical legal studies and the Law in Context movement offer many models for approaching traditional subjects in a broader way; the chapter on Evidence suggests one way of approaching the practical problems of arguing from evidence in legal contexts without exaggerating the importance of the exclusionary rules (Chapter 14); Atiyah and McAuslan provided examples of rethinking a legal field (Chapter 12); there are suggestions about how to teach particular topics and how to think about legal education more generally (Chapter 16) and how to consider the implications of globalisation for one's own work.

I have sometimes styled myself 'a legal nationalist'. I have argued that Law as a discipline deserves respect and a fair share of resources; that its subject matters are pervasive, fascinating and important; that its heritage of concepts, texts, examples and controversies has much to offer other disciplines, and that, provided that it realises its potential as a humanistic discipline, Law should be accorded a more central place in our general culture rather than continue to be hidden away at the back of a few larger book shops.[92]

Notes on the plates

1. The author. Photograph by Karen Twining Fooks.
2. The TANU Building, Party Political Headquarters, the first home of University College Dar-es-Salaam. Photographer unknown, early 1960s.
3. The First Fourteen, University College, Dar-es-Salaam, 1961. The first fourteen students were Messrs. Bakilana, Chiponde, El Kindy, Kakuba, Khaminwa, Kisese, Kivuitu, Kwikima, Miruka, Njenga, Ouma, Tibamanya, one other, and Ms. Manning. The expatriate staff were: front row: the author, Cranford Pratt (Principal of UCD), A. B. Weston and J. Russin; second row at side: Dr A. Slee (Extra Mural); back row: J. P. W. B. McAuslan. I infer from the dress that this was taken very early in the life of UCD as ties, gowns and shorts soon went out of fashion. Within a few years nearly all of the staff were East African.
4. President Nyerere opening Dar es Salaam University campus. This event doubled as the first degree ceremony and the President and Visitor is presenting her degree to the first Tanzanian woman Law graduate, Julie Manning.
5. Jeremy Bentham. Side view of the Auto-icon. © University College London.
6. H. L. A. Hart. Cover of *H. L. A. Hart* by Neil MacCormick (2nd edn, 2008) (Jurists series). Photograph by Ramsay and Muspratt, reproduced by permission of Stanford University Press.
7. Karl Llewellyn. The photograph depicts a bust of Llewellyn by the Russian sculptor, Sergei Konenkov, who later came to be regarded as one of the leading Russian artists of the twentieth century. Karl and Betty Llewellyn befriended Konenkov in New York in 1924 and helped him to obtain commissions for busts of leading American luminaries, including three Supreme Court Justices. (See M. T. Lampard, J. E. Bowlt and W. R. Salmond, *The Uncommon Vision of Sergei Konenkov 1974–1971: A Russian Sculptor and His Times* (2001); KLRM 421, 447). The original of the Llewellyn bust is in the University of Chicago Law School and a cast is in the University of Miami Law School. © Cambridge University Press.
8. Soia Mentschikoff. Photographer unknown. Probably mid-1970s.

9. Terry Anderson. This is a photograph of Terry Anderson who represented federal Judge Alcee Hastings pro bono in the case of *United States v Hastings* for over a decade from the early 1980s. He is giving a talk about the case. The photograph is signed by Hastings as a token of gratitude to his principal counsel. © Reproduced by permission of T. Anderson.

10. John Henry Wigmore. This picture was taken not long before the end of his Deanship at Northwestern (1901–29). For an account of his life, character and works generally, see William Twining, *Theories of Evidence: Bentham and Wigmore* (1986). © Courtesy of Northwestern Pritzker Law School.

11. Human Rights Southern Voices, Jordanstown 2008. Four Southern Voices: Symposium Transitional Justice Institute (TJI), Jordanstown (June 2008). From left to right: back row: Abdullahi An-Na'im, the author, Francis Deng, Upendra Baxi, Yash Ghai; sitting: Fionnuala Ní Aoláin (Director, TJI), Catherine Turner (TJI). © With permission from the Transitional Justice Institute, University of Ulster.

12. Lowering the Flag – a post-colonial image. Iffley Village has one shop which is run entirely by volunteers, including my wife. When she has the 3.30 to 5.30 p.m. slot she has to shut up the shop. Penelope is unable to reach the flag hanging outside, which needs to be taken down for several reasons, so I help by standing on a tub and lowering the flag. Photograph by Karen Twining Fooks.

Notes to the text

The following is a select bibliography of works by the author, many of which are substantially discussed in the text and notes to the text, where they are referred to by abbreviations. A comprehensive bibliography of the author's published works up to 2014–15 by Penelope Twining is published in LEGTC at 367–78. Full text access to some of the articles and papers is obtainable through standard providers such as LexisNexis and Heinonline. Some can be downloaded through www.ucl.ac.uk /laws/people/prof-william-twining and links there.

ACD	'A Cosmopolitan Discipline? Some Implications of "Globalisation" for Legal Education' (2001) 8 Int'l J Legal Profession 23–36 (2001) (also in (2001) 1 J Commwh L & Leg Ed 13–29) (translated into Italian in (2001/3) XXVII Sociologica Del Diritto 17–36)
'Afterword'	KLRM, 2nd edn (2012), 'Afterword', 388–443
Analysis	*Analysis of Evidence*, 2nd edn, with Terence Anderson and David Schum (Cambridge University Press, 2005); 1st edn, with Terence Anderson (Little, Brown, and Weidenfeld and Nicolson, 1991); with Teachers' Supplement (Northwestern University Press, 1998)
Bernstein Lecture	'Normative and Legal Pluralism' (Bernstein Lecture 2009) 20 Duke J Comp & Int'l L (2011–12) 473–517
BMR	'The Bad Man Revisited' (1975) 58 Cornell LR 275 (reprinted in GJB, Ch. 3)
BT	*Blackstone's Tower: The English Law School*, Hamlyn Lectures (Sweet & Maxwell, 1994), socialsciences.exeter .ac.uk/law/hamlyn/lectures/es
EIE	*Evidence, Inference and Enquiry*, ed. with P. Dawid and M. Vasilaki (Oxford University Press, 2011)
EIHL	*Evidence and Inference in History and Law*, ed. with I. Hampsher-Monk (Northwestern University Press, 2003)
EK	*Essays on Kelsen*, ed. with R. Tur (Oxford University Press, 1986)
	'Intellectual Journey' Entrevista M. Atienza and R. Gama, 'An Intellectual Journey with William Twining: An Interview' in LEGTC, Ch. 1 (Spanish version in (2010) 32 Doxa 713–27)

EMS	'Evidence as a Multidisciplinary Subject', Cardozo Conference, New York (2003) 2 Law, Probability and Risk 91–107, rev. version in RE2, Ch. 15
FiL	*Facts in Law* (Franz Steiner Verlag, 1983)
GCompL	'Globalisation and Comparative Law' in E. Örűcű and D. Nelken (eds.), *Comparative Law: A Handbook* (Hart, 2007), Ch. 3
GJB	*The Great Juristic Bazaar* (Ashgate, 2002)
GJP	*General Jurisprudence: Understanding Law from a Global Perspective* (Cambridge University Press 2009)
GLL	'Globalization and Legal Literature' (2011) Osgoode LJ 353–73 (review article on R. Domingo)
GLS	*Globalisation and Legal Scholarship*, Montesquieu seminars (Tilburg, 2011)
GLS	*Symposium* on William Twining's Montesquieu Lecture (2013) 5(4) Transnat'l Leg Theory
GLT	*Globalisation and Legal Theory* (Butterworth, 2000)
Granada	'General Jurisprudence', in M. Escamilla and M. Saavedra (eds.), *Law and Justice in Global Society*, XXII World Congress on Philosophy of Law and Social Philosophy (Granada, 2005), 645–88 (rev. edn (2007) 15 U Miami Int'l & Comp LR 1–59)
HCWT	'Have Concepts, Will Travel: Analytical Jurisprudence in a Global Context'(2005) 1 Int'l J Law in Context 5–40
HRSV	*Human Rights: Southern Voices* (Cambridge University Press, 2009) (see also Macdonald Lecture)
HTDTWR	*How to Do Things with Rules*, with David Miers, 1st edn (Weidenfeld & Nicolson, 1976); 2nd edn (1982); 3rd edn (1991); 4th edn (1999); Italian translation by Carlo Garbarino sub. nom. *Come far Cose con Regole* (1990)
JJM	'Karl Llewellyn's Unfinished Agenda: Law and Society and the Job of Juristic Method', Chicago Papers in Legal History, Llewellyn Centenary Lecture (University of Chicago Law School, 1993), reprinted in GJB, Ch. 6
KLP	*The Karl Llewellyn Papers* (University of Chicago Law School, 1968)
KLRM	*Karl Llewellyn and the Realist Movement*, 1st edn (Weidenfeld & Nicolson, 1973); reissued (1985); 2nd edn, with 'Afterword' (2012)
LEGTC	*Law's Ethical, Global and Theoretical contexts: Essays in Honour of William Twining*, eds. U. Baxi, C. McCrudden and A. Paliwala (Cambridge University Press, 2015)
LFTP	*Legal Fictions in Theory and Practice*, ed. with M. Del Mar (Springer, 2015)

LiC	*Law in Context: Enlarging a Discipline* (Oxford University Press, 1997)
LRIC	*Legal Records in the Commonwealth*, ed. with Emma V. Quick (Dartmouth, 1994)
LRJ	'Legal R/realism and Jurisprudence: Ten Theses' in Elizabeth Mertz, Stewart Macaulay and Thomas W. Mitchell (eds.), *The New Legal Realism* (Cambridge University Press, 2016), vol. I, Ch. 6
LTCL	*Legal Theory and Common Law*, ed. (Basil Blackwell, 1986)
LTV	'Law Teaching as a Vocation' (2003) 1 Speculum Iuris 161–80, reprinted in GJP, Ch. 17, www.cambridge.org /twining
Macdonald	Lecture 'Human Rights:Southern Voices' (Macdonald Lecture, University of Alberta) (2007) 11 R Const Stud 203–79 reprinted in Abdul Paliwala (ed.), Law, Justice and Social Development (LGD) Number 1, www.war wick.ac.uk/fac/soc/law/elj/lgd/2007_1/, short version in GJP Ch.13 (See HRSV)
MBL	'Moving Beyond Law: Interdisciplinarity and the Study of Evidence' in EIE, 73–118
OPP	'Other People's Power: The Bad Man and English Positivism 1897–1997' (1997) 63 Brooklyn LR 189 (shortened version included in GLT, Ch. 5)
PCLEA	*The Place of Customary Law in the National Legal Systems of East Africa* (University of Chicago Law School, 1964)
RDPS	'The Ratio Decidendi of the Parable of the Prodigal Son' in K. O'Donovan and G. Rubin (eds.), *Human Rights and Legal History: Essays for Brian Simpson* (Oxford University Press, 2000), 149–71, reprinted in RE2
RE1	*Rethinking Evidence* (Blackwell, 1990/Northwestern University Press, 1994)
RE2	*Rethinking Evidence*, 2nd edn (Cambridge University Press, 2006)
SSDL	'Social Science and Diffusion of Law' (2005) 32 JL & Soc 203–40
TEBW	*Theories of Evidence: Bentham and Wigmore* (Weidenfeld & Nicolson and Stanford University Press, 1985)
TFS	'Taking Facts Seriously' in N. Gold (ed.), *Essays on legal Education* (Butterworths, 1982), reprinted in (1984) 34 J Leg Ed 22–42; RE 2, Ch. 2; and LiC, Ch. 5
TFSA	'Taking Facts Seriously – Again' in P. Roberts and M. Redmayne (eds.), *Innovations in Evidence and Proof* (Hart, 2007), 65–86, reprinted in (2005) 55 J Leg Ed 360–80; and RE 2, Ch. 14

Preface

1. On field concepts see further p. xiv and GLS, 714–20.
2. 'The law is not the place for the artist or the poet ... The law is the calling of thinkers.' 'The Path of the Law' (1897) 10 Harv LR 457.
3. Holmes was an American judge-jurist, as were Cardozo, Learned Hand, and more controversially, Judge Jerome Frank. There is less of a tradition of judge-jurists in England, but Blackstone, Lords Devlin, Goff and, perhaps, Denning and Bingham would qualify. So would influential treatise writers for whom Jurisprudence was a secondary interest, like Pollock or Salmond or Dicey or other kinds of reflective practitioners.
4. Andrew Halpin reminds me that 'jurist' has a long history and several shades of meaning. It is distinct from 'jurisconsult', meaning someone qualified to give legal advice. It has sometimes been used to distinguish between thinking and unreflective lawyers (*jurisperiti*). The term has also been used disparagingly in some contexts to suggest approaches that are too academic or abstract or not grounded in practice. In this context a jurist is someone who reflects about matters legal, a species of thinker.
5. This was not as self-deprecating as it may seem. It was among other things an allusion to John Stuart Mill, who had opened his own very celebrated *Autobiography* (1873) with a similar disclaimer: he had nothing to offer, he said, apart from an account of the origin and growth of his philosophical convictions, and 'the reader whom these things do not interest, has only himself to blame if he reads further'.
6. Alan Bennett, *The History Boys* (2004).

1. Jurisprudence: a personal view

1. Robert K. Merton, 'Theories of the Middle Range' in On Theoretical Sociology (1949), 47.
2. I. Calvino, *Mr Palomar*, trans. William Weaver (1983), 1, 47.
3. Ibid.
4. I. Calvino, *Invisible Cities*, trans. William Weaver (1974), 121–3.
5. Of course, one needs to make use of bold but verifiable hypotheses, speculative models and images, and other methodological tools, provided these are treated with appropriate scepticism. Today a jurist needs to grapple with both whole views and local practical knowledge and lots of in-betweens. This is also an era in which the simplifying tendencies of IT and Big Data pose a particular threat.
6. In London some courses were called 'Jurisprudence and Legal Theory' but the difference was never clear.
7. What constitutes 'understanding' depends on context. A soldier ordered to 'Turn Right' understands enough if he can obey the order, even if he does not know the reason for it. It is adequate for use. In more general contexts the concept can occasion difficulty; for instance, the idea of

scientific explanation in philosophy or comprehension in Psychology. Here we can keep it simple. John Adams and Roger Brownsword state, that in the context of English legal education 'An "understanding" of law is provided primarily by an ability to conceptualize legal phenomena ... to account for the way in which law operates, and to evaluate its operation.' J. Adams and R. Brownsword, *Understanding Law* (1992). Here the key point is that, in my view, 'understanding law' involves all of these and is incomplete – indeed, potentially misleading – if the focus excludes any of these three ingredients, i.e. concepts, values and social facts. See further below, Ch. 13.

8. On field concepts see p. xiv. On judicial reasoning see Ch. 10.
9. On ladders of abstraction see HTDTWR, 299–304, 386–7.
10. On 'isms' see GJP, Ch. 16.
11. In his important book, *A Realistic Theory of Law* (2017), Brian Tamanaha reminds us that since Plato's *Minos* three types of conceptions of law, reflecting three branches of Jurisprudence, have generally been recognised, but that in modern times what he characterises as 'historical-sociological' jurisprudence has tended to be marginalised. The purpose of his book is to reinstate this 'Third Pillar' of Jurisprudence and develop it in the form of a realistic 'theory of law'. As we shall see, Tamanaha and I are close allies in the cause of integrating empirical understandings into the discipline of Law, but we follow different strategies, see below, pp. 255–6.
12. An alternative metaphor for capturing the landscape of jurisprudential activities is that of a huge bazaar consisting of many more or less informal, often overlapping, groups involved in competition, conversations, debates and disputes internally, occasionally allying with or attacking others, claiming more territory, or as with the popular image of Positivists and Natural Lawyers (and other anti-positivists), engaged in almost perpetual warfare with no discernible outcomes – a bewildering Babel of mutually uncomprehending voices that I satirised in a paper called 'The Great Juristic Bazaar' (1977, reprinted in GJB, Ch. 11); see further below, p. 160.
13. On 'theories of law', see pp. 276–9. On different kinds of theorising, see LiC, Ch. 6, esp. 129–30.
14. Cf. John Gardner, *Law as a Leap of Faith* (2012), Preface. 'I don't have a theory of law ... I have quite a lot of thoughts about law in general and I can only hope that they turn out to be consistent with each other. That they form any more perfect union than that is neither necessary nor desirable.' See further below, Ch. 20, n. 68.
15. I did not come across Robert Merton's work until the late 1960s, but I immediately felt a strong affinity. I was particularly impressed by *On Theoretical Sociology* (1967 [1949]). Over time I drew on some of his best-known ideas, including theories of the middle range, self-critical functionalism, manifest and latent functions, unintended consequences,

self-fulfilling prophecies, social roles, role sets and reference groups. I do not know how many of these originated with Merton or were popularised by him. On the seeming lack of connection between Llewellyn and Merton see GJP, Ch. 4. My interpretation and refinement of Llewellyn's 'law jobs theory' in terms of 'thin functionalism' is consciously Mertonian.

16. See pp. 246–8.
17. See Ch. 14.
18. See Ch. 12.
19. See Ch. 12.
20. See Ch. 18.
21. On 'rafts' see p. 2.
22. Merton's concept of 'theories of the middle range' was restricted to empirical ones. But in Jurisprudence concepts and values can also to be conceived in terms of working assumptions at varying levels of abstraction, generality and appropriateness.
23. 'Some Jobs for Jurisprudence' (Inaugural Lecture, University of Warwick) (1974) 1 Br J Law & Soc 149, discussed below, Ch. 13.
24. See JJM.
25. This passage eventually found its way (slightly changed) into a report published by the International Legal Center, *Legal Education in a Changing World* (1975), discussed below, pp. 219–21.

2. Childhood and schooling (1934–52)

1. The Programme of The Infant Welfare and Public Health Exhibition, Held in Kampala on 28, 29 and 30 May 1934. Dr H. M. Twining (Secretary of General Committee, Hon. Sec. Executive Committee).
2. See Anne Baker, *A Question of Honour* (1996) and *Morning Star: Florence Baker's Diary* (1972). See also, Brian Thompson, *Imperial Vanities: The Adventures of the Baker Brothers and Gordon of Khartoum* (2014); Susanna Hoe, *Travels in Tandem* (2012).
3. These included four or five women who had trained as doctors with my mother, Evelyn DuBuisson (my godmother and guardian) whom my father treated as an intellectual sparring partner, and several more who either had careers or were prominent in public life or both; for example, Dr Cicely Williams and Mary Trevelyan. What they had in common was they stood up to my rather domineering father, occasionally treating him as an overgrown school boy. During my childhood, adolescence and beyond I probably assumed that they were the superior gender. I don't think this view has changed. It was asserted in the family that 'William is good with great aunts.'
4. I have sometimes said that 'I had a colonial childhood, an anti-colonial adolescence, a neo-colonial start to my career, and a post-colonial middle-age.' This succinctly captures an important theme in my story, but it is too

glib, first, because the terms are both vague and ambiguous; and second, because, especially in respect of literature, the term has acquired a specific political meaning different from what I originally intended. On the first three terms my usage should be clear from the context: my father was a colonial administrator and my upbringing was fairly typical of such children; the process of rejection of my parents' benevolent paternalism was a slow process which came to a head when I was 21, linked to both a growing political awareness, a concern for personal autonomy and mixing with embittered African students in London and Paris (Ch. 3); the ambiguities and ambivalences of working as an expatriate in two newly independent countries are explicitly dealt with in Chs. 5 and 6, including enthusiastic 'nationalism' and an underestimation of the power of path-dependency and the extent of hybrids. In my original claim I meant 'post-colonial' in an apolitical sense, now typified as 'post-post-colonial by, for example, by the Booker Prize-winner, Marlon James in *A Brief History of Seven Killings* (2015), distancing himself from the more strongly anti-colonial forms of 'postcolonial' literature, while recognising that the colonial and neocolonial hangovers are still with us. What I can claim is that from about the age of 21 I have been committed to trying to make modest contributions to the processes of decolonisation (HRSV, Chs. 5, 6 and 20; and Plate 12 herein, 'Lowering the Flag').

5. Ashley Jackson, *War and Empire in Mauritius and the Indian Ocean* (2001), Ch. 6, 'Censorship, Radio Propaganda and Code-breaking'.

6. There were several memoirs of Charterhouse in the immediate post-war period. The one that squares best with my memories is Frederick Raphael, *Spoilt Boy: A Memoir of Childhood* (2003), except that he was in a different house and I am not Jewish. The quotation is at p. 164. The most famous accounts are the semi-fictional ones by Simon Raven, who was an almost exact contemporary of my brother and in the same house, almost immediately before my time there. He is particularly vicious about William Rees-Mogg, later editor of *The Times* and father of an even more conspicuous son.

7. Why so coy? This exercise has taught me how much I had imitated my parents: early rising, afternoon naps, other routines; a taste for good whisky; a sense of fun; making lists. Even writing was in the family. Great-uncles Sam and Val Baker published books; my grandmother Agatha published *A Child's History of Westminster Abbey* (1910) and similar works, her eldest brother, Professor Gilbert Bourne, published books on zoology and anatomy, as well as *Memoirs of an Eton Wet-bob of the Seventies* (1933); my grandfather William Twining published some family history and his elder son, Stephen, quietly corrected it; my father wrote some impressive books on coronations and regalia as a hobby; he also loved to plunge into archives in search of lost crowns and then challenge museum directors to explain their absence; my mother published several

matter-of-fact practical pamphlets on child welfare, how to dig latrines and the like; and my brother wrote light verse and one musical comedy (unpublished). Given this background it is a mystery why, as a teenager, I kept my ambition to be a 'writer' very quiet indeed. Was it because for my family writing was a side-line and I wanted to *be* one? Or that I secretly aspired to write fiction or that I was interested in ideas? Or was it just banal peer pressure?

8. Raphael, in *Spoilt Boy*, dwells on his experiences of anti-Semitism; I encountered this prejudice, but (perhaps remarkably) did not know what it meant; there were too few non-whites for colour to be an issue and Richard Sorabji was the only contemporary I kept in touch with after leaving. He was in another house, but he is still a good friend.

3. Oxford and after (1952-7)

1. A. J. Ayer (ed.), *The Revolution in Philosophy* (1956). Nicola Lacey's *A Life of H. L. A. Hart: The Nightmare and the Noble Dream* (2004) brilliantly captures the general context and Hart's life in intimate (for some, too intimate) detail.

2. (1954) 70 LQR, reprinted in *Essays in Jurisprudence and Philosophy* (1983), Ch. 1.

3. On doctrine, see further Ch. 13.

4. A. W. B. Simpson, *Reflections on the Concept of Law* (2011).

5. On MacCormick, see Ch. 15.

6. Cited by Lacey, *A Life of H. L. A. Hart*, 157.

7. As a result of these encounters at Lincoln's Inn I started on a scheme or campaign to improve the lot of overseas students in London, especially those reading for the Bar. I got as far as an appointment with the Master of the Rolls, and made a few waves, but I had no idea how to make this effective and it petered out. Mary Trevelyan was a friend of my parents and the well-known founder of International Students House and the Goats Club for overseas students. She admonished me for having bright ideas and then leaving them around for others to implement. She was right, but I am an ideas person.

8. In the period 1954-7 I slowly moved away from support of my father's multiracial policies, partly because of a better understanding of nationalism, partly because I felt 'fancy franchises' would not work and partly because of my experience of embittered African students in London and Paris; also because of the inevitability of a rapid move to Independence – the winds of change were unstoppable. In private my father moved in that direction (see Colin Baker, *Exit from Empire* (2010), 186–92), but by 1957 I had gone much further in my sympathy for African nationalism.

9. If my conversion can be placed in 1956–7, my 'anti-colonial adolescence' started at 21. A late developer, once more. My friend Nicola Lacey admits

that she was similarly slow on the uptake as regards feminism ('Companions on a Serendipitous Journey' (2017) 44 JL & Soc 283). Contrast the thoughts on nationalism of another friend, Neil MacCormick, below, p. 212.

10. C. K. Allen, *Law in the Making*, 4th edn (1946), 45.

4. University of Chicago I (1957–8)

1. In Chicago the first Law degree (the JD) was much more prestigious than the LLM, which was mainly for aliens. As I later discovered, it was Law School policy to steer foreign graduate students towards courses that were unique or special to Chicago. Commonwealth Fellows, who were offered the privilege of completing the JD in one year, had to take some mainstream courses in competition with 'real' JD students, especially first-year basic courses such as Torts and Property that I considered that I had already done.

2. In retrospect, I am surprised at the strong stand I took on this small issue of 'academic freedom', because I am slow to stand on principle until pushed quite far. I was right to object, but I now regret that I did not take the course, for three reasons. First, I missed an opportunity to obtain a grounding in micro-economics, a deficiency I never really made good and which has handicapped me both professionally and more generally, for I believe that economics is an important part of understanding both law and politics. Secondly, Director was a leading pioneer of the Law and Economics movement that has become one of the dominant forces in American academic law. He was the conduit and hatchet man for Milton Friedman and I missed the opportunity to witness the beginnings of this movement at close quarters. Thirdly, when the Chicago School of Law and Economics came into its own, I was ill-equipped to fight it on its own ground – significantly, years later Ronald Dworkin took private instruction in economics in order to equip himself in this way. It pays to study the opposition and I missed a rare chance.

3. For a further clash with Director, see pp. 79–80.

4. I took courses given by Nicholas de Belleville Katzenbach, Edward Shils and Edward Levi, Malcolm Sharp, J. B. Schneewind, William Winslow Crosskey, Alison Dunham and Max Rheinstein, as well as a course on International Commercial Transactions taught by the formidable team of Katzenbach, Llewellyn, Mentschikoff and Steffen. Subsequently, several prominent federal judges (Scalia, Posner, Easterbrook, and Bork), two US Attorneys-General (Katzenbach and Levi) and one President of the United States (Obama) had been members of faculty at the University of Chicago Law School before moving on.

5. Except Aaron Director and William Winslow Crosskey, a Casaubon-like legal historian who devoted his life to 'proving' a dubious premiss about the original intent of the US Constitution. He was the worst teacher that I ever had during my legal education. He made us buy and read vol. I of his treatise, while he read from the manuscript of the second volume, which he did not make available to us. He virtually refused to answer questions. All this made him memorable.

6. George W. Liebmann, *The Common Law Tradition: A Collective Portrait of Five Legal Scholars* (2005), 305.

7. Ibid., 304–6.

8. LiC, 6.

9. KLP, 7.

10. Adapted from KLP, 7–8.

11. 'Law in Our Society: A Horse-sense Theory of the Institution of Law' (1950 edn). Lengthy extracts from this remarkable manuscript are published in KLRM, Appendices B and C.

12. KLP, 9.

13. KLRM, 173.

14. Cited in KLRM, 172; from 'Law in Our Society', 11, reprinted in KLRM, 2nd edn, at 560.

15. On 'theories of law' and working assumptions, see pp. 276–9; see also 'rafts' at pp. 2 and 20.

16. KLRM, 264–6.

17. A doctoral student, J. Gillis Wetter, did something similar in comparing the styles of judgments of the highest courts in five countries. He tried to formalise his analysis too much for my taste. In 1957–8 I suspect that Wetter and I were rivals for the position of Llewellyn's favourite son. I had taken an instant dislike to him, which I sensed was reciprocated. He was very formal in social style and cast of mind and I thought that he was trying to squeeze Llewellyn's free-flowing ideas into a formalistic black box. There are signs of this in his book (J. Gillis Wetter, *The Styles of Appellate Judicial Decisions* (1960)), which nevertheless is still well worth reading. We were civil to each other and he was my host on a lecture tour in Sweden in the 1970s. He became a leading figure in international commercial arbitration and, inter alia, Solicitor Royal in Sweden. He died suddenly in 1995 at the age of 63.

18. Adapted from JJM; for longer discussions see KLRM, 15–84.

19. On Llewellyn's illuminating choice of 'trouble' rather than dispute see GJP, 105 n. 79.

20. K. N. Llewellyn, (1934) 34 Columbia LR 1. A shortened version was reprinted in Llewellyn's *Jurisprudence: Realism in Theory and Practise* (1962), 233–62. See further, W. Twining, 'Constitutions, Constitutionalism and Constitution-mongering' in I. Stotzky (ed.), *Transition to Democracy in Latin America* (1993).

21. See p. 86 and JJM. Hart later popularised the fallacy that the American Realists were 'rule sceptics' who believed that 'talk of rules is a myth'. I have defended Llewellyn against this absurd charge in several places (especially KLRM and 'Afterword'). He treated rules as one means of doing the law jobs, but only one; he rejected radical indeterminacy, but talked of 'leeways' for interpretation and limits of the leeways; he drafted several codes including the UCC; his book *The Theory of Rules*, ed. F. Schauer (2011) has been published posthumously; anyone who calls Llewellyn a 'rule-sceptic in Hart's sense is being unscholarly.

22. GJP 184 and JJM.

23. On the heuristic value of the idea of law jobs, see GJP 184 and JJM.

24. On 'the job of juristic method' see JJM.

25. 'Can't-helps' was a favourite term of Oliver Wendell Holmes Jr; see, for example, M. Lerner, *The Mind and Faith of Justice Holmes* (1923).

5. Khartoum (1958–61)

1. Mohamed Omer Beshir (1926–92) was a significant scholar and public intellectual as well as administrator at the University of Khartoum and later at Ahlia University in Omdurman, which he helped to found. M.O.B., as he was generally known, was a key link between the expatriate staff of the University of Khartoum and the wider local intellectual community. He remained a close friend until his death in 1992.

2. Edward Atiyah, *Black Vanguard* (1952). In an interview, Sir Michael Atiyah spoke of his father as follows: 'My father's main dream was to go to Oxford. He wanted to convert himself into an Englishman. It didn't quite work out. When he came back to Sudan, he found he wasn't part of the English class structure, he was regarded as one of the lower classes, although he was Oxford-educated and regarded himself as culturally English. That turned him over a bit. He became an Arab nationalist to some extent. All his life was divided between wanting passionately to be English and yet sympathising with the Arab political position within the British empire.' Interview 1986, cited in Wikipedia.

3. *An Introduction to the Law of Contract* (1st edn, 1961; 6th edn, with S. A. Smith, 2006). The recontruction in the text of what he said is based on memories quite close in time to the actual events.

4. *The Rise and Fall of the Freedom of Contract* (1979). See further below, Ch. 12.

5. See further, 'Yale, 1965' in Ch. 7.

6. My note written in 1960 reads as follows: '*Insha'Allah Sept 1960* One evening during my visit to Halfa, we were sitting on the roof, drinking *limoun* and watching the sun go down. Someone began wailing in a neighbouring house; the wailing spread to several other houses and people – mainly women – came rushing down the street also wailing. Zaki went to ask what this was

about and reported that a father had beaten his son at lunch-time, the boy had fled towards the desert at the edge of the town, and had not been seen since. The women were mourning his death. I asked Zaki, have they found his body? Are there search parties out? No, they have given him up for dead. It was getting dark, but not yet. I was shocked. I suggested that we – Zaki and I – should organise a search party with torches and lights. No, said Zaki, *Insha'Allah*, he will either turn up or he won't. It is a matter of fate. I interpreted this as an extreme example of fatalism – passive acceptance, giving up easily, which I found distressing – even infuriating. I find this in a much weaker form with my Irish in-laws in sharp contrast with my 'do something' instincts. Later that night the boy crept back home. He had been hiding in a railway siding.' Interestingly: my diary contains four pages of entries from the Halfa visit but does not mention this.

7.   There is a substantial literature by and about al-Turabi, mainly in Arabic, but with enough in English and French to reconstruct his life and ideas in some detail.

8.   This hardly squares with al-Turabi's professed views: 'Khartoum's bars and discos are shuttered. Women who dare to walk the streets in slacks or without a head-covering are often stopped by the front's security force and taken to police stations. Young couples courting in public say they are frequently harassed as well. College students said the police break up parties in private homes and confiscate liquor, and have at times horse-whipped the organizers.

The nation's laws now embrace shari'a, a Koranic code that includes harsh penalties for some crimes, like death by hanging for adulterers and the amputation of a hand for thieves.

Some here say the Islamisation has been largely cosmetic. Judges have proved reluctant to impose the penalties shari'a prescribes, and it is difficult to prove a crime under the law. To prove adultery, for instance, four grown men must witness the sex act at the same time. 'I have not heard of anybody who was hanged or stoned to death because of adultery', said Chief Justice Obeid Hag Ali, explaining that shari'a is 'more of a threat intended to regulate society'.

9.   W. J. Berridge, *Hasan al-Turabi, Islamist Politics and Democracy in Sudan* (2017) contains an interesting account of his ideology, scholarly writings and his extraordinary role in Sudanese politics. It is very informative about his ideas and public political stances, but rather thin on biographical and personal detail. It confirms the view that it is hard to reconcile his Islamist ideology (which some proclaim as 'liberal') with his extraordinary political career, in and out of gaol, switching allegiances, falling in and out of favour with the military regimes and responsible for the harsh Islamisation of Law.

10.   The author was a Scottish classicist, who was educated in Glasgow and Oxford and who spent most of his academic career at Columbia University

in New York. This combination of Scottish, Oxonian and American-type humanities traditions (influenced by Robert Maynard Hutchins of Chicago) appealed to me and I used it almost as a desk-book.

11. 'Legal Education Within East Africa' in *East African Law Today* (1966), 115.

12. For a more detailed account see GLT, 142ff.

13. M. F. Massoud, *Law's Fragile State: Colonial, Authoritarian, and Humanitarian Legacies in Sudan* (2013).

14. 1st edn 1937 (still in print in 1973). A central theme was that political theory is itself part of political action.

15. *KMC v Michel Cotran* (1958) SLJR 85, discussed in W. Twining, 'Khartoum Municipal Council v Cotran – a study in judicial techniques' (1959) SLJR 229. Although this was only my second published article, on returning to it after nearly sixty years I find that I rather like it – a bit prolix, but it makes some interesting points.

16. In Issa Shivji (ed.), *Limits of Legal Radicalism* (1986) (25th anniversary of Law Faculty in Dar es Salaam), reprinted in LiC, Ch. 2.

17. *Sudan Govt v El Baleila Bala Baleila and others* (1958) SLJR 2.

18. 'Law Reporting in the Sudan' (1959) 3 J Afr L 176.

19. E.g. A. W. B. Simpson, *Cannibalism and the Common Law* (1985); cf. W. Twining, 'What Is the Point of Legal Archeology?' (2012) 3 Transnat' Leg Theory 166.

20. Mainly through the SAILER Program (Staffing of African Institutions for Legal Education and Research), on which see Jayanth K. Krishnan, 'Academic SAILERS: The Ford Foundation and the Efforts to Shape Legal Education in Africa, 1957–77' (2012) 52 Am J Leg Hist 262.

21. See p. 260.

22. See n. 17.

23. As recorded from memory over twenty years later.

24. I think that his episode took place in 1960, but this account was written down over ten years later after numerous retellings.

25. Our co-examiners in 1959 were Coulson, Powell, Fitzgerald, Sir David Hughes Parry, de Smith, Gower, Crane, Keeton, Schwarzenberger, Nokes, Lloyd, Graveson and Bland. A team of substance.

26. In fact, Lennie Hoffman (later Lord Hoffman, the most intellectual judge of his generation) got the Stowell Fellowship at Univ., so I would almost certainly have missed that one.

27. I celebrated the fiftieth anniversary of this first publication by writing an article critically examining its underlying assumptions about 'reception'. (See further, pp. 246–8.)

28. For details see Krishnan, 'Academic SAILERS'.

29. See p. 230.

30. Discussed, and doubted in Krishnan, 'Academic SAILERS', but who knows?

31. HRSV.

32. P. Collinson, *The History of a History Man* (2011), 160.

33. See n. 13.

34. T. S. Eliot, 'Burnt Norton' (one of the *Four Quartets*) and *Murder in the Cathedral* (1935).

6. Dar es Salaam (1961–5)

1. For a longer account of the early years in Dar es Salaam see my 'Legal Education Within East Africa' in *East African Law Today* (1966), 114–51.

2. J. Harrington and A. Manji, '"Mind with Mind and Spirit with Spirit": Lord Denning and African Legal Education' (2003) *Journal of Law and Society* 376–99.

3. Speech at the Opening Ceremony of University College Dar es Salaam, 25 October 1961 at p. 12, reprinted in J. K. Nyerere, *Freedom and Unity* (1966).

4. I notice in my papers that an early staff list shows that of the first eleven senior staff, A. B. Weston, the Dean of Law, was the only one without prior African experience. Most of the early law staff had Oxford Law degrees and some had also worked in North America.

5. The Law Faculty celebrated its twenty-fifth, fortieth and fiftieth anniversaries, each of which produced quite substantial publications, including Issa Shivji's *The Limits of Legal Radicalism* (1985). Professors Ambreena Manji and John Harrington are doing historical work on some anglophone law schools in Africa, including Dar es Salaam.

6. In the Arusha Declaration (1967) President Nyerere outlined TANU's creed and its policies of socialism and self-reliance (Ujamaa). This marked the start of a more radical approach by TANU and the government, including extensive nationalisation of public services and parts of the private sector and the controversial policy of 'villagisation' which back-fired.

7. The University College Dar es Salaam, *A Guide for Schools* (1964), pp. 16–17. This is sometimes attributed to A. B. Weston, as Dean, and he would certainly have read and commented on it, but the first draft was in fact by McAuslan (it is in my possession!). Cf. a similar statement prepared for the Warwick Law School prospectus in the 1970s.

8. On 'context' see Ch. 13; on 'skills' see Ch. 17; on 'development' see Ch. 18.

9. This is based on notes made shortly once after I heard AB retell this story. The actual words are imagined, but close to what he reported.

10. See Plate 3.

11. See T. Zartaloulidis (ed.), *Land Law and Urban Policy in Context: Essays on the Contributions of Patrick McAuslan* (2016), which contains further details and includes the Encomium for Julie Manning.

12. Ibid.

13. For further details see ibid., *passim*.

14. Yash and I have coincided and worked together in New York, Uppsala, Warwick and with the Commonwealth Legal Education Association and the Commonwealth Human Rights Initiative (Ch. 17); he was one of my four 'Southern voices' (Ch. 20 and GJP, 406–23) and, despite all that, we have remained close friends. Loaded with honours (including a CBE and FBA from UK). He still jets around the world fixing conflicts and negotiating constitutional settlements. His work on the Basic Law in Hong Kong and constitutional reform in Kenya has been especially influential.

15. T. Ranger, *Writing Revolt: An Engagement with African Nationalism 1957–67* (2013).

16. Rodney taught in Dar es Salaam in 1966–7 and having been declared as *persona non grata* in Jamaica in 1968, he returned to Dar as Professor of History until 1974. He was killed by a bomb in his car in Guyana in 1980. An interesting summary of Dar's role as 'a beacon' for global revolutionaries in the 1960s and 1970s is: 'When Dar, the Haven of Peace, was the Mecca for Revolutionaries', *The East African*, 5–11 January 2013, reported in the Bulletin of the Britain-Tanzania Society.

17. Henry Kissinger is credited with saying: 'University politics are so vicious precisely because the stakes are so small'; in the story of the gowns the debates were well-mannered, but the protagonists treated the issue as emblematic of the contradictions and confusions of working in a neocolonial context.

18. K. E. Svendsen, Professor of Economics, memorandum to the Academic Board of UCD (Minutes of Special Meeting held on 8 July 1964).

19. See Plate 2.

20. I had personal contact with E. E. Evans-Pritchard, Godfrey Lienhardt, Tom Fallers, Philip Gulliver, Sally Falk Moore, Paul Bohannan and some of the younger generation, such as Neville Dyson-Hudson; in Khartoum, Elizabeth Hopkins, Marguerite Johnston and Mary Nicholson. I also knew Ad Hoebel, Laura Nader and Max Gluckman in other contexts. When Max visited Makerere, his host was a young economist, Cyril Ehrlich. At short notice he invited Gluckman to address a meeting of the Uganda Society (which my father had helped to found in the 1930s). Max read a very witty, polished paper. It went down very well. Cyril asked him if he could publish it in the *Uganda Journal*. 'Young man,' said Gluckman, 'how long have you been in academic life? ... Do you not know that the first principle of the wandering scholar is: "NEVER publish your party piece"' (as reported to me by Ehrlich). I have tried to follow this principle, but have generally failed.

21. H. Cory, *Sukuma Law and Custom* (1953), *Customary Law of the Haya Tribe*, with M. Hartnoll (1945), *African Figurines* (1956). He had a large collection of figurines at his home in Mwanza, some of which were so obscene that when I was sixteen my mother had unsuccessfully tried to shield me from seeing them. Cf. N. Miller, (1968) 11 Afr Stud Bull 195 (Hans Cory Collection).

22. This is attributed to Sheikh Amri Abedi, then Minister of Justice, at a Conference on Local Courts and Customary Law in 1963. The exact wording of this dictum is variously reported. See W. T. McLain (ed.), *African Conference on Local Courts and Customary Law* (1963), a record of the proceedings of the Conference held in Dar es Salaam, Tanganyika in September 1963, under the Chairmanship of the Minister of Justice of Tanganyika, Sheikh Amri Abedi (I was one of the rapporteurs).

23. Published as *The Place of Customary Law in the National Legal Systems of East Africa* (1964).

24. In some African countries it has been government policy not to post magistrates to their own areas.

25. I have heard this story several times, but have seen no published version. It possibly relates to the Giriama people of the Coast Province in Kenya, but I am unable to confirm this.

26. Adapted from my Bernstein Lecture, 489ff.

27. Cf. Sir Rupert Cross on 'abolishing' his subject (Evidence), see p. 178.

28. The fullest development of this was later, e.g. Martin Chanock, *Law, Custom and Social Order: The Colonial Experience in Malawi and Zambia* (1985).

29. GJP, Ch. 12.

30. On the American Restatements and the controversy surrounding them, which included some harsh criticisms by American Realists, see GJP, 306–12.

31. See Twining, *The Place of Customary Law in the National Legal Systems of East Africa*, 16–17.

32. This passage is adapted from 'McAuslan in Context – Early Days at Dar es Salaam and Warwick' in Zartaloulidis (ed.), *Land Law and Urban Policy in Context*.

33. In teaching Torts, I used the excellent Canadian book of cases and materials by Cecil A. ['Caesar'] Wright, of Toronto, *Cases on the Law of Torts* (1963 [1954 and 1958]), supplemented by East African cases. This was before E. Veitch (ed.), *East African Cases on the Law of Tort* (1972).

34. The classic example of the advantages of a historical approach to law in times of rapid change is Claire Palley, *The Constitutional History of Southern Rhodesia 1888–1965: with special reference to imperial control* (1966). Ian Smith declared UDI while the book was at the proof stage. The publishers allowed the author to add another chapter to bring the

narrative up to date. The book reputedly became the 'bible' of the three nationalist leaders, Mugabe, Nkomo and Sithole when they shared a prison cell – the standard joke being: 'Who will sleep with Dr Palley tonight?' This contrasts sharply with expository books on African constitutional law which have anchored in specific texts and soon became outdated, sometimes even before publication.

35. Before arriving in Dar, I urged AB to push for a four-year LLB and to think seriously about the use of vacations and students' use of time. I still have the letter, written from Khartoum in July 1961. It starts 'Dear Arthur' – probably the only time I used that vocative. He supported my lobbying, but we lost on both counts. On four-year undergraduate degrees in the UK see Ch. 17. In 1963 Ford Foundation financed a short US study tour for me to learn about work-study programmes at Antioch and elsewhere. I was impressed, but was never able to persuade colleagues to take the idea of a forty-hour week study year seriously. In the UK Buckingham and commercial institutions like BPP, who make more use of the calendar year, have been often treated with scorn as not being 'proper universities', but nearly all 'proper ones' are set in their ways in respect of structure, finance, expectations, length of terms and the convenience of academics. Some use this approach to reduce the period of the degree to under three years. Later, at Warwick some administrators proposed cutting the length of terms to increase conference revenue; I moved an amendment suggesting that we abolish terms altogether and become a conference centre. The original motion was defeated, but my basic argument had some resonance with colleagues – bureaucratisation was not yet complete.

36. Laski to Holmes (15.X.32): '[A] remark of mine that we should look at the work of Harvard produced from an eminent silk the comment that the American inability to cope with crime was a sufficient comment on Harvard; I imagine that this takes its place among the best non-sequiturs in history.' M. Howe (ed.), *Holmes–Laski Letters* (1953), vol. II, 1410. The context in Nairobi was whether a Harvard Law degree should be given partial recognition in Kenya.

37. African Jurisprudence, Jurisprudence in an African context, Jurisprudence for Africa, a student book for African law schools? This was never clear or adequately thought through.

38. I had in fact registered for an External PhD on Llewellyn at UCL, with Dennis Lloyd as supervisor, but never followed this up.

39. When I returned to Dar, some people thought that I was being disloyal to my father. He did not think that and we remained on very good terms during his last years despite our political differences.

7. Llewellyn again: American interludes (Chicago 1963–4, Yale 1965, Philadelphia 1971)

1. Hart to Twining, cited by Nicola Lacey in *H. L. A. Hart: The Nightmare and the Noble Dream* (2004), 233. The context was an invitation to visit Belfast to give some classes in 1967, when he indicated that he was willing to talk about almost anything 'except that wretched book'.

2. 'Afterword', 404–9. Much of this chapter substantially overlaps with the detailed account in the 'Afterword' to KLRM (2012) of my work on Llewellyn in Chicago and elsewhere from 1963 (my second visit to Chicago) to 1973 (the publication of KLRM). I have adapted pp. 390–404 with only minor changes and cuts, because it is directly relevant to my narrative here. However, pp. 404–43 mainly deal with the aftermath of KLRM as it relates to posthumous publications of Llewellyn's works, writings about Llewellyn and American Legal Realism between 1971 and 2011, developments relating to the UCC during that period, detailed Excursuses on Llewellyn and Hart and on the course on 'Elements'. Most of these topics are at least touched on in other chapters of this book, but in less detail.

3. Reproduced from 'Talk about Realism' (Dewey Lecture, 23 October 1984) (1985) 60 NYU L Sch R 329–84, reprinted in GJB, Ch. 6.

4. Of course, I cannot vouch for the exact words used on this occasion, but this reconstruction is based on my contemporaneous notes.

5. I included the poem in KLP despite Gerhard Casper's advice that it was embarrassingly bad and unpublishable.

6. In 1964 I also had grants from the Ford and Rockefeller Foundations to visit institutions and work-study programmes in the United States in connection with my job in Dar es Salaam.

7. KLP, 11–13. The story of Llewellyn's 'war adventure' is told in Appendix A of KLRM.

8. There were two publications connected with this collection: W. Twining, *The Karl Llewellyn Papers* (1968) (KLP) and R. Ellinwood Jr, *The Karl Llewellyn Papers: A Guide to the Collection* (1967), both published by the University of Chicago Law School. There is now a comprehensive catalogue of both the Llewellyn and Mentschikoff papers online at University of Chicago Special Collections.

9. Mark de Wolfe Howe of Harvard Law School was the main exception. He was known to be working on a multi-volume biography of Oliver Wendell Holmes Jr. Two were published: *Justice Oliver Wendell Holmes: The Shaping Years, 1841–1870* (1957) and *The Proving Years* 1870–1882 (1963). Unfortunately, he died in 1967, aged 60, without completing his project. I arranged to meet him at Harvard, but he did not seem interested in my project and offered me no advice.

10.   This excursus is reprinted from the 'Afterword' to KLRM. Soia was known professionally as Soia Mentschikoff, but socially she liked to be called Mrs Karl Llewellyn. The main sources, apart from first-hand knowledge and numerous obituaries, are Connie Bruck, 'Soia Mentschikoff, The First Woman Everything' (Oct. 1982) The American Lawyer 36; Symposium in Honor of Dean Soia Mentschikoff, (1983) 37 U. Miami L. Rev.; Zipporah Wiseman, 'Soia Mentschikoff' in R. M. Sakolar and M. L. Volcansek (eds.), *Women in Law* (1996) and in *American National Biography* (1998). See also Robert Whitman, 'Soia Mentschikoff and Karl Llewellyn: Moving Together to the University of Chicago Law School' (1992) 24 Connecticut LR 1119. For a bibliography of her main published writings see Wiseman (1996). Some of her professional papers are in the Special Collections of the University of Chicago Library, others are in the possession of the University of Miami Law Library. www.lib.uchicago.edu/e/scrc/findingaids/view.php?eadid=ICU.SPCL.MENTSCHIKOFF.

11.   S. Mentschikoff and I. Stotsky, *The Theory and Craft of American Law – Elements* (1981). Llewellyn took over the first year 'Elements' course when he arrived in Chicago and continued teaching it until his death. Soia exported her own version to Miami (where it still survives, at least in name, sometimes more than that). See further 'Afterword', 411–18. Our course on 'Juristic Technique' in Belfast had a similar function, but was very different, as is obvious comparing the Mentschikoff-Stotsky book with *How to Do Things with Rules* (see below, Ch. 11).

12.   Mentschikoff was associated with the UCC project in various capacities from 1942 until the 1970s.

13.   The University of Chicago forbade joint appointments of spouses (a nepotism rule), so Soia did not become a tenured professor until Karl died. This did not appear to faze her.

14.   Cited by Bruck 'Soia Mentschikoff, The First Woman Everything'.

15.   She was twice nominated by her former colleague, Nicholas de Belleville Katzenbach.

16.   Her personal style is evident in 'Reflections of a Drafter' (1982) 43 Ohio State LJ 537 in which the term 'horsing around' is used more than once to describe the behaviour of members of a legal elite during the preparation of the UCC. See also the posthumous lectures (reconstructed by Irwin Stotzky) 'The Last Universal Discipline' (1986) 54 U Cincinnati LR 695 and I. Stotzky, 'Soia's Way: Toiling in the Common Law Tradition' (1984) 38 U. Miami L. Rev. 373.

17.   Cited by Bruck, 'Soia Mentschikoff, The First Woman Everything'.

18.   Ibid.

19.   E.g. Manfred Weis, review of KLRM, (1990) Archiv für civilistische Praxis 90 ff; cf. Colin Tapper: 'remarkably detached' (review (1973) JSPTL (NS) 168–9).

20. She also made a significant contribution to the biographical chapter (KLRM, Ch. 6). Here the initiative was mine. I plied her with questions about Karl's childhood and family (there was little in the papers) and quirks, and I used her as a sounding-board to check that both my facts were accurate and my judgements were on the right track. Towards the end I consulted Ernie Haggard, a psychologist, who had worked closely with both Karl and Soia, as to whether my take on Karl's personality was plausible. Without any hint of a Freudian interpretation, he made some helpful suggestions. I did not meet Betty, Llewellyn's first wife, and had only one perfunctory interview with his second wife, Emma Corstvet, who understandably did not give me access to her papers. So I did not get a balanced picture of Karl's marital relations – but this did not matter much, because I was not trying to write a rounded biography. Later Schlegel learned a lot from interviews with Corstvet (John Henry Schlegel, *American Realism and Empirical Social Science* (1995), index under Corstvet). On Robert Whitman et al. and the Corstvet papers see 'Afterword', 427–2.

21. Of course, I cannot recall her exact words, but I am confident about the punchline.

22. KLRM, 458, n. 6.

23. See, however, 'Symposium: Origins and Evolution: Drafters Reflect Upon the Uniform Commercial Code' (1982) 43 Ohio State LJ 535. Also, Homer Kripke, 'The Importance of the Code' (1990) 21 U Toledo LR 591 and ALI Audiovisual History No. 2, 'Homer Kripke' (American Law Institute, 1991). In my view Ch. 9 of KLRM is incomplete, especially in respect of internal disagreements, but it can claim to be an authentic, if thin, account of Soia's version of events. See further her 'Reflections of a Drafter'.

24. However, Peter Winship of Southern Methodist University has had a project on this for some years.

25. 'Talk About Realism' (1985) 60 NYU LR 329–84, reprinted in GJB Ch. 5.

26. JJM reprinted in GJB, Ch. 6.

27. KLRM, Preface, xxiv.

28. *Präjudizienrecht und Rechtssprechung in Amerika* (1933). The main text has been translated into English and published as Paul Gewirtz (ed.), *The Case Law System in America*, trans. M. Ansaldi (1989), reviewed in (1991) 100 Yale LJ 1093.

29. (1967–8) 30 MLR 165.

30. See pp. 88–92.

31. In addition to a joint letter from the group, signed by Leff, I met two of the three students in the group, Duncan Kennedy and Richard Danzig. They were friendly and polite, but confirmed that it was dull.

32. Sadly, Arthur Leff died young, but this was the start of a long, but fragmented, friendship with Duncan Kennedy – whom I met for the first time during riots on campus at Yale in 1968.

33.   When I presented a copy of KLRM to my mother, she seemed to be surprised that any son of hers could have produced something like this; she made it clear that she had no intention of trying to read it. However, she left it lying around her sitting room like a coffee-table book and I may once have caught her surreptitiously stroking it.

34.   KLRM, 190–3. Some commentators treat socio-legal *research* as the main or exclusive basis for empirical understandings; as any student of Evidence knows such findings are only a small part of the 'stock of knowledge' and 'general experience' on which background generalisations and many specific practical decisions have to be based in practice. See RE2, 438–46 and *Analysis*, 273–9.

35.   K. Llewellyn, 'The Adventures of Rollo' (1953) 2(1) U Chicago L Sch Record 3–4, 20–4.

36.   R. Kipling, 'The Disciple' (1932) discussed below, Ch. 18.

37.   At various times we considered a move to the United States, especially after the teenage period for our children, but Penelope drew the line at 'cold places'. It happened that at the relevant times only cold places exhibited an interest in me as a regular faculty member, so we never made the plunge. I flirted with Miami on a couple of occasions but decided against. There are several advantages in being a Visitor – one's only obligations are teaching and making oneself available; no committee meetings, no academic politics, one can usually write one's own ticket so far as teaching is concerned. One is quite well paid, but usually without the generous benefits that accrue to tenured Faculty, such as pension and other rights, health insurance and security until one becomes incompetent. Obtaining visas and being enrolled afresh each time is tedious and one *feels like* a perennial guest rather than a part of the community. And there are great advantages in being an academic in a small country.

38.   See further Chs. 14 and 15.

39.   This is how I tried to reported the interview not long afterwards: 'In 196[5] the author visited Corbin at his home in Hamden in order to interview him about Llewellyn. By then Corbin was [over] 90; his hearing was impaired and he could only read with considerable effort. He had just completed work on a supplement to his monumental treatise on contracts. Beside his chair was a box of manila cards on which each new decision affecting contracts was noted with care in longhand as the advance sheets came in. In the previous six months, Corbin said, he had noted approximately two thousand cases in this fashion. Long after most scholars would have handed over such "mechanical" work (Corbin would have rejected this description of it) to younger men, he had ploughed on relentlessly and had only stopped when it became a physical impossibility to continue. This patient, careful, relentlessness was Corbin's cardinal virtue.' On Corbin, see KLRM, esp. Ch. 2, and (2015) 47 Yale JL & Humanities 101.

40. KLRM, 27–34, 395–7; 'Looking Back, Looking Forward: A Letter from Arthur Corbin to Soia Mentschikoff on the Death of Karl Llewellyn' (2015) 47 Yale JL & Humanities 101.

41. Corbin to Llewellyn (letter dated 1 December 1960, copy in possession of the author).

42. On 'rule-scepticism' see p. 139.

43. See p. 42.

44. See p. 230.

45. For a longer account see W. Twining, 'Reflections on Law in Context' in Peter Cane and Jane Stapleton (eds.), *Essays for Patrick Atiyah* (1991); see further below, n. 47.

46. B. Abel-Smith and R. B. Stevens, *Lawyers and the Courts* (1967) and *In Search of Justice* (1968). Stevens also collaborated with an Economist, R. Stevens and B. Yamey, *The Restrictive Practices Court* (1965). In England in the 1960s he was the leading pioneer of cross-disciplinary legal studies.

47. The story of the launch of the series and the thinking behind it is told in LiC, Ch. 3. On Robert Stevens see the Symposium in (2009) 16(1) Int'l J Legal Profession.

48. See p. 98.

49. Taken from a novel Eric Hodgins, *Mr Blandings Builds his Dreamhouse* (1946), which later became a popular film. The casebook was less popular.

50. This resulted in a symposium on recent literature on Law in Eastern Africa, written mainly by the students ((1971)119 U Penn LR 1062).

51. On an encounter with Erving Goffman at Penn, see below, p. 121.

8. The Queen's University Belfast (1966–72)

1. This account is based mainly on hearsay from three or four informants. I have not been able to research the background to 'the Montrose affair', which may well have been much more complicated.

2. See p. 2.

3. See pp. 300–1. When Claire Palley was appointed to a Chair at Queen's in 1972 she was the first woman to be appointed as a Professor of Law in the UK. Later she became the first woman Law Professor in England. In 1972 I heard someone ask: 'Can a woman be a Professor of *Law*?' We firmly answered yes. In fact, Frances Moran had been Regius Professor of Law at Trinity College Dublin since 1944. See further, Fiona Cownie, 'The United Kingdom's First Woman Law Professor: An Archerian Analysis' (2015) 42 JL & Soc 127.

4. For a history of the University see Brian Walker and Alf McCreary, *Degrees of Excellence: The Story of Queen's, Belfast, 1845–1995* (1994).

5. From Penelope's course I learned that the seven faculties and departments involved in teaching it had different cultures and styles: the medics were the best communicators; Agriculture students threw snowballs at an assistant lecturer in Economics; the part-timer outsourced by Law had no sense of the students' incomprehension. These academic tribes seemed to belong to different universes. From her social work on both sides of 'the Peace Line' it seemed that problems of poverty were quite similar for Protestants and Catholics.

6. I bought a £50 share in *Fortnight* and when pressed to return it, refused as I felt that it was a piece of history. Some queried whether *Fortnight* was compatible with Hadden's full-time appointment at Queen's. Some of this criticism was political, some administrative. As his Head of Department, I defended Tom, emphasising his extraordinary energy and his academic publication record, as well as arguing that Queen's badly needed public intellectuals. I worked closely with Tom and Kevin and became the latter's mentor and close friend. Both are now well-known beyond Northern Ireland, but that is another story.

7. Zander, a lecturer at LSE was a regular columnist for *The Guardian*; Robert Stevens, based at Yale, co-authored with a sociologist two books that were highly critical of the then legal establishment (see p. 306).

8. *Report of the Committee on Legal Education in Northern Ireland* (Armitage Committee Report) (Cmnd 579, 1973). See BT, *passim* and (2014) 48 The Law Teacher 94.

9. This was the form of oath at Queen's in my day. The actual wording of the Act is: 'Every professor upon entering into office shall sign a declaration in a form approved by the Commissioners jointly under this Act, securing the respectful treatment of the religious opinions of any of his class.' I reluctantly signed this declaration six months after I had taken up my post; later I challenged the practice of administering this oath to lecturers.

10. Published in LTCL, Ch. 14.

11. Expanded in 'Reading Bentham' (Maccabean Lecture) (1989) LXV Proceedings of the British Academy 97, reprinted in GJB, Ch. 7.

12. LiC, Ch. 12, discussed below, Ch. 10.

13. An idea borrowed from Herbert Hart, see p. 21.

14. See p. 103.

15. Discussed at pp. 218–19.

16. See now LiC, Ch. 3.

17. 'Ernie and the Centipede' (with Katherine O'Donovan and Abdul Paliwala, in Tony Jolowicz (ed.), *The Division and Classification of Law* (1970)). On classification of subjects in legal education, see further below, pp. 152–6.

18. See Ch. 12.

19. 'Some Jobs for Jurisprudence' (1974) 1 Br JL & Soc 149; see also *New Society*, 27 June 1974.
20. See further below p. 174.

9. Normative Jurisprudence

1. GJP, esp. Chs. 1.7 (Positivism), 5 (Utilitarianism and Theories of Justice), 6 (Human Rights as Moral, Political and Legal Rights), 7 (Meeting the Challenges to Human Rights: Griffin, Tasioulas and Sen), 11.4 (The Millennium Development Goals) and 13 (Human Rights: Southern Voices).
2. GJP, Chs. 6 and 7.
3. Normative Jurisprudence as a broad field encompasses general questions about values and law. It deals with the relations between law, politics and morality, including debates between and among positivists and others about the relationship between law and morals, whether law is at its core a moral enterprise, and about political obligation and civil disobedience. It includes questions about the existence, scope, and status of natural, moral and non-legal rights; the relationship between needs, rights, interests and entitlements; theories of justice; constitutionalism and democracy; and standards for guiding and evaluating legal institutions, rules, practices and decisions. (See GJP, 122.)
4. My most extensive general discussion of the area is GJP, Chs. 5–7.
5. On cultural relativism, see GJP, 129–32. As an example, despite some knowledge of the contexts of female genital mutilation (FGM), I have been convinced by arguments condemning the practice and part of my charitable giving has in recent years been directed to reducing it.
6. Cf. Llewellyn's 'fighting faiths' and Holmes's 'can't helps' (Ch. 4). On the idea of working assumptions as 'rafts', see further pp. 2 and 20.
7. The main texts I studied were most of the essays leading up to *Punishment and Responsibility* (1968); 'Immorality and Treason', *The Listener* (30 July 1959) (Hart at his best as a public intellectual); and *Law, Liberty and Morality* (1963).
8. Hart, 'Bentham and the Demystification of the Law' (1973) 36 MLR 2, at 16–17, reprinted in *Essays on Bentham* (1982), Ch. 1.
9. A. J. Ayer, 'The Principle of Utility' in G. W. Keeton and G. Schwarzenberger (eds.), *Jeremy Bentham and the Law* (1948).
10. See W. Twining, 'The Contemporary Significance of Bentham's *Anarchical Fallacies*' (1975) 61 Archiv Für Rechts und Sozialphilosophie 325. A new version of what was previously referred to as *Anarchical Fallacies* is now included, as part of the *Collected Works*, as *Nonsense Upon Stilts* in P. Schofield et al. (eds.), *Rights, Representation and Reform* (2002).

11.   Cmd 4901 (1972). The Parker Report concluded that the five techniques were unlawful, but not unjustified and made a dubious distinction between ill-treatment and brutality. Lord Gardiner wrote a minority report rejecting the techniques on moral as well as legal grounds. I am grateful to Richard Carver for this point.

12.   The group included Tom Hadden, Desmond Greer, Reginald Weir and, among the students, Christopher McCrudden and Mary Leneghan (later, as Mary McAleese, President of Ireland) both of whom subsequently played important roles in Irish politics on both sides of the border. Two colleagues, David Trimble and Kevin Boyle, committed activists on each side, stayed away.

13.   *Emergency Powers: A Fresh Start*, Fabian Tract, 416 (1972).

14.   W. and P. Twining, 'Bentham on Torture' (1973) 24 NILQ 305, reprinted in M. James (ed.), *Bentham and Legal Theory* (1973).

15.   On the complexities of the concept of torture, see HTDTWR. pp. 162–4. In the eyes of some critics, Bentham's argument was skewed by his definition of torture, which was wide in not limiting the concept to excruciating pain (he talked of 'violent pain') and narrow in confining it to inflicting bodily pain for the purpose of coercion. He used pinching a baby to stop it harming itself as an example of coercive torture. This usage is different from how the term is used in modern law and debates. However, in defence of Bentham he realised that intensity of pain, as in punishment, is a matter of continuous variation, as are other dimensions of pain such as duration, fecundity and purity – in short that torture is a vague and complex concept. Bentham was concerned to compare torture to punishment differentiating them by their purposes rather than any other aspect.

16.   On more effective means of preventing torture as an institutionalised practice, see pp. 112–13.

17.   'Torture and Philosophy' (1978) Aristotelian Society, Supp. Volume LII, 143–68.

18.   I was probably unfair to Amnesty. At the time they had developed strict procedures in order to ensure their reputation for independence, accuracy and objectivity. The priority was to focus on rigorous documentation of individual cases in a few countries. Over time there was continuing internal and external controversy about what their role should be with two main competing models: maintaining their reputation for careful investigation underlying factual reporting and campaigning for individuals or expanding into a more broadly focused political organisation fighting for a wider spectrum of human rights. So far as I can tell, bringing social perspectives and techniques to bear did not feature much on either side in these disagreements. Put off by my concerns being dismissed as 'academic', I did not join Amnesty. In retrospect I should probably have joined and put my arguments

more forcefully from within. Amnesty did in fact discuss 'themes' and in 1984 developed a strategy which has proved to have been quite realistic about prevention, although it was based mainly on anecdotal evidence and impressions from a few countries (see below).

19. Serious studies about the American episodes include Karen Greenberg and Joshua Drakel (eds.), *The Torture Papers* (2005); Philippe Sands, *Torture Team* (2009), with epilogue; and Jeremy Waldron, *Torture, Terror and Trade-offs: Philosophy for the White House* (2010).

20. Publicity for the Warwick Castle Dungeon a few years ago. Recent online advertising seems a bit less ill-judged, but when last accessed still states: 'For obvious reasons this scary fun is not for everyone ... but promises interactive, participative experience ... for the bravest people with strongest stomachs. Therefore we recommend that this attraction is unsuitable for children under the age of ten years old.'

21. Carver wrote several reports. The main source is now R. Carver and L. Handley (eds.), *Does Torture Prevention Work?* (2016).

22. Ibid., 1.

23. Emphasis added. The passage continues: 'There are, of course, notable exceptions to this statement. Langbein and others have traced the history of torture in Europe and attempted to account for its decline. Einolf emphasizes the degree to which democratic institutions have had a positive effect on the incidence of torture in the past two centuries; and pointed out that the theories that have explained its decline after the European Enlightenment do not explain its resurgence in the twentieth century. Rejali has documented the persistence of torture in modern democracies. Hathaway's work has prompted a flurry of studies that attempt to explain the impact (or, more usually, lack of impact) of UNCAT. This scholarship intersects with a broader debate between international relations scholars on why states comply (or not) with international human rights law' (ibid., 11–12).

24. Carver and Handley, using a new measuring mechanism (Carver-Handley Torture Score (CHATS), conclude that the incidence of torture in sixteen countries declined steadily during the study period, but they are careful to stress the limitations of this measure and the difficulties of extrapolating beyond the countries studied (ibid., Ch. 3). Nevertheless 'we believe it reasonable to conclude that a general decline in the incidence of torture has probably occurred' (ibid., 45–6). However torture is still endemic in a majority of countries in the world (ibid., 18). For a short overview see ibid., 99–101.

25. Recent research in Brazil led to requiring a mandatory hearing within one day of arrest which enabled some judicial control over the prevention and tackling of police torture. However, 'the enactment of perjury laws and plea bargaining in the Brazilian criminal procedure would also improve police control by enhancing dialogue in good faith between

prosecutors and criminal defendants' (P. Fortes et al. (eds.), *Law and Policy in Latin America: Transforming Courts, Institutions, and Rights* (2017), 257).

26. Ibid., 627.

27. The bibliography in Carver and Handley (eds.), *Does Torture Prevention Work?* suggests some increase in sophistication recently, but the criticism still holds.

28. M. Kramer, *Torture and Moral Integrity: A Philosophical Enquiry* (2014), Ch. 2.2.

29. Ibid., 132–49, commenting on Shue's article, 'Torture in Dreamland: Disposing of the Ticking Bomb' (2006) 37 Case Western J Int'l L 231 and other similar articles. Empirical claims about the probability of almost inevitably overreaching claims to illegitimacy are admittedly not based on evidence and at that level of abstraction need a sound empirical base, but at least Shue ventured into the world of routinised and institutionalised torture, which is central to Carver and Handley's account of 'the real-world problems'. Their account does not commit them to a position on consequentialist and absolutist arguments about legitimacy, but it does enable them to diagnose very important aspects of the actual problems.

30. Torture treated analytically, away from actual practices, may be philosophically interesting in respect of absolute prohibitions, but so are many other examples; my suggestion is that a philosophy can contribute to efforts to reduce the incidence of torture, but if this is treated as separate from the practicalities, the analysis tends to get skewed. The focus of attention on extreme cases is an example of this.

31. See GJP, 187–9; see Bentham's *Anarchical Fallacies*, above n. 10.

32. See further HRSV (esp. Ch. 4) and GJP Chs. 6, 7 and 13.

33. GJP, 159–67.

34. Especially, A. Sen, On Economic Inequality (1997 [1976]); Poverty and Famines (1982); *Development as Freedom* (1999); *The Idea of Justice* (2009); and his work with Martha Nussbaum and Jean Drèze.

35. Sen, *The Idea of Justice*.

36. Edmond Cahn, *The Sense of Injustice* (1949); cf. Judith Shklar, *The Faces of Injustice* (1990), a rather abstract, but a more nuanced account of the psychological and philosophical aspects. At Stanford I had lengthy discussions with Guilhelmina Jasso (NYU) who had done interesting empirical work on the topic.

10. Standpoint, questioning and 'thinking like a lawyer'

1. D. Lodge, *The Art of Fiction* (1992).

2. 'The Path of the Law' (1897) 10 Harv LR 457. Taken out of context, this has been used as the main support for the idea that Holmes subscribed to

a prediction theory of law. The context refutes this, but if Holmes or anyone else did have such a theory, it is very easily criticised and is hardly worth discussing (see GJB, Ch. 3).

3.   GJP, 32–5.

4.   See 'Law in context' in Ch. 13.

5.   W. Twining, 'Academic Law and Legal Philosophy: The Significance of Herbert Hart' (1979) 95 LQR 557.

6.   There is considerable debate about Collingwood's idea of History. I was innocent of that debate and mainly picked up the idea of reconstructing the thought of a writer or actor. On the question whether this is over-rationalistic and some other reservations about some of Collingwood's ideas see n. 11 and p. 120. The overwhelming victory at Trafalgar has often been attributed to Nelson's unorthodox tactics, to which a lot of attention has been given by historians, some of whom question this explanation. Presumably a Collingwoodian approach to History fits attempts to rationally reconstruct his strategy, tactics and specific decisions, but would be less helpful, though not irrelevant, to explaining the outcome of the battle.

7.   R. G. Collingwood, 'On the So-called Idea of Causation' (1937–8), Proceedings of the Aristotelian Society 85, at 96.

8.   E. M. Forster, *Aspects of the Novel* (1927).

9.   Percy Lubbock, *The Craft of Fiction* (1954 [1921]), 251. I read the 1954 edn; cf. Lodge, *The Art of Fiction*.

10. Forster, *Aspects*, pp. 147–8. Henry James, *The Ambassadors* (first published 1903). Forster acknowledges that 'There is a masterly analysis [by Percy Lubbock] from another standpoint in *The Craft of Fiction*' (*Aspects*, 141). Forster was, I think, making two points: that emotions, biases and predispositions of the actor need to be taken into account as well as rational thought; and, secondly, that staying with one standpoint in a novel is artificially limiting. I agree that Collingwood's version of standpoint is highly intellectualised and hardly accommodates individual actors' emotional states or intuitions; however, there is nothing in my interpretation of Collingwood to restrict this kind of analysis to a single standpoint. The important thing is to differentiate them. See further pp. 119–20.

11. Although strongly influenced by Collingwood, I did not accept all of his ideas uncritically. For example, I am sceptical about the claim that every statement presupposes a question – that all statements can be interpreted as answers to questions ('the logic of question and answer'). However, heuristically it is often useful to ask: to what question is this proposition or sentence an answer?

12. On the vagueness and ambiguity of 'standpoint' see pp. 122–30.

13. J. Bentham, *A Fragment on Government*, ed. J. H. Burns and H. L. A. Hart (1977); J. Rawls, 'Two Concepts of Rules' (1955) 64 Phil

R 3; H. L. A. Hart, *Punishment and Responsibility* (1968 [1959]), Ch. 1; see also the useful Introduction by John Gardner to the 2008 edn; H. Lasswell and M. MacDougal in several works, e.g. McDougal (1962) 61 Yale LJ 915; O. W. Holmes, 'The Path of the Law' (1897) 10 Harv LR 457 – see generally GJB, Ch. 3.

14. Especially in Juristic Technique (Ch. 8), Evidence (Ch. 14) and 'conversing' with juristic texts (GJB, Ch. 7). On the whole I focused, like Collingwood, on rational, purposive actors, but I also encouraged students to think dialectically and to use this to become aware of their biases. In providing normative guidance on how rational actors think, I have usually focused on classes of actor and their putative roles rather than specific individuals.

15. Once a Philosophy student who attended some of my classes on utilitarianism told me that he had never before been asked to make *a decision* in class when studying the topic.

16. RE2, 249–54.

17. See Steven Pinker, *How the Mind Works* (1999). Of course, neuroscientists treat this distinction as simplistic, but it is useful in the present context to differentiate novelists' concerns, like those of Lodge and Lubbock, from more intellectual uses.

18. In later chapters we shall also encounter particular applications in relation to rules (Ch. 11), evidence, evidence-based policy-making (Ch. 14), interpreting texts, the idea of 'legal method' in legal education (Ch. 17) and the implications of adopting a global perspective (Ch. 18).

19. See Holmes, 'The Path of the Law'.

20. I could have extended the criticism further in terms of Holmes not being realistic about the psychology, sociology and situations of actual deviants.

21. BMR and OPP.

22. Esp. W. Twining, 'Law and Literature: A Dilettante's Dream?' (2017) 1 Journal of Oxford Centre for Socio-legal Studies; HTDTWR *passim*; *Analysis*, esp. 117, 124–5, 225; LiC, Ch. 12.

23. See GJB, *passim* index under standpoint.

24. See pp. 363–4.

25. E.g. the American Law Institute's Restatements, discussed in GJP, 306–12.

26. On the tacit knowledge of expositors, see pp. 122–3.

27. E.g. how far should local and institutional factors affect answers to such questions?

28. A good example is debates about '*the ratio decidendi*' (or holding) of a case – that is, the proposition(s) for which a precedent is an authority. Much of the literature on the *ratio decidendi* gets side-tracked into puzzles about judicial discretion or else tries to resolve the puzzle without any reference to standpoint. But if one adopts the standpoint of an

advocate arguing in court, much of the puzzlement can be dissolved. For an advocate all past relevant precedents are either favourable to her case or hostile to it or irrelevant. Her role in interpreting the precedent is to present the most plausible interpretation that is consistent with winning. The opposite applies to her opponent. Similarly, the Cautious Solicitor to start with may take a pessimistic (e.g. narrow) view of what a potentially favourable case stands for, but later in the proceedings may argue for a more optimistic interpretation (HTDTWR, Ch. 9.6). See further below, pp. 142–3.

29.   See Thomas Nagel's brilliant *The View from Nowhere* (1986), which explores the issues in great depth without coming up with many firm answers.

30.   R. Kipling, *The Elephant's Child* (1900/2).

31.   This is partially developed in 'The Reading Law Cookbook' (LiC, Ch. 12 – see also Ch. 11), which is about putting different kinds of legal texts to the question.

32.   I found a wide range of writers, including R. G. Collingwood, Charles Hamblin, Arthur Koestler, Jaakko Hintikka, Michel Meyer, Herbert Simon, David Schum and John Searle moderately helpful in different ways but none quite met my concerns. A useful recent survey of the literature is Charles Cross and Floris Roelofsen, 'Questions' in the *Stanford Encyclopedia of Philosophy* (2016).

33.   On tacit knowledge see pp. 122–3, 171.

34.   David Lodge, *Changing Places* (1975), 45.

35.   The seven liberal arts consisted of the quadrivium (arithmetic, geometry, music and astronomy) and the trivium (grammar, logic and rhetoric). These intellectual skills were seen as distinct from professional or technical techniques or capabilities.

36.   I was a member of the Hoffman Working Party (CLE) on the vocational stage for the Bar (1987), which recommended a skills-oriented course (BVC) in lieu of the old-style bar examinations. Archived in Records of Legal Education (IALS) (TWIN/02/04/04).

37.   On self-criticism see pp. 245–8.

38.   W. Twining, 'Taking Skills Seriously', Commonwealth Legal Education Newsletter, No. 43, reprinted in N. Gold, K. Mackie and W. Twining (eds.), *Learning Lawyers' Skills* (1989); 'Intellectual Skills at the Academic Stage: Twelve Theses' in P. Birks (ed.), *Examining the Law Syllabus: Beyond the Core* (1993); and Papers of the Tenth Commonwealth Law Conference (Nicosia, 1993).

39.   On 'instrumentalism' see GJP, Ch. 16.

40.   LiC, Ch. 10, 'Karl Llewellyn and the Modern Skills Movement'.

41.   K. Llewellyn, 'The Study of Law as a Liberal Art' in *Jurisprudence* (1962), 377.

42.   I. Rutter (1961) 13 J Leg Ed 301.

43. Llewellyn, 'The Study of Law as a Liberal Art', 376.
44. ABA, *Legal Education and Professional Development – An Educational Continuum* (1992) (McCrate Report).
45. See pp. 127–32.
46. R. Meagher QC, 'How Can You Learn Practice in Theory?', Papers of 7th Commonwealth Law Conference, Hong Kong, September 1983, at 173–5.
47. LiC, Chs. 4–12.
48. Even in the late 1950s in Chicago there were specialised courses on basic writing skills to compensate for this deficiency in their prior education.
49. See Chs. 19 and 20.
50. H. Simon, *Models of Thought* (1989), vol. III, 278, discussed in LiC, 335.
51. It is one thing to learn about Dworkin's theory of argumentation in dealing with questions of law; it is quite another to start to learn how to emulate his ideal judge Hercules. I have even criticised Karl Llewellyn for conflating such ideas ('Afterword', pp. 416–18). This is an example of conflating methodology (the study of method) and actually mastering a method oneself.
52. The Certificate in Legal Method at Birkbeck College (Extra Mural Dept.). Sharon Hansen's excellent *Legal Method, Skills and Reasoning*, 3rd edn (2009) grew out of this course.
53. This is mainly because employers, graduates and educators tend to have different expectations of a new graduate. Cf. R. Harris, 'Misleading Talk of What Is a Graduate', *Times Higher Education Supplement*, 21 June 1996.
54. HTDTWR, Ch. 9.
55. Karl Llewellyn, *The Common Law Tradition: Deciding Appeals* (1960), 62–120 ('The Leeways of Precedent').
56. Later in courses on Jurisprudence I regularly asked students to write additional judgments for Lon Fuller's Case of the Speluncean Explorers, in order to illustrate different approaches to and styles of judicial reasoning – but that was more a matter of 'learning about'. See LiC, pp. 213–21; (1949) 62 Harv LR 616. Fuller's classic piece has stimulated collections of further opinions on the case itself and beyond, especially by feminists in several countries, including a Feminist Judgement Project (see C. M. Hunter and B. Fitzpatrick, 'Feminist Judging and Legal Theory' (2012) 46 The Law Teacher 255).
57. In teaching Torts in Dar es Salaam I used to hold hour-long mini-moots on hypothetical problems with pairs of students acting as advocates and two others sitting with me as judges. Etiquette, procedure and piles of law reports were set aside so that these exercises could involve active learning of one kind of reasoning applied to Torts by six students at a time. This was a quite economical way of stimulating active learning.
58. HTDTWR, xiii–xiv.
59. See n. 42.

60. See, however, p. 269.

61. In teaching we concentrated on developing usable intellectual skills and techniques, but some of the theoretical aspects are developed in RE.

62. I plan to develop this with Dr Raquel Barradas de Freitas in order to deal in more detail with some of the issues mentioned in the text at nn. 63 and 64.

63. RE2, Ch. 10; GJB, Part B. Over many years I tried to persuade Neil MacCormick to take evidential reasoning seriously and to relate it to reasoning about questions of law. In his later writings he made some mentions of this, and developed some ideas about coherence, but he never carried this very far. See, however, N. MacCormick, *Rhetoric and the Rule of Law* (2005), Chs. 9–11.

64. E.g. Ronald Dworkin's ban on policy and consequentialist arguments by judges (*Taking Rights Seriously* (1977), Chs. 2 and 4) can be read as a thesis about their admissibility. The Thayer-Wigmore view that there are no rules of weight (see below, Ch. 14) can illuminate issues about balancing, cogency and strength of arguments about questions of law.

65. On tacit knowledge see pp. 122–3.

66. Ch. 19.

67. For a fuller account of its use see (1999) 25 JL & Soc 603.

68. LiC, 203–4.

69. E.g. students studying Contract or Succession complained that they were rarely if ever asked to read actual contracts or wills, or analyse really complex ones. They were rarely asked to draft such documents. The only will I drafted in my life (paired with Bob Carswell a future Lord Chief Justice of Northern Ireland) was in Max Rheinstein's course in Decedents' Estates in Chicago. I never drafted a single clause of a complex contract, let alone a whole document, in the course of my formal legal education.

11. Social and legal rules

1. Robert Frost, 'The Silken Tent' (1939).

2. Karl Llewellyn, 'Ballade of the Glory of Rules' in *Put in His Thumb* (1931).

3. This section is adapted from the Bernstein Lecture.

4. Here, roughly assumed to be the co-existence in the same time-space context of multiple systems or bodies of norms or rules or of institutionalized normative orders – concepts that need closer examination in relation to legal pluralism. See pp. 252–3.

5. Here I treat 'rules' and 'norms' as synonyms (see p. 138). Some people treat 'norms' as the generic category and 'rules' as more specific, e.g. as categorical precepts.

6. F. Schauer, *Playing by the Rules* (1993 [1991]).

7. For example, I shall argue later that some of the main puzzles about 'legal pluralism' are best treated under the more general topic of normative pluralism. See pp. 136–8.

8. See p. 262.

9. On the questions whether all norms are general prescriptions that fit the logical form: 'If X (protasis) then Y (apodosis)? Can all social rules be restated in Hohfeldian terms: I may (not), I can/cannot (power), I must/should/might; others must (my claim); others can (cannot)? See GJP, pp. 49–54 and Andrew Halpin, forthcoming.

10. On the concept of 'doctrine' and its relationship to rules, see Ch. 13.

11. A classic example is *Rylands v Fletcher* (1868) introducing strict liability in Torts. The original perceived problem was how to regulate bursting reservoirs; but as Brian Simpson has elegantly shown, the rule was never again applied to dams, but took on a life of its own in other contexts. A. W. B. Simpson, *Leading Cases at Common Law* (1995), Ch. 8.

12. The complete poem runs to four stanzas. It is mainly a play on the names of several American Realists and Chicago sympathisers: Green, Sharp, Frank, Kalven, Dunham, Blum and even Fuller, a critic of Realism. It was also intended as a satire on criticisms which attributed the idea of 'rule-scepticism' to American Legal Realists, including Llewellyn.

13. The fact that Montrose had chosen this name for the course rather than 'Introduction to Law' or 'Sources of Law' signalled a link to Llewellyn because both emphasised a combination of theory and skills in handling legal materials, but Llewellyn's concept of Juristic Method was broader than Montrose's. Llewellyn had given me some insights into the leeways and techniques of interpretation of cases and statutes and their limits. Although England allegedly had a stricter doctrine of precedent, on close examination it did not amount to much; and it was doubtful that most of the so-called rules of statutory interpretation deserved the status of rules (see further Ch. 8).

14. Over time I deviated from tradition in teaching students a systematic approach to reading cases and statutes and, later, other materials of law study. The first step was to realise that the best starting point is not rules of interpretation, but standpoint. The second, that interpreting involves asking questions about the nature of the object of interpretation; the third, that one is reading, interpreting and using certain kinds of *text* and one needs to know something about the characteristics, and limitations of the text and how it is constructed. The fourth point is to realise that there are many shared aspects of *interpreting* legal texts and other kinds of texts; the fifth, that the *rules of interpretation* of legal texts do not amount to much, but that there are some special aspects of the contexts and techniques of legal interpretation to do with the purposes for which they are constructed and published and the uses to which they are put. Finally, and most important, the factors giving rise to doubts about

a particular interpretation are many and various. On the idea of 'legal method', see further Ch. 10.

15. GJB, Ch. 16; HTDTWR, Ch. 11.6.

16. Five editions: 1976, 1982, 1991, 1999 and 2010 with a possible sixth being planned.

17. Now Professor Emeritus of Cardiff University and known as a leading expert on legislation in the UK, as a prominent member of the Study of Parliament Group and as a specialist on Gaming Law and compensation for victims of crime.

18. HTDTWR, xiii–xiv; see above, Ch. 10.

19. The Domestic Violence and Matrimonial Proceedings Act, 1976. In the fifth edition this was put on the link to the web, with two other case studies on MPs expenses and The Hunting Act, 2004: www.cambridge .org/twiningandmiers.

20. This example does not imply that all rules can be treated as responses to problems, but in this kind of rationalist analysis the idea is a very useful one. On rules as responses to perceived problems see HTDTWR, Ch. 2.

21. Ibid.

22. On the sub-optimality of nearly all rules see Schauer, 'The Convergence of Rules and Standards', 31–44, 86n. *et passim*.

23. A nice example is how not wearing a seat-belt came to be counted as contributory negligence as they became more established. I am grateful to James Goudcamp for this point.

24. The most systematic text in the literature for practitioners is Francis Bennion's *Statutory Interpretation: A Code* (2008 [1984]). Bennion's approach was partly based on ours, but later editions of his main book became more of a reference work than a student book.

25. Especially 'The Ratio Decidendi of the Parable of the Prodigal Son', reprinted in RE2, Ch. 13 and GJP, Ch. 16.

26. The rather condensed treatment of interpretation deals succinctly with a number of topics: different meanings of 'interpretation'; the distinction between law and fact; the distinction between interpretation and application; other kinds of rule handling, some of which involve interpretation (e.g. avoidance, evasion, compliance) and some which do not (e.g. promulgate, enforce, repeal); who interprets? (an extension of standpoint); the relationship between rule-makers and interpreters (not necessarily one of co-operation); 'legalism'; and leeways for interpretation and application. In a theoretical treatise we could have expanded on each of these topics, some of which could sustain one or more doctorates. The next chapter on 'Imperfect rules' deals with topics that are familiar to jurists: the factual context of rules; intentions, purposes and other reasons in interpretation; rules and language; and the open texture of rules. Again, the treatment is compressed and use is made of 'non-legal' as well as 'legal' examples. Here there is an already extensive legal

literature, some of excellent quality, but nevertheless there are many lines of enquiry needing further exploration.

27. English edition, trans. D. Kunzle (1975).
28. See n. 17.
29. The nature, scope and processes of law-making in UK are dealt with in detail in Ch. 7. Chapter 8 combines practical advice with a sustained application of the key theoretical elements in our approach including routine and problematic readings – the why? what? how? – of reading legislation, standpoint, identification of the conditions of doubt and the construction of arguments.
30. Esp. RE2, Ch. 13. See above, pp. 313–14, n. 28.
31. See further pp. 259–73 on 'unfinished business'.

12. Warwick (1972–82)

1. M. Beloff, *The Plateglass Universities* (1968), 11.
2. M. Bradbury, *The History Man* (1975).
3. R. Hugo, *The Triggering Town* (1979).
4. On the 1966 conference see F. Cownie and R. Cocks, *A Great and Noble Occupation!: The History of the Society of Legal Scholars* (2009), 104–5.
5. G. P. Wilson, 'The English Law School' (1966) CLJ 148–9.
6. Discussed below, Ch. 17.
7. Geoffrey Wilson, 'English Legal Scholarship' (1987) 50 MLR 818, at 819, discussed LiC, Ch. 17. I thought that some of Wilson's polemics were overstated. Even Cambridge was not monolithic: it was strong in International Law and Legal History, it had an Institute of Criminology, and it was the home of Maitland and Maine; some individuals such as Glanville Williams and R. M. Jackson had also deviated from the strict doctrinal tradition. Some of Geoffrey's young contemporaries at Cambridge, including Tony Bradley (who later spent two years in Dar), were also restive, especially about the undergraduate curriculum.
8. *Cases and Materials on Constitutional and Administrative Law* (1976 [1966]) was noted for its use of a much broader range of sources than orthodox casebooks ('and materials' can be attributed to American influence). Later his *Cases and Materials on the English Legal System* (1973) went beyond the formal structures of the courts to cover a wider range of institutions with details of how they worked in practice. In these and other works Geoffrey tended to hide his light under a bushel. These two books contained many insights hidden in the form of anthologies for students. A largely unnoticed theme of the second was the sceptical question: call this a system? Perhaps his most admired work was his chapter on constitutional conventions in Lord Nolan and

Stephen Sedley, *The Making and Remaking of the British Constitution* (1997), Ch. 7.

9.   On four-year degrees, see pp. 223–4.

10. On the difficulties of 'fact-based classification' see below, n. 14.

11. Commercial and Consumer Law, International Law and Jurisprudence were all compulsory. Perhaps even more significant were the names of the first-year subjects: *Structure and Methods* of the English Legal System; (2) *Methods and Functions* of the Criminal Law; (3) *Basic Techniques of the Common Law* in Contract and Tort; (4) *Introduction to the Law of Property*. Ironically, the label of McAuslan's first-year course was more traditional than the other three.

12. Edward Thompson's *Warwick University Limited* (1970) is mainly about the troubles on campus in the late 1960s, but the political atmosphere on campus was still fraught in the mid-seventies.

13. GJP, Ch. 10.1.

14. On 'fact-based classification' see n. 17. Bernard Rudden in his famous article 'Torticles' (1991–2) 6/7 Tulane Civ LR 10 dissected common law Torts law methodology and commented famously that 'the alphabet is virtually the only instrument of intellectual order of which the common law makes use'. In the first two curricula for the LLB at Warwick a lot of thought was given to the best labels for individual courses, but some pragmatic compromises were, perhaps inevitably, accepted.

15. On the continuation of 'the creeping core' from 1970 to the present see Ch. 17, and BT, Ch. 7. It is worth noting that although we resisted the imposition of Equity and Trusts as a full core subject, two of the best Warwick books, by Michael Chesterman, were about Trusts and became recognised as a path-breaking work. See further below, n. 30.

16. After the first syllabus revision the title of first-year course was 'Basic Techniques of the Common Law in Contract and Tort', with provision made for more Contract in 'Law and the Consumer' (compulsory) and for specific Torts in various courses.

17. The outcome was that we would be recognised as 'covering' Torts and could keep Equity as a half-course, provided we added a topic on 'Duties of Directors and Trustees compared' to Company Law. I also gained acceptance that up to 50% of student results could be based on assessment rather than unseen exams. Years later I realised that not all of our students had quite fulfilled this pact, mainly because some of the previously compulsory courses had become optional, but also because some had done less than 50% of their assessment by closed-book examination; it seems that some students had not technically earned their exemptions. Nobody noticed.

18. See comments on aspects of Legal Education and Training Review (LETR) in (2014) 48 Law Teacher 84 and (2015) 49 Law Teacher 38. See further below, pp. 269–73.

19.   Law in Context series authors and titles with a substantial connection with Warwick included Atiyah, Cranston (2), Davies and Freedland, Lacey, Wells and Meure, Moffat, Chesterman, Norrie, Picciotto, Snyder, Twining (4) – up to 1997, ten apart from my own. Some of these went into several editions.

20.   P. Atiyah, *Accidents, Compensation and the Law* (London: Weidenfeld and Nicolson, 1970); it is still in print, now in its 8th edition (2013), with a 9th edition forthcoming (Cambridge University Press, edited by Peter Cane and James Goudcamp). There is a useful entry in *Wikipedia* under 'Atiyah's *Accidents, Compensation and the Law*'. Patrick came to Warwick in 1973 because of this book, but it is quintessentially 'a Warwick book.' Sadly, Patrick Atiyah died on 30 March 2018, as this book was in production. An assessment of his contributions by James Goudcamp will appear in *Scholars of Tort Law* (forthcoming, 2019).

21.   *The Damages Lottery* (1997) in which the author seemed to change his mind, proposing personal safety insurance instead of a state-run system, both involving abolition of most of the Law of Damages.

22.   This is not true of some attempts to articulate the philosophical underpinnings of Tort (not Torts). For example, neither the bibliography nor the index of J. Oberdiek (ed.), *Philosophical Foundations of the Law of Torts* (2014) contain a single reference to Atiyah, or settlement, but does have some discussion of insurance. Strangely, the bibliography under Peter Cane does not mention any of his editions of *Accidents, Compensation and the Law*.

23.   Cf. LiC, Ch. 3.

24.   His posthumous unpublished book, *Land and Empire* (there are several potential titles), may eventually come to be recognised as his masterpiece.

25.   Patrick and I were friends as well as colleagues; I think that his courses and outside work on land and planning were extraordinary achievements; but I have constructed a 'McAuslan legend' which theorises, perhaps idealises or goes beyond his actual practice in teaching and advising. I use it as one model for rethinking a field. I think that 'legend' is better than 'myth' here as the story has its basis in fact.

26.   On 'fact-based' classification, see above, n. 14.

27.   In 1969 McAuslan taught Land Use Planning at the University of Wisconsin Law School. He acknowledged that he was much influenced by the approaches of Charles M. Haar, Myrres McDougal and David Haber, *Property, Wealth and Land* (1948) and the temporary edition (never published) of materials on Land Use Planning by the late Jake Beuscher. McAuslan's book on Planning in England in the Law in Context series was called *Land, Law and Planning* (1976). He is now best known for his work on land reform and urban planning in the Global South; see T. Zarkaloudis (ed.), *Land Law and Urban Policy in Context: Essays on the Contributions of Patrick McAuslan* (2016).

28. A protest in Caledon (Dungannon) in 1968 about unfair allocation of council housing is often said to mark the start of the Civil Rights Movement in Northern Ireland.

29. See further, LiC, 53–8.

30. Michael Chesterman, *Trusts Law: Text and Materials* (1988), now in its sixth edition as Graham Moffat, Rebecca Probert, Gerry Bean and Jonathan Garton, *Trusts Law: Text and Materials* (2015). *Charities, Trusts and Social Welfare* (1979) is another good example of rethinking.

31. This theme is developed in W. Twining et al., 'The Role of Academics in the Legal System' in Peter Cane and Mark Tushnet (eds.), *The Oxford Handbook of Legal Studies* (2003), Ch. 41.

32. On the Bentham Project and the Society of Public Teachers of Law, see below, Chs. 15 and 16 respectively.

33. TEBW, RE1 and *Analysis*. These were all published while I was at UCL, but most of the groundwork was done in the 1970s.

13. Jurisprudence, law in context, realism and doctrine

1. H. Melville, *The Confidence Man* (1966 [1857]), 16.

2. See pp. 35–6.

3. Hart viewed Philosophy of Law as an activity addressing problems, more than as a heritage, but he directed it to a narrow range of questions, concepts and topics. *Essays in Jurisprudence and Philosophy* (1983), Ch. 3, discussed GJB, Ch. 4.

4. On the tensions involved in being a follower of both Hart and Llewellyn see 'Afterword', 404–9.

5. This view was best expressed in my 'The Great Juristic Bazaar' (1978) 14 JSPTL (NS) 185–200 (reprinted in GJB, Ch. 11), a satirical paper for The World Congress on Philosophy of Law and Social Philosophy in Sydney in 1977. It was interpreted by one of the organisers as an offensive attack on the Congress and by a Marxist judge as a subversive dismissal of all bourgeois Jurisprudence. My intention rather was to ridicule the pretensions and reductionism of all Grand Theories, the practice of caricaturing opponents in polemical Jurisprudence and, less consciously, the narrow parochialism of the main Anglo-American practices of legal theorising. On the story behind the paper see GJB, Introduction, 9–11.

6. Delivered November 1973, published as 'Some Jobs for Jurisprudence' (1974) 1 Br JL & Soc 149–74.

7. '[O]ur intellectual heritage, our main arena (the Law School) and our clientele remain virtually unchanged' (167).

8. The conduit function, i.e. one role of Jurisprudence was to serve as a conduit between disciplines and traditions – Stone's idea of 'the lawyer's extraversion': J. Stone, *Legal System and Lawyers' Reasonings* (1964), 16.

9. The published version included an extended interpretation of 'law in context' and a deliberately non-confrontational account of the Warwick aspiration with what I thought was a quite restrained critique of 'the Expository Tradition' and the varied reactions against it. I emphasised both the dominance of the former and the diversity of the latter. See further p. 173.

10. On rereading it after a long gap, I was disconcerted, not so much by my having used the male gender for all academic lawyers, nor by my rather court-centric treatment of Evidence, but rather because my ideas had changed so little.

11. The emphasis on the limitations of 'high theory' (i.e. abstract Legal Philosophy) and on the importance of 'middle-order theorising' partly explains my approach to Evidence and American Legal Realism and why I opted out of the (Analytical) Jurisprudence mainstream for about twenty-five years, only returning to it in 2005, towards the end of my project on 'globalisation' (HCWT). See below, pp. 253–5.

12. My Warwick inaugural, like 'Pericles and the Plumber' in Belfast and 'Evidence and Legal Theory' at UCL (1984), was programmatic and assertive, as inaugurals should be. It gives a rather good picture of the state of my ideas in mid-career. I included the exuberant passage on 'the case for Law' quoted in pp. 5–6.

13. See pp. 91–2.

14. See pp. 154–5.

15. D. J. Galligan, *Law in Modern Society* (2007), Ch. 3, has a very good account of 'the contextual contingencies' of social and legal rules. I differ slightly on some points (see below, nn. 20, 42), but this is a very useful summary.

16. On theorising about 'context', see n. 21.

17. The next paragraphs are adapted from my entry on 'The Law in Context Movement' in Peter Cane and Joanne Conaghan (eds.), *The New Oxford Companion to Law* (2008), 680–2.

18. Including Wolfgang Friedmann, J. L. Montrose, L. C. B. Gower, Otto Kahn-Freund, Julius Stone and R. M. Jackson.

19. W. Twining, 'Law and Social Science: The Method of Detail', *New Society*, 27 June 1974.

20. Cf. Galligan, *Law in Modern Society*, 62–3, 67–8. His interpretation is insightful with regard to law interpreted in terms of rules and doctrine. But how 'law' is interpreted in 'law in context' also depends on context. For example, studies of lawyers, legal services, legal architecture and famous trials or leading cases have all been the subject of contextual studies and fall within the purview of the discipline of Law. In such studies doctrine is neither the starting point nor the centre. And 'contextual' is often used to mark a break from the doctrinal tradition

without going to the extreme of saying doctrine is not important. Cf. Philip Selznick (2003) 30 JL & Soc 177–8.

21. The concept of context in the Social Sciences has been explored by Teun A. van Dijk in *Discourse and Context* (2008) and *Society and Discourse* (2009) which came to my attention too late for comment here.

22. On 'isms', see GJP, Ch. 16.

23. I remember walking in the Blue Mountains (NSW) with David Farrier and Dirk Meure, discussing for hours whether the substantive law of crimes could best be understood as part of a larger field of Criminal Justice which would include institutions and procedures and have close links with criminology and penology; and then, how to make teaching and writing about this subject manageable – another example of being self-conscious about organising categories. The first book on Criminal Law in the Law in Context series was N. Lacey, C. Wells and D. Meure, *Reconstructing Criminal Law: Cases and Materials* (2010 [1990]). (Celia Wells is a Warwick Graduate.)

24. See pp. 226–7.

25. See pp. 367–8.

26. C. K. Allen, *Law in the Making*, 4th edn (1946), 45.

27. Discussed in Ch. 7.

28. Wouter de Been, *Legal Realism Regained: Saving Realism from Critical Acclaim* (2008).

29. See 'Afterword', 431–3, 440–1; and LRJ, 128 n. 25 and 133 n. 41.

30. In LRJ I discuss recent reinterpretations of 'Realism' by Brian Leiter and Hanoch Dagan. They are well worth extending, but the status of their claims is unclear: as historical accounts of what those individuals commonly identified as Realists said, they are over-generalised and contain significant omissions (e.g. Frank on fact-finding, Llewellyn's law jobs, ideas about an empirical science of law) (GJB, Ch. 5). As attempts at theory construction they are unnecessarily tied to the historical texts, producing a juristic hybrid, neither clearly historical nor conceptual. They continue to tend to treat 'R/realism' as an American exclusive and focus mainly on 'adjudication', interpreted as being solely concerned with questions of law. Freed from the historical texts a contemporary attempt to construct a contemporary 'realist jurisprudence' need not be limited in these ways.

31. On NLR see generally, Elizabeth Mertz, Stewart Macaulay and Thomas W. Mitchell (eds.), *The New Legal Realism* (2016), and (2015) 2 Leiden J Int'l L (special issue).

32. On 'understanding' in this context, see pp. 288–9.

33. See 155.

34. The term 'law in action' is useful as a broad term designating a focus on empirical aspects of law as social fact. But its vagueness is revealing. Leaving aside the indeterminacy of 'law' in this context (*what* is in action?), what does *action* encompass? Surely it need not be limited to just

behaviour (e.g. Donald Black) or attitudes, but also beliefs, values, techniques, skills, knowledge and opinion about law, unintended consequences, impact etc. Can there be action and agency without *meaning*? Are not rules important *sources* of meaning? *Whose* action? Surely not only appellate judges: that must rank 'high among the unrealities' both about the tasks of judging and about other law-related actors, subjects and victims, e.g. lawmakers, law interpreters, appliers, expositors, enforcers, users, avoiders, evaders, victims, deviants, inspectors, regulators and observers – individuals, legal persons and collectivities (see Ch. 10). On the much-debated distinction between 'the gap' between law in books and law in action, see GJP, 318–20. One aim of realist and contextual approaches has been to get more of the action into the books.

35. I have usually treated the relationship between American and Scandinavian 'Realisms' as not much better than a pun – the word 'realism' is generally being used in quite different senses, the underlying concerns were very different, and there was no historical connection until secondary commentaries linked them. At the level of epistemology, a tenuous connection might be explored, except that it is unclear which ALR scholars are under consideration. When I interviewed Karl Olivecrona in Lund he distinguished between his real work (philosophy) and his book on Marine Insurance which was 'just to earn money' and, in his view, totally disconnected with his theory of law. One of his students is credited with being a pioneer of Sociology of Law in Sweden, but the connection is not clear to me. Olivecrona was branded by his support for Nazi Germany in World War II and was largely avoided thereafter. I did not know about this when I interviewed him.

36. See, however, the caveat that formal or social scientific empirical legal studies are only one route to empirical understandings (e.g. 'lessons of experience', p. 332.

37. See 135.

38. See LFTP, *passim*.

39. HTDTWR, *passim*.

40. R. Dworkin, *Justice in Robes* (2006), 4, citing his *Law's Empire* (1986), 102–8.

41. D. Galligan, *Law in Modern Society* (2007), 103.

42. Ibid., 103. Chapter 6 and pp. 347–50 of that book are particularly illuminating on social spheres generally. Galligan rightly cautions that rules *normally* can only be understood in the context of a given social sphere involving shared understandings, but he allows for exceptions. It is easy to think of examples where a simple rule-statement is understandable for a given purpose without any elaboration of context. For example, a peremptory sign saying 'Keep off the grass' can normally produce conformity without more. However, this example opens up the

floodgates of borderline cases, tacit knowledge and clues that may be involved in understandings and misunderstandings.

43. Even strong versions of realism in this sense will concede that context and awareness of how a particular piece of doctrine operates in fact or is likely to do so may not be necessary in all contexts, e.g. in routine interpretation or application of a particular rule in a simple situation. But even there, questions of tacit knowledge arise; see p. 131.

44. On some standard dichotomies and tensions within the social sciences see GJP, 258–62. In the context of particular enquiries, it is sometimes straightforward to identify important aspects of reality that are adequate for the purpose of that enquiry (or decision). However, in many enquiries what empirical aspects are relevant, essential, important, adequate or useful is part of the challenge.

45. In short, strong realism and strong doctrinalism are difficult to reconcile. Here moderate 'doctrinalism' refers to the proposition that knowledge and understanding of legal doctrine is a necessary but not a sufficient condition of understanding law and legal phenomena.

46. H. L. A. Hart, 'Dias and Hughes on Jurisprudence' (1958) JSPTL (NS) 149.

47. 'Law in Context: A Tentative Rationale' (1967), first published 1991 (in a *festschrift* for Patrick Atiyah), reprinted in 1997 in LiC, Ch. 3.

48. 'Is Your Textbook Really Necessary?' (1973) 11 JSPTL (NS) 267.

49. T. B. Smith, 'Authors and Authority' (1972) 12 JSPTL (NS) 3. This contains a fascinating and nuanced account of the Scottish tradition.

50. 'Treatises and Textbooks: A Reply to T. B. Smith' (1972) 12 JSPTL (NS) 267. See further David Sugarman's much-cited paper, 'Legal Theory, the Common Law Mind and the Making of the Textbook Tradition' in LTCL, Ch. 3.

51. For a good recent account of the Scottish treatise writers and their relationship to Blackstone, see Michael Lobban, *A History of the Philosophy of Law in the Common Law World, 1600–1900* (2016), Ch. 4.

52. The first two are field concepts, but neither 'law in context' nor realism as here interpreted as *a field* (except perhaps when it is itself the subject of study).

53. *Justice in Robes* (2006) and (2006) Harv LR Forum 95.

54. For criticism of other aspects of Dworkin's 'doctrinal concept of law', see pp. 211–12.

55. A. Halpin, *Definition in Criminal Law* (2004), Ch. 1.

56. It is probably fair to say that both Scotland and the United States have stronger traditions of doctrinal writing than England. Their leading expositors have had a richer conception of doctrine than the mere organising and description of blackletter categorical precepts. One can acknowledge that pioneering English textbooks, such as Anson on

Contract and Pollock on *Torts*, although rather simplistic, laid a basis for the disciplined study of law in the universities.

57. Even Sir Rupert Cross, whose approach to Precedent and Evidence I have sometimes criticised for being too narrowly focused on doctrine, had a Law Lord as a brother and good contacts with the practising Bar, so that he has rightly been praised for having a good sense of what issues leading practitioners and judges felt to be important and of their tacit working assumptions.

58. Renaud Colson and Stewart Field, 'Socio-legal Studies in France: Beyond the Law Faculty' (2016) 43 JL & Soc 285, at 287–8. Cf. a different story in Germany, by Alfons Bora, 'Sociology of Law in Germany' (2016) 43 JL & Soc 619. Cf. B. Frydman, *Les Sens des Lois*, 3rd edn (2011) – a pragmatist interpretation – and C. Stolker, *Rethinking the Law School* (2014), esp. 202–4. There is a very extensive, often introspective literature within the civil law tradition about the scientific credentials of Law as a discipline. For an interesting recent approach to legal dogmatics and 'legal science' by an Argentinian jurist see Alvaro Nunez Vaquero, 'Five Models of Legal Science' (2013) 19 J Const Theory & Phil L 53–81. The perspective is very different from mine, but his analysis of 'what legal academics do; what they should do; and what they can do' (at 3.2) I find quite suggestive.

59. Colson and Field, 'Socio-legal Studies in France'.

60. Morton White, *Social Thought in America: The Revolt against Formalism*, 2nd edn (1957). For a more cautious interpretation in relation to ALR see Brian Tamanaha, *Beyond the Formalist-Realist Divide* (2009).

61. There is nothing in ALR or realism that involves denial of the importance of ritual, forms, or formality in some contexts. For example, the writings of Victor Turner and Mary Douglas in anthropology, emphasising symbolism, are not antithetical to realist perspectives. Forms have functions. On the ubiquity of standard forms see Brian Tamanaha, *A Realistic Theory of Law* (2017), 139–42. Cf. R. S. Summers, *Form and Function in a Legal System – A General Study* (2006).

62. HTDTWR, 370–5.

63. EK, Introduction. Similarly, Hart's concept of law as a system of rules is about structure and validity of primary rules, rather than their content. Exposition involves substance. There are in fact very difficult questions about the methodological foundations of exposition of legal doctrine, with long-standing internal controversies, but I will not dwell on them, because my concern here is with scholarly practices rather than their methodological foundations.

64. Fiona Cownie, *Legal Academics: Cultures and Identities* (2004), esp. Ch. 3.

65. GJP, 24–5, 56–70.

66. Ibid., 56–60.

67. Herbert Hart had reluctantly supported the setting up of the Oxford Centre for Socio-Legal Studies under pressure from his friend Jean Floud, a sociologist but, as Nicola Lacey makes clear in her biography, he was highly sceptical about, if not hostile to, sociological approaches to law, he shared Oxford academics' general scepticism about sociology and really believed that armchair conceptual analysis could proceed independently of involvement with social sciences. Nicola Lacey, *H. L. A. Hart: The Nightmare and the Noble Dream* (2004), 229–31, 260–1, 322.

14. Rethinking Evidence

1. J. Bentham, *Works* (Bowring edn), VI 5.
2. J. B. Thayer, *Treatise* (1898), discussed below.
3. D. Schum, Preface to *Evidential Foundations of Probabilistic Reasoning* (1994).
4. RE2, Ch. 14, 418.
5. The idea of cognitive competence was developed by Jonathan Cohen in his campaign to attack 'the cult of the expert', e.g. L. J. Cohen, *The Probable and the Provable* (1977). Recently Brexiters and Climate Change deniers have used different 'arguments' to discredit 'experts', including the most vulnerable, viz. economists, pollsters and other futurologists. See generally, Susan Haack, *Evidence Matters* (2014). On the ideas of 'common sense', cognitive competence and cognitive consensus as problematic, see RE2, 85, 334–5, 444; *Analysis*, 265–80.
6. Jeffrey Goldberg, *The New Yorker*, 10 February 2003, 40–7. See further, RE2, 436–8.
7. This passage is adapted from RE2, Ch. 14 (TFSA). I suspect that my two papers on 'Taking Facts Seriously' (RE2, Chs. 2 and 14), which were explicitly addressed to non-specialists, were perceived as being about Evidence and so nothing to do with them – a common *non sequitur*; see below, n. 41.
8. Reasoning about questions of fact in litigation (and beyond) is a prime example of a neglected topic in the area of Reasoning in Legal Contexts (Ch. 10).
9. See Ch. 10.
10. See Ch. 18.
11. See Ch. 20; EIE; and RE2, Ch. 15.
12. On the implications of transnationalisation for the study of Evidence in Legal Contexts see p. 356.
13. See especially, J. Frank, *Courts on Trial* (1970 [1949]). I treat Jerome Frank as a Hedgehog with One Big Idea. He was a successful practitioner, a judge, a public intellectual and a demi-mondaine academic who attracted a lot of attention. His writings were eclectic, polemical,

sometimes self-contradictory and highly repetitive. But his big idea was a good one: variously expressed in terms of 'The Upper Court Myth', 'fact-skepticism' and 'appellate court-itis', the basic point was that far too much attention was paid in legal education, legal theory and legal literature to decisions on questions of law in the upper reaches of the American legal system, whereas the main action and sources of uncertainty were in trial courts. I used this thesis as the starting point in my Evidence project, but criticised Frank for 'court-itis', i.e. placing too much emphasis on contested trials to the virtual exclusion of earlier stages in litigation, non-litigious practice by lawyers and many other legal contexts in which fact-finding, evidential reasoning, evidential enquiries, construction and reasoning play an important role. On Frank generally see A. W. B. Simpson (ed.), *A Biographical Dictionary of the Common Law* (1984), 190–3; and RE2, *passim* and index under Frank, Jerome.

14.   Frank also estimated that trial courts determined nearly all disputed cases: 'a 2% tail wagged a 98% dog', (1948) 13 L & Contemp Probs 369, at 374. This is a typical Frank wild speculation and takes no account of cases ended earlier in litigation. The exact figures are immaterial, because the basic point is both true and important. For about a decade Frank taught a course on fact-finding at Yale, as part of his campaign to move towards 'clinical lawyer schools'; like so many initiatives in this area, neither the course nor the general idea really caught on. 'Clinical legal education' is a pale shadow of what Frank proposed, but in its early days Antioch Law School, where Terry Anderson was Associate Dean, approached it. (I once drafted an incomplete paper comparing Antioch and Dar es Salaam as law schools that tried to do something different.)

15.   It is unclear whether Frank invented this term, or merely used it along with phrases such as 'the Upper Court Myth' and 'fact-scepticism' to make essentially the same point.

16.   In the late 1970s I enquired of Wildy's, the famous law book shop in Lincoln's Inn Passage, whether copies of the John Stuart Mill edition of Bentham's *Rationale of Judicial Evidence* (1827) ever came their way. After checking in their box of card-index cards for pending orders, they said that they were on the look-out for it, but there was one person ahead of me – this turned out to be Rupert Cross, the doyen of English Evidence scholars – who had enquired about it before World War II. If the date is correct, Cross was only in his late twenties at the time. So far as I know, he never read or cited Bentham.

17.   Such cases were a staple for Wigmore exercises in teaching. See RE2, *passim* and the work of bodies such as the Criminal Cases Review Commission (UK), www.gov.uk/government/organisations/criminal-cases-review-commission. There is, of course, a massive secondary

literature on individual cases and more generally. It is of variable quality and few adopt a really systematic approach, a partial exception being R. Nobles and D. Schiff, *Understanding Miscarriages of Justice* (2000).

18. RE2, 117–22; and W. Twining (ed.), *Facts in Law* (1983). For a useful survey see P. Roberts and A. Zuckerman, *Criminal Evidence* (2004) (new edition forthcoming). From 1984 for many years, Philip Dawid, Professor of Statistics at UCL gave a three-week introduction to this topic in my Master's course in Evidence and Proof. See *Analysis*; Appendix. Patrick Atiyah had contributed to the topic on a smaller scale in the course at Warwick.

19. For a fuller account of the project and most of the topics touched on here see RE2.

20. Some of the basic concepts of the Law of Evidence and of Evidence and Proof in Legal Contexts are shared (such as materiality, relevance, probative force and admissibility), but others are seen as special to one part, unless one considers (as I do) that understanding inferential reasoning is an essential element in both parts. See *Analysis*, Glossary, 379–87. The topic of probabilities and proof fits under Wigmore's conception of 'the logic of proof', but his treatment was simplistic.

21. The Preface of a leading American coursebook on Evidence (G. Fisher, *Evidence* (2002)) is a clear example of this view of the subject: 'Evidence Law is about the limits we place on information juries hear.' See RE2, 440–1.

22. Cf. p. 24 and my remarks on *Salmond on Torts*.

23. I treated confessions as an important topic in teaching, but never published much on it (see RE2, 268 n. 79). My approach to the topic was similar to that on identification (RE2, Ch. 5).

24. 'Goodbye to Lewis Eliot: The Academic Lawyer as Scholar', Presidential address, SPTL 1978, (1980) 15 JSPTL (NS) 2–19; RE2, Preface, pp. 3–4.

25. See now A. Powancher, *John Henry Wigmore and the Rules of Evidence: The Hidden Origins of the Modern Law* (2016). Later I placed more emphasis on the influence of James Bradley Thayer, Wigmore's teacher at Harvard; see RE2, 61–3, 202–10. In retrospect I think that I should have treated him in more depth. See Eleanor Swift, 'One Hundred Years of Evidence Law Reform: Thayer's Triumph' (2000) 88 *Calif LR* 2439.

26. RE2, Ch. 4.

27. Ibid., Ch. 6; *Analysis*, Ch. 11.

28. On the various meanings of 'free proof', see RE2, 203–4, 241–2; and W. Twining (1996) 31 Israel LR 439–63.

29. J. Bentham, *A Treatise on Judicial Evidence*, ed. E. Dumont (1825), 180. On two minor caveats to his anti-nomian thesis, see RE2, 43–4.

30. E.g. M. Tonnelli, 'Integrating Evidence into Clinical Practice: An Alternative to Evidence-based Approaches' (2006) 12 J Evaluation of Clinical Prac 248–56. See RE2, 439 and 452 n. 8. In political contexts

the related notion of 'evidence-based policy' is widely used often very loosely, but there is a rapidly expanding, largely bureaucratically oriented literature. See e.g. EIE, Chs. 10 and 11.

31. RE2, 39–41.

32. Ibid., 202–6. Thayer, *Treatise*, 314.

33. 'The counsel who uses this book [C. C. Moore, *A Treatise on Facts: On the Weight and Value of Evidence* (1908)] to induce the judge to a ruling of law upon credibility is committing moral treason to our system.' Wigmore, Review of Moore's *A Treatise on Facts* in (1908) 3 Illinois LR 477, see RE2, 69–71.

34. RE2, Chs. 3, 4, 7 and 15; and FiL, *passim*.

35. See *The New Wigmore: A Treatise on Evidence* (multiple vols. and editors) (2001–).

36. Wigmore prefaced the book with the following quotation: '"How do you mean?", asked the Home Secretary, rather puzzled, but with a melancholy smile. "I should hardly speak of it as a science. I look at it as common sense".'
'Pardon me, sir. It is the most difficult of all the sciences. It is indeed rather the science of sciences. What is the whole of inductive logic, as laid down (say) by Bacon and Mill, but an attempt to appraise the value of evidence, the said evidence being in the trails left by the Creator, so to speak?
The Creator has (I say it in all reverence) drawn a myriad of red herrings across the track. But the true scientist refuses to be baffled by superficial appearances in detecting the secrets of Nature.' Israel Zangwill, *The Big Bow Mystery* (1892). Neither Wigmore nor Zangwill used 'science' in any strict sense in this context.

37. Especially RE2, Ch. 6 and *Analysis*, Chs. 3, 8, 10, 11.

38. RE2, 15–19.

39. Including similar facts, standards for decision (including standards of proof), hearsay, improperly obtained evidence and identification evidence.

40. RE2, 258–69, and Ch. 6 (ibid.).

41. In 1970 I spoke to a non-specialist audience on 'Taking Facts Seriously' which was published in several places, including (1984) 34 J Leg Ed 22 and reprinted in RE2, Ch. 2. 'Taking Facts Seriously – Again' was also widely published, including in the generalist J Leg Ed (vol. 55(3) (2005)). The original lecture and paper were received politely, but failed to persuade, perhaps because it fell between audiences: practitioners quite liked it, but it was about legal education; many academic lawyers perceived it as addressed to specialists in Evidence and so no concern of theirs; some Evidence teachers perceived it as a radical and undiplomatic critique of traditional courses on the Law of Evidence; while others saw it as poor salesmanship for improbable Wigmore charts.

42. E.g. RE2, Chs. 2 and 14.

43. See further pp. 363–4.

44. 'Some Scepticism about Some Scepticisms', RE2, Ch. 4.

45. See RE2, *passim* and Ho Hock Lai, *A Philosophy of Evidence Law – Justice in the Search for Truth* (2008) 55–7.

46. RE2, Ch. 3.

47. The role of narrative in legal discourse and questions about the relations between narrative, reasoning, argumentation and persuasion are distorted if narrative and stories are only considered in relation to disputed questions of fact in adjudication. Stories and story-telling are also important in investigation, mediation, negotiation, appellate advocacy, sentencing and predictions of dangerousness, for example, as well as in secondary discourse (e.g. writing or telling history). They also feature in arguments about disputed questions of law. As Karl Llewellyn emphasised: in appellate cases the statement of facts by advocates and judges is 'the heart of the argument' (K. Llewellyn, *The Common Law Tradition* (1962), 126–8, discussed in RE2, 296–306). Some of these topics have been canvassed rather eclectically under the heading of 'Law and Literature'. See below, p. 366 n. 62, and e.g. Leonora Ledwon, 'The Poetics of Evidence: Some Applications to Law and Literature' (2003) 21 Quinnipiac LR 1145.

48. Susan Haack, a philosopher, has also explored in depth the relationship between the philosophy of science and scientific evidence, expertise and pseudo-science. Susan Haack, *Evidence Matters* (2014).

49. Some commentators conflate empirical understandings of law in action or of context and findings of disciplined socio-legal research. That is too narrow. The Genn Report (H. Genn et al., *Law in the Real World: Improving our Understanding of How Law Works* (2006)) stressed that mainstream legal scholars can assimilate and use socio-legal and other social science findings without having to do the research themselves. Doctrinal scholars can reasonably worry when there is often no or very little empirical research on topics they are interested in. However, as Llewellyn emphasised, 'knowledge does not have to be scientific, to be useful and important' (see KLRM, 188–96). In Evidence it is generally recognised that in drawing inferences one has to rely on the best information that is available from our 'stock of knowledge' which ranges from repeated controlled clinical trials through various kinds of expertise, 'horse sense' and common sense to unreliable or biased or speculative working assumptions. As suggested in Ch. 17, in Law we could explore further 'the lessons of experience', because so many judgements that are required in policy-making, description and explanation cannot be based on 'scientific' research. See GJP, 238–42.

50. (1984) 47 MLR 261, reprinted in abbreviated form in LiC, Ch. 6.

51. Viz. Intellectual History, High Theory, middle-order theorising, both prescriptive and descriptive (including working theories for participants), interdisciplinary relations (the conduit function), and the integrative or synthesising function (Ch. 1).

52. RE2, 248–54. This was potentially illuminating in sketching connections with decision theory, information theory and theories of litigation, but it did not catch on. Moreover, it did not capture all the lines of enquiry that I was reaching for – after all, law is concerned with much more than formal processing of disputes; e.g. 'litigation' is only one part of lawyers' practices and the label is awkward.

53. Denis Galligan, 'More Scepticism about Scepticism' (1988) 8 OJLS 249, for a partial response see RE2, 257–61.

54. See Ch. 20. Much of my effort was in fact invested in developing ways of teaching a set of skills (Modified Wigmorean Analysis (MWA) see p. 188) linked intimately to a different conception of the field than was traditional. The details of this are discussed in the next section. But there is an intimate connection between legal theory and the quite practical matter of teaching students how to construct, reconstruct, marshal, criticise and present arguments about questions of fact. This involves 'close analysis of a selective kind', but not only of concepts.

55. The concept of common sense in relation to background generalisations is problematic as are the related ideas of cognitive competence and cognitive consensus, see RE2, Ch. 11 and 443–6 and *Analysis*, Ch. 10.

56. From course description for Analysis of Evidence (Miami) and Evidence and Proof (London).

57. This approach is developed at length in *Analysis* (2nd edn, 2005).

58. Traditionally lawyers have used several analytic devices for organising data in preparing for trial. These include chronological tables, narratives, classification by source, and more or less elaborate "trial books", which combine several methods (see *Analysis*, Ch. 4 and pp. 317–24). Today, they can use sophisticated records management, indexing and support systems. Wigmore's chart method is different from all of these in that it is the only one which operates in a framework of argument. Generally speaking, these methods are complementary rather than rivals.

59. I used this formulation regularly in handouts in teaching and other presentations of MWA.

60. The main modifications have been to reduce the number of symbols; to systematise the method through a flexible seven-step intellectual procedure; to emphasise clarification of standpoint; to treat story construction as a complementary rather than as a rival method; to broaden the focus from contested jury trials to all phases of legal process; and to extend its application to all enquiries into particular past events (e.g. history, genocide) and some other enquiries (e.g. intelligence analysis, spotting insurance fraud). See *Analysis*, Ch. 2 and D. Schum, *Evidence and*

Inference for the Intelligence Analyst, 2 vols. (1987). See now: G. Tecuci, D. Schurn, D. Marcu and M. Boicu, *Intelligence Analysis: Connecting the Dots* (2016). On the application of MWA to Archaeology see T. Anderson and W. Twining in Robert Chapman and Alison Wylie (eds.), *Material Evidence: Learning from Archaeological Practice* (2015), Ch. 15.

61. E.g. Peter Murphy, *Evidence, Proof and Facts* (2003), 3–4.
62. David Schum has taught the technique to engineers, intelligence analysts and students in other disciplines in single-semester modules. In a blind testing of a complex exercise designed for intelligence analysts two third-year Miami law students produced better results than a collection of police officers, academics from several disciplines, and even experienced intelligence analysts. This is an experiment that deserves to be repeated.
63. On expanding the idea of 'Legal Method' in legal education and training to include inferential reasoning from evidence, see p. 228.
64. See further Ch. 16.
65. See EIE, *passim.*
66. See Ch. 10, pp. 130–1.
67. After the Millennium Dave Schum, Terry and I were involved in an ambitious attempt at UCL to develop an integrated cross-disciplinary field, led by a statistician, Philip Dawid. This was a mixed success. I consider it still to be unfinished business and will deal with it in Ch. 20.

15. Bentham's College (1983–99)

1. UCL (originally the University of London) earned its 'Godless College' epithet because it was the first university institution in England to admit students who were not members of the Church of England (London Standard Editorial), including Jews, Catholics, Muslims, Quakers and Hindus. This label was popularised as 'The Godless institution of Gower Street'.
2. Pigeon-holes are allegedly proof of one's academic existence; loss of one's pigeon-hole marks Academic Death: one becomes a non-person. A few years ago, a bureaucratic error killed off all of the Emeritus Professors in the UCL Faculty of Laws. We appealed and were *resurrected* – an innovation in academic doctrine.
3. 'Butler tours' were organised by Bill Butler, Professor of Comparative Law at UCL, the leading anglophone specialist on Soviet/Russian Law and Socialist Legal Systems. In exchange for listening to lectures by the visitors, our hosts arranged visits to various legal institutions in their respective countries. This elevated form of legal tourism was instructive, sometimes surprising, and nearly always fun. Clearly, we got the best of the deal. Meanwhile Professor Butler regularly disappeared to augment his unique collection of bookplates.

4. The subtitle is revealing: *Being a Collection of Papers, Explanatory of the Design of an Institution, Proposed to be Set on Foot, Under the Name of the Chrestomathic Day School, Or Chrestomathic School, for the Extension of the New System of Instruction to the Higher Branches of Learning, for the Use of the Middling and Higher Ranks in Life.* This subverts claims to classlessness and illustrates why many find JB's style off-putting. UCL charged fees from the start.

5. See Plate 5.

6. Esp. GJB, Ch. 8.

7. President Mary Robinson, 'Imaginative Possessions', John Foster Galway Lecture, UCL, October 1995, www.rothschildfostertrust.com /materials/lecture_robinson.pdf.

8. *Auto-icon*: JB's own comments on it are evidence of his sense of humour: 'Auto-icon; or, Of the Farther Uses of the Dead to the Living'. See Philip Schofield, *Utility and Democracy* (2006), 337–42.

9. Cited ibid., Ch. 10.

10. Esp. Negley Harte, *The University of London 1836–1986* (1986); John North and Negley Harte, *The World of UCL 1828–2004* (2004); F. M. L. Thompson (ed.), *The University of London and the World of Learning 1856–1986* (1990).

11. John Baker, 'University College and Legal Education 1826–1976' (1977) Current Legal Problems 1–13. This section draws heavily on my sesqui-centennial lecture, '1836 and All That' (1987), discussed below.

12. Interpretations of Austin are contested, in particular in what sense he was a 'positivist'. On 'Austinian Myth' see W. L. Morison, *John Austin* (1982), at 170–7. Morison's interpretation is itself controversial, based on the approach of the Australian philosopher, John Anderson. That need not concern us here, where the relevant point is that Austin considered his role as Professor of Jurisprudence to include both eluci-dation of abstract concepts that are a necessary part of the law as it is *and* utilitarian guidance and evaluation of the law as it ought to be (the Art of Legislation). These were to be kept separate, but both were to be dealt with. Morison goes further in arguing that on his interpretation Austin also provided a philosophical basis for empirical approaches to law.

13. See '1836 and All That', and my report on the Intercollegiate LLM (1994).

14. Bob Hepple, *Young Man with a Red Tie: A Memoir of Mandela and the Failed Revolution 1960–1963* (2013).

15. These joint degrees span four years; I approved of the length, but thought that opportunities were being missed in the design and implementation of the syllabuses, which were sometimes little more than the Foundation subjects studied twice plus a foreign language. It is not clear to what extent in practice the students are asked to make regular comparisons at

various levels of abstraction and to think theoretically about such matters. On four-year undergraduate Law degrees see Ch. 17.

16. See n. 11.

17. Overall reported numbers for the LLM can be misleading because the programme involved a mixture of full-time, part-time and occasional students among others.

18. I treat 'Jurisprudence' and 'Legal Theory' as synonyms (Ch. 1). What the distinction is meant to indicate is obscure. Today it serves no purpose.

19. Glanville Williams was one of my academic heroes at the start of my career, mainly for his writings on Torts. He made some workmanlike contributions to Jurisprudence, but is still mostly remembered for his work on Criminal Law, though sometimes criticised by criminal law specialists for not being 'theoretical' enough.

20. The Chair also led to invitations to sit on University Committees, some *ex officio*, some voluntary, such as the Management Committee of IALS and the Committee for External Students.

21. See p. 200.

22. I cannot do justice here to this talented and congenial bunch of colleagues; but the early ones deserve a special mention. They included Michael Freeman, an energetic polymath, leading defender of children's interests, sociologically inclined. He was very popular as a lecturer, but rather too wedded to coverage for my taste. He has made outstanding contributions to family law and feminist legal thought. See *Law in Society: Reflections on Children, Family, Culture and Philosophy: Essays in Honour of Michael Freeman*, ed. A. Diduck et al. (2015). Stephen Guest on the other hand was a single-minded disciple of Ronald Dworkin, a meticulous teacher, a careful scholar, a good institution-person, who found it difficult to break away from his hero's perspective, but was very fair in his treatment of Bentham and Hart. Later he did an excellent book on Dworkin for the *Jurists* series. In her first job, Niki Lacey, whose main field is Criminal Law, had been strongly influenced by Hart's work on punishment and responsibility. By 1982 she was breaking away from the narrow Hartian perspective and just beginning to emerge as a leading feminist jurist. She and I have been close allies in trying to bridge the chasm between Analytical Legal Philosophy and Socio-legal Studies (see p. 255). On her biography of Herbert Hart see p. 292. See also 'Companions on a Serendipitous Journey' (2017) 44 JL & Soc 283–96. Andrew Lewis, a Roman Law specialist and legal historian, for whom Jurisprudence was an avocation, was quite flexible in adapting to a new broom, but quietly continued to do his own thing; David Hutchinson, a young international lawyer, mainly interested in political theory, left after my second year to follow a distinguished career in the United Nations, where he became Principal Legal Officer in the Department of Legal Affairs. Freeman and Lacey became Fellows at

the British Academy. Later Philip Schofield, an outstanding Editor and Director of the Bentham Project, taught regularly on the Jurisprudence course.

23. See p. 21.

24. In 1994 Stephen Guest introduced and mentored *The UCL Jurisprudence Review*, written and edited by students, to begin with by undergraduates, later including postgraduates, and from 2011 a few contributions from outside UCL. Now nearing its twentieth anniversary, with the best essay being awarded the Stephen Guest Prize, it is splendid evidence of what students can do when given the chance (cp. *The Dim Student Fallacy* which is still abroad in English law teaching).

25. Despite the strong support of all the Jurisprudence teachers and the Dean, I narrowly lost the battle to move Jurisprudence into the second year. Some colleagues were hostile to the idea of Jurisprudence being required, some strongly defended their particular territory and some took the line 'if it ain't broke, don't fix it' (I thought that it was broke). So far as I could tell almost none were willing to think about the curriculum as a whole – in my experience that is the main difficulty of curriculum planning in Law, for we law teachers tend to be very territorial. We lost by a narrow margin on more than one occasion and that was one reason why I decided to step aside from the Quain Chair and become a Research Professor. Jurisprudence is still compulsory, but it is now in the second year.

26. We used the newspaper exercise (Ch. 1), although some colleagues were not comfortable with it.

27. I handed out a list of words, only a few of which were too difficult conceptually for a dictionary to be adequate for the purpose. My main objective was to weaken the exaggerated idea that legal discourse is a foreign language and to encourage the habit of consulting a law dictionary. In some years I also taught in the Legal System course, usually organised by Michael Freeman. This gave me a bit more scope for catching them young.

28. See p. 263.

29. Instead, I later helped to design and produce materials for an Access course, organised by Birkbeck College's Extra Mural Dept. That I felt was a really worthwhile venture, it was built along the same lines as *How to Do Things with Rules*, named 'The Certificate in Legal Method' and was, I thought, a great success. It still continues.

30. See further Ch. 17.

31. LLM Review: Final Report (University of London) (1993). This was preceded by two more detailed Interim Reports and some working papers.

32. GJB, 366.

33. See RE, Ch. 32 and *Analysis*, Ch. 7.

34. A provisional version of *Analysis of Evidence* was completed in the mid-1980s, but the first edition was not published until 1991. Twenty-four years later, having recruited David Schum as co-author, we published a substantially revised second edition in 2005.

35. See p. 214. After that I always circulated a short handout so that I could get my message in first and this has been my practice for nearly all performances elsewhere.

36. In particular I owe much to Susan Haack, Patrick Gudridge and Ken Casebeer.

37. I shall not enter here into the question about the extent to which ABA accreditation really limited innovation. Cf. the exaggeration of the constraints imposed by 'core subjects' in England and Wales (Ch. 12).

38. For an early critique see GLT, 161–5. On indicators generally see pp. 204, 235.

39. See LiC, 300.

40. For a very controversial polemic about the economics of American legal education, see Brian Tamanaha, *Failing Law Schools* (2012), which also argues for greater flexibility and variation.

41. At one stage the Faculty at Miami unanimously voted that I should be offered a half-time tenured position. I was ambivalent, but I would probably have accepted. However, this was vetoed by the then Dean. My first reaction was: if you treat me like a visitor, I shall behave like a visitor. If I had been appointed I would have gained financially (benefits), but I would have felt a sense of obligation to teach mainstream courses and to work to improve the institution, including fighting hard to make the Law School distinctive. For me the main positive outcome was that I wrote much more.

16. Four contrasting relationships (Bentham, Dworkin, MacCormick, Anderson)

1. Dates: Jeremy Bentham (1748–1832); Ronald Dworkin (1931–2013); Sir Neil MacCormick (1941–2009); Terence Anderson (1939–).

2. GJB, 281.

3. See Ch. 9.

4. *Anarchical Fallacies* is the title by which it is best known, but this has now been published in the *Collected Works* as *Nonsense Upon Stilts* as part of *Rights, Representation, and Reform*, ed. P. Schofield, C. Pease-Watkin and C. Blamires (2002).

5. GJP, Ch. 6.5.

6. *Bentham: Selected Writings of John Dinwiddy* (2003).

7. H. L. A. Hart, *Essays on Bentham* (1982), 39. However, Hart felt greater empathy for Bentham as a person and as a phenomenon and was more of a hard positivist (see below at p. 342). I am inclined more to the pluralism of Isaiah Berlin's 'the crooked timber of humanity', with

greater emphasis on history, tradition, intuition and context (Llewellyn) and complexity (Calvino).

8. GJP, Ch. 6.

9. GJB, 214–15, 262–63.

10. For three different interpretations by leading Bentham scholars see G. Postema, *Bentham and the Common Law Tradition* (1986); Paul Kelly, *Utilitarianism and Distributive Justice* (1990); and *Bentham: Selected Writings of John Dinwiddy*.

11. The Bentham Project has been fortunate to have had four outstanding scholars as General Editors: James Burns, John Dinwiddy, Fred Rosen and Philip Schofield. Whether each of these has been a Benthamite utilitarian is unclear. What is clear is that a great debt is owed to all of the editors for their dedication, ingenuity and textual skills in labouring on an extraordinary mass of material to produce excellent and elegant texts with invaluable furniture and secondary works. As was mentioned above, I decided long ago that I was unsuited to this kind of textual scholarship; but I treasure the association with the Bentham Project, which has been my most important point of reference for careful scholarship.

12. There is also a troubling question about Bentham's relevance to twenty-first-century and future issues. One of my first essays on Bentham was titled 'The Contemporary Significance of Anarchical Fallacies' (1975), but later I struggled to differentiate textual, contextual, conversational, anachronistic and contemporary reading together with non-reading and speculating about how Bentham might have reacted to twentieth-century events and projects. I even allowed for fruitful non-reading, exemplified by Foucault and Marx, who both helped to make him notorious without having read many pages (GJB, Ch. 7). Late in life Marx probably read some more.

13. There was a brave effort by Mary Mack, *Jeremy Bentham: An Odyssey of Ideas* (1963). I rather like it, but it is quite adventurous. It has been criticised as being too speculative and that may have contributed to the unwillingness of the next generation to undertake this important task. Philip Schofield, *Utility and Democracy: The Political Thought of Jeremy Bentham* (2006) comes nearest to achieving this, but it does not claim to be comprehensive, focusing mainly on the political ideas.

14. JB prioritised publicity and what we now call transparency. In later work he explicitly linked it to representative democracy, which allows for 'some *eventual faculty of effective resistance* and consequent change in government, which is purposely left, or rather given to the people'. See Schofield, *Utility and Democracy*, Ch. 10. *Panopticon* was just one example of 'architecture as a means of securing publicity, while publicity was a means of securing responsibility' (ibid., 259) through inspectors of

all kinds of institutions, asylums, schools, poor houses and factories. Cf.
JB on the Public Opinion Tribunal and freedom of the press (ibid.).

15. Nicola Lacey, *H. L. A. Hart: The Nightmare and the Noble Dream*
(2004), 186.

16. In Oxford it was considered irregular to be involved in choosing one's
successor; some might consider it suicidal or noble to promote one's
chief critic. However, it was not unprecedented to pick out an unknown
with few publications: Hart himself had set the precedent. Both proved
to be inspired appointments. Tragically, Hart became obsessed with
Dworkin's strictures, never answered them convincingly and ignored
most of his other critics.

17. Cf. Lacey on Hart: 'as it was, Herbert's sensitivity to Dworkin's criticisms
was fuelled by a sense that there was something wilful or even lacking in
honesty about Dworkin's reading of his work' (Lacey, *H. L. A. Hart*, 330).

18. For Dworkin, judicial interpretation consists of two phases: 'fit' with
existing authoritative materials, and when this is doubtful, 'justification'
according the basic principles which give a system both its legitimacy and
its integrity. Both 'fit' and 'substance' are 'interpretive concepts' – that is,
concepts that refer to practices 'that have a point'; for example, courtesy: in
some cultures the point of bowing to superiors is to show respect. See
S. Guest, *Ronald Dworkin*, 2nd edn (1997) for an admirably clear explanation of these concepts. The basic principles are principles of political
morality; the key standpoint is that of the appellate (American/common
law/Western?) judge – all other standpoints are subordinate or parasitic;
and the central focus of legal thinking is interpretation and application of
legal doctrine, propositions of law. In a late formulation he stated 'our
main question [to be]: whether and when morality figures in the
truth-conditions of propositions of law'. For Dworkin this one question
was about law in the doctrinal sense (*Justice in Robes* (2006), 4). See
below n. 21.

19. In introducing Hercules, Dworkin states: 'I suppose that Hercules is
a judge in some representative American jurisdiction' (*Taking Rights
Seriously* (1977), 10). This is to illustrate the idea of 'a lawyer of super-
human skill, learning, patience and acumen' (ibid.) in concrete terms
rather than limit the application of the idea of Hercules to the United
States. However, Dworkin claims that his kind of interpretive theory 'is
by its nature addressed to a particular legal culture generally the culture
to which their authors belong'(*Law's Empire* (1986), 102); cf. Rawls,
'The aims of political philosophy depend on the society it addresses'
('The Idea of an Overlapping Consensus' in *Collected Papers* (1999), 1).
Although Hercules' derivation is clearly American he could be interpreted to fit broadly with aspirational models for reasoning at least in
higher courts in the European Union, Federal Germany and no doubt
some other countries. He can also be a model of argumentation for some

other participants in legal systems to which they are committed, so long as institutional differences are ignored. These complex issues are discussed in GLT, 44-7, 71-5. Cf. J. Raz, *Between Authority and Interpretation* (2009), 92 ('Talk of *the* concept of Law really means *our* concept of law'). I think that Hercules is an important contribution to theorising about reasoning about questions of law and interpretation. My differences with Dworkin are of another kind.

20.   On the theme that the concept of 'judge' does not travel well across legal traditions and jurisdictions with differing institutional arrangements see p. 360 n. 45.

21.   Dworkin's distinction between 'the doctrinal concept of law' and 'the sociological concept of law' (e.g. in *Justice in Robes*, Introduction) is so silly about the latter that one wonders whether it was written tongue in cheek or in a moment of stress. I have criticised this in 'Legal R/realism and Jurisprudence' (LRJ, at 124-8) and do not repeat it here.

22.   For a robust defence of Dworkin against all the main criticisms, see Guest, *Ronald Dworkin*.

23.   I have dealt in other chapters with some negative aspects of his legacy (see Index).

24.   See, however, GJP, 56-60 ('the olive-branch thesis').

25.   See Guest, *Ronald Dworkin*.

26.   See pp. 356-7 n. 5.

27.   See Ch. 13.

28.   On 'appellate court-itis', see pp. 121, 166 and p. 329 n. 13.

29.   When I wrote some detailed comments on the manuscript of *Law's Empire* (mainly about standpoint) he acknowledged this in the Preface, but paid no attention to them. I think he only cited me in relation to Llewellyn, whom he misrepresented.

30.   Ronnie did me one favour. I had been told by UCL that I would have to retire at 67. However, shortly afterwards they appointed Dworkin to the Quain Chair (part-time). I was allowed to continue for a bit longer. Moral: always be succeeded by an older man. Later he moved sideways and he chose, no doubt tongue in cheek, to take the title of Bentham Professor.

31.   'Neil MacCormick, 1941-2009', *Biographical Memoirs of Fellows of the British Academy* (2012), vol. XI, 449-71.

32.   A major reference point for him was G. Davie, *The Democratic Intellect* (1961).

33.   D. N. MacCormick, *Legal Right and Social Democracy* (1982), 253. Some of Neil's most interesting work stemmed from the tension between his commitment to Scottish nationalism and the European Project, culminating in what many consider to be his best book, *Questioning Sovereignty: Law, State and Nation in the European Commonwealth* (1999). This was published in the same year that he was elected to the

European Parliament and considerably enhanced his standing within the EU.

34. D. N. MacCormick, 'The Democratic Intellect and the Law' (Presidential Address, SPTL) (1985) 5 Leg Stud 177, at 181.

35. N. MacCormick and W. Twining, 'Theory in the Law Curriculum' in LTCL, Ch. 13. I think that it was during this collaboration that Neil told me that Karl Llewellyn's 'The Normative, the Legal and the Law-jobs' (1940) 49 Yale LJ 1355 – Llewellyn's fullest statement of the law-jobs theory – was a game-changer in his intellectual development: ('You could hear the sound of scales clattering as I read it.').

That is one reason why we included Llewellyn's 'A Required Course in Jurisprudence' ((1940) 9 Am L Sch R 590) as a kind of appendix to our joint paper in LTCL. Cf. Llewellyn: 'My brother Patterson and I have lived in amity for years, until this matter of a course in Jurisprudence came up. Then we became as two prowling tom-cats in the spring. Jurisprudence is Philosophy of Law!, said Patterson. Jurisprudence is Philosophy of Legal Institutions! said I, and prepared to sling a chair. Yet there were only two class hours to work with. And Jurisprudence is really both and a good deal more.' Llewellyn (ibid.) reprinted in LTCL, Ch. 14, 258. Neil and I had both reached the view in the last sentence before we collaborated.

36. See first paragraph of previous note.

37. Among less important issues on which we disagreed was making sense of the concept of 'the ratio decidendi' of a case (HTDTWR, 304–12).

38. In his own words: 'Perhaps under the influence of Finnis, however, but also in ways linking back to my Scottish philosophical training, it made Hart seem more of a natural lawyer than he (Hart) wanted to be, as he once told William Twining. In due course, the new Preface to the second edition of [The] *Concept of Law* that was published post-humously showed how Hart had hardened the positivistic line in his own thought. This ran counter to the ideas I had suggested as the most attractive line of development of certain principal ideas in *The Concept of Law*.' 'MacCormick on MacCormick', an informal autobiographical fragment published in A. J. Menéndez and J. E. Fossum (eds.), *Law and Democracy in Neil MacCormick's Legal and Political Theory* (2011), 17–24.

39. W. Twining, 'Institutions of Law: Globalization, State Law and Legal Pluralism' in M. Del Mar and Z. Bankowski (eds.), *Law as Institutional Normative Order* (2009). Neil is quite explicit that the four volumes of *Law, State and Practical Reason* are underpinned by his moral views.

40. *Legal Reasoning and Legal Theory* (1994).

41. *Practical Reason in Law and Morality* (2008), 4; cf. 209.

42. This section draws on 'Celebrating Terry Anderson' (University of Miami Law School, 7 November 2013).

43. Neither Terry nor I can vouch for the exact words, but these fit his style and we agree that he thumped the table. This was first encounter with the Miami convention of interrupting speakers early on. Thereafter I always prepared a handout so that my message could be communicated.

44. There were two main reasons why each version took so long: first, there were no deadlines. Terry, a practitioner at heart, only works to deadlines and does not respect those unless there are sanctions involved; so more immediate matters took priority, such as admissions, teaching, helping students, appointments, minority affairs, faculty politics, trial competitions, *pro bono* legal advice and representation, and, of course, the epic Hastings impeachment case (see below). Secondly, Terry is a perfectionist at heart and will relentlessly revise until forced to stop.

45. But for health reasons and our differences in age we might have entered for the World over-80s table tennis competition, as depicted in the wonderful documentary film *Ping Pong* (2013).

46. As an admirer of Mirjan Damaska's work on Comparative Evidence and Procedure (M. Damaska, *The Faces of Justice and State Authority* (1986)), I was better prepared than Terry, but I also experienced some shocks even after six months, especially when visiting institutions and inspecting dossiers of criminal appeals and revisions.

47. See EIHL, Chs. 3 and 4.

48. T. Anderson, *The Battles of Hastings: Four Stories in Search of a Meaning*, Uhlenbeck Lecture 13 (1996).

49. *United States v Hastings* (multiple proceedings). There is masses of material, much of it drafted by Terry. Some is in the public domain, and a certain amount is on the Internet. It is probably too late for Terry to construct a coherent book about a case which deserves more than one volume. Terry's main published account is *The Battles of Hastings*. It is fascinating and remarkably detached, but too short to capture all the twists and turns of a compelling legal saga that needs to be better known.

50. Formally, 'from 1981 until 1993, Professor Anderson served as principal counsel to former United States (now Congressman) Alcee L. Hastings on all matter affecting his rights as a judge in proceedings before federal courts and judicial administrative bodies and before the House of Representatives and the Senate of the United States and from 1989, in proceedings to determine the validity and consequences of his removal from judicial office'. Programme for the Uhlenbeck Lecture in 1995 (see above).

17. Legal Education

1. For them a First in Greats or Mathematics plus the despised bar exams were enough. This is still reflected in nine-month conversion courses for graduates with Upper Seconds or Firsts in Arts or Science which do little

more than cram in the core subjects without much pretence of under-standing or intellectual skills.

2. This chapter discusses Legal Education (capitalised) as a field of study, research and scholarly debate; 'legal education' (lower case) refers to the complex and varied arrangements, practices and institutions concerned significantly with learning about law. There are, inevitably, some border-line cases.

3. The LETR published several major documents, together with responses from professional associations. See http://letr.org.uk. Five years since its final report (2013) the issues are still being debated.

4. Reprinted in LiC, Ch. 4. The subtitle 'lawyer education' was deliberate, as part of the argument was that a liberal education is important for intending lawyers even in an avowedly 'professional' law school.

5. K. Llewellyn, *Jurisprudence* (1962), 376. This is, of course, part of the more general themes of 'law in context', broadening the study of law, and what Harry Arthurs has called 'humane professionalism', which is the central idea behind the important Arthurs Report in Canada, *Law and Learning* (1983). See further '"Globalization" as Framing Concept: Some Implications for Legal Education' in S. Archer, D. Drache and P. Zumbansen (eds.), *The Daunting Enterprise of the Law: Essays in Honor of Harry Arthurs* (2017).

6. Revisited in 'Pericles Regained?' LiC, Ch. 16 (a review of A. Kronman's *The Lost Lawyer* (1993)). I have also been mildly critical of some other simplistic images of 'the products' of legal education and training, including 'the lawyer' as problem-solver and all-purpose fixer, and Lasswell and McDougal's aggrandising vision: 'It should need no empha-sis that the lawyer is today, even when not himself a maker of policy, the one indispensable adviser of every policy-maker of our society' ((1947) 52 Yale LJ 1345). Each of these images is overstated, but contains an important core of truth (LiC, 194–5, 334–5). On problem-solving in the abstract see above, pp. 128–9 (Herbert Simon).

7. A good starting-point for understanding the diversity of modern uni-versity systems as a crucial context for understanding modern law schools is W. Rueg (ed.), *A History of the University in Europe*: IV, *Universities since 1945* (2010). 'Law schools by their very nature, tend to think locally not globally': C. Stolker, *Rethinking the Law School* (2014). This informative book by a former Dean and Rector Magnificus at Leiden University amply illustrates the diversity of uni-versity law schools transnationally, while arguing for a more cosmopo-litan perspective. This was interestingly reviewed by N. Johnson, (2017) 51 The Law Teacher 107.

8. Cf. e.g. Brian Tamanaha's powerful critique of the modern American scene (*Failing Law Schools* (2012)) with the rather more optimistic

account of the situation in England and Wales in the LETR Report (2013).

9. ILC, *Legal Education in a Changing World* (1975). There has, of course, been considerable diffusion of ideas and practices and networking within the common law world. Plans are in train for an interesting project to explore the influence of elite American law schools (especially Harvard) and their ideas about legal education in a selection of common law and civil law jurisdictions in terms of diffusion.

10. The drafting committee for the ILC Report was James C. N. Paul (USA), Yash Ghai (Kenya, Oxford and Harvard), Andrés Cuneo (Valpairaiso, Stanford and Harvard), and myself (Oxford and Chicago).

11. In respect of formal legal education this was probably almost true during the Cultural Revolution; but from a broader perspective it is almost certainly false in respect of informal learning about law, on which see pp. 272–3.

12. For controversies surrounding the ILC Reports, especially that of the Research Committee, see LiC, 16 n. 43.

13. See pp. 265–71.

14. Nearly all of these institutions were outside the remit of LETR (see pp. 269–72). On the diversity of legal education providers in Germany, see the Wissenschaftsrat Report (English translation), *Prospects of Legal Scholarship in Germany: Current Situation, Analyses, Recommendations* (2012). See also Stolker, *Rethinking the Law School*, Chs. 1 and 3, focusing mainly on universities and whether Law belongs in 'proper' universities.

15. The ILC Report (*Legal Education in a Changing World*, 35–9) argued that Law schools of the future should be viewed as multi-purpose resource centers dealing with all levels of legal education and staffed by a corresponding variety of specialists. This idea has been criticized for expecting too much of a single law school. The report was primarily concerned with countries that had only one national law school (which is now increasingly rare). This model is best interpreted as an ideal type for university law schools *collectively* in a larger (national, provincial, or regional) 'system', with plenty of space for collaboration, competition, niche specialisms, and centres of excellence within it.

16. 'As legal education is perceived to be a panoply of programs and educational efforts calling for diverse expertise, . . . The faculty of a law school might better be perceived as a team of specialists working in a complex system of education' (ibid., 23–4).

17. W. Twining, 'Professionalism in Legal Education' (2011) 18 Int'l J Legal Profession No. 1 and 2 165–72; 'LETR: The Role of Academics in Legal Education and Training; Ten Theses' 48 The Law Teacher (2014) 94–103. See also 'Bureaucratic Rationalism and the Quiet (R)evolution' (1996) 7 Legal Education Rev. 291–308 (book review). With the

bureaucratisation of higher education, Deans and Heads of Department are increasingly perceived as middle management, accountable to 'line managers'. Some are even given orthodox management training, which probably does not include much of the kind of advice offered in F. M. Cornford's classic, *Microcosmographia Academica* (1908, now online).

18. If higher education is largely about self-education, *a fortiori* law teachers ought to be able to inform themselves adequately about the basics without formal instruction. Any individual law teacher can quite easily take the first step of achieving an awareness of the standard literature on education (including legal education), and of the range of possible objectives that can be pursued and the range of standard devices and techniques which can help to achieve these objectives. This does not require formal certification, which might entrench a rigid orthodoxy. It has been and can be primarily a matter for self-education, complemented by attending courses and events. A good starting point for the UK is C. Ashworth and J. Guth (eds.), *The Academic Lawyer's Handbook* (2016). See also Roger Burridge, Karen Hinett, Abdul Paliwala and Tracey Varnava (eds.), *Effective Learning and Teaching in Law* (2002); Stolker, *Rethinking the Law School*; it is interesting to compare these with the German Wissenschaftsrat Report of 2013.

19. For the UK see the website of the Legal Education Research Network (LERN) at http://ials.sas.ac.uk/about/leadership-and-collaboration /legal-education-research-network-LERN. Such research is by no means restricted to degree-level education. For example, in relation to public legal values, private ethics, professional and judicial legal ethics, and professional responsibility and discipline (categories that are too often conflated) the literature has burgeoned transnationally. On some topics needing more attention see below p. 273.

20. In particular that the history, politics and culture of law schools are in some important ways unique or special and that 'generic' approach to pedagogy in higher education misses these important factors.

21. One commentator on this chapter, committed to the values of liberal education, in effect said: 'It is OK for a few academic lawyers to specialise in Legal Education as a field of research and policy-making, but as a teacher I try to help my students to learn how to think independently and critically through legal materials. I did not need training to learn how to do this, and I am (very) good at it.' No doubt, many excellent law teachers fit this model; some are reflective practitioners; I myself was an auto-didact so far as legal education was concerned; but I think that some formal education in pedagogical techniques and dealing with students can be very helpful for everyone (unless it is too bureaucratic or doctrinaire); some need such help; and most important for the future, we are near the start of several revolutions and the next generation of

academic lawyers need to understand their situation, its history and the challenges facing their profession (Ch. 20). It is particularly in these respects that standard short courses for university teachers seem to differ from the UCL Law Teachers Programme in prioritising pedagogical techniques over contextual awareness, especially in respect of the differing tribes and territories of the various disciplines.

22. R. Cocks and F. Cownie, 'A Great and Noble Occupation': *The History of the Society of Legal Scholars* (2009), reviewed W. Twining, (2010) 37 JL & Soc 542.

23. See p. 147.

24. This 'small jurisdictions project' (otherwise known as my 'coral islands project') included smaller jurisdictions of the British Isles, several Commonwealth countries, Canadian provinces, and even Sudan which was 'small' because of the size of the market for local legal literature. This harked back to the *Sudan Law Journal and Reports*, which relied heavily on government funding. Publications resulting from these activities included W. Twining and J. Uglow (eds.), *Law Publishing and Legal Information*: (1981); W. Twining and J. Uglow (eds.), *Legal Literature in Small Jurisdictions* (1981). 'Servicing the Legal System' (Northern Ireland), stimulated by Colin Campbell, also grew out of this work (http://pure.qub.ac.uk).

25. The politics and diplomacy of the proposed amalgamation or, at least extension of membership, were complicated partly because of the conservatism of our older members, but also because some in the ALT felt that they would not feel at home in the stuffier and more pretentious SPTL. The story is well told in Cocks and Cownie, 'A Great and Noble Occupation'.

26. This was before the Research Excellence Exercises (RAE, REF, etc.) reversed this view and created the recent REFomania.

27. In response, in order to make the Dinner memorable, I tried to rent Warwick Castle (and some other castles) for the Dinner; they proved to be too small and we had to settle for a modern hotel in Coventry.

28. Thanks largely to Jenny Uglow who produced several informative working papers and advice (unknown at the time) on presenting a book proposal to a publisher, which I still use.

29. I delivered a paper on 'Four-Year Degrees in Law' to several seminars and conferences, but I do not think that I ever published it.

30. I also persuaded Warwick (and later UCL) to provide an opt-in provision to spend four years over their LLB with the possibility of a mandatory grant. There was very limited take-up, although there were not severe financial implications for students. I was appalled by the negative attitudes (of some students and even colleagues) to the idea that an opportunity to spend a fourth year at University would be a good thing. Very few students at Warwick and UCL opted in, some

saying that they would want a Master's degree for a fourth year, ignoring the points that an extra year at university could be a benefit in itself, would give them a better legal education, the chance of a good class in their degree and that postgraduate grants were very hard to come by. Very few of my colleagues encouraged opting in, which suggests something about their attitudes to their job and the value of learning. The situation has changed with the new arrangements for University funding and student debt. However, four years' Honours is still generally favoured over three years' Pass Degrees in Scotland. Sadly, in 1991-2 Queen's, Belfast succumbed to pressure and reduced their Honours LLB to three years. On a recent visit to Warwick I was delighted to find that the four-year opt-in provision was still in place and was sometimes being used. Any Law School in England and Wales or Northern Ireland can consider introducing such an option in anticipation of further radical changes in university funding.

31. The fact that the Commonwealth Secretariat was in London was mildly embarrassing, as our officers and staff were very conscious of the sensitivities surrounding the idea of the Commonwealth and tried hard to avoid being seen as neocolonial or nostalgic – with mixed success.

32. See LiC, *passim* and the Bibliography in LEGTC for the period 1983-97, at pp. 373-6.

33. On some quite strident antipathy to customary law in some Commonwealth circles, see GJP, 358.

34. See p. 232.

35. See 'Punching our Weight? Legal Scholarship and Public Understanding' (SLS Centenary Lecture) (2009) 29 Leg Stud 519.

36. The Conference papers were published in D. Mitchell (ed.), *Legal Studies and Legal Education for Non-lawyers* (1979).

37. 'Legal Education for All' in Mitchell (ed.), *Legal Studies and Legal Education for Non-lawyers*, 1-13. This was the year of Kerry Packer's World Series, set up as a rival to official arrangements. This had enormous implications both for the governance of cricket and for the employment conditions of professional cricketers.

38. Including launching two fallacies: the Dim Student Fallacy – the assumption that anyone who is not a university student is incapable of understanding anything unless it is dumbed down; and the Dull Subject Fallacy, viz. that the lower down the educational ladder you go the duller the subject has to be made. On educational fallacies, see p. 365 n. 48, and LiC, 89-90, 131-2, 237-8.

39. Gil Boehringer had taught at Queen's before moving on to Dar es Salaam and later to MacQuarie University in Sydney. He had successfully ruffled feathers in all three institutions and I was sometimes blamed for having recruited him.

18. Globalisation and Law

1. Unpublished draft entitled 'Notes on Basic Value Judgments in Preliterate Custom and Law' (1964) (9 pp.) to be deposited in the Perelman Centre.

2. On the Commonwealth, see pp. 224–5.

3. Jane Collier and June Starr (eds.), *History and Power in the Study of Law: New Directions in Legal Anthropology* (1989) was, in part, based on this colloquium.

4. Teaching and other activities in Sudan or Dar es Salaam could be classified under 'capacity-building'. Most of the relevant topics have been dealt with above under different labels especially in Chs. 5, 6 and 16.

5. GJP, Ch. 11. The main headings are 1. Introduction; 2. 'Law and development': an historical excursus; 3. Contemporary perceptions of the role of law in development: five models; 4. The Millennium Development Goals (MDGs); 5. The Millennium Development Goals and Uganda: A case study; 6. Non-state law: the forgotten factor; 7. Conclusion.

6. In Tanganyika (later Tanzania) the overriding objectives of enterprises in which I was involved were sometimes expressed in terms of 'nation building' and 'national legal development', i.e. *development of law rather than by law* and the focus was national rather than global, regional or transnational. The title of my Taylor Lectures in Lagos was 'Academic Law and Legal Development'; it was assumed that the audience was only lawyers.

   In the early 1960s in Tanganyika/Tanzania the meaning of 'nation-building' was reasonably clear. The first priority was security: externally to consolidate and defend the newly won national sovereignty; internally to build national unity in order to preserve stability and to mobilise people to join the war on 'poverty, ignorance, and disease'. Expatriates were welcome to help, provided that they supported the national effort and did not overstay their welcome. Foreign aid was acceptable so long as it did not threaten national sovereignty. However, terms like 'development', 'less-developed countries' etc. were considered to represent foreign, patronising, often neocolonial perspectives. On my callow attempts to make prescriptions for the future of law in the Sudan, see Ch. 5.

7. In 1964 I had 'inspected' the Law School in Addis Ababa; in 1971 Jim Paul and I had an adventurous tour of Lesotho, Botswana and Swaziland in order to write a report on where a shared law school might be, a highly political exercise; when serving as External Examiner in various African countries I often was asked for informal advice about the institution or some aspect of its programme; later I was part of a team that conducted a review of the National Law School University in Bangalore, one of the most interesting law schools in my experience (1996). In 1977 I spent about three weeks in Papua New Guinea advising on legal information, especially in the lower courts (Report on 'Information about Law' (Law Information Centre, PNG Law Reform Commission, 1977). These were

at least within my area of professional expertise. I was also involved in various activities to do with preservation of legal records (e.g. LRIC). On FILMUP see below.

8. See pp. 224–5.

9. GJP 327–8, 340–46.

10. GJP 330–32. I used to respond "That is rather like asking: what is the role of water in marriage? The answer is obvious: a necessary pre-condition, but beyond that there is no general answer, for the uses of water in this context are manifold, serendipitous, and not very interesting."

11. *Tanzania – Financial and Legal Management Upgrading (FILMUP) Project*. Washington, DC: World Bank, http://documents.worldbank .org/curated/en/895911468129890599/Tanzania-Financial-and-Legal-Management-Upgrading-Project, Legal Task Force Legal Sector Report (January 1996, M. Bomani, Chairman). Copies of the Tanzania and Uganda Reports and background materials will be deposited with other East African papers in the Bodleian Special Collections. For an appraisal of the approach pioneered in FILMUP, see Kithinji Kiragu, *Tanzania: A Case Study in Comprehensive and Programmatic Approaches to Capacity Building* (2005) (dealing with Tanzania's PRSP for the Millennium Development Goals).

12. Government of Uganda/Crown Agents, *Review of the Criminal Justice System: Final Report*, 2 vols. (December 1997). I do not have access to a copy of the second report.

13. See esp. Immanuel Wallerstein et al., *World Systems Analysis: Theory and Methodology* (1982). On economic models, see n. 21 below.

14. B. de Sousa Santos, 'Law as a Map of Misreading', reprinted in *Toward a New Common Sense* (1995).

15. GLS, 21–5.

16. Even as a field concept 'global law' is an aberration: does it cover Public International Law? And Islamic Law? And Canon Law? And Space law? And common law? None of the great legal traditions has ever been worldwide, except in their claims.

17. Revised edition, *Toward a New Legal Common Sense* (2002).

18. *Caldeirada*: Portuguese monster fish stew.

19. 'Globalisation, Post-modernism, and Pluralism: Santos, Haack and Calvino' (GLT, Ch. 8, reprinted in GJB, Ch. 9). Two important books by Brian Tamanaha, who soon became a close friend and ally, were more directly related to mainstream Jurisprudence, with a valuable social scientific frame of reference (esp. *General Jurisprudence of Law and Society* (2001) discussed in a long review article (W. Twining, (2003) 37 Law and Society Rev. 199). See now B. Tamanaha, *A Realistic Theory of Law* (2017), discussed below in Ch. 20.

20. Paul Hirst and Grahame Thompson, *Globalisation in Question* (1999 [1996]) was preceded by several influential articles.

21. 'One was the emergence of a globalized economy involving new systems of production, finance and consumption and worldwide economic integration. A second was new transnational or global cultural patterns, practices and flows, and the idea of "global culture(s)". A third was global political processes, the rise of new transnational institutions, and concomitantly, the spread of global governance and authority structures of diverse sorts. A fourth was the unprecedented multidirectional movement of peoples around the world involving new patterns of transnational migration, identities and communities. Yet a fifth was new social hierarchies, forms of inequality, and relations of domination around the world and in the global system as a whole.' William Robinson, 'Theories of Globalization' in George Ritzer (ed.), *The Blackwell Companion to Globalization* (2007/8). Cf. the treatment of 'law and development' theories in GJP, 330–48.

22. Jokes can be made about World Cups at football (almost genuinely 'global'), and cricket (ten Full Members, expanding), and the World Series at baseball, recently extended to an instant 'World Baseball Classic' invented in 2006. A recent historical study claims that 'Japanese pitcher Hideo Nomo's contract with the Los Angeles Dodgers initiated the globalization of baseball' (Thomas W. Zeiler in Akila Iriye (ed.), *Global Interdependence* (2014), 203.

23. Rafael Domingo, *The New Global Law* (2010), reviewed in GLL.

24. Neil Walker, *Intimations of Global Law* (2015), reviewed W. Twining, (2016) PL 540.

25. B. Frydman and Arnaud van Waeyenberge (eds.), *Gouverner par les standards et les indicateurs: de Hume aux Rankings* (2014).

26. See GJP, 251–3.

27. For early critiques of rankings see GLT, 157–65 and GJP, 251–8. Since then I have been influenced, but not entirely persuaded, by David Restrepo Amariles's fascinating ongoing work on 'the numerical turn', indicators and the application of management theory to legal topics. David Restrepo Amariles (with Julian McLachlan), 'Legal Indicators in Transnational Law Practice: A Methodological Assessment' (2018) 58 Jurimetrics J. 163–209; ' Supping with the Devil? Indicators and the Rise of Managerial Rationality in Law,' 13(4) Int'l JL in Context (2017), 465–84; 'The Mathematical turn: l'indicateur Rule of Law dans la politique du développement de la Banque Mondiale' in B. Frydman and Arnaud van Waeyenberge (eds.), *Gouverner par les standards et les indicateurs: de Hume au Rankings* (2014), 193–234.

28. See p. 204.

29. Synthesised in GJP, Part B.

30. I offered this course about a dozen times (1998–2012) mainly in Miami, but also in Boston and as a series of lectures in UCL as part of a first-year course on 'World Legal Orders'. The stated aim in Miami was to widen

the horizons of American law students about law in the world outside the United States. That aim was largely thwarted by the fact that most of the students who chose the course were reasonably well-travelled or from abroad, so it did not reach those who needed it most. Many of the students were mature. The course drew on a wide range of their experiences and was both instructive and fun for all of us. To start with I had envisaged this as a theory course, but most of those taking it were innocent of abstract legal theory and wished to remain so. I had to make it quite concrete, with the focus on an eclectic range of transnational issues which to a large extent followed the students' interests and prior knowledge. But I allowed some theory to infiltrate.

31. I let them choose to present and write papers from a wide range of particular topics such as *lex mercatoria*, sex trafficking, the Millennium Development Goals, topics in international commercial arbitration, alleged 'global law firms', a right to development, the legal problems surrounding Antarctica and the Arctic, Amartya Sen's theories of justice and capabilities or the impact of diffusion on some aspect(s) of their own national legal system. At this level they performed reasonably well and, I hope, by the end had had their horizons extended and some working assumptions challenged. When time allowed we held special sessions on topics that varied from year to year, such as the Pinochet case, human rights, southern voices, *lex mercatoria* and the ideas of Brian Tamanaha. Thus, each student was exposed to a broad range of topics held together by some overarching themes.

32. Instead I use other terms such as transnational, cross-border, North/South, supranational, subnational, regional, provincial, intercontinental, multinational, widespread, far-flung, general, mostly and universal in an empirical sense. None of these is entirely adequate; e.g., taken literally, several exaggerate the importance of the national, but they are less susceptible to the temptations of g-words. This helps to restrict 'global' to genuinely worldwide without being pedantic.

33. In other contexts, this can be used to equate Hans Kelsen with the Captain ('The Bellman').

34. GJP, 171, now greatly weakened by recent events in the Arctic (see e.g. https://ubaltciclfellows.wordpress.com/category/arctic/).

35. But where to draw the boundaries of non-state law? Would not any definitional stop be arbitrary? Would we include legal orders so small that they would not be visible on a large map of the world? Or legal orders with disputed borders or overlapping jurisdictions? How to depict legal pluralism (especially cross-border) and hybrid legal orders? In short, many of the problems arising with analysing or defining conceptions of law reassert themselves in this context. This is discussed at length in GJP, esp. Chs. 3, 4 and 12.

36. See p. 238.

37.   E.g. M. Bavinck and G. Woodman, 'Can There Be Maps of Law?' in
       F. v Benda-Bekman et al. (eds.), *Spatialising Law* (2009), discussed GJP,
       74–6.

38.   I have written quite a lot about mapping law (e.g. GLT, 136–73, 233–9; GJP,
       Ch. 3). Some commentators and critics have made the error of assuming
       that I think that this kind of mapping can provide a distinct theory of law or
       the basis for one. That was never my idea (see p. 369). Traditional mapping
       is mainly concerned with depicting the extent, distribution and relations
       between already identified units. A world historical atlas of law might
       presuppose, implicitly or explicitly, some concept of law or some working
       assumptions about law's nature and scope appropriate to the context.
       Anyway, what exactly would such a world historical atlas be good for?
       More useful than CNN world weather maps? My general answer is mainly
       to set a broad context for more particular enquiries.

39.   Santos, 'Law as a Map of Misreading'.

40.   E.g. Edward Tufte, *Envisioning Information* (1983).

41.   As a classroom exercise this worked rather well. It can be illuminating to
       think of law spatially and historically. It also illustrated how context can
       guide one's uses of the concept of law; some of the criteria of exclusion
       were largely pragmatic – e.g. how much could you squeeze in? Only after
       the mapping exercise did we spend some time discussing different
       conceptions of law in this context. By then we had a wide range of
       examples to play with. This becomes even more elusive if one accepts,
       as I do, that individuating legal and normative orders as well as traditions
       is highly problematic. See p. 168.

42.   I shall deal with these as examples of middle range theorising in the
       next chapter, linked to the thesis that Comparative Law as a sub-
       discipline is moving rapidly from being perceived as a marginal
       specialist subject to having a central role for all jurists in adapting
       our discipline to the challenges of an era of accelerated globalisation
       (see further p. 250).

43.   For an interesting example of crowd-sourced mapping used to help in
       the fight against FGM in Tanzania, see https://crowd2map.wordpress
       .com/. This is one of my favourite charities.

44.   The trouble was to do with quality and the conceptual and data bases for
       generalisation. In my extended gap period in 1955–7 I had studied and
       reflected on Arnold Toynbee's *A Study of History* (the abridged edition,
       not all twelve volumes). I was fascinated by it, but was left uneasy by his
       main concepts, especially 'civilisation', and his sweeping generalisations.
       During that time, I also read regional histories and studies of Africa and
       Europe, including John Gunther's popular *Inside Africa* (1955), but on
       the whole felt that these were little more than high-grade tourism.
       At least Gunther did not talk about 'Africa' as one place, a practice that
       I reacted against strongly early on. Later I came across 'World Systems

Theory', including Marxist or Marxian versions, such as the writings of Immanuel Wallerstein. Again, I found them too reductionist for my taste. Later I found Fernand Braudel's *A History of Civilisations* (1993 [1987]) and Eric Hobsbawm's grand European trilogy of Ages covering the period 1789–1991 to be helpful, not least because they were conceptually more sophisticated and had access to much more data than their predecessors. I could probably have made more use of Braudel. I discovered the work of Jürgen Osterhammel and his associates too late to use them (see next note). If my project had begun twenty years later it might have been quite different, but I would still echo Robert Merton: Jurisprudence is not yet ready for its Einstein, because it has not yet found its Kepler (see quotation above, p. 1).

45.   If I were advising someone entering this area for the first time I would recommend Jurgen Osterhammel's *Transformation of the World: A Global History of the Nineteenth Century* (2014 [2009]) together with Akire Iriye (ed.), *Global Interdependence: The World after 1945* (2014) as a possible starting point. The latter book is the first in a projected series on 'The History of the World' edited by these two scholars. One would, of course, need to cast a critical eye on their main working assumptions.

46.   Brian Tamanaha's 2017 book (discussed below, pp. 255–6) adopts a different perspective from Glenn's and is more clearly linked to Historical Jurisprudence.

47.   In 2005 I helped to organise a substantial symposium on the book in *The Journal of Comparative Law* (2006), vol. I. A *festschrift* in memory of Patrick Glenn (1940–2014) is being prepared in McGill Law School (forthcoming).

48.   E.g. economic and cultural globalisation; 'the clash of civilisations'; corruption; fundamentalism; diffusion and convergence; nationalism and identity politics; universalism, relativism and incommensurability; multivalent logic; and even chaos theory. In addition, Glenn uninhibitedly breaks free from twentieth-century comparatists' aversion to social theory and philosophy, but in a somewhat idiosyncratic fashion. Some recent texts have taken globalisation seriously, e.g. M. Siems, *Comparative Law* (2014), and W. Menski, *Comparative Law in a Global Context: The Legal Systems of Asia and Africa*, 3rd edn (2006).

49.   GLS.

50.   See pp. 241–2.

51.   J. Bentham, 'Place and Time in Legislation' (ed. P. Schofield) in Stephen Engelmann (ed.), *Selected Writings by Jeremy Bentham* (2011).

52.   See p. 244.

53.   See also GJP, Ch. 4.2.

54.   In particular some neglected texts by Kant, Leibniz, Vico, Bentham, Jenks, Jessup and others have attracted fresh attention.

55. Rudyard Kipling, 'The Disciple' (1932).
56. *One World: The Ethics of Globalisation*, The Terry Lectures (2004 [2002]), discussed GLT, 65–9.
57. John Rawls, *The Law of Peoples* (1999), discussed GLT, 69–75.
58. E.g. Martha Nussbaum, *Women and Development: The Capabilities Approach* (2001); Amartya Sen, *Development as Freedom* (2001).
59. Brian Tamanaha, *A General Jurisprudence of Law and Society* (2001), reviewed (2003) 37 L & Soc R 199.
60. Brian Tamanaha, *A Realistic Theory of Law* (2017), discussed Ch. 19 n. 53.
61. HCWT, summarised in GJP, 43–54.
62. Edward Shils, *The Academic Ethic* (1984); (ed.), *Remembering the University of Chicago* (1994).
63. GJP, 1.3.
64. Ch. 13.
65. Ch. 4 was called 'Constructing Conceptions of Law: Beyond Hart, Tamanaha and Llewellyn'. This chapter led me into trouble. Because it dealt with concepts of law, whose importance I had argued was overrated, my wife urged me to drop the chapter completely; otherwise, she suggested, many people, especially analytical jurists, would focus on that, perhaps to the exclusion of all else. She was right. At two seminars in Oxford and in several commentaries, analytical jurists tried to divine from Ch. 4 what was 'Twining's theory of law' or his 'concept or conception of law' despite repeated denials that I have a general theory or a single general conception of law outside a given context (see below, pp. 276–9). As noted above, the idea of using a thin functionalist interpretation of Llewellyn's law-jobs theory was intended as a framework for imagining a historical atlas of law in the world, NOT as a general theory of law. This distracted attention from the more original parts of the book especially in Part B. In some instances, the critic had clearly skipped the first two chapters; and Part B has hardly received any attention, except from specialists, probably because it falls outside narrow conceptions of 'Jurisprudence'.
66. This was mainly a response to Simon Roberts's polemics 'Against Legal Pluralism' and 'After Government?' criticising jurists for trying to interpret social phenomena through lawyers' lenses.
67. I have not given much attention to the implications of transnationalisation and globalisation in relation to the subject of Evidence in Legal Contexts except in relation to diffusion (e.g. the story of the Indian Evidence Act 1872, GJP, 280–5). Insofar as the subject is tied up with inferential reasoning and 'free proof', I am sceptical of ideas of multiculturalism in relation to epistemology, and agree with Susan Haack that 'there is no real relativity of standards of evidence [as contrasted with legal standards of proof], though disagreements in background beliefs,

and consequential disagreements about evidential quality, can make it look as if there is'. S. Haack, *Manifesto of a Passionate Moderate* (1998), 144. On multiculturalism and feminism in relation to epistemology see, ibid. Chs. 7 and 8 and *Putting Philosophy to Work* (2008), 32–5. The recent work of John Jackson and collaborators on Comparative Criminal Evidence is significant; see e.g. J. D. Jackson and S. S. Summers, *The Internationalisation of Criminal Evidence: Beyond the Common Law and Civil Law Traditions* (2012).

68. Including LRJ, my Bernstein Lecture, 'Afterword' in KLRM and reviews of important works by Raphael Domingo and Neil Walker (see above). GLS was the subject of a symposium in Toronto, to which I responded in 2013 ((2014) 4 Transnat'l Leg Theory 714).

69. See further pp. 232, 276–91.

70. The general direction of my thinking in this area is indicated in the form of some deliberately provocative propositions that I set out as a basis for discussion at a conference on 'The Law of the Future and the Future of Law' in 2011. As an exercise in futurology, it is subject to the usual disclaimers. W. Twining, 'Globalisation and Law: Ten Theses' in S. Muller et al. (eds.), *The Law of the Future and the Future of Law*, 2 vols. (2012), vol. II, prepared by the Hague Institute for Innovation in Law (HiiL). These two volumes, later publications and HiiL's website (www.hiil.org) are a useful indicator of transnational thinking in this area.

19. General Jurisprudence

1. F. Wieacker, (1981) 4 Boston Coll Int'l & and Comp LR n. 12.

2. E.g. in the title of my book, *General Jurisprudence Understanding Law from a Global Perspective*.

3. GLT, Ch. 2.

4. This is not quite the same as one common usage in Continental Europe, where 'general jurisprudence' (*théorie générale du droit, algemeine rechtlehre*) has sometimes been conceived as a sub-discipline that tried to establish itself between abstract legal philosophy and legal dogmatics. In this civilian interpretation 'legal philosophy' is abstract and metaphysical, removed from the details of actual legal systems, while 'general jurisprudence' was empirical, concerned with analysing actual legal systems (Mark van Hoecke, *What Is Legal Theory?* (1986)). 'General' in that context refers to level of abstraction rather than to geographical reach and 'general jurisprudence' is interpreted as a kind of middle-range theorising.

5. Some of Hart's successors have applied the term 'General Jurisprudence' to the idea that a general descriptive theory of law is one that applies to all actual and possible legal systems (though often implicitly limited to state

law). This claims to be universal and conceptual rather than empirical or normative or a combination of these. Some would suggest that by doing so some analytical legal philosophers, without regard to history, have requisitioned the term to apply to a very narrow and abstract part of the field of Jurisprudence as most other jurists conceive it. The terminology is not very significant outside academic politics, but it is important to emphasise that my usage is very different from this narrow one. I recently came across a paper entitled: 'Is General Jurisprudence Interesting?' by David Enoch. He turned out to be using the term in this narrow sense, and I was pleased to find that his answer was 'No' from a philosophical point of view. Having recently published a book called *General Jurisprudence* (2009) (GJP), I was surprised, but also rather pleased, to have been completely ignored in that paper ((2011) 1 Oxf Stud Phil L 1–38).

6.   In scholarly practice there is a tendency to move rather indiscriminately from discussing doctrine of a single municipal legal system (e.g. England and Wales, Alabama), to discussing Anglo-American common law (including both state and Federal Law), sometimes common law generally. On the dangers of assuming that the institutional and other contexts for such generalisations is shared across jurisdictions, see GJP, 57–9.

7.   E.g. Denis Galligan, 'Concepts in the Currency of Social Understanding of Law: A Review Essay on Later Work of William Twining' (2015) 35 OJLS 373; Brian Tamanaha, 'Enhancing Prospects for General Jurisprudence' (2007) 15 U Miami Int'l & Comp LR 69. I have no General Theory of Law (see below, pp. 276–9), nor do I aspire to one, but Galligan assumes that I do and Tamanaha treats my conception of General Jurisprudence as a framework which regulates enquiry rather than as a deliberately vague field concept, covering many different lines of enquiry and many levels of abstraction.

8.   Emphasis on the limitations of 'high theory' (i.e. abstract Legal Philosophy) and on the importance of 'middle-order theorising' is significant for my story because it explains first, my approach to Evidence and my interpretations of legal realism and 'law in context' and, secondly, why I opted out of the (Analytical) Jurisprudence mainstream for about twenty-five years, only returning to it towards the end of my project on 'globalisation'. This re-emphasis on conceptual analysis was germinated during the year at Stanford in 1999–2000, hinted at in GLT, but most clearly marked by HCWT which was not published until 2007, later condensed in GJP, Ch. 2. In arguing that I was mistaken in taking Analytical Jurisprudence as my *starting point*, Denis Galligan (in 'Concepts in the Currency of Social Understanding of Law') ignored the introductory chapters of GJP (which restated a conception of Jurisprudence different from his) and overlooked the fact that I had

returned to doing Analytical Jurisprudence after a prolonged gap. Galligan was closer to the mark in suggesting that I had downplayed the importance of social theory, on which see below, p. 278.

9. See pp. 4–5.

10. For some time, such 'rethinkings' have been taking place to a significant extent; e.g. in the late 1980s anthropologists, including legal anthropologists, recognised that they had often erred in treating small-scale societies as timeless, self-contained units and have since then been more sensitive to the broader contexts of history and geography (see p. 229). In International Law the writings of Philip Allott, Richard Falk, Martii Koskenniemi, Tony Carty and American critical theorists (TWAIL), among others, have been prominent. They are clearly contributions to General Jurisprudence.

11. A. Watson, *Legal Transplants and European Private Law*, (2000)4(4) Electronic J Comp L www.ejcl.org/ejcl/44/44–2.html.

12. B. Latour, *Aramis or the Love of Technology*, trans. Catherine Porter (1996).

13. 'Diffusion is the process by which an innovation is communicated through certain channels over time among the members of a social system' (Everett Rogers, *Diffusion of Innovations*, 4th edn (1995), 5) (innovation means new to recipients). In the present context most talk of diffusion of law is transnational, while early diffusion studies were largely confined to the USA or anthropology.
    Reception/Transplants/Diffusion as labels. When I first studied it in the late 1950s the topic was known as 'Reception', typically of foreign law; Alan Watson's lively writings on the theme that imitation is the main engine of legal change gave currency to the metaphor of transplantation; I have used 'diffusion' since 1999 because this links the legal topic to the literature of sociological diffusion studies. Some social scientists have moved away from this category which implies a single starting point or source. Neighbouring 'network analysis' has developed exponentially in a number of fields since the 1970s. See further GJP, Ch. 9 and (2005) 32 JL & Soc 203.

14. Discussed GJP, Ch. 10.

15. R. Benford and D. Snow, 'Framing Processes and Social Movements: An Overview and Assessment' (2000) 26 *Ann R Soc* 611–39.

16. Ibid.

17. Franz Wieacker's great book, *A History of Private Law in Europe*, trans. Tony Weir (1995 [1952]) gives a Weberian account of the 'reception' of Roman Law in Europe. It can be exempted from being caught up in the naïve model of reception; see e.g. the quote on 'Prolific misunderstanding', above, p. 244. On Wieacker, see (2005) 32 JL & Soc 203, 209 and 227.

18. GJP, 277, for another formulation see ibid., 270–1.

19. Rogers, *Diffusion of Innovations*.

20. At first sight Table 1, by emphasising the variety and complexity of processes of diffusion, can seem rather daunting. Indeed, more than one person has commented to me that this analysis makes the subject of diffusion unmanageable. That is to confuse the method of analysis, which is quite straightforward, with the phenomena of diffusion, which are indeed complex and varied. Rather, the table provides a quite simple tool for analysing particular instances of diffusion. Based on standard concepts in social science diffusion theory, it suggests a series of questions that a scholar can apply to almost any example. For a similar use of a single ideal type with variations for each element for a complex concept (torture) see HTDTWR (5th edn, 2010), 163–4.

21. Cited by K. Zweigert and H. Kötz, *An Introduction to Comparative Law*, 3rd edn (1998), 33.

22. Ibid., 33–4.

23. This section, adapted from GLS, is a condensed version of several papers, especially GLT, Ch. 7, and GCompl. For an interesting critique of my views on Comparative Law from a Nietzschean perspective see B. Salman, 'William Twining on "Reviving" Comparative law: Some Reflections Inspired by Friedrich Nietzsche', Bocconi Legal Papers No. 2009–09/EN (2009). I am not sufficiently familiar with Nietzsche to comment.

24. CLLT, 21.; cf. GLT, Ch. 7. Although first published in 2000, the basic work was done in 1995–7.

25. A. Watson, *Legal Transplants* (1993 [1974]); W. Ewald, (1995) 43 Am J Comp L 489; P. Legrand, *Fragments on Law-as-Culture* (1999).

26. We ran a Comparative Common Law programme at Queen's for a few years, but it did not develop very far.

27. I made such a claim (e.g. Twining, 'Comparative Law and Legal Theory, the Country and Western Tradition', 70), but it has sometimes been misunderstood to mean that there is no room for specialist courses, organisations or literature on Comparative Law.

28. See p. 128.

29. Quoted p. 249.

30. This version is from GJP, 5–7.

31. GJP, 6.

32. This is a summary statement of views expressed in 'Normative and Legal Pluralism' (Bernstein Lecture) and 'Legal Pluralism 101' in Brian Tamanaha et al. (eds.), *Legal Pluralism: Scholars and Practitioners in Dialogue* (2012), 112–28. Both of these were written after the completion of GJP. These supplement and gloss, but do not entirely supersede the discussions of pluralism in GJP and GLT.

33. E.g. F. M. Deng, *Tradition and Modernization; A Challenge for Law among the Dinka of the Sudan* (1971); and HRSV, Ch. 2 (esp. references to *Sudan Democratic Gazette*).

34. See pp. 136–7.

35. B. de Sousa Santos, *Toward a New Common Sense* (1995), 385, 473.

36. Similarly, an observer or other actor considering this situation will consider this to be a situation of legal pluralism. 'Bottom-up perspectives' on the topic, e.g. adopting the standpoint of a subject or user, are sometimes referred to as 'radical legal pluralism'. In my view, the topic of normative and legal pluralism is the least problematic and easy to grasp from this standpoint. So why 'radical'?

37. For more detailed accounts and citations see the Bernstein Lecture.

38. See p. 47.

39. The situation of Muslim women in Britain who have gone through the ceremony of 'niqab', but have not officially registered a civil marriage, has been explored extensively in the campaign 'Register Our Marriage', led by Aina Khan, a solicitor (www.registerourmarriage.org).

40. Esp. GJP, Ch. 2–4; GLT, Ch. 2.

41. See p. 211.

42. HCWT, summarised in GJP, 43–54.

43. E.g. under the headline: 'Is Britain among Europe's worst for employing female judges?' 'Only Azerbaijan has a lower proportion of women judges than Britain', *The Independent*, 20 September 2012. The source of this league table was the OECD programme on Gender Equality in Public life which produces generally excellent data in this area. There is substantial gender inequality in the *senior* judiciary in UK, as Baroness Hale has made very clear. The point here is that the concept of 'judiciary' means different things in different countries. Feminists do not need bad arguments to make their case. The press, as in this example, often conflates England, Britain and the United Kingdom. The judiciaries in Scotland and Northern Ireland are differently organised from that for England and Wales.

44. GJP, Ch. 15, including persons, subjects, groups, communities and related concepts, www.cambridge.org/twining.

45. See p. 211.

46. My general views on 'Empirical dimensions of law and justice' are set out in GJP, Chs. 8 and 11 and are not repeated here.

47. See 'Afterword', pp. 404–9.

48. On 'formalism' see p. 172.

49. See p. 325.

50. This has been a constant theme of Nicola Lacey's writings, e.g. N. Lacey, 'Analytical Jurisprudence versus Descriptive Sociology Revisited' (2006) 88 Texas LR 945; see also GJP, 57–9.

51. H. Berman, *Law and Revolution I: The Formation of the Western Tradition* (1983); *Law and Revolution, II: The Impact of the Protestant Reformations on the Western Legal Tradition* (2004).

52. See pp. 255–7.

53. B. Z. Tamanaha, *A Realistic Theory of Law* (2017). The author presents this as a 'third pillar' as if it were a discrete theory separate from the other two pillars (characterised in terms of positivism and Natural Law), but his argument is that all three are essential to the enterprise of understanding law.

54. See pp. 209–11.

55. See p. 260.

56. Other examples include basing an enquiry on false or outdated or otherwise dubious working assumptions; ignoring developments in other branches of scholarship or other legal traditions; the lack of access of monolinguistic anglophones to huge expanses of 'foreign' literature (Ch. 20, n. 5); and the uneven gaps between surface law and the law in action (GJP, Ch. 10).

20. 'R/retirement'

1. GJP, 258–62.

2. In fact, Rutter had said that I would probably become an essayist, 'like Goldsworthy Lowes-Dickinson'. At the time he and I were both immersed in the Bloomsbury Group. 'Goldie' was a hanger-on – I recently learned from *Wikipedia* that he was a foot-fetishist and secret homosexual who has been credited with the idea of a League of Nations, but not much else. I was offended at the time; I aspired to be more like a combination of Virginia Woolf and John Maynard Keynes rather than a third-rate essayist, only remembered because E. M. Forster had written his biography without mentioning his sexuality or foot-fetishism.

3. Discussed in earlier chapters, especially Chs. 14, 17, 18 and 19. Publications since 1999 include new editions of HTDTWR, RE, *Analysis*, the 'Afterword' to KLRM, and GLT, GJB, HRSV, GLS, GJP, several edited books and numerous papers.

4. This is intended to refine and begin to test the common-sense hypothesis that over half of humankind do not have a working knowledge of the official or operative language(s) of their state legal system, including non-litigious legal transactions.

5. The projects on linguistic diversity and Southern Voices are discussed by Abdul Paliwala and the author, in S. Adelman and A. Paliwala (eds.), *The Limits of Law and Development* (forthcoming).

6. http://ials.sas.ac.uk/research/areas-research/legal-records-risk-lrar-project. The main objective for this is to construct a national strategy for private sector legal records in England and Wales in conjunction with The National Archive's plans for a new strategy for preserving private sector records more systematically. See Clare Cowling, *Legal Records at Risk: A strategy for legal records* (forthcoming, 2019).

7. See pp. 10–11. See also LRIC, the Records of Legal Education Archive at the Institute of Advanced Legal Studies and miscellaneous other publications.

8. These include a half-finished manuscript on *Reading Law* (an expansion of the Seegers Lectures in Valparaiso (1988/9) and *The Reading Law Cookbook* (LiC, Chs. 11 and 12)) and some other writing projects.

9. I prefer to use norms and rules as generic synonyms referring to all types of prescriptions. Some others treat rules as more specific than norms; e.g. Ronald Dworkin treated 'rules' as peremptory precepts and in my view unfairly attributed that usage to Hart.

10. I was once invited to be an expert witness on Dinka law in a homicide case; I declined because of my lack of expertise, not because I reject the idea of Dinka law.

11. For a useful bibliography up to about 1990, see Schauer, *Playing by the Rules*, 234–47; *The Stanford Encyclopedia of Philosophy* entry on 'Social Norms' (C. Bicchieri and R. Muldoon, 2011) contains a rather shorter bibliography of social science literature and some useful links. Today some of the literature in fields such as Artificial Intelligence, Cognitive Psychology and Neuroscience is becoming more relevant.

12. Kate Fox, *Watching the English: The Hidden Rules of English Behaviour* (2004). This genre goes back at least as far as Geoffrey Gorer's snide book *The Americans* (1948) which I read just before I first went to Chicago; it slowed down my integration into American culture.

13. These materials (including books) will be deposited in an archive of my professional papers at the Perelman Centre in Brussels.

14. This idea was suggested by F. M. Cornford's *Microcosmographia Academica* (1908). One rough hypothesis is that law examiners can be divided into four categories: those who want rules, interpret them literally and enforce them strictly ('the ruley'); those who want rules but interpret them liberally, find ways round them or disregard them in other ways; those who want few rules, perhaps because they interpret them literally and enforce them strictly; and those who do not want rules and disregard those that exist (the unruly). These can be further subdivided in respect of both attitudes and behaviour. University law examiners in my experience are an example of rule-handlers who have a good deal of power and discretion in contrast with markers for institutionally prescribed exams such as SATS and GCSEs. The key distinction, not always observed in discussions of legalism, is between the standpoints of rule-makers and standard-setters, on the one hand, and rule-interpreters, appliers and enforcers and users or subjects of rules, on the other.

15. Paul Dresch and Hannah Skoda (eds.), *Legalism: Anthropology and History* (2012); Fernanda Pirie and Judith Scheele (eds.), *Legalism: Community and Justice* (2014); Paul Dresch and Judith Scheele (eds.),

Legalism: Rules and Categories (2015). The series of seminars is continuing in 2018.

16. See p. 182.

17. See p. 266.

18. Jeremy Waldron, 'How to Do Things with Standards', LEGTC, Ch. 16. There has been an extended debate about standards in the USA stimulated in part by Kathleen Sullivan, 'The Supreme Court, 1991 Term – Foreword: The Justices of Rules and Standards' (1992) 106 Harv LR 22. Much of the debate can be traced back to Henry M. Hart and Albert. M. Sacks's idea of 'reasoned elaboration' in their materials on *The Legal Process* (eventually published in 1994), 102–58. On indicators, see above, p. 235.

19. E.g. A. Burrows, *Improving Statutes*, The Hamlyn Lectures (2017).

20. This is an extension beyond the paper on 'Rethinking "Legal Reasoning": A Modest Proposal', discussed in pp. 1302–4.

21. This can be framed as a simple linear ideal type or total process model, see pp. 19–21. On non-linear processes of litigation and dispute processing see RE2, 353–8.

22. On questions see Ch. 10, pp. 24–6.

23. HTDTWR (5th edn, 2010), Ch. 11, esp. 353–8.

24. The nearest substantial body of work that came close to my interests was the 'New Rhetoric' of Chaim Perelman and others and I have been very pleased to be associated with the Perelman Institute in Brussels in recent years. See esp. Ch. Perelman and L. Olbrechts-Tyteca, *A New Rhetoric: A Treatise on Argumentation*, trans. J. Wilkinson and W. Weaver (1973). See also J. L. Golden and J. J. Pilotta (eds.), *Practical Reasoning in Human Affairs* (1986).

25. HTDTWR, esp. 356–8, entry on 'Legal Reasoning and Argumentation' (2001) 2 IESBS 1145–51.

26. FiL.

27. RE2, Ch. 4.

28. E.g. S. Lloyd-Bostock (ed.), *Psychology in Legal Contexts* (1980); *Law and Psychology* (1981); *Evaluating Witness Evidence* (1983); *Law in Practice* (1988).

29. RE2, Ch. 5.

30. The formulation was deliberately provocative, but I do not remember anyone at NIAS seriously challenging it; this contrasts with the UCL project in which there was no consensus about its working assumptions and Schum's approach was challenged (see below).

31. W. Twining and I. Hampsher-Monk (eds.), *Evidence and Inference in History and Law* (2003) (EIHL). The title reflects the fact that nearly every contributor adopted the standpoint of 'the historian', but the contributions exemplify the varieties of historiography, including papers

on Theatre Iconography, Musicology, the History of Ideas, Labour History and Assyriology, as well as Law.

32. See pp. 175–6.

33. RE2, Ch. 15 and *Analysis*, 46–55 illustrate how evidence is central to understanding 9/11, especially in relation to the restructuring of American intelligence services.

34. See Jason Davis, 'Disciplining the Disciplines' in EIE, Ch. 3.

35. EIE.

36. EIE, Ch. 4 (my post-mortem on the project). When I listed fourteen questions that I thought that such a project should address, Susan Haack commented in effect: 'Why do you need funding for that? Answer them yourself.' A good question, but it would need a team. I did not participate as much in the UCL programme as I had hoped. A combination of ill-health and my commitments in Miami were partly to blame, but the times of meetings were also inconvenient and I disagreed with some of the directions taken.

37. Colin Aitken, Paul Roberts, Graham Jackson and Roberto Puch-Solis: 1. *Fundamentals of Probability and Statistical Evidence in Criminal Proceedings: Guidance for Judges, Lawyers, Forensic Scientists and Expert Witnesses* (2010); 2. *Assessing the Probative Value of DNA Evidence* (PDF), (2012); 3. *The Logic of Forensic Proof: Inferential Reasoning in Criminal Evidence and Forensic Science* (2014); 4. *Case Assessment and Interpretation of Expert Evidence* (2015). All published by the Royal Statistical Society.

38. As Editor of the *Jurists* series I invited proposals for books on non-Western jurists; I received several proposals and even more promises, but so far only one book has been published: Colin Imber, *Ebu's-Suud: The Islamic Legal Tradition* (1997). See also, J.-M. Barreto (ed.), *Human Rights from a Third World Perspective* (2013).

39. Limitations of my expertise and linguistic competence narrowed the options. Possibly within my competence was an edited collection of important texts by African nationalist leaders, such as Nkrumah, Nyerere, Kaunda, Mandela, including founders of the *négritude* movement, including Léopold Senghor and Aimé Césaire.

40. Macdonald Lecture.

41. H. Patrick Glenn, *Legal Traditions of the World: Sustainable Diversity in Law*, 3rd edn (2007), Ch. 10.

42. 'They respect cultural diversity and value tolerance, but this involves no commitment to "tolerating the intolerable". Each believes in the value of dialogue, but with different emphases: Deng, the diplomat, has always relied on persuasion and mediation; An-Na'im stresses the importance of internal dialogue; Ghai points to the value of human rights discourse as a framework for political negotiation and compromise between people

with different interests, concerns, and ethnicities; Baxi, more pugnacious, sees dialogic human rights as the gentler part of struggle.' HRSV, 218.

43.   Published as *Human Rights: Southern Voices* (2009).

44.   I thought of including the acceptance speeches of two Nobel Prize-winners, Shireen Ebadi and Aung Sang Suu Kyi, but decided that this would be mere tokenism. Instead I tried to stimulate at least one sister volume and still hope that this will emerge in due course – there could easily be several.

45.   Oscar Guardiola Rivera has responded with a fascinating piece on applying the approach to Latin America (LEGTC, Ch. 5). See Barreto (ed.), *Human Rights from a Third World Perspective*. Abdul Paliwala has plans for a follow-up project based at Warwick, including a website and a small library and archive. See further S. Adelman and A. Paliwala (eds.), *The Limits of Law and Development: Neoliberalism, Governance and Social Justice* (forthcoming). In similar vein, but probably confined to translations from European languages, is a new series published by Routledge (Glasshouse Press) and edited by Mariano Croce and Marco Goldoni. The first volume rendered as *The Legal Order* by Santi Romano (2017, edited by M. Croce) fills a significant gap in the literature on legal pluralism.

46.   R. Susskind, *Tomorrow's Lawyers* (2017), citing the first edition (2013).

47.   In addition to being a member of one committee and doing some lobbying, I wrote a few pieces, see (2014) 48 The Law Teacher 94; (2015), 49 The Law Teacher 388–406 (a prequel to this section); and 'Foundation Subjects Must Go', a polemic which was quite widely circulated and included in the second paper. A more substantial piece for the ALT's Annual Lord Upjohn Lecture, 'Rethinking Legal Education' (2018) 52 *The Law Teacher* 241. This section is a prequel to that lecture.

48.   See e.g. LiC, Ch. 15. The Xanadu Report also attacked some common fallacies or skewed working assumptions in legal education discourse: 1. the football league model; 2. the primary school image; 3. the private practitioner image; 4. the numbers game; 5. the professional snob syndrome; 6. the cheap subject fallacy (LiC, 300–1, cf. ibid., 294–6).

49.   E.g. 'Pericles' (1967), the ILC Report (1975) and even the 'Law for non-lawyers conference' (1977) (discussed above) had not followed through on the implications of focusing on learning rather than teaching and informal legal education 'from cradle to grave'. Pericles was mainly about American law schools; the ILC Report focused on institutions, teachers and courses; even discussions of public understanding were focused on us-for-them activities.

50.   The distinction between 'formal' and 'informal' is highly problematic. In the present context 'formal' is restricted to taught courses and

specialised institutions, but there is a need for further conceptual refinement. See p. 273.

51. LiC, Ch. 15.

52. L. Friedman, 'Law, Lawyers and Popular Culture' (1989) 98 Yale LJ 1579, at 1598. I am grateful for Peter Twining for help with framing these ideal types, but the responsibility is mine alone.

53. See p. 220.

54. Adapted from (2014) 48 The Law Teacher 97.

55. When I used the Library of the Institute of Education (IOE) in preparing for *Blackstone's Tower*, I found a lot on higher education, but virtually nothing on legal education. Of course, IALS, which is next door, has some library holdings and the Records of Legal Education archive, but I would surmise that there has been little traffic between the two buildings.

56. It is worth bearing in mind that practising lawyers often seek information from non-lawyers, e.g. by phoning or emailing the local Planning Officer or a non-lawyer accountant or insurance specialist.

57. See now 'Rethinking Legal Education' (see above, n. 47).

58. For my position in relation to some common 'isms' see GJP, 16; and GJB, Ch. 11, esp. 370.

59. The phrase is from Tony Becher's *Academic Tribes and Territories*, 1st edn (1989), which has influenced my approach especially in *BT*.

60. See Ch. 1; and LiC, 24–5.

61. Cf. the Genn Report (2006) which found, regretfully: '[I]t is from within Law Schools that the majority of UK empirical researchers emanate and it is from within Law Schools that the majority of UK empirical legal researchers operate' (discussed GJP, 238–42).

62. This theme is developed in 'Law and Literature: A Dilettante's Dream', a lecture delivered at Wolfson College, Oxford in November 2013. Part A was a critique of some general discussions of 'Law and Literature'; so far it is unpublished, as I think that I overstated the scepticism. Part B, drawing on drafts for this book, deals with standpoint, narrative and argument in fact-finding and Italo Calvino as an inspiration for jurists. See now (2017) 1 J Oxf Centre for Socio-leg Stud.

63. S. Roberts, 'After Government? On Representing Law without the State' (2005) 68 MLR 1, discussed GJP, Ch. 12; and R. Cotterrell, *Law, Culture and Society: Legal Ideas in the Mirror of Social Theory* (2006).

64. 'It is easy to explain in what sense legal philosophy is universal. Its theses, if true, apply universally, that is they speak of all law, of all legal systems; of those that exist, or that will exist, or even that can exist though they never will ... Moreover, its theses are advanced as necessarily universal ... A claim to necessity is in the nature of the enterprise.' J. Raz, *Between Authority and Interpretation* (2009), 91–2 and see also 17, 24, 97. Cf. J. Raz, *The Authority of Law* (2009), 104–5. For a good discussion see Michael Giudice, *Understanding the Nature of Law*

(2015), Introduction, citing Joseph Raz, Scott Shapiro and Julie Dixon as exemplars of this view. That makes Legal Philosophy seem like a rather restricted enterprise; happily, in their practices they use analytical methods to deal with a range of questions, not all of which are necessarily staging posts on the way to an all-encompassing Grand Theory. On Raz's late acknowledgements that jurists should also pay attention to non-state law and that 'Talk of *the* concept of law really means our concept of law' (*Between Authority and Interpretation* (2009), 32, 95–98) see also J. Raz, 'Why the State?' in N. Roughan and A. Halpin (eds.), *In Pursuit of Pluralist Jurisprudence* (2017), Ch. 7, discussed by Brian Tamanaha in LEGTC, Ch. 17, and several papers by Frederick Schauer, e.g. 'The Social Construction of the Concept of Law' (2005) 25 OJLS 493. It is tempting to treat these recent moves by Raz as a kind of retreat, but much of this might be interpreted in terms of the problematic emic/etic distinction in anthropology (see GJP, 41–3, 372), a point that I cannot pursue here.

65. See GJP, Chs. 3, 4 and 12.

66. Roger Cotterrell, 'Does Global Legal Pluralism Need a Concept of Law?' in LEGTC, Ch. 14.

67. Joseph Raz acknowledges that there are 'theories of law' of other kinds than his own narrowly focused and culturally relative one. See further above n. 64.

68. Cf. J. Gardner, *Law as a Leap of Faith* (2012), Preface. Gardner and I are quite close to each other on this matter, as on many others, except that he is mainly interested in Philosophy of Law. Later he chides me for sometimes suggesting that all theorists should have the same special interests as I have. 'Twining veers dangerously close to a Dworkinian diktat about what is "interesting"', pp. 296–7 n. 75. My point was not about freedom of enquiry for individuals. There are also collective responsibilities or 'jobs' concerning the health of one's discipline and what and how we offer to students. Where Gardner and I might disagree is about what constitutes 'health' in legal scholarship and legal theory and, perhaps especially, legal education.

69. A German Reviewer of KLRM criticised me for not making clear what was Llewellyn's 'system' (M. Weis, (1974) 174 Archiv fur Civilistische Praxis 90–2). My immediate reaction was that Llewellyn was not a systematic thinker and that he was worthy of attention for a wide range of particular ideas and for specific insights and contributions to various topics. He had begun to outline his 'Whole View', but even if he had completed it, this would not have presented all of his thought as a coherent whole. In my view it would have been a distortion to systematise Llewellyn in much the same way that it is not very illuminating to try to pin Shakespeare down to a single world view.

70. This is why in introducing undergraduates to the field, like many others, I have followed Collingwood in focusing on specific texts set in context

rather than on 'schools' or 'isms' or 'chaps'. If individual thinkers and their texts are difficult to summarise accurately, the dangers are even greater in generalising about schools or tendencies or trends. Sometimes such generalising can be useful, provided the necessary caveats are made clear. With 'isms' and 'ists' a sensible practice is to specify in terms of one or more discrete proposition(s) as Hart did with 'positivism' and I have done with 'realism' (above, p. 166). On 'isms' and 'ists' see GJP, Ch. 16 and GJB, Ch.11, esp. 370.

71. Recently in casual talk in Oxford I have heard a distinction being made between 'ambitious' and 'modest' legal theory, the former seemingly referring to activities designed to reach the heights of a Grand Theory of the Nature of Law (a philosophical question) and the latter to those who are content to wander in the foothills of middle-order theory (hardly worth the name of theory and not philosophically interesting). A story is told that Rupert Cross and Brian Simpson once offered a seminar on 'Low-brow Jurisprudence', but this title was rejected by the authorities.

72. See further GJP, Chs. 4 and 12, 64–6, 84–5.

73. Rather less attention is paid to questions such as 'plurality of what?' or 'what kind of "ism" is this'? See Bernstein Lecture, 477–8, 482–3.

74. It is clear that if one adopts state law as a working concept for the purpose, that narrows the topic and excludes much of the literature; but that may be quite sensible in some contexts; e.g. if one's main focus, as an official or legal scholar, is on state legal pluralism or how a particular state deals or should deal with non-state normative orders. If one adopts for a given purpose some kinds of 'non-state law' this may or may not involve specifying a definitional stop – for some purposes whether a particular normative order counts as 'legal' or not may or may not be of theoretical or practical importance.

75. The tendency to assume that the aim of Jurisprudence is to produce theories of law is linked to an unwillingness to discuss or debate the nature and role of Jurisprudence as a field. This book argues that Jurisprudence can contribute to the health of our discipline in several important ways and in an era of rapid change there are important jobs to be done.

76. Some commentators may subscribe to the view, elegantly expressed by Filmer Northrop, that everyone has a philosophy, but not everyone knows what their philosophy is. F. Northrop, *The Complexity of Legal and Ethical Experience* (1959), 6. In other words, when talking, thinking and writing about law we have certain working assumptions, even if we are not conscious of them. Of course, I have working assumptions, but they are not uniform across contexts. Cf. Gardner, *Law as a Leap of Faith.*

77. In GJP I speculated about how one might set about compiling a historical atlas of law in the world. I suggested that such an atlas would be mainly useful for setting a broad context for more specific enquiries and for illustrating the diversity of legal phenomena and the complexity of their relations. Some commentators have assumed that this was envisaged as a step towards constructing a general theory of law. But such mapping would *assume a working concept of law* for that purpose. A good historical world atlas of law would have its uses, but also considerable limitations. It should not be treated as a basis or substitute or a starting point for a general theory of law. An atlas presupposes some criteria for inclusion and exclusion suited to its purposes (whatever they are) and it would be difficult to avoid quite pragmatic criteria of inclusion and exclusion for a particular map or atlas. See p. 353.

78. D. Galligan, 'Concepts in the Currency of Social Understanding of Law: A Review Essay on Later Work of William Twining' (2015) 35 OJLS 373.

79. See pp. 257-8.

80. 'Law Teaching as a Vocation' (2003) 1 Speculum Iuris 161.

81. E.g. The Rationalist Tradition (RE2, Ch. 3); the concept of torture (HTDTWR, 123-4); conceptions of Legal Education as a field (above pp. 271-2); Lord Upjohn Lecture, above n. 47); GJB, Ch. 9; human rights 'schools' (HRSV, Ch. 6); and sets of working assumptions (above, Ch. 19). See further the index under 'ideal types'.

82. D. Dennett, *Darwin's Dangerous Idea* (1995).

83. Cf. The Bellman's Map, above, p. 236.

84. Italo Calvino, *Invisible Cities*, trans. William Weaver (1974), 131-2.

85. Like Llewellyn. In respect of doctrine, one of the main planks of American Legal Realism was 'the belief in the worthwhileness of grouping cases and legal situations into narrower categories than has been the practice in the past' (K. Llewellyn, *Jurisprudence* (1962), 55-7). However, he was not dogmatic about such narrow-issue thinking and in Article IX of the UCC (Secured Transactions) he did the reverse, substituting one broad category for a collection of narrow ones (KLRM, 79, 331-5).

86. Katherine Hume, 'Grains of Sand in a Sea of Objects: Italo Calvino as Essayist' (1992) 87 *MLR* 72, at 75; and *Calvino's Fictions: Cogito and Cosmos* (1992).

87. The recent writings of Stephen Pinker (*The Better Angels of Our Nature* (2011) and *Enlightenment Now* (2018)) usefully synthesise reasons for optimism about the future. I am more sceptical about futurology and am more inclined to think the world will end in fire (or ice) relatively soon.

88. LiC, 281.

89. Quoting GJP, 5-7.

90. See p. 255.

91. Cf. 'Adopting a global perspective shows up some of the limitations of
    what is in many respects a rich tradition of Western Comparative Law.
    It should also alert us to the extent of our collective ignorance and warn
    against unfounded, often ethnocentric, generalisation about matters
    legal. Such a perspective reminds us of the diversity and complexity of
    legal phenomena, but it is mainly useful in setting a broad context for
    more particular studies. Most of the processes of "globalization" occur at
    sub-global levels. Even in an interdependent world, the comparative
    study of law needs to focus mainly on detailed particulars that are
    local, practical, and embedded in specific cultural contexts' (GCL, 85).
    See also GJP, Ch. 14.
92. Cf. BT, Ch. 1 and ibid., 199.

Index